D1179436

THE EPIGRAMS OF SIR JOHN HARINGTON

For
Charlotte, Eleanor and Beatrice,
Safiya, Hester and Aliya

permitte divis cetera, qui simul
stravere ventos aequore fervido
deproeliantes, nec cupressi
nec veteres agitantur orni

The Epigrams of
Sir John Harington

GERARD KILROY

ASHGATE

Published by
Ashgate Publishing Limited
Wey Court East
Union Road
Farnham
Surrey, GU9 7PT
England

Ashgate Publishing Company
Suite 420
101 Cherry Street
Burlington
VT 05401-4405
USA

www.ashgate.com

British Library Cataloguing in Publication Data
Harington, John, Sir, 1560–1612
    The Epigrams of Sir John Harington
    I. Title II. Kilroy, Gerard, 1945–
    828.3'02

Library of Congress Cataloging-in-Publication Data
Harington, John, Sir, 1560–1612.
    The Epigrams of Sir John Harington / [introduced and edited by] Gerard Kilroy.
       p.   cm.
    Includes bibliographical references and index.
    1. Harington, John, Sir, 1560–1612 – Criticism and interpretation.
    I. Kilroy, Gerard, 1945– II. Title.
    PR2284.A4 2009
    821'.3–dc22
                               2008053168

ISBN 978-0-7546-6002-6

Printed and bound in Great Britain by
MPG Books Group, UK

Contents

Preface

Sir John Harington (1560-1612) presented his *Epigrams*, arranged in four 'bookes' and framed by emblems and royal 'Elegies', to King James VI of Scotland, in 1603, and two years later, to Henry, Prince of Wales. The *Epigrams* constitute a moral, political and theological critique of the state of the nation, so it is easy to see why Harington might have hesitated to have them printed. While Harington was no fool, he studiously, and successfully, cultivated the appearance of one: a mask, perhaps, for some of the dangerous literary transcription and circulation in which he was engaged. Harington, in the *Epigrams*, several times expresses admiration for those who, like Ulysses or Lucius Junius Brutus, 'fayned madnes' or pretended stupidity, and it is clear that he identified with those who used folly to survive tyrannical monarchs, from Tarquinius Superbus to Henry VIII. His own admiration for the Queen whose godson he was, did not prevent him from seeing the strange changes of temper to which she was subject, and whose daughter she was.

Harington's disguise ensured his survival in a politically turbulent time, but it has prevented later centuries from appreciating him. Part 1 aims to locate the *Epigrams* in their biographical, literary and historical context. Chapter 1 is less a brief biography than an account that uses Harington's own letters, anecdotes and observations to reveal the man behind the mask. Harington may have been a courtier of Queen Elizabeth, but his life was profoundly shaped by the experience of his father at the court of Henry VIII, and most of his heroes belong to the Henrician period. Chapter 2 examines the models for the *Epigrams*, and shifts the perspective from Martial to the tradition that stemmed, through Alciati, Erasmus, Thomas More and John Heywood, from the Greek Anthology. These authors, thanks to Erasmus, formed part of the weekly diet of Elizabethan schoolboys. Chapter 3 offers an interpretation that is designed to reveal the intricate architecture of the *Epigrams*: their patterns, groups and sequences. A thematic commentary (rather than notes or glossary) should enable readers to supply the profound analysis each epigram deserves. Chapter 4 provides a detailed bibliography of the manuscripts and of the posthumous printed editions, and attempts a picture of how Harington was being read from 1590 to 1680, in manuscript and in print. The chapter ends with a detailed account of the conventions of this edition.

The poems have never before been printed in full, or in the order in which Harington so carefully arranged them. I have chosen as my copy text Folger MS V.a.249 (*F*), an elegant transcription made for presentation to the eighteen-year-old Prince Henry, and dated by Harington himself: *19 June 1605*. The four 'bookes', each of a hundred epigrams (with attendant dedications, 'Elegies' and emblems) in this collection are substantially the same, and in the same order, as in the other complete manuscript, BL Add. MS 12049 (*BL*). This working copy, in secretary hand, equipped with the author's own first-line index and table of contents, appears to have been corrected and revised by Harington over a number of years. In a third manuscript, Cambridge University Library Adv. b.8.1 (*C*), dated in his own hand *19 December 1600*, Harington selected fifty-two epigrams for a beautifully bound presentation copy for his wife and mother-in-law, transcribed in the same italic hand as *F*.

This edition, the first to be based solely on these three extant and closely related manuscripts, all of which Harington himself ordered and revised, aims to provide the modern reader with an uncluttered text of the *Epigrams* that, as nearly as possible, approximates to *F*. I have used the other two texts to provide corrections only where the scribe has made an obvious error or to supply one omission of three epigrams (fully discussed in Chapter 4). All changes to the copy text are recorded in the Critical Apparatus, which shows both authorial revision (including deletion) and alternative readings. This is not a composite text, nor does any emendation come from outside these three manuscripts.

I have preserved the original spelling, lineation and punctuation (however variable) of *F*. Demands of space and modern typography meant that it was impossible to preserve the original pagination, but it is indicated on the right of the text. Since *F* (like the other two manuscripts) has clearly identifiable autograph revisions, this edition concentrates on indicating to the reader where and how Harington has amended the text. I have included the corrections Harington made to the numbering of the 'decades': the forty theological poems that, on every tenth poem, form the skeletal backbone of the entire collection. I have, therefore, treated the numbers and their variable 'pointing' as part of the text. Autograph revisions, to text and to numbers, are in italics, the only italics (apart from running heads, sigla, *bis* and *ter*) in the text, Apparatus and Appendix.

After 1596, Harington chose to print none of his major compositions, in prose or poetry. All five printed editions of the *Epigrams*, from 1615 to 1930, are posthumous, and not only lack Harington's authority, but changed the spelling, silently omitted poems (some a great many) and progressively scrambled the order. A critical edition of these muddled and defective texts would be of limited value.

The first-line index and table of contents, the first ever to accompany the poems in print, have been transposed from Harington's own (untitled) index in *BL*. Since every printed edition has invented its own scheme of numbering, and since the most recent edition has become a standard scheme of reference, I have also added a concordance of the numbering of the *Epigrams*, in print and manuscript, at the end of the book (Table 1). The first-line index and tables should make it possible to find individual poems, and see at a glance how the various editions selected, and successively disordered, the *Epigrams*. For the first time in print, the common reader can see the *Epigrams* as the coherent and intricate work of art that Harington designed and meticulously shaped with his own hand.

List of Illustrations

Watermark 1: Folger MS V.a.249, pp. 1–172: watermark of Hans Durr, owner of the Upper Schliefe Mill, St Albantal, Basel, from 1604 to 1635. *Painted by Simon Mathers.*

Sigla

Folger Shakespeare Library MS V.a.249	*F*
British Library Add. MS 12049	*BL*
Cambridge University Library Adv. b.8.1	*C*
Arundel Harington Manuscript	*AH*
Bodleian MS Rawlinson D. 289	*R*
Holkham Hall MS 437	*H*

Abbreviations

Beal	*Index of English Literary Manuscripts*, I: *1450-1625*
BL	British Library
Briquet	C. M. Briquet, *Les Filigranes*, 4 vols
CSPD	Calendar of State Papers Domestic
CUL	Cambridge University Library
CWE	*Collected Works of Erasmus*
CWTM	*Collected Works of Sir Thomas More*
Folger	Folger Shakespeare Library
HMCR	Historical Manuscripts Commission Report
May	*Elizabethan Poetry: A Bibliography and First-line Index of English Verse, 1559-1603*
ODNB	*Oxford Dictionary of National Biography*
PRO	Public Record Office
TLS	*Times Literary Supplement*

Watermark 2: Folger MS V.a.249, pp. 173-266: watermark of Nicolas Lebé of Troyes. *Painted by Simon Mathers*.

Acknowledgements

The generous support of the Grocers' Company over the last four years has made the research for this book possible, and I should like to thank this ancient Company, their Clerk, Peregrine Rawlins, and his successor, Robert Pridham, who have made my visits to Grocers' Hall such a pleasure. It was a singular privilege to give a talk there in 2006 on the feast of Edmund Campion, the most distinguished Grocers' Scholar. I owe almost everything else to the Folger Shakespeare Library which, under its Director, Gail Kern Paster, awarded me Fellowships in 2005 and 2008, and which has been a second home and family. This book was largely written there. The remarkable Librarian, Richard Kuhta, and all his staff, especially Betsy Walsh and all the Reading Room staff, looked after my scholarly needs with their unique combination of warmth, humour and efficiency. I was not only given prolonged access to my copy text, Folger MS V.a.249, but able to benefit from the knowledge, help and support of Erin Blake, Ron Bagdon, Carol Brobeck, Rachel Doggett, Steven Galbraith, Barbara Mowat, Frank Mowery and Georgianna Ziegler. Heather Wolfe gave me superb advice, provided whatever sound basis there is in my editorial policy and read through sections of my introduction.

I wish to express a special debt to two other scholars, both of whom had earlier set out on the task of transcribing this text. The first is Robert H. Miller, whose transcription provided an invaluable control and corroborative evidence for difficult readings. The second is Jason Scott-Warren, who generously passed to me his corrections of Miller's text, notes on the evidence of ink colour, migration of epigrams, and countless bibliographic details, and who kindly helped me eliminate a number of errors by reading through my entire draft.

There are many others without whose advice this text would be less accurate. I wish especially to thank Michael Kiernan, who has not only been a good companion in hot Folger days, but whose expert editorial advice has helped me solve many a problem; Steven W. May who has given me invaluable advice at critical stages in the editorial process; Hilton Kelliher whose eagle eye spotted, in the Bodleian, a third Harington transcription of Campion's poem; and Peter Beal, who helped me with numerous manuscript terms, told me of useful miscellanies and read through my final draft. There are many other scholars without whose encouragement, friendship and advice this would never have been finished: Clare Asquith, Dom Aidan Bellenger, Timothy Billings, Peter Davidson, Eamon Duffy, Tom Freeman, Philippa Glanville, Andrew Hegarty, Grace Ioppolo, Phebe Jensen, Sean Keilen, Arthur Marotti, Randall McLeod, Jean-Christophe Mayer, Robert

Miola, John Mulryan, Petr Osolsobe, Aysha Pollnitz, Robert L. Reid, Dom Geoffrey Scott, Alison Shell, Deirdre Serjeantson, John Sutherland and René Weis.

As I wrestled with the wealth of sources, several talks on Sir John Harington's *Epigrams* helped me reduce the material to manageable shape: to the Renaissance Society of America in Miami, in March 2007, to the Institute of Historical Research, Senate House, London, in June 2007, to the conference on Robert Southwell at St Edmund's Hall, in April 2008, and to the conference on Sir Thomas More and William Tyndale at Liverpool Hope University in July 2008.

I should like to thank Elizabeth Fuller, Librarian of the Rosenbach Library, Philadelphia, and Mark Farrell, Librarian of the Robert H. Taylor Collection, Princeton University Library, Peter Young, Archivist at York Minster Library (which still contains the collection of Archbishop Matthew) all the librarians and staff of the British Library Manuscript Room, whose endless patience and kindness with the collation and research has been such a help, of the Bodleian Duke Humfrey Library, the Rare Books Room of Cambridge University Library, and of Bath City Library, which generously allowed me access to Harington memoranda and the 1598 edition of John Heywood's *Workes* in their Buxton Collection. I should like to thank all my family and friends, who have been so tolerant of my prolonged immersion in Sir John Harington and his writings; my students and colleagues at King Edward's School, Bath, who certainly heard more about him than they needed; and my editors at Ashgate, Erika Gaffney and Kirsten Weissenberg, who have been models of patience as I struggled to keep the text and commentary within a gradually increasing allocation of space, and who provided me with a superb copy editor in Maria Anson. Finally, I should like to thank my three daughters, Charlotte, Eleanor and Beatrice, and my three grand-daughters, Safiya, Hester and Aliya, for making me sing nursery rhymes down the telephone and tell absurdly redemptive stories of giants and dolphins.

Gerard Kilroy.
Folger Shakespeare Library, 2009.

PART 1
The Pleasant Learned Poet

Chapter 1

The Courtier in the Margins

A most learned knight

In the only major political event in which Sir John Harington played a part, he deliberately portrays himself as a marginal figure. Harington (Plate 3), aged 39, had been 'speciallie commended' by the Queen to accompany the Earl of Essex on his expedition to Ireland.[1] Harington joined Sir William Warren on 18 October 1599, the second day of his diplomatic completion of the controversial treaty that Essex had struck with the Irish rebel, Hugh O'Neill, Earl of Tyrone. The O'Neill, after sharing with Harington reminiscences of their shared friends among the English nobility, returned to the business in hand:

> After this he fell to private communication with Sir William, to the effecting of the matters begun the day before; to which I thought it not fit to intrude myself, but took occasion the while to entertain his two sons, by posing them in their learning, and their tutors, which were one Fryar Nangle, a Franciscan; and a younger scholer, whose name I know not; and finding the two children of good towardly spirit, their age between thirteen and fifteen, in English cloths like a nobleman's sons; with velvet gerkins and gold lace; of a good chearful aspect, freckle-faced, not tall of stature, but strong, and well set; both of them [learning] the English tongue; I gave them (not without the advice of Sir William Warren) my English translation of "Ariosto," which I got at Dublin; which their teachers took very thankfully, and soon after shewed it to the earl, who call'd to see it openly, and would needs hear some part of it read. I turn'd (as it had been by chance) to the beginning of the 45th canto, and some other passages of the book, which he seemed to like so well, that he solemnly swore his boys should read all the book over to him. (248–50)

Harington presumably read not only from his *ottava rima* translation of *Orlando Furioso*, but from his own commentary on this canto, which recalls that Elizabeth, 'the Queenes most excellent Majestie that now is', had been an imprisoned princess

> that wrate in the window at Woodstocke with a Diamond:
>   Much suspected by me}
>   Nothing proued can be} quoth Elizabeth prisoner.[2]

Ostensibly, Harington is telling O'Neill and his sons – and other readers of *Orlando Furioso* – that he and '*M. Thomas Arundell* and Sir *Edward Hobby*' translated this epigram into Latin; indirectly, he is emphasizing the unjust accusation and dramatic changes of fortune that can afflict even princes. A princess in prison one moment can, he argues, become 'a crowned Queene, with greater applause then either *Lewes* in France, or *Coruino* in Hungarie'.[3] Harington is not just being loyal to the young princess whom his father had protected so faithfully, but also instructing, through his sons, an aspiring political leader.

This story is an emblem of how Harington dealt with affairs of state: not 'intruding' but using the book to read moral lessons to rulers. The poetic text of the book may be a *commedia*, but its commentary uses historical and personal anecdote to reflect on mutability. From the beginning to the end of his life, Harington used his position as a marginal commentator, on the page and at court, to mask the seriousness of his moral, political and theological message.

After the execution of Essex on 25 February 1601, the Queen descended into what Harington describes (in an intimate letter to his wife, Mary) as a 'most pitiable state' full of 'choler and greife' (322–3). Amidst several scenes when he describes the Queen as enraged with courtiers and ministers, Harington was summoned to 'the chamber', where

> Her Majestie enquirede of some matters which I had written; and as she was pleasede to note my fancifulle braine, I was not unheedfull to feede her humoure, and reade some verses, whereat she smilede once, and was pleasede to saie; – "When thou doeste feele creepinge tyme at thye gate, these fooleries will please thee lesse; I am paste my relishe for suche matters; thou seeste my bodilie meate dothe not suite me well; I have eaten but one ill tastede cake since yesternighte." (322–3)

He is still able to evoke a smile in a dark period where she 'stamps with her feet at ill news, and thrusts her rusty sword at times into the arras in great rage' (318). Harington's position as a wise fool, 'that witty fellow, my godson' (317), now makes him an unthreatening courtier, upon whose loyalty, as upon his father's, the Queen may depend. It becomes easy to see why Harington adopted this mask if one examines his inheritance.

John Harington was born into the court of Queen Elizabeth on or about 1 August 1560, the date he put on the autobiographical title page of his *Orlando Furioso* (Plates 1 and 8); he was certainly christened on 4 August at Allhallows, London Wall; the Queen was his godmother and William Herbert, the Earl of Pembroke, his godfather.[4] He was the first son to be born to Isabella Markham, the second wife of John Harington of Stepney; she remained a gentlewoman of the Privy Chamber from her marriage in 1559 until her death in 1579. His father, a courtier, survived a religious and political whirligig: the capricious cruelty of Henry VIII, two spells in the Tower, first under Edward VI and then under Mary and, finally, the increasing severity of Elizabeth's Privy Council during the 1570s.

Harington's father, who was first married to an illegitimate daughter of Henry VIII, had devoted himself to transcribing the poetry of Sir Thomas Wyatt and Henry Howard, Earl of Surrey, both of whom had been imprisoned and accused of treason: Surrey was executed, as was Wyatt's son. John Harington of Stepney (as the father is usually known) was 'much skilled in musicke, which was pleasing to the King, and which he learnt in the fellowship of good Maister Tallis, when a young man' (184). He wrote a translation of Cicero's *De Amicitia* (On Friendship) while in his first confinement to the Tower for his support for the 'Lord Admirall', Thomas Seymour. It was his father's experience of loyalty among this imprisoned group, 'the old Admiraltie (so he called them)', that Harington remembers in the 'Morall' of Book XIX of *Orlando Furioso*. His father 'but a weeke before he died' recalled 'that noble peere', some 'fortie yeares since that noble man was put to death', and translated the first stanza of this canto, on loyal friendship, as especially apt, 'for his servants who loued him so dearely, that euen in remembrance of his honourable kindnesse, they loued one another exceedingly', even though some 'were but meane men'.[5]

Harington elides his memories with those of his father, as in this account of his father's second imprisonment, in 1554, under Bishop Gardiner:

> My father, only for carrying of a letter to the Ladie Elizabeth, and professing to wish her well, he [Gardiner] kept him in the Tower twelue months, and made him spend a thousand pownd ere he could be free of that trouble. My mother, that then servd the said Lady Elizabeth, he caused to be sequestred from her as an Heretique, insomuch that her own father durst not take her into his house, but she was glad to soiourne with one Mr. Topclife; so as I may say, in some sort, this bishop persecuted me before I was borne.[6]

While his father was in the Tower, he attended on the young imprisoned Princess, a kindness and loyalty which she never forgot, and from which the younger John Harington benefited throughout his life. In turn, he never ceased to 'blesse her memorye, for all hir goodnesse to me and my familie'(355).

His father's experience of the fickleness of fortune left a profound impression on the courtier son. When he sent his *Epigrams* to King James VI of Scotland, he reminded him of an earlier King of Scots who had been imprisoned at Nottingham Castle, and there engraved the mysteries of the Rosary on the walls.[7] The poem was meant to remind King James, and later Prince Henry, not only of their Catholic past, but of what it is like to be a prisoner, especially a royal prisoner whose life is likely to be taken. The great unspoken subject here is Mary, Queen of Scots (see *Epigrams* III.44). These are not merely tropes on the wheel of fortune; they spring from an inherited sense of the dangers of life at court, for princes and courtiers.

In 1602, writing to Tobie Matthew, then Bishop of Durham, Harington recalled his father's judgement on Henry Walpole's poem on Edmund Campion, who 'though he had the death of a Traytor, yet there was an Epitaph written fitt for a Martyr, and in my fathers Iudgement . . . It was the best Englishe verse and I think the last Englishe verse that euer he redd'.[8] His father's admiration for Edmund Campion, the leading Oxford scholar of the 1560s, Jesuit theologian, poet, orator, martyr and friend of Sir Philip Sidney, may be a development of this sympathy with those denounced as 'traitors'. It is significant that in the year of his death,

1582, John Harington of Stepney, royal courtier, was intensely concerned with paying tribute to two 'traitors': Thomas Seymour and Edmund Campion.

There is no indication of when Harington's own devotion to Campion began, but he refers in glowing terms to him in every prose work from 1596 to 1608: from *A New Discourse*, where he mocks the 'Campiano μαστιξ' [Campion scourge], Dr Laurence Humphrey of Magdalen, to *A Supplie or Addicion*, where he quotes Campion's *Ten Reasons* in his piece on Tobie Matthew.[9] The father passed to his son a transcription of a long Latin poem on the early history of the church by Campion.[10] Harington had at least two more copies made of this poem. His scribe copied the poem in what is now Holkham MS 437 (*H*), sometime after 1586, and again, sometime after 1604, in Bodleian MS Rawlinson D. 289 (*R*).[11]

Harington bases his own admiration for two Henrician courtiers sentenced to death for treason – Sir Thomas More ('what neede hee care, that cared not for death?') and John Heywood ('that scaped hanging with his mirth') – on their attempt to use wit to stand up to, and in Heywood's case to evade, the wrath of a tyrant.[12] It is not surprising that the view of religion Harington received from his father focused on the 'unstable wheele' of fortune. In 1602, he writes to Tobie Matthew (and Matthew has underlined):

> of these fower chaunges in religion, all fower capitall, all 4 within litle more then 14 yeare, as my father (who lyved in all of them, and was persecuted in the third) hath often remembred.[13]

The influence of a literary group of humanist courtiers, many of whom were fellow prisoners with his father in 1550 or 1554 – Sir John Cheke (nine of whose letters Harington transcribed or preserved), Roger Ascham, John Feckenham, last Abbot of Westminster, and John Heywood – shaped Harington's love of learning and his own detachment from the *cursus honorum* of the court. In *A New Discourse*, the first book cited is *Castalios Courtier*.[14] Sir Thomas Hoby, the father of Harington's schoolfellow Edward, made a celebrated translation of *The Courtier* in 1561 (and the first edition includes a letter from Sir John Cheke). Castiglione's advice is:

> To eschew as much as a man may, & as a sharp and daungerous rock, *Affectation*, or curiosity & (to speak a new word) to use in euery thyng a certain *Recklessness* (*una certa sprezzatura*), to couer art withall, & seeme whatsoeuer he doth & sayeth to do it wythout pain, & as it were not myndyng it.[15]

Two of the earliest tributes to Harington refer to him as *doctissimus* (most learned), but he masked this learning, as Castiglione suggests, with *sprezzatura*.[16] He carried on his father's task of collecting poetry and prose in manuscript, and he remains one of the most important transcribers of Sir Philip Sidney's *Arcadia*, the Countess of Pembroke's translation of the Psalms, Henry Constable's sonnets for *Diana* and the poetry of Edmund Campion.[17]

If he inherited from his father a sense of the fragility of court life, Harington was as shaped by his mother's family, the Markhams, which had links with the Nevilles and Lady Margaret Beaufort. Through them he was introduced to the dangers and discomforts of the Catholic recusant community. Just as Sir Thomas Wyatt had been denounced by Bishop Bonner for his alleged links with Cardinal Pole (a relative of the Beauforts), so Thomas Markham was now being libelled by Justice Young. *A New Discourse* is disguised as a prose discourse on 'how vnsauerie places may be made sweet' (sig. L1), but is actually a complex allegorical and emblematic study of the corrupting impact of political 'libell'.[18] Harington devotes twelve pages – the longest section in the book – to clearing his uncle from the 'libell' put about by Justice Young, that he is a 'Mal-content'; Young is twice glossed, in Harington's own hand, as a *promooter*, the real *stercus* (excrement), and savagely accused three times of lying: 'You lye, like a lowt lewd Maister Libeller'.[19] He writes, in his own hand, to Markham, 'I wil not say moche to you in the beginning of my booke because I have sayd perhaps more then enough of yow in the end.'[20]

A vivid picture of Isabella Markham is given us when Harington cites an incident from the beginning of Elizabeth's reign, when:

> neither were they called papists but the old religion, and the new, and to speake of the furthest of my memorye, I remember how the Lord Haistinges of Loughborrowe came to dynner to my fathers, who lay then at Stepney, and while prayers were saieng he walked out into the garden, which my mother taking ill, for she was euer zealous in her faith, said to hir brother Mr. Thomas Marckham (who brought the same Lord Haistings thither) that if he brought guestes thither that scorned to pray with her, she would scorne they should eate with her.[21]

His mother's desire for unity forms the essential argument of Harington's *Epigrams* and *A Tract on the Succession*, but the connections of the Markham family brought the dangers of recusancy very close to home. Isabella's sister, Frances, married Henry Babington, whose son, Anthony, was executed in 1586 as the author of the plot to rescue Mary, Queen of Scots. Her brother, Thomas Markham, married Mary Griffin, and their son, Sir Griffin Markham, was sentenced to death in 1603 (and then pardoned on the scaffold) for his part in the Bye Plot. More importantly, Thomas Markham's daughter, Elizabeth, married Edward Sheldon, son of Ralph Sheldon of Beoley, whose wife was Anne Throckmorton, one of the four daughters of Sir Robert Throckmorton of Coughton (the three others were married to Sir William Catesby, Sir Thomas Tresham and Edward Arden, executed in 1584). Harington, close in age to Edward Sheldon, dedicated *A New Discourse* to him, addressing him as 'My good cousin Philostilpnos' (lover of cleanliness).[22] He is obviously as anxious to clear Ralph Sheldon as his own uncle, Thomas Markham, from the libels heaped on him.[23]

Harington was, in this way, linked to a network of recusant families in Warwickshire and Worcestershire, the very group that sheltered Campion, and

whose sons went on to devise the 'Powder Treason'. Biographical accounts of
Harington normally emphasize the ancient lineage and courtly grandeur of his
family; I wish to suggest that Harington's inherited memory was of the instability
of court life and the mortal dangers incurred by close family on account of their
religion.

Harington was also deeply influenced by his closeness to the Arundells. Sir
Matthew Arundell, of Wardour Castle, was a leading Catholic recusant, and his
wife, glossed by Harington himself as *the Lady | Arundel a | Wiloughby*, was a
Lady of the Privy Chamber.[24] The Willoughby family was connected to the family
of Sir Robert Markham, so it is not surprising that Harington treats the Arundells
as if they were his own family. Harington shared his schooling at Eton, which he
began in 1570, with Thomas Arundell. The relationship was sufficiently close for
familial banter as, in a marginal note in Lord Lumley's copy of *A New Discourse*,
Harington has glossed Thomas as *Peleus son | a better man | then his fa|ther.* (sig.
O1ᵛ). Harington compares the way the Queen 'loveth to see me in my laste frize
jerkin, and saithe *'tis well enoughe cutt'*, with her insult to Sir Matthew Arundell:
'I do remember she spit on Sir Mathew's fringed clothe, and said, *the fooles wit
was gone to ragges*' (167). Clearly both men tried to bring a touch of rural
simplicity into the life of the court. 'Peleus' is the pseudonym he gives Sir
Matthew in three amusing epigrams (I.26, 49; III.15). The banter concealed a more
serious involvement. In the winter of 1583–84, a government spy wrote from Bath,
concerned that 'yong harrington' was among a network of 'playfellowes,
companions therein and confederates' of Charles and Matthew Arundell, and
involved with them in importing 'nawghtie bookes . . . from beyond the seas'.[25]
Harington's one-eyed servant, James Baker, was apprehended for using a
commission given to Harington's father to 'range about the contreye from place to
place with Edmund Campions bookes'.[26]

That the connection with the Arundells remained central to Harington's life is
proved by autograph marginalia in the copy of *A New Discourse* belonging to Lord
Lumley (now in the Folger), listing the five others present when this emblematic
work or 'devise was first both thought of and discoursed of, with as brode termes
as any belongs to it, in presence of six persons':

> *Erl of Southamp.| Sʳ Mat. Arundel |Count Arundel.| La Mary Arundel| Sʳ Hary Davers.|
> Warder Castle.*[27]

The conception of *A New Discourse* at Wardour Castle can, therefore, be dated to
before October 1594, when Sir Henry Danvers had to flee abroad.[28] The presence
of the Earl of Southampton and his devoutly Catholic sister, Lady Mary
Wriothesley, who had married Thomas Arundell in 1585, gives the whole
inspiration of the 'device' a strongly recusant ring. Harington's most famous work,
A New Discourse, emerges from the heart of the Arundell and Southampton
families, and sets out to clear his own Catholic relatives, Thomas Markham and

Ralph Sheldon, of libels being put on them for their recusancy. That the allegory struck home, making Harington flee the court, is an indication of its power.[29]

If Harington's family background shaped his desire for religious unity, his education at Eton, and later at King's College, Cambridge, made him at home in Greek, Latin, French, Spanish and Italian literature. Eton, like all great schools in this period, was fortunate to be following a programme largely determined by Erasmus (see Chapter 2). By the 1560s every good school in the country was following the plan contained in three books of Erasmus: *De Ratione Studii*, first produced for John Colet of St Paul's in 1511; *De Copia,* first published in 1512; and finally the grammar produced by William Lily and Erasmus, that became known as 'Lily's Grammar'.[30] We know from the anecdote cited above that Harington was already composing Latin epigrams at Eton. At the end of the *Epigrams*, we find 'The Authors farewell to his Muse written at Eaton the 14 of Aprill. 1603.' Harington leaves behind the comic Muse which was born at Eton (*Te nunc Ætonæ, namque hinc es nata relinquo*).

The Queen evidently took an interest in the education of her godson, because Harington records receiving a speech of hers, addressed to 'Boye Jacke', a gift sent 'because thy father was readye to sarve and love us in trouble and thrall' (127–8). Harington, as he tells us in *Orlando Furioso*, also received advice and poetry from 'That wise and honorable counseller, Sir Walter Mildmay'.[31] From one heavily deleted epigram in *BL* we learn that, contrary to Erasmian principles, boys were beaten: 'Who tells tales out of school somtimes is beaten | such was the fashion of the schoole of Eaton'.[32]

Many of Harington's memories of Eton surface in his *A Supplie or Addicion to the Catalogue of Bishops to the Yeare 1608*, since many of his schoolmasters went on to become bishops. Harington remembers with affection William Wickham, later Bishop of Winchester (then 'Viceprovost of Eaton') who

> in the Schoole maisters absence) would teach the Schoole himselfe, and dyrect the boyes for their exercises; of which myself was one, of whom he shewd as fatherly a care, as if he had bene a second tutor to me.[33]

There is less affection for a former Provost, William Day. Harington remembers this avaricious collector of benefices falling from a horse, and a number of 'waggish schollers, of which I thinke my selfe was in the *Quorum*, would say it was a iust punishment' because the horse 'was giuen hym by a gentleman to place his sonne in Eaton, which at that tyme we thought had bene a kinde of sacriledge'.[34] Day became Dean of Windsor, and was one of Campion's opponents in his 'Conferences' in the Tower, for which he wrote the official account.[35]

Harington went up to King's College, Cambridge, in 1576, where 'my good Jacke' received another letter of advice, this time from Lord Burghley, recommending 'for the Latin tongue, Tullye chieffelie, if not onlie; for the Roman story, (which is exceedinge fitt for a gentleman to understande,) Lyvie and Caesar; for logycke and philosophie, Aristotle and Plato'(131–2). The Earl of Essex was one of his contemporaries.[36] Vivid pictures of Harington's life at Cambridge are provided in *A New Discourse*, where he describes the scene in hall at 'commencement feasts' when the 'Bibler' (reader) began and they all hissed *s't tacete*.[37] A glimpse of Harington's interest in university theatre is given us when he compares himself to

> our stage keepers in Cambridge that for feare least they should want companie to see their Comedies, go vp and downe with vizers and lights, puffing and thrusting and keeping out all men so precisely; till all the towne is drawne by this reuell to the place; and at last, tag and rag, fresh men and subsizers, & all be pakt in together, so thicke, as now is scant left roome for the Prologue, to come upon the stage. [38]

Harington was even more interested in theology and, in 1607, he recalled two academic topics of debate. The first was when he 'was a truantly scholer in the noble Vniversity of Cambridge', on whether the language of scripture 'is not barbarous'.[39] The second, 'some 25 yeares since' in Cambridge, asked whether sermons could be adorned with 'Rhetoricall figures and tropes, and other artificiall ornaments of speach taken from prophane authors, as sentences, Adages, and such like'. Harington clearly endorses the views of 'my learned tutor Doctor Flemming' that 'we shoud not dispise the helpe of any humane learning'.[40] 'About 12 yeare after this, the verie same question in the same manner was canvased at Oxford', in a sermon by Dr Walter Howse, when Dr John Reynolds, 'Bellarmins Corrector', was on the opposite side.[41] This must have been one or two years after the lecture by Reynolds that is ridiculed in *Epigrams* I.20, and dated in autograph as *1592*.

Harington took his Master of Arts degree in 1581, and entered Lincoln's Inn on 27 November. He was, therefore, in London seven days after Campion's trial and four days before his execution. His transcription in the Arundel Harington manuscript of the Walpole poem on Campion contains one change that suggests that he may have been a witness to one or both of these momentous events. Where Walpole sharpens the focus of the impact of Campion's death from the whole of Europe to England and London, Harington alters 'London must needes' to 'And London most', as if he remembered the charged atmosphere of the capital, like one who was present: 'England was filled with rumore of his end. | And London most for yt was present then.'[42]

On 26 June 1583, Harington came into possession of his inheritance, which included the estate at Kelston. He married Mary Rogers (Plate 4), daughter of the widowed Lady Rogers of Cannington, Somerset, on 6 September 1583. All the evidence is that this marriage was extraordinarily successful:

> The Queene did once aske my wife in merrie sorte, "how she kepte my goode wyll and love, which I did alwayes mayntayne to be trulie goode towardes her and my childerne?" My Mall, in wise and discreete manner tolde her Highnesse, "she had confidence in her husbandes understanding and courage, well founded on her own stedfastness not to offend or thwart, but to cherish and obey; hereby did she persuade her husbande of her own affectione, and in so doinge did commande his." (177–8)

The elaborately bound gift-book of epigrams (*C*, Plate 7) celebrating their marriage, their minor rows, their witty exchanges and their love-making, is a lasting testimony to a marriage of equals. Two of their nine children died, and four epigrams movingly refer to their deaths. In III.80*bis*, he tries to comfort his wife for her loss, but his own grief is evident in two autograph revisions elsewhere. He amended a line, in both *F* and *C*, to read, 'two souls, sweet souls, were to *too* fleeting' (III.11), and in *C* deleted 'Nine', writing *Seavn* above the line (III.91). Finally, in *BL*, he prefaces the collection with an epigram describing how Lady Rogers is now joining her dead grandchildren in a triumph over Death:

> their soules in hands of god from death are free
> their flesh must rise agayne to conquer thee.[43]

Harington and his wife moved into the estate he had inherited at Kelston, where it seems that he completed the construction begun by his father. This included the addition of a fountain beneath which, it is said, the Queen, in 1592, 'dined right royally'.[44] Collinson's *History of Somerset* contains an engraving of the fountain (Plate 10), on top of which is Harington's own humorous rebus, which Thomas Combe engraved in 'An Anatomie', a hare holding a ring above a tun, inscribed '1567', from which water flows into a bowl and then into a square basin, which is raised off the ground on four columns, and decorated with the Harington coat of arms and a theatrical mask at each corner.[45] From Collinson we also learn that:

> The old manor-house stood near the church, and was erected in 1587 by sir John Harington, after a plan of that celebrated architect James Barozzi, of Vignola. This house sir Caesar Hawkins pulled down [in 1764], and about twenty years since erected an elegant mansion southward of it.[46]

The fountain in Harington's translation of *Orlando Furioso* seems to reflect the fountain at Kelston as much as that in Ariosto.[47] The prefatory 'Letter' in *A New Discourse* from 'Philostilpnos' (Edward Sheldon) particularly mentions 'a Fountaine standing on pillers, like that in Ariosto, under which you may dyne and suppe', among the attractions of 'your house, of your picturs, of your walks, of your ponds'.[48] Harington writes how he came 'home to Kelstone, and founde my Mall, my childrene, and my cattle, all well fedde, well taughte, and well belovede', and makes this contrast: ''Tis not so at cowrte; ill breeding with ill feedinge, and no love but that of the lustie god of gallantrie, Asmodeus' (166), where there are 'false hope, false friends, and shallow praise' (168). 'Now what findethe he who lovethe the "pride of life," the cowrtes vanitie, ambition's puff ball? In soothe, no more than emptie wordes, grinninge scoffe, watching nightes, and fawninge daies' (170). By contrast, when he arrives home from the expedition to Ireland, he writes: 'Thank heaven! I am safe at home, and if I go in suche troubles againe, I deserve the gallowes for a meddlynge fool' (179). In a letter to Sir Anthony Standen, written just after his return from Ireland, he declares:

In December I came hither, but since, I hear little and do nothing but sit by a good fire, and feed my lean horses, and hearken for good news, but hear none, save the certain expectation of peace with Spain . . . Let this suffice from a private country knight, that lives among clouted shoes, in his frize jacket and galloshes, and who envies not the great commanders of Ireland, but hereby commends himself to them. (310–11)

From Kelston, after the Queen's death, he writes in pastoral and elegiac vein, of how he will 'tende my sheepe like an Arcadian swayne, that hathe loste his faire mistresse' (180).

Such comments persist into the reign of James; in a letter written to Lord Thomas Howard in April 1603, soon after the accession of James, Harington contrasts the sycophantic 'sportes at newe cowrtes' (337) with his life in the country where, like Horace, he enjoys a life of scholarly reading and verse composition:

I am now settynge forthe for the countrie, where I will read Petrarch, Ariosto, Horace and suche wise ones. I will make verses on the maidens, and give my wine to the maisters; but it shall be such as I do love, and do love me. I do muche delight to meete my goode freindes, and discourse of getting rid of our foes. Each nighte do I spende, or muche better parte thereof, in counceil with the aunciente examples of lerninge; I con over their histories, their poetrie, their instructions, and thence glean my own proper conducte in matters bothe of merrimente or discretion; otherwyse, my goode Lorde, I ne'er had overcome the rugged pathes of Ariosto, nor wonne the highe palme of glorie, which you broughte unto me, (I venture to saie it) namely, our late Queenes approbation, esteeme, and rewarde. Howe my poetrie maye be relishde in tyme to come, I will not hazard to saie. (338)

In a letter from the same period to Dr John Still, 'the Bishoppe of Bathe and Welles' he expresses sympathy for the disgraced Ralegh, adding:

but hereof enowe, as it becomethe not a poore countrye knyghte to looke from the plow-handle into policie and pryvacie. I thanke Heavene, I have been well nighe driven heretofore into narrowe straits, amongste state rocks and sightless dangers; but if I have gained little profitte and not moche honoure, I have not adventured so far as to be quite sunken herein. I wyll leave you all now to synke or swym, as seemethe beste to your own lykinge; I onlie swym nowe in our bathes, wherein I feel some benefyt and more delyghte . . . God commend and defend your Lordshippe in all youre undertakynges. He that thryvethe in a courte muste put halfe his honestie under his bonnet; and manie do we knowe that never parte that commoditie at all, and sleepe wyth it all in a bag. (343)

By contrast, Harington was fully involved in the life of the city of Bath and the affairs of the county of Somerset. He succeeded his friend, Sir Hugh Portman, as High Sheriff in 1591.[49] Bath had just been given 'a new charter, declaring it to be a sole city of itself'.[50] Harington, concerned with the lamentable state of Bath Priory (now Bath Abbey), campaigned for its restoration over a period of some fifteen years. He recounts how it came to be in such deplorable condition in his notes on

Bishop Oliver King, where he tells with horror of how the townsmen, when given the chance to buy the whole church from Thomas Cromwell's Commissioners for 'vnder 500. Marks', thinking they were being tricked, 'vtterly refused yt'.[51] The church, having been sold twice over, had 'become ruinous, and stript of . . . every thing else that could be sold for money'.[52]

> Wherevpon certaine merchants bought all the glass Iron, bells and leadd of which leadd alone was accompted for, As I haue crediblie heard 480. tunne worth at this day .4800[li].
> . . . Thus speedily it was pulld downe, but how slow it hath rysen againe I may blush to wryte, Collections haue bene made over all England, with which the Chauncell is coverd with blew slate, and an Alms house built *ex abundantia*, but the whole church stands bare *ex humilitate*. The rest of the money never comming to the Townsmens hands is layd up as I suppose with the money collected for Pauls steeple, which I leave to a *Melius inquirendum*. And thus the Church lyes still like the poore travailer menciond in the 10. of Luke spoyled and wounded by theeues. The priest goes by the Levites go by but doe noe thing. Only a good Samaritan honest Mr. Billet [Thomas Bellot] (worthy to be billeted in the new Ierusalem) hath powrd some oyle in the wounds and maintaind yt in life.[53]

In a letter to Lord Burghley, as early as 1595, Harington describes the progress of the restoration:

> Our work at the Bathe dothe go on *haud passibus aequis*: – we sometimes gallop with good presents, and then as soon stand still, for lack of good spurring; but it seemeth more like a church than it has aforetime, when a man could not pray without danger of having good St. Stephen's death, by the stones tumbling about our ears, and it were vain to pray for such enemies. (185)

Harington's success in this project is praised by his cousin, Lord Harington of Exton who, with Lord Burghley, is in Bath hoping for a cure: "You are not dead to good works, for even now this churche doth witness of your labour to restore it to its ancient beauty" (237). In a letter of June 1608 to 'Mr Thomas Sutton founder of the Charter-house School', Harington outlines the progress so far of the restoration and appeals for funds:

> Do somewhat for this church; you promised to have seen it e're this; whensoever you will go to Bathe, my lodgings shall be at your commandmente: the baths would strengthen your sinews, the alms would comfort your soule.
> The tower, the quire, and two isles, are allready finished by Mr. Billett, executor to the worthie Lord Treasurer Burleigh; the walls are up ready for covering.
> The leade is promised by our bountiful bishop, Dr. Montague; timber is promised by the earl of Shrewsburie, the earle of Hartford, the lord Say, Mr. Robert Hopton, and others.
> There lacks but monie for workmanship, which if you would give, you should have many good prayers in the church now in your life-time. (378–9)

The only memorial in Bath Abbey to Harington's long campaign is one anecdote:

> Conversing one day with bishop Montague, near the abbey, it happened to rain, which afforded an opportunity of asking the bishop to shelter himself within the church. Especial care was taken to convey the prelate into that aisle which had been spoiled of its lead, and was nearly roofless. As this situation was far from securing his lordship against the weather, he remarked to his merry companion that it did not shelter him from the rain. "Doth it not, my lord?" said Sir John, "then let me sue your bounty towards covering our poor church; for if it keep not us safe from the *waters* above, how shall it ever save others from the *fire* beneath?"[54]

In summary, during the last twenty years of Elizabeth's reign, from 1583 to 1603, Harington was largely at home in Kelston with his beloved wife and his growing family, occupied with building his house and emblematic fountain. Harington's involvement with the 'Irish action' was thrust upon him rather than sought, and produced a flood of letters and poems detailing the intrigue, deception, military chaos, disorder and disloyalty. As Robert Markham's warning letter makes clear, there were 'overlookers' or spies on all sides, with the factional rivalry between Lord Mountjoy and the Earl of Essex at its peak (239–44). While, most of the time, he enjoyed the approbation of the Queen, he clearly found the poisonous factions and sycophancy of the court in the 1590s distasteful. He was heavily involved in local affairs as High Sheriff and a Justice of the Peace, and was a central figure in the long campaign to raise funds for the restoration of Bath Abbey.

Books dominated the life of this scholarly knight. Before 1591, he 'spent some yeares, and months, and weekes, and dayes | In englishing th'Italian Ariost' (*Epigrams* I.48). The 30,000 lines of *Orlando Furioso*, together with the commentaries, engravings and hand-ruled margins, must have taken at least five years to compose and set to print. During the next ten years, he composed and circulated over four hundred epigrams; organized and indexed them into four 'bookes' (including a special gift copy for his wife and Lady Rogers); wrote *A New Discourse* (producing annotated large-paper copies for a small group of friends and relatives); and wrote a remarkably irenic piece on resolving the religious divisions of the nation that he sent to Tobie Matthew in 1602, and which we now know as *A Tract on the Succession*. He was also engaged in transcribing the whole of Sir Philip Sidney's *Arcadia* (BL Add. MS 38892), two copies of a translation of the Psalms by Sir Philip and his sister, the Countess of Pembroke (BL Add. MSS 12047 and 46372), and in adding to his father's collection of poetry in manuscript the works of men like Henry Constable and Edmund Campion (*AH*, *H* and *R*: see Chapter 4). This is a formidable literary output in a life of cultivated, scholarly and literary interest. Harington's works show a profound and detailed knowledge of the Bible, St Augustine, St Thomas Aquinas, Virgil, Horace, Ovid, Cicero, Plutarch, Dante, Petrarch, Ariosto, Erasmus, Castiglione, Sir Thomas More, Alciati, Rabelais and John Heywood, which would require a considerable library. His autograph list of playbooks, compiled in 1610, includes 129 plays, bound in thirteen volumes.[55]

As Craig argues, 'Harington had collected a respectable proportion of all the plays printed in London between 1588 and 1600, and had a remarkably complete collection for the years from 1600–1610.'[56]

Harington's bibliography reflects his preference for living in the margins of court life. His entry into the world of print, the translation of *Orlando Furioso* (1591), was 'a publishing as well as a literary event'.[57] According to Alfred Pollard, it was 'the most ambitious [English] book illustrated with metal plates in the [sixteenth] century.'[58] Yet Field published a separate, large-paper edition, which Harington used for gift copies, some with coloured title page and engravings (see Plate 8). In Lord Burghley's copy, the printed text has been surrounded, on every single page, with hand-ruled red margins; Lady Arabella Stuart's copy has not only the title page, but all the engravings, the initial letters of each canto, the printer's decorations and even the colophon, beautifully hand-coloured.[59] Even with all the resources of print available, Harington seems keen to retain the more personal attributes of manuscript, and subvert the plurality and uniformity of print.

We can catch Harington in the act of subversion, if we examine closely the title page of *Orlando Furioso*, engraved by Thomas Coxon for the first edition in 1591, and compare it with the title page of the First Folio of *The Workes of Beniamin Ionson* printed by William Stansby in 1616 (Plates 1 and 2). In a fine architectural design by William Hole, Jonson presents himself, with two quotations from Horace, as a classical author, surrounded by laurels and triumphal arches, images of tragedy and comedy, and of the *Theatrum*. Jonson's declaration, in his chosen epigraph from Horace, that he is not writing for the vulgar crowd but for a select readership – *neque, me, vt miretur turba laboro: Contentus paucis lectoribus* (Nor do I work so that the crowd may admire me; rather I am content with a few readers) – complements his presentation of the classical origins of drama in the Thespian wagon and the Greek amphitheatre or *Visorium*.

> The presence of the obelisks, which are monuments, and the laurels, the traditional crown of the poet, is surely to signify the author's desire that the folio may bring him a poet's immortality. The pictures of the ancient theatre and the sentences from Horace proclaim the allegiance to the reverend models and precepts of the classical drama and classical poetry by which his works, too learned for the vulgar, have deserved eternal fame.[60]

Jonson the playwright, the engraving proudly proclaims, is a court poet working within a classical tradition.

Twenty-five years earlier, Harington uses the same classical framework, but wittily subverts it. First he uses a very different quotation from Horace, which makes it clear he is not going to flatter the Queen at court: *Principibus placuisse viris non vltima laus est* (The greatest praise does not come from having pleased princes). Secondly, he puts a portrait of himself, which is 'one of the earliest if not the earliest example' of transferring the portrait from the verso to the title page itself.[61] Finally, Coxon has created a chequered ground beneath the classical arch to allow Harington's dog Bungey to remind him of 'Olivero whose deuise is the spaniell, or lyam hound couching with the word, *fin che vegna*' (*vntill he commeth*, Canto XLI, st. 30) coming from the dog's mouth on a banderole that touches his sleeve.[62] That this original and self-deprecating humour made an impact on contemporaries we know from Sir John Davies's epigram which refers to 'Lepidus his printed dogge'. The printed text of Harington's *Orlando Furioso* itself moves attention from the *ottava rima* of the translation to the prose commentary (the 'Morall', 'Historie', 'Allegorie' and 'Allusion') often full of revealing personal anecdote and fascinating cross-reference.

In his next work, *A New Discourse of a Stale Subiect, called the Metamorphosis of Aiax* (1596), Harington went even further. In this emblematic study of the corrupting impact of political libel, he furnished the printed text, in the first large-paper edition, with handwritten marginal glosses.[63] While selected and named readers, like Thomas Markham and Lord Lumley, see a text elucidated by autograph marginalia, the Privy Council and the common reader see, through a glass darkly, an opaque text shrouded in enigmatic marginal spaces.[64]

Thereafter Harington turned almost exclusively to presentation manuscripts. He prepared at least two gift copies of Edmund Campion's *Sancta salutiferi nascentia semina verbi*, supplied with copious marginal glosses.[65] He presented to Lady Rogers, his mother-in-law, and his wife, Mary, a selection of epigrams, bound with his *Orlando Furioso* (*C*), as many of the 'toyes I haue formerly written to you and your daughter, as I could collect out of my scatterd papers'.[66] These poems are no more 'scatterd' than Petrarch's carefully organized *Rime sparse* (scattered verse); nor are they as purely domestic as the inscriptions on the binding suggest. This copy also has annotations, ruled margins and a painted title page (Plate 8; see Chapter 4). As Harington looked to a Scottish succession, he dated this collection, in his own hand, *19 December 1600*, keying it six months from the King's birthday. He dated to the same day a selection of his epigrams to Lucy (Harington), Countess of Bedford. This was followed by *A Tract on the Succession* sent to Tobie Matthew (18 December 1602).[67] The next three handwritten texts were all dedicated to Prince Henry. All the royal gifts are presented as if they are the rewriting of an earlier work, and prefaced by a complex double dedication to Prince and King.

In bibliographic terms, Harington moves from witty self-presentation on the title page of *Orlando Furioso*, through the marginal spaces of *A New Discourse*, into the more private realms of eight handwritten texts. Here bibliography reflects biography: I wish to suggest that the margins, on the page and in life, were a carefully chosen rhetorical space for Sir John Harington. The threat of the Star Chamber (see *Epigrams*, I.87, omitted in *F* and deleted in *BL*) that met the publication of *A New Discourse* and the prolonged 'exile' from court, may have contributed to this shift from printed text into elaborately bound, beautifully produced and privately circulated manuscript books. Certainly, Harington identified himself in an autograph gloss in the *Epigrams* that he presented to Prince Henry with (Lucius Junius) *Brutus*, who survived tyranny by pretending to be a fool.[68] Yet Harington's move to the margins of the book – and of the court, away from 'pleasing princes' – was a triumph of the self-effacing courtesy of an art form that found its full expression in manuscript commentary, and a moral integrity that kept him free of 'the cowrtes vanitie, ambition's puff ball' (170).

Harington was sending gifts to the Scottish King even before the end of Elizabeth's reign. We know from the *Epigrams* that they (and 'a darke lanterne') were sent to James as a 'Newyeares guift to the Kings M$^{tie.}$ of Scotland. Anno. *1602*'. Now that James I is on the throne of England, Harington focuses his attention on the young Prince Henry, but makes each offering echo an earlier gift to the King. In June 1604, he gave his translation of *Aeneid* VI to Prince Henry, claiming 'to revyse a worke I had formerly taken payn in for my sonns better understandinge'.[69] Once again, the *mise-en-page* of this beautiful manuscript is significant. Harington surrounds Thomas Combe's italic transcription of the Latin text of a poem that prophesies the future of Rome with a commentary drawn largely from a text that reflects on the fall of Rome, St Augustine's *De Civitate Dei*. Virgil's prophecy of the Roman *imperium* is textually surrounded by his mediated version of Augustine's reflections on the limitations of worldly power. The verse translation, in *ottava rima*, is on the facing page.[70] The translation and commentary are both in his own secretary hand, a feature that enhances Virgil's text, and gives more emphasis to the commentary's mixture of casual anecdote, light humour and learned reference to his sole authorities, the Bible and 'Snt Awgustin'. He presents the commentary at the end as merely 'a few lynes following' (actually, six essays on major theological subjects), a supplement to 'the marginall notes of this booke . . . unparfet for the lacke of space'.[71] In the first of these essays, 'Of Enchauntments and prophecies', Harington establishes an agreement with the King's own view of witches, before arguing that the Cumaean Sibyl 'prophecyed owr savyor Cryste as proove her verses cyted by *Snt Austin* in the 18 booke *de Civitate dei*'.[72] In educating the Prince, Harington was still careful to acknowledge the new King by a letter of dedication, 'To the Kings most excellent Mat^{ie}', that also seems to belong to the King's birthday.[73] The book certainly received the King's stamp and, for a time at least, seems to have been in the royal library.[74]

The following year, on the King's birthday, 19 June 1605, Harington presents 'all my ydle Epigrams' to Prince Henry, but encloses a substantial amount of earlier dedicatory material (poetic and artistic) to King James. This gift, like the translation of the *Aeneid*, is presented as a fresh transcription of an earlier work. This 'Collection or rather Confusion' is far from confused. Disguised as 'Idle lynes', as Sir Thomas More calls his *Epigrammata*, mixing the homely and the personal, the earthy and the anecdotal, this elaborately ordered collection points to the need for the Prince to unite the kingdom, recognize the importance of a unified church, bring an end to simony and protect church property.

His third literary gift to Prince Henry is dated 18 February 1608, the eve of the Prince's birthday. *A Supplie or Addicion to the Catalogue of Bishops to the Yeare 1608* is presented as an elaborate series of notes to Bishop Godwin's history of the church. It advertises the conversational mode of these notes on the Elizabethan and Jacobean church, and turns occasional commentary and autograph marginalia, which run through printed text and manuscript, into an art form. Still adopting the role of reader to princes, Harington apologizes to Prince Henry at the end that

> this vnworthie supplie of mine . . . is grown into greater lengthe then I expected by reason I tooke some kinde of pleasure with the paine of wryting hereof, supposing I was all the while as it were telling a Story, in your highnes presence & hearing./[75]

Harington disguises his biographical accounts of bishops as postscripts to Bishop Godwin's *A Catalogue of the Bishops of England* (1601), and succeeds in infusing them with his own blend of humour and anecdote. Less history than a conversation that we are invited to join, it uses its colloquial form to pass devastating verdicts on those who have disgraced the office of bishop. Starting his account of Bishop Gardiner with the mild 'Because I will not alwayes be praysing', Harington reveals the contradictions in this churchman and the basis of his own resentment.[76] Over fifty years after Bishop Gardiner's imprisonment of his father and isolation of his mother, Harington describes 'his terrible hard vsage', which he 'cannot yet skarce thinke of with charitie, nor wryte of with patience'.[77] To emphasize Gardiner's 'too great crueltie', he quotes in full the 'sawcie Sonnet' his father sent to him:

> Elev'n months past and longer space
>   I haue abid your develish drifts,
> While you haue sought both man and place,
>   and set your snares with all your shifts.[78]

Elsewhere, Harington ends his damning indictment of William Day's avarice with an apparent afterthought that uses the see of Winchester to portray the Elizabethan church as sliding into an accelerating catalogue of bishops:

> By the way I think this worth the noting that whereas in the yeare of our lord 1486. being the first of king Henry the seaventh yt was found that three bishops successiuely held this bishopprick, six score yeares saue one, namely Wickham Bewfort and Wainfleet. Now in Queene Elizabeths raigne there had bene seaven bishops in forty yeare, 5 in 17. yeare, and three in fowr yeare.[79]

These three books – the *Epigrams*, *Aeneid* VI and *A Supplie or Addicion* – are all in the tradition of Erasmus's *Institutio Principis Christiani* (Instruction of a Christian Prince): attempts to influence both the present and the future King, particularly in his treatment of the church, religion and justice (see Chapter 2). All three books seem to have been transcribed (and in one case painted) by Scribe A in beautifully prepared gift copies. In addition, in a letter of 1609 to Prince Henry, Harington indicates that he has 'sente my "Ariosto" for your Highnesse entertainment' (389). Harington's literary artifice is to present each work as if it has already formed part of a previous dialogue, to enclose verse in prose commentary, to add emblems to allegory disguised as Erasmian humour; to use a translation of Virgil as a way into Saint Augustine's *De Civitate Dei*, to present a collection of *Epigrams* as if they were 'ydle', when their underlying aim is to educate the King and his young Prince; to construct a comprehensive survey of the failings of the church by making it look like an occasional series of marginal and amusing anecdotes.

Harington was here following the advice of Castiglione, who in Book Two of *The Courtier* advises the courtier who wishes to gain the ear of his prince to use the disguise of humour. Castiglione goes on to use the image of a mask (see the masks on Harington's fountain, Plate 10), 'Because to be in a maske bringeth with it a certaine libertie and lycence', disguising 'the principall matter' under *una certa sprezzatura*, so that the onlookers are delighted 'whan they behold afterward a farre greater matter to come of it then they looked for under that attire'.[80]

Harington describes a drunken reception by King James I of the Danish King, in 1606, when his Majesty 'was carried to an inner chamber and laid on a bed of state', and contrasts this with 'what passed of this sort in our Queens day; of which I was sometime an humble presenter' (351–2). He concludes that 'the gunpowder fright is got out of all our heads, and we are going on, hereabouts, as if the devil was contriving every man should blow up himself, by wild riot, excess, and devastation of time and temperance' (352), adding characteristically, 'I wish I was at home' (353). He does, however, go to read to the King, hinting subtly at the King's egotistical obsession with the public opinion of his 'lernynge'. When the King does not turn the conversation back to his own reputation, Harington deftly does it for him:

> The Prince did nowe presse my readinge to him parte of a canto in "Ariosto;" praysede my utterance, and said he had been informede of manie, as to my lernynge, in the tyme of the Queene . . . His Majestie, moreover, was pleasede to saie much, and favouredlye, of my good report for merth and good conceite: to which I did covertlie answer; as not willinge a subjecte should be wiser than his Prince, nor even appeare so. (368)

Harington, again in his pose of reading to a ruler, clearly finds in King James much that makes him nostalgic for 'the tyme of the Queene'. In a letter of 1606 to his cousin, Robert Markham, he gives a fascinating retrospect, starting with the Queen's anger at Essex, of his relationship with her:

> The elements do seem to strive which shall conquer and rise above the other. In good soothe, our late Queene did enfolde them all together. I blesse her memorye, for all hir goodnesse to me and my familie; and now wyll I shewe you what strange temperament she did sometyme put forthe . . . When she smiled, it was a pure sun-shine, that every one did chuse to baske in, if they could; but anon came a storm from a sudden gathering of clouds, and the thunder fell in wondrous manner on all alike. I never did fynde greater show of understandinge and lerninge, than she was bleste wyth; and whoever liveth longer than I can, will look backe and become *laudator temporis acti*. (355–62)

It must have been hard not to 'praise times past' in the presence of such a capricious and superficial King. Lord Thomas Howard urges Harington to 'get a new jerkin well borderd, and not too short' (391) since the King is 'nicely heedfull of such points and dwelleth on good looks and handsome accoutrements' (392); in the absence of the youth and good looks of the King's favourites, Howard suggests that Harington's 'Latin and your Greek, your Italian, your Spanish tongues' (396) may be a recommendation.

Harington, only just forty-three, makes several references in letters to his 'lameness' during these early years of James's reign. 'But, my good Lorde, I will walke faire, tho a cripple' (339). 'My lameness is bettered hereby, and I wyll shortlie set forwarde to see what goethe on in the citie, and prie safelie amonge those that trust not mee, neither wyll I truste to them . . . I am too well strycken in yeares and infirmyties to enter on new courses'(343). Robert Cecil recommends him to avoid London, 'Too much crowdinge doth not well for a cripple'(346). He says to Robert Markham in 1606, 'I growe olde and infirme' (362).[81]

While Harington was, as we have seen, heavily occupied with restoring Bath Abbey, and raising funds for its redecoration, books were clearly his main comfort during these years. To Sir Hugh Portman he says, 'I am in liking to get Erasmus for your entertainmente' (319). His treatment of his copy of Petrarch is ingenious. To Lord Thomas Howard he writes of how he will 'point oute to you a special conveyance' necessary 'for in these tymes, discretion must stande at oure doores, and even at our lippes too' (339). Thomas Combe is associated in Harington's letters with bringing him his copy of Petrarch. 'Send me Petrarche by my man, at his returne' (363), he writes to Robert Markham, and to his wife, 'Send me up, by my manne Combe, my Petrarche. Adeiu, swete Mall' (324). In Lyly's *Euphues and his England* (1580) Petrarch is used for carrying secret correspondence: 'This letter Camilla has stitched into an Italian Petracke she had.'[82] It looks as if Harington is using Combe and his copy of Petrarch to convey his confidential letters. In the introductory epistle to *A New Discourse*, Edward Sheldon (Philostilpnos) asks Harington (Misacmos) 'to cause your man M. Combe (who I vnderstand can paint pretily) make a draught, or plot thereof to be well conceaved.'[83] Clearly Combe is no ordinary 'man'. From the winter of 1583–84, when he was distributing 'Edmund Campions bookes', to 1608, the 'most learned' Harington seems adept at exploiting every aspect of the book.

In the reign of King James, Harington turned to making his own translations of the Psalms. Several transcriptions by him of the Psalms of Sir Philip and Mary Sidney (Herbert), most of them laid out for daily recitation, may also belong to this period.[84] He seems also to have been making a verse translation of the *Schola Salernitana*, to educate his son and Prince Henry.[85] Harington's carefully cultivated mask of 'witty poet' and failed courtier belongs to the elaborate subterfuge that kept him, just, safe from the Star Chamber.

Harington's output as scholar and writer is, by any standards, prodigious. Yet only three of the works were printed in his lifetime. Both the scale and the seriousness of his works have been underestimated. Beneath the mask recommended by Castiglione, he used his wit to comment on the injustices of his time. Brought up among men of learning whose conscience had led to imprisonment and, in some cases, death, Harington turned to the 'pleasant' scholars of his father's time: Alciati, Erasmus, Sir Thomas More and John Heywood. Harington's originality was to create an art whose form invited readers to relax among the humour and ambiguity long before they realize that they have taken in a much more serious message. Concealed amid the anecdotes of the commentaries on *Orlando*, hidden in the spaces of the marginal glosses of *A New Discourse*, attired in the leather binding of the *Epigrams*, is a moral philosophy by which prince and pauper alike may judge their own actions and the values of their time. Harington disguises as postscripts to Godwin's *Catalogue of Bishops* a devastating analysis of what has produced the high and low points of the church in England. In both life and literature, Harington followed Castiglione's advice: using *una certa sprezzatura* to disguise his serious content, and delighting his readers because they discover *molto maggior cosa* ('a farre greater matter') emerging with 'grace'.[86]

Scott-Warren also ends his scholarly analysis of Harington's writing by focusing on 'Castiglione's *sprezzatura* (the art that hides art, the extra labour that makes a hard-won skill look easy)', but then asks, 'why did Harington's career fail to happen?'[87] My answer is that Harington chose to live and write in the margins, away from 'ambition's puff ball'(170). This kept him safe and, in the end, secured him a privileged position where Elizabeth could see him, like his father in the Tower, 'readye to sarve and love us in trouble and thrall' (128).

Notes

1   Thomas Park, ed., *Nugae Antiquae*, 2 vols (London: Vernon and Hood, 1804), vol. 1, p. 245. Hereafter all references to this first volume will be page numbers in the text.

2   *Orlando Furioso in English Heroical Verse by Iohn Harington Esquire* (London: Richard Field, 1591), STC 746 (large-paper edition), p. 393; Sir John Harington, *Orlando Furioso*, ed. Robert McNulty (Oxford: Clarendon Press, 1972), pp. 541–2. Henceforth all references will be to the first, large-paper, edition by Field, followed by McNulty's edition in parenthesis.

3   Ibid.

4   *Orlando Furioso*, sig. ¶1r; Ruth Hughey, *John Harington of Stepney: Tudor Gentleman* (Columbus: Ohio State University Press, 1971), pp. 58–60; D. H. Craig, *Sir John Harington* (Boston MA: Twayne, 1985), p. 5.

5   *Orlando Furioso*, Canto XIX, 'Morall', p. 151 (ed. McNulty, p. 217), where Harington also tells us that the translation of the first stanza, on the constancy of real friends in misfortune, is 'almost word for word . . . my fathers'.

6   Sir John Harington, *A Supplie or Addicion to the Catalogue of Bishops to the Yeare 1608*, Royal MS 17.B.XXII, p. 38; ed. R. H. Miller (Potomac MA: Turanzas, 1979), p. 67. Henceforth references will be to the MS, then to Miller in brackets.

[7] See below, *Epigrams*, p. 162.

[8] York Minster Library MS XVI.L.6, pp. 237–8; Sir John Harington, *A Tract on the Succession to the Crown (1602 A.D.)*, ed. Clements R. Markham (London: Roxburghe Club, 1880), pp. 104–5. All references will be to the York MS (*A Tract* in parenthesis).

[9] Sir John Harington, *A New Discourse of a Stale Subiect, Called the Metamorphosis of Aiax* (London: Richard Field, 1596), STC 12779, p. 29; ed. Elizabeth Story Donno (London: Routledge & Kegan Paul, 1962), p. 105; *A Supplie or Addicion*, p. 164 (ed. Miller, pp. 175–8). Henceforth, all references to *A New Discourse* will be to this edition, paginated only till p. 128 (end of the 'Metamorphosis') and (in parenthesis) to Donno.

[10] BL Add. MS 36529, fols 69v-78r. A full account is to be found in my *Edmund Campion: Memory and Transcription* (Aldershot: Ashgate, 2005), pp. 149–93.

[11] The first is Holkham MS 437 (*H*), on paper manufactured by Niklaus Heusler, who owned the Zunziger Mill, Basel, 1586–1613. A second manuscript has now come to light, thanks to Hilton Kelliher, Curator of Manuscripts (retired) at the British Library. Bodleian MS Rawlinson D. 289 (*R*) contains the poem with no attribution or dedication. The hand is the same as *F* and *H*, and is written on paper that shares the same watermark as the first eleven quires of *F*, that of Hans Durr who owned the Upper Schliefe mill, thirty metres from the Zunziger mill in Basel, from 1604 to 1635.

[12] *A New Discourse*, p. 27 (ed. Donno, pp. 101–2).

[13] York MS XVI.L.6, p. 239 (*A Tract on the Succession*, p. 106).

[14] *A New Discourse*, 'The Answer', sig. A6r (ed. Donno, p. 61).

[15] Count Baldessar Castiglione, *The Courtyer of Count Baldessar Castilio. diuided into foure bookes*, trans. Thomas Hoby (London: W. Seres, 1561). sig. E2: hereafter *The Courtyer* (1561). Hoby later produced a parallel text version in Italian, French and English: *The Courtier of Count Baldesar Castilio, devided into foure bookes*, trans. Thomas Hoby (London: John Wolfe, 1588) STC 4781. See also, J. R. Woodhouse, *Baldesar Castiglione: A Reassessment of The Courtier* (Edinburgh: University Press, 1978), pp. 76–7.

[16] Joannis Stradlingi, *Epigrammatum Libri Quatuor* (London: George Bishop and John Norton, 1607) STC 23354, p. 32. *Epigrammatum Ioannis Owen Cambro-BritanniLibri Tres Editio Tertia, prioribus emendatior* (London: Humfrey Lownes, 1607), STC 18986, Bk II.34.

[17] H. R. Woudhuysen, *Sir Philip Sidney and the Circulation of Manuscripts 1558–1640* (Oxford: Clarendon Press, 1996), pp. 106–9, 164, 290–91, 380–84, 397–9; Ruth Hughey, *The Arundel Harington Manuscript of Tudor Poetry*, 2 vols (Columbus: Ohio State University Press, 1960), vol. 1, pp. 244–54; my *Edmund Campion*, pp. 39–120 and 195–208.

[18] Ibid., sig. L1 (ed. Donno, p. 187).

[19] *A New Discourse* (STC 12779, Lord Lumley's copy), glosses on sigs O6r-v (ed. Donno, pp. 243–5); for defence of Markham, see sigs O5r-P3v (ed. Donno, pp. 245–50).

[20] From Harington's autograph dedication to Thomas Markham's annotated copy, which is now in the Robert H. Taylor Collection, Princeton University Library, STC 12779.

[21] York MS XVI.L.6, pp. 234–5 (*A Tract on the Succession*, pp. 102–103).

[22] Harington's autograph gloss in the Nares-Folger edition of *A New Discourse* confirms his identity as 'Edward Sheldon' (sig. A4r).

[23] *A New Discourse*, sigs O4v-O5r (ed. Donno, pp. 238–40).

[24] Ibid. (Lord Lumley' copy), sig. O1v (ed. Donno, pp. 233–4).

25 PRO SP 12/164: fol. 183r; *CSPD 1581–90*, p. 142.

26 PRO SP 12/167: fol. 14r; *CSPD 1581–90*, p. 150. See my *Edmund Campion*, p. 68.

27 *A New Discourse* (listed in margin of Lumley's copy), p. 113 (ed. Donno, p. 174).

28 See Donno, p. 59, note 29.

29 For this interpretation of *A New Discourse*, see my *Edmund Campion*, pp. 89–96.

30 The full title was *De Octo Orationis Partium Constructione Libellus, tum elegans in primis, tum dilucida brevitate copiosissimus* (Strasbourg: Martin Schurer, 1515).

31 *Orlando Furioso*, Canto XXII, p. 175 (ed. McNulty, p. 249).

32 In *BL*, p.192 (see Appendix below).

33 *A Supplie or Addicion*, p. 55 (ed. Miller, pp. 80–81).

34 Ibid., p. 58 (ed. Miller, p. 83).

35 Alexander Nowell and William Day, *A true report of the Disputation or rather private Conference had in the Tower of London, with Ed. Campion Iesuite, the last of August. 1581.* (London: Barker, 1583), STC 18744; for Sir Thomas Tresham's account see BL Add. MS 39828, fols 38r-41r.

36 *Orlando Furioso*, Canto XIV, 'Allegorie', p. 111 (ed. McNulty, p. 163).

37 *A New Discourse*, p. 69 (ed. Donno, p. 138).

38 Ibid., sig. N3v (ed. Donno, p. 221).

39 *A New Discourse*, pp. 7–8 (ed. Donno, pp. 85–6).

40 *A Supplie or Addicion*, p. 132 (ed. Miller, p. 147).

41 Ibid. For Harington's long, chiastic account of these 'two brothers of one name', see also York MS XVI.L.6, p. 248–50 (*A Tract on the Succession*, pp. 112–13).

42 For a full account of the text and transcriptions see my *Edmund Campion*, pp. 195–207.

43 *BL*, sig. Ai; for a full transcription, see Appendix below.

44 John Nichols, *The Progresses and Public Processions of Queen Elizabeth*, 3 vols (London: 1788–1807; repr. J. Nichols and Son, 1823), vol. 3, pp. 250–51.

45 John Collinson, *The History and Antiquities of the County of Somerset*, 3 vols (Bath: R. Cruttwell, 1791), vol. 1, p. 41 (Plate 10).

46 Ibid., vol. 1, p. 128.

47 *Orlando Furioso*, Canto XLII, stanzas 71–5, p. 356 (ed. McNulty, pp. 488–9).

48 *A New Discourse*, sig. A2r-v (ed. Donno, p. 55).

49 Collinson, *Somerset*, vol. 1, p. xxxvii.

50 Ibid., vol. 1, pp. 22–3.

51 *A Supplie or Addicion*, p. 89 (ed. Miller, p. 111).

52 Collinson, *Somerset*, vol. 1, p. 57.

53 *A Supplie or Addicion*, pp. 89–91 (ed. Miller, pp. 111–12).

54 *Nugae Antiquae*, vol. 1, pp. xvi-xvii. Park gives no source for this anecdote, now recorded on Bishop Montague's tomb.

55 BL Add. MS 27632, fol. 43r-v: Harington's autograph list, for thirteen bound volumes.

56 See Craig, *Sir John Harington*, p. 14. For a printed list, see F. J. Furnivall, 'Sir John Harington's Shakespeare Quartos', in *Notes and Queries*, 7th series, 9 (1890), 382–3.

57 Steven W. May, *The Elizabethan Courtier Poets: The Poems and Their Contexts* (Columbia and London: University of Missouri Press, 1991), p. 158. McNulty, *Orlando Furioso*, examines at length the printing and engraving of this work, pp. xlii-xlvii.

58 Alfred W. Pollard, *Early Illustrated Books: a history of the decoration and illustration of books in the 15th and 16th centuries,* 2nd edn (London: K. Paul Trench, 1893), p. 249, quoted by McNulty, *Orlando Furioso*, p. xlvii.

[59] Burghley's copy is now in the BL: C.57.h.1, sig. Ai. 'ESQUIRE' has been tipped in (and partially lost) beneath Harington's name on the title page; autograph corrections, 'The table' and 'The tales', have been added to 'An Advertisement', as in Folger, STC 746, Copy 1 (inscribed *PTyrwhitt*). Lady Arabella Stuart's copy is in a private collection.

[60] Margery Corbett and Ronald Lightbown, *The Comely Frontispiece: The Emblematic Title-Page in England 1550–1660* (London: Routledge & Kegan Paul, 1979), pp. 144–50 (p. 150).

[61] Ibid., p. 43.

[62] *Orlando Furioso*, Canto XLI, p. 349 (ed. McNulty, p. 480).

[63] The paper of this edition, like part of *F*, was made by Nicolas Lebé (see Chapter 4).

[64] The only two complete annotated copies known to survive are Lord Lumley's, in the Folger, and Thomas Markham's, at Princeton. See my *Edmund Campion*, pp. 90–96.

[65] Holkham MS 437 and Bodleian MS Rawlinson D. 289. See Chapter 4 below.

[66] CUL, Adv. b.8.1., fol. 204v (verso of Field's colophon).

[67] York MS XVI.L.6 (*A Tract on the Succession*).

[68] *Epigrams*, 'The Elegie of the Lanterne', 1 (p. 254).

[69] Trumbull Add. MS 23 (now in a private collection in New York), sig. A2r. *The Sixth Book of Virgil's Aeneid, Translated and Commented on by Sir John Harington*, ed. Simon Cauchi (Oxford: Clarendon Press, 1991), p. 1.

[70] Ibid., p. liv (illustrated on pp. lviii-lix).

[71] Ibid., p. 61–2.

[72] Ibid., p. 65.

[73] Ibid., p. lvii. Cauchi notes that the date 'June 9th 1604' is given in a mid-seventeenth century copy. Jason Scott-Warren, *Sir John Harington and the Book as Gift* (Oxford: University Press, 2001), p. 214, suggests that '9' could be a scribal misreading of '19', the date of the King's birthday.

[74] Ibid., p. lv. The manuscript, bound in vellum, has the stamp of James I on both covers.

[75] *A Supplie or Addicion*, p. 179 (ed. Miller, p. 189).

[76] Ibid., p. 35 (ed. Miller, p. 64).

[77] Ibid., p. 38 (ed. Miller, p. 67).

[78] Ibid., p. 40 (ed. Miller, p. 69).

[79] Ibid., p. 60 (ed. Miller, p. 84).

[80] Castiglione, *The Courtyer* (1561), sig. M3; *The Courtier* (1588), sig. L1r-v (Italian).

[81] There is a dubious anecdote, told by Dr Henry Harington, that Lord Burghley said, when visited by Harington in Bath, 'Sir John nowe doth one cripple come to visit another', BL Add. MS 46381, fol. 48r, quoting Peck's *Desiderata Curiosa*.

[82] Quoted by Jason Lawrence, *'Who the devil taught thee so much Italian?': Italian Language Learning and Literary Imitation in Early Modern England* (Manchester: University Press, 2005), p. 30.

[83] *A New Discourse*, sig. A3r (ed. Donno, pp. 56–7).

[84] BL Add. MSS 12047 and BL Add. MS. 46372. The text of the seven penitential psalms in BL Egerton MS 2711, fols 104–7 was probably begun earlier.

[85] *The Englishmans Docter or The School of Salerne* (London: Helme and Busby, 1607), a slight verse translation in 24 pages, was published anonymously, but originally existed in a lost parallel text manuscript, see Scott-Warren, *Sir John Harington*, p. 215, note 98.

[86] Castiglione, *The Courtyer* (1561), sig. M3; *The Courtier* (1588), sig. L1r-v (Italian).

[87] Scott-Warren, *Sir John Harington*, p. 240.

Chapter 2

Models and Sources

Discussion of Harington's models has usually started, and often finished, with the poet Martial, the Spanish-born master of the Latin epigram who wrote some twelve books of epigrams in Rome between AD 86 and 102. Norman Egbert McClure puts forward no other model.[1] Even Jean McMahon Humez took 'A Study of the Epigram Volumes of Martial, Harington and Jonson' as the title for her seminal thesis.[2] I wish to argue that Harington's collection of *Epigrams* looked to a more meditative and philosophical tradition: the Greek Anthology, although he used Martial as his cover, 'Hyding a iewell rich in hollow cane'.[3]

Johannes Lascaris published the first printed edition of the Greek Anthology in 1494; in 1503, Erasmus's friend, Aldus Manutius, published an edition based on the sole autograph manuscript, Marcianus 481, transcribed by the monk Planudes in 1320, and then in St Mark's library, Venice. Within thirty years, Alciati, Erasmus and More had all published Latin translations of these epigrams. Under the influence of Erasmus who wrote his *De Ratione Studii* for John Colet and his new school at St Paul's in 1511, the Greek Anthology became familiar to every English schoolboy, who practised 'variation' as a creative way to learn verse translation under the influence of great writers. Epigrams from the Greek Anthology, along with Latin versions by Martial and sixteenth-century practitioners like Alciati, Erasmus and Thomas More, formed a standard part of the school curriculum in England by the time Harington started at Eton, sometime around 1570.[4] The *ratio studiorum* laid down for Eton in the 1560s included this Friday afternoon prescription for the Fourth Form: 'Before five the master reads: 4th [form] Apophthegms, or Epigrams of Martial, Catullus, or Thomas More.'[5] In 1581, G. H. (Gabriel Harvey) records a list of grammar school texts being read in London. The same combination as at Eton occurs:

Legunt Erasmi Apophthegmata, Parabolas, Chiliades, Moriae Encomium . . . Horatii Odas, Epistolas, Satyras: legunt Epigrammata Martialis . . . Alciati Emblemata.[6]

The *Apophthegms*, *Parables*, *Adages* and *Praise of Folly* of Erasmus, the *Odes*, *Epistles* and *Satires* of Horace, the *Epigrams* of Martial and *Emblems* of Alciati: this combination of texts forms the basis of education in all the best schools in the country.

The notebook of William Badger, who was at Winchester College (1561–69), has the following entry, dictated by Christopher Johnson, the master, that shows the eminence of the epigram:

Inter omnia scriptorum genera nullum est quod magis ingenium probet atque exerceat, quam carmen quod . . . Epigramma appellatur.
[Among all kinds of writers, none tests and exercises the intelligence so much as the poem called the Epigram.][7]

Badger was given an epigram from the Greek Anthology, then versions of it by Martial, Alciati, Sleidan, by the master himself, and then asked to provide his own version: *Vos experimenta date* (Now you have a go).[8]

John Stockwood, Headmaster of Tonbridge, published his *Progumnasma Scholasticum* in 1597, based on the indexed and annotated edition of the Greek Anthology by Henri Estienne.[9] Each epigram is provided with a page reference to Estienne's edition; the parts of speech are explained, and then follow translations. A good example is an epigram that seems to have left its mark on Dr Johnson (an admirer of the *Epigrammata* of both More and Erasmus), *In nuptias* (on marriage), followed by the Latin translations of Erasmus, More and Alciati:

> *Ab Erasmo*
> *Altera connubium experto cui ducitur uxor*
> *Hic fracta repetit aeqora saeua rate.*
> [The man who takes a second wife after trying matrimony is a man who takes to rough seas when his raft has been broken.]

> *A Moro*
> *Qui capit uxorem defuncta uxore secundam*
> *Naufragus in tumido bis natat ille freto.*
> [The man who takes a second wife after the death of his first is like a shipwrecked man who takes to the rough sea for a second time.]

> *Ab Alciato*
> *Coniunx cui periit piro, & connubia rursus*
> *Prosequitur, rursus naufragium patitur.*
> [The man who loses his wife and pursues a second marriage suffers again a second shipwreck.][10]

I wish to argue that these Latin translators of the Greek Anthology, Alciati, Thomas More and Erasmus, who formed an integral part of the school curriculum, were Harington's most important influences, but it is also true that Martial was, as much as Cicero, part of the literary air in early modern England. So what influence did Martial exercise, and what did Harington take from him?

The first edition of Martial seems to have been printed in Venice between 1469 and 1473, and there were at least twenty-six editions by the time Sir Thomas More came to publish his own *Epigrammata* in 1518. The earliest copy owned by the Folger Shakespeare Library was printed in Venice in 1493. This is an elegant folio copy of 159 leaves, where the text is surrounded by the commentary of Domizio Calderino and Giorgio Merula.[11] The commentary early draws attention to a strand which runs through the history of the epigram, attention to the reader's reception:

Ambiguitate in primis suspensum auditorem circumscribit: quem uni intentum parti altera occupat. Denique delectat omnes: alienat neminem, nam eum quoque qui dicto laedit: risu uetinet [retinet].

[The epigram at first holds the reader suspended with its ambiguity; when one part distracts the hearer, another seizes him. Then it pleases everyone, alienates no one. For the man whom it stings with a word, it holds with a laugh.] [12]

An inscription on the title page makes clear that the book was owned by the Jesuit College in Paris, a fact confirmed by two partially cropped annotations: *Collegii. Paris. Soc[ie]tis Iesu* and *Ad usum Rhetorum.*[13] For Saint Ignatius had commissioned Father André des Freux to prepare an expurgated edition of Martial for school use. Edited by Father Edmond Auger, it appeared in 1558, and was printed, as the title page makes clear, at Rome:

Epigrammata paucis admodum vel reiectis, vel immutatis nullo Latinitatis damno, ab omni rerum obscenitate, verborumque turpitudine vindicata.

[The Epigrams, only a few of which have been rejected or changed without damage to the Latin, stripped of every sort of obscenity and raised above every distasteful form of language].[14]

The professors of Rhetoric in Paris obviously had the 1493 text to consult for the missing poems or lines. The Jesuits, therefore, were teaching Martial about a century before the first school edition in England, printed for Westminster School in 1655; a further sixteen Westminster editions followed before 1790. There was no printed edition of Martial published in England before the Farnaby edition of 1615, a copy of which Ben Jonson sent to his friend Richard Briggs in 1623:

Est Farnabij mei Martialis. Non ille Jesuitarum castratus, eviratus, et prorsus sine Martiali Martialis. [The book is my Farnaby Martial, not that castrated and emasculated edition of the Jesuits, which is, frankly, Martial without Martial.][15]

The vigour with which Jonson inveighs against the castrated Jesuit version suggests that this was the edition he had used as a schoolboy at Westminster.

While it is true that Harington completely omits the frequent and flagrant obscenity in Martial, he uses some of the obscene poems, but translates them in such a way as to rob them of any offence. He had certainly seen a full text of Martial, for Harington's 'Of Galla going to the Bath./' (II.51) is derived from Martial's epigram, III.87, not included in the Jesuit version, which reduces the very obscene Book III of Martial to a mere thirty-seven epigrams. Harington, however, omits the two offensive words, *fututam* and *cunno* and, instead of the image of Chione lifting her undergarment to hide her face, surprises the reader with the innocent final couplet:

But yet one foule and vnbeseeming place
she leaues vncouered still: what's that? her face./

In an apostrophe to the book that imitates Martial, at the start of his own selection of *Epigrammes* in the 1616 Folio, Jonson declares his intention of avoiding what people might expect from the title *Epigrammes*:

> It will be look'd for, booke, when some but see
>   Thy title, Epigrammes, and nam'd of mee,
> Thou should'st be bold, licentious, full of gall,
>   Wormewood, and sulphure, sharpe, and tooth'd withall. ('To my Booke')

Although Jonson's epigrams avoid both the obscenity and the savage vitriol of Martial, the autograph marginal annotations of his 1619 edition of Martial make clear his knowledge of both.[16] Equally, some eighty of Harington's epigrams, Humez argues, 'are based, in whole or in part, upon a source in Martial – one in every five'.[17] His 'debt to Martial is profound and complex,' she adds, dismissing T. K. Whipple, who described Harington's translations of Martial as 'uninspired but not quite incompetent'.[18]

In some of the shorter poems, Harington preserves the spirit and the letter of Martial's wit. Two Harington epigrams are characteristic, both close to their originals in Martial, Book I.38 and 40. It is not an accident that John Budge chose these two lightweight epigrams to open his 1615 edition:

> The vearses Sextus thou didst reade are mine,
> But with bad reeding, thou maist make them thine./ (II.43)

> Who reed our lynes with visage sowr and grim,
>   I wish him envy me, none envy him. (II.73)

A more important contribution of Martial is that he frequently frames each book, which he makes us imagine as having a physical entity, on its way to readers. He starts with an apostrophe to *parue liber* the 'little book' (I.3; II.1; III.2, 4, 5; VIII.1; XI.1; XII.2) and ends each *libellus* with another (IV.86, 89: *Ohe, iam satis est, ohe, libelle* (Whoa, little book: whoa now, that's enough!); VII.97; VIII.72; IX.99; X.104.[19] Martial makes us imagine the moment his book is struck by a shower of rain (III.100) or, with the ink still wet, sent round as a gift (IV.10):

> While my little book is new, the edges not yet trimmed, and the page, not yet dry, afraid to be touched, go, my lad, and take a small present to a dear friend who deserves to be the first to have my trifles. Run, but go equipped. Let a Punic sponge accompany the book, it suits my gift. Many erasures cannot mend my jests, Faustinus, but one erasure can.[20]

He also describes his book replacing the usual Saturnalian gifts of napkins and jars of damsons (V.18).[21] There is no echo of that physical sense of the book in Harington, but he does involve the reader and the supposed recipient in the imagined moment, in what Humez calls the 'theatricality' of Martial.[22] Harington can makes us feel vividly close to the dramatically imagined moment of a supper guest using his writing 'tables' to take down a date, in 'Of table talke'(III.6):

> I had this day carrowst the thirtenth cup,
>   and was both slipper tongu'd, and ydle braynd,
> And said by chaunce that you with me should sup,
>   You thought hereby a supper cleerly gaind,
> And in your tables strayght you cote it vp,
>   Vncivill guest, that hath been so ill traynd,
>   Worthy thou art hence supperles to walke,
>   that tak'st advauntage of our table talke./

Harington too (III.98) invites his 'Frends' to share his choice of the 'pleasure' of 'toyes' (light poetry) as Martial does in V.16: 'You, my reader friend, are the reason, why I prefer to write what gives pleasure, when I could write of weightier matters, you who read and recite my verses all over Rome.'[23]

Yet the tone and overall effect is quite different from Martial's twelve books.[24] We find neither the sustained Saturnalian obscenity nor the abuse that runs through all twelve books of Martial's epigrams; Harington, by contrast, hints at ribald meanings, or makes the reader supply a 'wanton' word. Where Martial is sharply satirical, Harington is, with some rare exceptions, humorously exposing absurdity; where Martial is flagrantly obscene and often dealing with homosexual practices, Harington is mildly wanton, always heterosexual and never explicit about any sexual activity. Martial suggests only a fool thinks he can compete with Virgil (III.38, VIII.55). While Harington too plays down the artistry of his 'ydle Epigrams', he begins each book with an epigram on the prophetic role of the poet: himself (I.1), John Heywood (II.1), Thomas Bastard (III.1) and his own plea for a Stuart reform of England (IV.1).[25] Other poems humorously defend the epigrams against various critics and, as Humez says, 'represent skirmishes fought with the traditional opponents: bad poets, plagiarists, carping critics, or victims disgruntled by earlier epigrams'.[26]

While Harington's *Epigrams* cultivate the same sense of immediacy and artless spontaneity as Martial, they show a stronger awareness of the structure of each book. Examine the framing poems of Book III, for example. Harington clearly enjoyed 'Of two frayle Saynts', the poem that so amusingly closes Book III, and that included a Latin version in both manuscripts. Yet its subtle wordplay on the current usage of the word 'saynts' for the Puritan 'godly', and the abandonment of its use for the canonized blessed in Paradise, is revealed as a debasement that affects the whole society:

> How would the wicked and vngodly scoffe yt
> Yf they should fynd vs saynts getting a Prophitt.

If 'saynts' are engaged in such unholy 'venereous action', the last epigram of Book III suggests, poets need to be prophets, as its first epigram of the book so clearly asserts: 'a Poet is one step vnto a prophet' (III.1). In his prophetic role, Harington tightens the structure of each book, as he makes explicit in III.94, with a skeleton of ten theological poems. These forty 'decades' endow Harington's four books of *Epigrams* with a serious moral and political purpose that is completely original to him, and well beyond the scope and intention of Martial (see Chapter 3 below).

Sine Martiale Martialis (Jonson's phrase) could as well describe Harington's four books of *Epigrams*. Over eighty poems are concerned with religion and ecclesiastical abuse; a further fifty focus on justice and the state; over fifty, addressed to his wife and mother-in-law, are domestic, or familial in every sense of the word; a further thirty are addressed, lovingly, to friends and to fellow poets. In short, over half the poems have no parallel in Martial.

Harington sets out his models clearly in *A New Discourse of a Stale Subiect, called the Metamorphosis of Aiax* (1596). In the introductory letter prefacing his learned satire, he pins his colours to the tradition of Erasmus, who 'writes in prais of follie'.[27] In the body of the text he moves from Alciati, the emblematist, through the epigrams of Martial, to a longer discussion of the epigrams of More and Heywood.

The contributions of the friend of Erasmus, the great Milanese jurist, Andrea Alciati (1492–1550), to the *Selecta Epigrammata graeca latine versa, ex septem epigrammatum Graecorum libris* of Cornarius were first published by Bebellius in Basel in 1529, and thirty-one of these epigrams formed the basis of the first edition of Alciati's *Emblematum Liber* in 1531. This small book, which began as illustrated epigrams, expanded through a series of editions and was translated into French, German, Spanish and Italian. It was given its most famous commentary by the Dijon jurist, Claude Mignault in 1573 and, by 1621, had been published in 152 editions.[28] Harington begins his discussion of emblems and epigrams in *A New Discourse* with a long discussion of 'diuerse pretie emblems, of this excrementall matter. As that in Alciat'.[29] After two pages on 'Emblemes', Harington turns to 'Epigrams':

> And thus much for Emblemes. Now for poesie (though Emblemes also are a kind of poesie) . . . It is certaine, that of all poems the Epigram is the wittiest, & of all that writes Epigrams, Martiall is counted the pleasantest. He in his 38. ep. of his first book, hath a distichon, that is very plyable to my purpose; of one that was so stately, that her close stoole was of gold, but her drinking cup of glasse.
>
> 1.38   *Ventris onus puro, nec te pudet excipis auro:*
>   *Sed bibis in vitro, charius ergo cacas.*
>
> [Your bowels' burden you receive in pure gold and are not ashamed of it, yet you drink out of glass. So you defecate more dearly.][30]

Harington was singling out Alciati's most controversial, learned and complex emblem, *Aduersus naturam peccantes* (Of those sinning against nature), published by the Aldine press for the first and only time in the 1546 *Emblematum Libellus*:

Turpe quidem factu, sed & est res improba dictu
   Excipiat siquis chœnice uentris onus.
Mensuram, legisque modum hoc excedere sanctae est,
   Quale sit incesto pollui adulterio.
[It is certainly a shocking deed, but it is even disgraceful to describe, if someone were to empty the burden of his bowels into the city's corn measure. This is what transgressing the measure and limit of sacred law means: it is as serious as being defiled by incestuous adultery.] [31]

This emblem, unique to the Aldine edition, shows an old man defecating in front of the city or *res publica*. The sources for this include the Martial epigram he quotes (now I.37), Erasmus's *Adagia* (I.i.2), Plutarch's *Moralia* (12.E-F), the *Oneirocritica* (Interpretation of Dreams) by Artemidorus and the commentary of St Jerome. It suggests that the damage done to the state by those who transgress the system of law is as dreadful as defiling the corn measure. Harington transforms Alciati's juridical idea (whose reference to incest and adultery, based on Artemidorus, must have carried some political resonance in 1546) into his epigram, 'A godlie father, sitting on a draught' (I.90), and into the political critique of a corrupt and venal society that runs like a thread through the last fifteen epigrams of 'The first booke' and culminates in the last word of the book:

> they that devour whole churches and their rents
> I mean our Favorites and courtly Minions,
>   Voyd forts and Castles in their excrements./[32]

Harington's chosen pseudonym, in both *A New Discourse* and the *Epigrams*, is 'Misacmos': hater of filth. In using imagery drawn from this emblem of Alciati, Harington was giving a scholarly reference to one of the most learned international jurists of the century and his critique of extra-judicial excess, and applying it to Elizabethan society in the 1590s. The influence of Alciati on Sir John Harington and his servant, the emblematist Thomas Combe, was considerable. Thomas Combe transformed de la Perrière's courtly emblems into something closer to Alciati's moral discourse when he brought out *The Theater of Fine Devices*, published, in 1593, by Richard Field. [33]

After Alciati, Harington turns to 'Sir Thomas Mores Epigrams, that flie ouer all Europe for their wit and conceit'. [34] Erasmus encouraged his friend, the great Basel publisher Johann Froben, to print More's *Epigrammata, Pleraque e Graecis versa* (for the most part translated from Greek epigrams), in a joint edition with his *Utopia*. [35] This elegant volume, which also contained translations of Greek epigrams by Erasmus and More's English friend, William Lily, and illustrations by Holbein, was first published in 1518, and revised for a separate edition in 1520. The Froben edition is, in this way, an outward sign of the profound concordance of ideas between the two men at this period. Schurer had just published the expanded version of Erasmus's *Encomium Moriae*; Erasmus was elaborating his essay on Adage IV.i.1, *Dulce bellum inexpertis*, working on his *Enchiridion Militis*

Christiani, published independently for the first time in 1515, and working on *Institutio Principis Christiani*, first published by Froben in May 1516. The works by Erasmus and More in this period share a profoundly Christian and Platonic view of the folly of this world, the emptiness of power, the importance of just rulers, and a strong criticism of the wastefulness of warfare.

More's *Epigrammata* are prefaced by five poems originally dedicated to the young King Henry on his coronation in 1509. The five dedication poems welcome the new King as bringing law and light to a fearful kingdom, compare the new King's reign to the abuses of power by his father, Henry VII, and emphasize his role in uniting the factions in the kingdom, getting rid of *delatores* (informers), uniting two powerful kingdoms through his Queen and producing a male heir. They liken the new King to Phoebus Apollo (as Harington does later with James), and invoke Virgil and Plato to proclaim the return of a new golden age.

> *Aurea prima sata est aetas, argentea post hanc.*
>   *Aerea post illam, ferrea nuper erat.*
> *Aurea te, princeps, redierunt principe secla.*
>   *O possit uates hactenus esse Plato.*
> [The golden age was the first to be sown, after this the silver; after that came the bronze, and, more recently the iron age. With you on the throne, O Prince, the golden age has returned. May Plato, at least in this, be a true prophet.] [36]

The dedicatory framework, which makes clear the purpose of the 253 epigrams – to educate a prince and outline the ideals of a peaceful kingdom – ends with a poem on the imagery of the emblem of two roses united in one. In a presentation copy that has survived in the British Library, these congratulatory poems are accompanied by several illuminations, a decorated title page and two painted emblems of the Tudor rose and the Granada pomegranate.[37] In the prose letter, prefacing Froben's 1518 edition, More apologizes to the King for the long delay, which he amusingly blames on the attack of gout that afflicted the illustrator just when he was undertaking the task: *haud scio, maioremne gratiam uersiculis nostris pictoris manus adiecerint, an pedes ademerint* (I do not know whether the illustrator's hands added more grace to my verses or his feet took more away).[38]

More's *Epigrammata* are dedicated to the newly crowned King Henry, and re-dedicated to him nine years into his reign. Similarly, Harington's epigrams, originally dedicated to King James as a New Year's gift *1602* (6 January 1603), just before the transition from the old reign to the new, are re-dedicated, in 1605, to the young Prince Henry on his father's birthday. Harington's *Epigrams*, therefore, like More's, constitute a reminder of the high hopes expressed in the welcoming 'Elegies' to the new King and Queen. Harington's poems are accompanied by the painted emblem of 'the Lanterne' (like that of the Tudor rose) and a religious engraving. More's are prefaced, Harington's followed, by five celebratory elegies.

More's influence goes further. Twenty-six of More's epigrams, one-tenth of the total, are devoted to the topic of kingship, particularly the difference between tyrants and kings. While these poems are embedded in a general pattern of epigrams that focus on the mortality and folly of human beings, they tend to occur in sequences (21–4, 61–2, 91–103), a practice followed by Harington. One of those cited in full by Harington in *A New Discourse* (Ep. 21) states that wind held in the stomach too long can kill you, but let out, can make you live. 'A king can cause no more, a crack doth do no lesse.'[39] This is followed by a group of three poems on the vulnerability of kings and their equality with beggars before death. The last of these, *Venatus Araneae* (Spider Hunt), employs an image also used by Erasmus. The fly is rescued from the allegorical spider (or king) by a bird. The final couplet makes the allegory explicit, the Latin alliteration of *m* and *t* linking armed men with the fear of an evil tyrant:

> *Sic misero spes est plerunque secure sub ipsa,*
> *Inter et armatos mille malo metus est.*
> [Thus for a poor wretch under the very blade of the axe there is usually some hope, while the evil tyrant, even with a thousand armed guards, has reason to fear.][40]

The longest sequence in More's *Epigrammata* is right at the centre, from 91 to 103 where More first (Ep. 91) takes up a theme, repeated in the *Utopia*, of the distinction between a king and a tyrant, *Quid inter tyrannum et principem*:

> *Seruos tyrannus quos regit*
> *Rex liberos putat suos.*
> [A tyrant thinks of his subjects as slaves, a king as his own children.][41]

Fear plagues a tyrant (92), a true prince is a father of his people and not a lord (93), a good king is the head of the body of his people, and treats his people as the parts of his own body (94), a people often does not recognize how good a king is until his bad heir comes along (95), a slave and a tyrant are the same in sleep (96) and a bad king is not the shepherd of his people but the wolf (97). After a brief break between 98 and 100, the sequence resumes with a monumental poem (101), which has its roots in Plato and looks forward to *Hamlet*, on the futility of this life:

> *Damnati ac morituri in terrae claudimur omnes*
> *Carcere. In hoc mortem carcere nemo fugit.*
> [Condemned and about to die, we are all shut in the prison of this earth, a prison where no one escapes death.][42]

The final pair (102–3) argues that a king rules only with the consent of his people. A comparable sequence in Harington, focusing on justice and monarchs, occurs in *Epigrams*, III.38–45 (see Chapter 3 below).

Harington follows More in offering advice to the King, and there are many places where Harington directly echoes More's wider concern with justice in the kingdom, as in III.72, 'Of Sheepe whose sheapheards are Wolues./', where the grotesque metaphor of ravening sheep, 'Cotsold lions', comes straight from More's attack on the injustice of enclosures (particularly in wool-rich regions like the Cotswolds) in *Utopia*:

> "Your sheep," I answered, "which are usually so tame and so cheaply fed, begin now, according to report, to be so greedy and wild that they devour human beings themselves and devastate and depopulate fields, houses, and towns. In all those parts of the realm where the finest and therefore the costliest wool is produced there are noblemen, gentlemen, and even some abbots, though otherwise holy men, who are not satisfied with the annual revenues and profits which their predecessors used to derive from their estates. They are not content, by leading an idle and sumptuous life, to do no good to their country; they must also do it positive harm. They leave no ground to be tilled; they enclose every bit of land for pasture; they pull down houses and destroy towns, leaving only the church to pen the sheep in."[43]

Harington selects 'Pleasant Sir Thomas' as the model for the *Epigrams*, devoting several pages of *A New Discourse* to him. If Harington turned to the Latin *Epigrammata* of the circle of More and Erasmus for the moral, theological and familial quality of his poems, for the exact structure of a hundred poems and for proverbial, idiomatic wit, he drew on the English *Epigrammes* of the man who married More's niece, John Heywood (1496–1578). Harington explicitly links epigrams with resistance to tyranny by these two Henrician courtiers:

> my Muse . . . bad me wish my friends, that no man should follow Sir Th. Mores humour, to write such Epigrams as he wrate, except he had the spirit, to speake two such apothegmes as he spake, of which the last seemes to fal fit into our text.[44]

More's witty apophthegms did not save him from the King, as Harington's marginal gloss notes: 'He was beheaded'.[45] He contrasts More wittily, but fatally, standing up to Henry VIII with the 'harmless verses' of John Heywood:

> what thinke you by Haywood that scaped hanging with his mirth, the King being graciously and (as I thinke) truely perswaded, that a man that wrate so pleasant and harmless verses, could not haue any harmfull conceit against his proceedings, & so by the honest motion of a Gentleman of his chamber, saued him from the ierke of the six stringd whip.[46]

The most likely source for this unique account, and the most probable candidate for 'a Gentleman of the Chamber', is Harington's own father.[47] John Heywood had been a musician at Henry's court whose life was transformed by his marriage to Joan Rastell, the daughter of More's sister, Elizabeth, and the printer John Rastell. As he was a contemporary of John Harington senior at the court of Henry VIII, and shared a strong interest in music and poetry, and his son Jasper was brought up with the young Princess Elizabeth, Harington's connections with the Heywoods may have been many and complex. On 6 July 1544, Heywood was indicted for treason, but pardoned on condition that he made a public recantation at Paul's Cross. In a grisly mock execution, Heywood was taken from the Tower and laid on a hurdle before being reprieved. After this narrow escape, Heywood turned from writing plays or interludes to the safer task of writing epigrams. He gradually built up a series of six *hundred of Epigrammes*, first published as his *Woorkes* in 1562, and going into four further editions.[48]

Of course, Heywood's debt to More and Erasmus is both personal and literary. One of Heywood's most famous texts, *The Spider and the Flie* (like More's Ep. 24, discussed above), also takes its inspiration from a passage in the *Institutio Principis Christiani* where Erasmus advocates having as few laws as possible:

> It is best to have as few laws as possible; these should be as just as possible and further the public interest; they should be as familiar as possible to the people: for this reason the Ancients exhibited them in tables and on tablets in public places for all to see. It is disgraceful that certain men use the laws like a spider's web, plainly intending to entangle as many as possible, not in the interest of the state, but simply to catch their prey.[49]

Harington mentions Heywood by name ten times, more than any other historical character in his *Epigrams*, always with complimentary epithets (often the same one as applied to Sir Thomas More, 'pleasant'). In a marginal note Gabriel Harvey wrote that 'sum of Heywoods Epigrams are supposed to be the conceits & devises of pleasant Sir Thomas More.'[50] Harington also pays tribute to Heywood's son, Jasper (1535–98), a Fellow of All Souls who had translated three Senecan tragedies. As a Jesuit 'traitor', he was imprisoned in the Tower in February 1584, and visited by his sister, Elizabeth, accompanied by her son, John Donne, then aged twelve, and William Weston, his fellow Jesuit, in disguise.[51] 'Young Haywoods answer' (III.60*bis*) to another prison visitor, 'my Lord of Warwicke', who enquired 'what things with him were skannt', is worthy of his father's wit:

> Thanks to that Lord said he that wills me good
> for I want all things sauing Hay and wood./

In an ironic epigram on the two Heywood sons (III.57), Jasper and Ellis, both brilliant scholars, Harington records that

> Old Heywoods sonns did wax so wylde and youthfull,
> it made their aged father sad and ruthfull.

Ellis Heywood (1529–78) had also been a Fellow of All Souls. While secretary to Cardinal Pole during his exile in Italy, he published, in Florence, *Il Moro d'Heliseo* in 1556, a dialogue in the tradition of *Moriae Encomium*, in which the leading character is Thomas More, after he has resigned as Lord Chancellor.[52] He went into exile in 1566, joining the Jesuits, and his brother, at Dillingen, in Bavaria. John Heywood himself seems to have fled abroad around 1569–70 and, under the

act passed against fugitive Catholics, known as '13 Eliz. Cap. 3' (1570), his lands
and the inheritance of the sons had been confiscated by the state.[53] The multiple
ironies of III.57 are clear only to those who know this sorry tale of exile and
appropriation of family property by the Crown. The story is not that of a Prodigal
son, who has an even more corrupt younger brother, because there is no inheritance
to squander, and the only 'wylde'-ness of these sons is that they are Jesuits.

Harington specifically allies himself with Heywood in 'Englishing' a classical
form for the first time, and gives him pride of place at the start of Book II of the
Epigrams:

> Old Haywood wrytes and proues in some degrees
> that one maie well compare a booke with Cheese.

These two Tudor courtiers, Heywood in the 1540s and Harington in the 1590s,
choose a genre that, for all its idiomatic and understated English irony, is fiercely
subversive at its core, but looks light and graceful. As Humez argues:

> Heywood's epigrams are for Harington a constant rich source of native English punnery
> and quibbles, colloquialisms and proverbs memorably formulated, and even certain
> structural rhythms.[54]

Like Heywood, Harington has chosen epigram as a form in which it is safe to write
in troubled times, and he 'identifies his role with Heywood's, if not with the
legendary and saintly More's'.[55]

Yet, even where he most closely echoes him, Harington transforms Heywood,
as when, in 'Of the excuse of Symony' (III.80), he turns Heywood's proverbial
'Where are no receivers, there are no theeves' (Heywood, 69, 'Of theft and
reciete') into his own chiastic, and much more satirical line.[56] Harington savagely
sharpens this saying of 'a right wise man' into a final couplet that links 'Symony'
with 'receiving' (and by implication, the establishment with thieves):

> I know a right wise man sayes, and beleeues,
> where no receiuors are there be no theeues./

Harington echoes the Latin learning of More, the proverbial English wit of
Heywood and the radical critique of power in More's circle.

For the presiding genius of the *Epigrams* is Erasmus (c.1467–1536), whose
towering intellectual influence in the period it may now be necessary to stress.
Harington not only puts Erasmus at the head of the list of 'Dutch, French and
Italian' masters in *A New Discourse*, but singles him out for praise at the
conclusion of the introductory 'letter' of Misacmos:

> Wherefore to conclude, I dare undertake, that though my discourse will not be so wise as
> the first of those seuen I spake of, that prayses folly . . .[57]

If his influence is acknowledged in *A New Discourse*, his presence is pervasive in the *Epigrams*. The dedications to Prince Henry and King James, the 'disticks' on the Rosary and the accompanying emblems, may be in the literary tradition of More's *Epigrammata* and the philosophical tradition of Alciati's *Emblems*, but their colloquial, licensed wit places Harington's *Epigrams* in the conversational mode of the *Colloquies*, the wisely foolish mode of *In Praise of Folly* and, in their princely frame, the politically didactic tradition of *Institutio Principis Christiani*.[58]

Erasmus dedicated his *Institutio* (Education of a Christian Prince) to a young prince, the future Charles V, then aged sixteen. It went into ten separate editions in Erasmus's lifetime and was translated into many languages.[59] 'There was never boke written in latin', as Sir Thomas Elyot wrote in his *Governour* (1531), 'that in so lytle a portion contayned of sentence eloquence and vertuous exhortation a more compendious abundaunce'.[60] In the Aldine edition of 1518, it is followed by the *Panegyric* to Philip of Burgundy, and a dialogue of Plutarch, *On distinguishing a true friend from a flatterer*, dedicated to Henry VIII.[61] Erasmus and More were trying to educate Christian princes across Europe. The climax of the *Institutio* is a peroration against war, echoing his essay on the adage, *Dulce bellum inexpertis*, published separately the previous year, 1515, which Harington obviously knew well enough to parody in a wholly ironic epigram:

> I praisd the speach but cannot now abide it
> That warr is sweet to them that haue not tride it. (III.38)

Erasmus's influence is more than just a series of verbal echoes. It was he who gave such an important place to the epigram in his *De Ratione Studii*. Erasmus here advises the *praeceptor* (schoolmaster) what qualities he should highlight in the epigram:

> *velut in epigrammatis argutam breuitatem laudari, tum iocandi rationes, quas Fabius & Cicero tradunt, indicabit. Hoc genus praecipue gaudere epiphonematis, commode in fine adiectis, quae cogitationem velut aculeatam in animo lectoris relinquant.*
> [So, for example, he will point out that in the epigram a sharp brevity is to be praised, explain the types of humour which Fabius and Cicero hand down, and especially the delight of the *epiphoneme*, which is subtly added at the end in such a way as to leave a stinging reflection in the mind of the reader.][62]

What drew Harington to Erasmus, I wish to suggest, is not only that he used wit and folly as a mask for moral instruction but that he consciously involved the reader. Erasmus's *Enchiridion Militis Christiani* (Handbook of a Christian Soldier) 'virtually reborn in Froben's types' (as Erasmus says) in 1518, ran to seventy editions in Latin. Early editions in the Folger Shakespeare Library make it clear that readers responded by annotating the text heavily in the margins.[63] Erasmus confirmed that this was the response he sought in a letter to More:

My *Enchiridion* is universally welcome; the bishop of Basel carries it round with him everywhere – I have seen all the margins marked in his own hand.[64]

Translations into Czech, German, Dutch, Spanish, French, Italian and English followed. The Spanish translation 'had a popular success without precedent in the history of Spanish printing up to that time'.[65]

> The translator himself wrote exultantly in a letter of 13 November 1527: "In the court of the emperor, in the cities, in the churches, in the convents, even in the inns and in the streets there is no one without a copy of Erasmus's *Enchiridion* in Spanish."[66]

It laid the foundation in Spain for the revival of interest in mystical theology and the flowering of meditational works like those of Luis de Granada. It quickly became a best-seller in England, even before it was translated by William Tyndale, as an Oxford bookshop's sales list of 1520 reveals:

> The outstanding feature of this list of sales of books, however, is the place occupied by the writings of Erasmus. One-ninth of the whole sales were of books written or edited by him. If the small primers, almanacs, ballads and so on and the grammars written by two popular Oxford grammar-school teachers be excluded, one customer out of every seven came to buy a book written by the great humanist. It is instructive also to notice what books of his command the largest sale. These are *Colloquia, De Constructione, Copia, Enchiridion Militis Christiani* and *Adagia*.[67]

The importance of reader response is even more obvious in the *Colloquies* (as they were known in England). The *Colloquies* (or *Familiarium colloquiorum formulae* with their origins in scholastic formulae) were virtually a new genre, and perfected the art of engaging the reader in a dialogue that was already in place, and then weaving into this banal form profound ideas destined to stimulate further debate among the readers. By 1522, the *Colloquies* had already run through thirty editions, and Froben added *Scholia* or *Aliquot loca explicata* (Glosses or some annotations) to the 1526 edition, giving formal recognition to the marginal glosses by readers. The *Colloquies* were immensely popular in England.

> From the 1520 lists of the Oxford bookseller, John Dorne, we know that he sold about 175 copies of works by Erasmus and that 48 of these were copies of the *Colloquies*. An Edinburgh bookseller had 625 copies of the *Colloquies* in stock in 1577; one in York bought 100 copies of an 'Epitome' of the *Colloquies* . . . An inventory of the 150 volumes belonging to the *curé* of a village near Antwerp in 1537 lists twenty-eight by Erasmus, two of them copies of the *Colloquies*. In the Latin school at Basel, which Thomas Platter the elder reorganized in 1541, the second class (grade) read the shorter colloquies of Erasmus three times a week.[68]

The first edition of the *Colloquies* in 1518 included what later became one of the most popular school texts of the sixteenth century, usually referred to simply as the *Copia* (*De duplici copia verborum ac rerum*) which was reprinted 150 times. The

Colloquies not only provided Harington with a general model, but one of them, 'The Soldier and the Carthusian', seems specifically to have inspired 'Of Caius hurts in the wars' (II.14), whose wounds 'came they not by dint of Pyke or Dart | But with a pot, a pynte, or els a quart.'[69] Perhaps even more pervasive in the *Epigrams* is the influence of another colloquy of Erasmus, *De captandis sacerdotiis* (In Pursuit of Benefices). Cocles welcomes back Pamphagus (who has an excessively large nose) from Rome, and hears of his failure to secure both benefices and a concubine. Cocles expresses surprise:

> Cocles: In my opinion men live more pleasantly if they have a pretty girl at home to make love to whenever they like.
> Pamphagus: Yes, and sometimes when they don't like! I prefer a lasting pleasure. The man who marries is happy for a month; the one with a rich benefice enjoys it all his life.[70]

This is particularly close to Harington's satirical investigation of the advantages of marriage for priests, III.7, a poem illustrated with painted manicules (Plate 6), but beyond that it seems to have inspired a whole sequence of poems where Harington attacks the clergy for being both venal and 'venereous'. In his apology for the 'Usefulness of the *Colloquies*', Erasmus (in a passage that Harington would surely echo) writes that, 'I'm not sure anything is learned better than what is learned as a game'.[71] Harington chooses the same disguise as Erasmus, Thomas More, John Heywood – and Lucius Junius Brutus: *sapiens stulti simulator* (a wise pretender of folly). Erasmus, in his fusion of *commedia* with theology, his desire to involve the reader and his concern to educate princes, is a perfect model for Harington.

In dealing with the religious divisions of the late sixteenth century, Harington turned to the giants of the Henrician period: Erasmus, More and Heywood, and the moral tradition derived from the Greek Anthology. He took over Heywood's idiomatic 'hundreds', and enriched them with his own structural core of four decades (or forty theological epigrams) to put before a prince the 'vices' which he must 'correct'. Martial and Erasmus provide models for the linguistic spontaneity, local immediacy and colloquial vigour of the *Epigrams*. Alciati and More both influence his use of emblems. While the painted 'Lanterne' emphasizes the ideal role of a king, the emblem of the fifteen Mysteries of the Rosary, as engraved by an imprisoned King of Scots, points to the structure of decades, the mutability of fortune and the importance of religious toleration. Harington's approach to religious division echoes More's emphasis on reason and moderation in *Utopia*:

> Moreover, even if it should be the case that one single religion is true and all the rest are false, he foresaw that, provided the matter was handled reasonably and moderately, truth by its own natural force would finally emerge sooner or later and stand forth conspicuously. But if the struggle were decided by arms and riots, since the worst men are always the most unyielding, the best and holiest religion would be overwhelmed because of the conflicting false religions, like grain choked by thorns and underbrush.[72]

In *A Tract on the Succession*, which contained several epigrams, and which Harington dated '18 December 1602' and gave to Tobie Matthew, shortly before he sent the *Epigrams* to King James, Harington wrote:

> Now to returne againe to my former purpose, which is not to define any matter in controuersy, but a little to allay the heate on all sydes, and as it were prepare them to a peaceble parley before their competent Iudge, I wishe as I said all rancour laid away on all sides, and that seing experience hath taught that <u>neither</u> the burning vsed in Queen Maries tyme, <u>nor</u> the hanging vsed in this tyme, <u>nor both</u> vsed in King Henries tyme, did any good at all. Neither of them might be vsed in the next Princes tyme, but all good meanes vsed to sifte the truthe for the satisfaction of all, for a full reconcilement and pacification if it be possible. And if some will still remaine scrupulous of anie side, as after so good meanes vsed there can be nothing so many as have bene, yet to pitie them rather then persecute them, and to vse salues to their soares, rather then swordes, if they be not verie contagious. The sworde is no good decider of questions in religion.[73]

Notes

[1] Norman Egbert McClure, *The Letters and Epigrams of Sir John Harington: Together with The Prayse of Private Life* (Philadelphia: University of Pennsylvania Press, 1930), pp. 46–53.

[2] 'The Manners of Epigram: A Study of the Epigram Volumes of Martial, Harington and Jonson', PhD dissertation (Yale University, New Haven, 1971), hereafter 'Humez'.

[3] 'The Elegie of the Lanterne translated into English', p. 252.

[4] D. H. Craig, *Sir John Harington* (Boston MA: Twayne, 1985), p. 6.

[5] T. W. Baldwin, *William Shakespere's Small Latine and Lesse Greeke,* 2 vols (Urbana: University of Illinois Press, 1944), vol. 1, p. 357, quoting *Etoniana* (1905).

[6] Baldwin, *Small Latine*, vol. 1, p. 436.

[7] BL Add. MS. 4379, fol. 12v; *dictata magistri Ionsoni | feliciter tradita in sexta classe | teste badgero puero*, fol. 189r; see Baldwin, *Small Latine*, vol. 1, p. 323.

[8] BL Add. MS. 4379, fol. 7v; see Hoyt Hopewell Hudson, *The Epigram in the English Renaissance* (Princeton NJ: Princeton University Press, 1947), p. 151.

[9] Estienne, Henri, *Ανθολογια διαφόρων Επιγραμματων . . . Florilegium diversorum epigrammatum veterum, in septem libros divisum* ([Geneva]: Huldrich Fuggerus, 1566).

[10] *Progumnasma Scholasticum*, ed. John Stockwood (London: Adam Islip, 1597), p. 43. For one epigram, a plea to Cupid, the *variatio* reaches 450 versions (pp. 413–49).

[11] *Martialis cum duobus commentis*, ed. Domizio Calderino and Giorgio Merula (Venice: B. de Zanis, 1493), Folger, Inc M269.

[12] Ibid., sig. a2; *uetinet* appears to be a misprint for *retinet*.

[13] Ibid., sigs a1 and a2.

[14] Martialis, *Epigrammata, paucis . . . vindicata* (Rome: Soc. Iesu, 1558).

[15] Martialis, *Epigrammaton Libri Animadversi, Emendati*, ed. Thomas Farnaby (London: William Welby, 1615).

[16] Martialis, *Nova Editio Ex Museo Petri Scriverii* (Lyons: John Maire, 1619). Martial ends II.28 (sig. A1v) by saying, disingenuously, *Nescio: sed tu scis res superesse duas.* Jonson has written in the margin: *Fellator Cunniling.*

[17] Humez, p. 133.

[18] Ibid.

[19] Martial, *Epigrams*, ed. and trans. D. R. Shackleton Bailey, 3 vols (London and Cambridge MA: Harvard University Press, 1993): all references are to numbers and pages in this Loeb edition; see also Humez, pp. 63–4.

[20] Martial, *Epigrams*, vol. 1, pp. 284–5 (translation adapted); *Martialis Epigrammata* (Venice: Aldus Manutius, 1517), sig. F8v.

[21] Martial, *Epigrams*, vol. 1, pp. 274–5 and pp. 284–5.

[22] Humez, pp. 38–57.

[23] Martial, *Epigrams*, vol. 1, p. 366, my translation, and reading *malim* as in Aldus, *Martialis*, 1517, fol. 55v.: *Seria cum possim, quod delectantia malim | Scribere, tu causa es, lector amice, mihi: | Qui legis, & tota cantas mea carmina Roma.*

[24] I am not including the *Liber de Spectaculis*, *Xenia* and *Apophoreta* in this number.

[25] Thomas Bastard (1566–1618) was a minister and epigrammatist.

[26] Humez, p. 165.

[27] *A New Discourse*, sig. A7r (ed. Donno, p. 63).

[28] The first complete edition of 211 emblems, with all but the controversial Emblem 80, *Aduersus naturam peccantes*, was published in Lyons in 1550.

[29] *A New Discourse*, p. 20 (ed. Donno, p. 95).

[30] Ibid., p. 22 (ed. Donno, pp. 97–8). In Martial, *Epigrams*, vol. 1, pp. 66–7, but reading *misero* for Harington's *puro*, and numbered I.37.

[31] Andrea Alciati, *Emblematum Libellus, Nuper In Lucem Editus* (Venice: Aldus, 1546), fol. 26v. The 1621 edition alters both text and engraving. See William S. Hecksher, 'Pearls from a Dung-Heap: Andrea Alciati's "Offensive" Emblem: "Adversus Naturam Peccantes"', in *Art the Ape of Nature: Studies in Honor of H. W. Janson*, ed. Moshe Barasch and Lucy Freeman Sadler (New York: Abrams, 1981), pp. 291–311.

[32] Accompanied by Thomas Combe's engraved emblem when reproduced in *A New Discourse*, pp. 18–19 (ed. Donno, p. 94).

[33] Thomas Combe, *The Theater of Fine Devices, containing an hundred morall Emblemes, First penned in French by Guillaume de la Perrière, and translated into English* (London, Richard Field, 1614), STC 15230.

[34] *A New Discourse*, p. 24 (ed. Donno, p. 99).

[35] For full text of title, see Bibliography.

[36] *The Latin Epigrams of Thomas More*, ed. and trans. Leicester Bradner and Charles Arthur Lynch (Chicago: University of Chicago Press, 1953), Ep. 3, p. 23, with my translation.

[37] BL Cotton MS Titus D. IV, fols 11v and 12v.

[38] *Latin Epigrams*, Bradner and Lynch, p. 15, with my translation.

[39] *A New Discourse*, pp. 25–6 (ed. Donno, p. 100).

[40] *Latin Epigrams*, Bradner and Lynch, p. 28, with my translation.

[41] Ibid., p. 48 (trans. p. 171).

[42] Ibid., p. 51, with my translation.

[43] *The Complete Works of St. Thomas More*, vol. 4, eds Edward Surtz, S.J., and J. H. Hexter (New Haven: Yale University Press, 1965), pp. 64–7. Harington's epigram, III.72, makes it clear that the depredation of the poor under Elizabeth is as severe as under Henry.

[44] *A New Discourse*, pp. 25–6 (ed. Donno, pp. 99–101).

45 Ibid., p. 25 (ed. Donno, p. 100).
46 Ibid., pp. 27–8 (ed. Donno, p. 102).
47 'My father . . . made the tune which my man Combe hath sent herewith; having been much skilled in musicke, which was pleasing to the King, and which he learnt in the fellowship of good Maister Tallis, when a young man.' *Nugae Antiquae*, vol. 1, p. 184.
48 *John Heywoodes Woorkes* (London: Thomas Powell, 1562), later reprinted in 1566, 1576, 1587 and 1598.
49 *CWE*, vol. 27, *Institutio Principis Christiani*, trans. Betty Radice, Neil M. Cheshire and Michael J. Heath, p. 273.
50 Humez, p. 178, citing Burton Milligan, *John Heywood's Works and Miscellaneous Short Poems* (Urbana: University of Illinois Press, 1956), p. 4.
51 William Weston, *The Autobiography of an Elizabethan*, trans. Philip Caraman (London: Longmans, Green, 1955), pp. 10–11.
52 Graves, T. S., 'The Heywood Circle and the Reformation', in *Modern Philology*, 10/4 (1913), 553–72 (p. 568).
53 Graves, 'The Heywood Circle', p. 571.
54 Humez, p. 183. See her Appendix A, pp. 440–52, for a full study of correspondences.
55 Ibid., p. 178.
56 *Three Hundred Epigrammes Vpon the Prouerbes*, 69. This is the first recorded use in Tilley, R53. Cf. Harington's II.1 with Heywood's 4.92, 'Of bookes and cheese'.
57 *A New Discourse*, sig. A8r (ed. Donno, p. 65).
58 *CWE*, vol. 27, *Institutio Principis Christiani*, pp. 199–288. Erasmus himself is joining a tradition that goes back to Xenephon's *Cyropaedia* and Plutarch's *Moralia* (p. 200).
59 Ibid., p. 201.
60 Baldwin, *Small Latine*, vol. 1, p. 209, quoting Sir Thomas Elyot, *The Boke named the Gouernour* (London: Berthelet, 1537) fols 41v-42r.
61 *Pacis querela, De regno administrando, Institutio principis Christiani, Panegyricus ad Philippum & carmen* . . . (Venice: Aldus, 1518). For full title, see Bibliography.
62 *Erasmi Roterodami, De Ratione Studii*, 2nd edn (Strasbourg: Matthew Schurer, 1513), fol. Xr (Bb2).
63 *Enchiridion Militis Christiani* (Mainz: Schoeffer, 1520). The Folger copy, extensively annotated in a contemporary hand, is bound together with Schoeffer's 1519 edition of *Colloquiorum Familiarium Formulae*.
64 *CWE*, vol. 66, *Spiritualia: Enchiridion*, trans. and annot. Charles Fantazzi, p. 3.
65 Ibid., p. 4.
66 Ibid., p. 5.
67 T. M. Lindsay, 'Englishmen and the Classical Renascence', *The Cambridge History of English Literature*, vol. 3, pp. 21–22, quoted by Baldwin, *Small Latine*, vol. 1, p. 103.
68 *CWE*, vol. 39, *Colloquies*, introd. Craig R. Thompson, p. xxxii (citing H. S. Bennett, *English Books and Readers 1558 to 1603* (Cambridge: University Press, 1965), p. 266.
69 *CWE*, vol. 39, *Colloquies*, pp. 328–43.
70 Ibid., p. 48.
71 *CWE*, vol. 40, *Colloquies*, p. 1098.
72 *Complete Works of St. Thomas More*, vol. 4, pp. 220–21.
73 York MS XVI.L.6, p. 244 (*A Tract on the Succession*, p. 109). The epigrams are II.8, III.44, IV.1. 'A tragicall Epigram' is on p. 257*bis*. The same pages, 256*bis* and 257*bis*, are double-numbered in *F*, where the scribe has also slipped a hundred in numbering.

Chapter 3

Patterns and Sequences

Each tenth Stanze: forty theological decades

'Neither length, purpose, nor structure adequately define Harington's widely diversified epigrams,' as Steven W. May argues.[1] Yet, beneath the surface of this dazzling variety, the *Epigrams* are subtly held together by a backbone: the elegant design where 'each tenth Stanze may seeme the Parsons part' (III.94). This great sequence of forty theological poems, carefully placed on every decade, supported by a further forty-five poems dealing with religious topics, creates a fruitful tension between order and spontaneity. In addition, each 'booke', as we have seen, begins with an epigram that sets out the prophetic role of the epigrammatist.

The sequence of theological decades in Book I castigates the new clergy for their inadequacy (I.10 and 30), derides their empty and combative 'learning' (I.20) and parodies the theology of Puritan 'election' (or predestined salvation) in Cinna and in Leda. The change of one letter (from 'elect' to 'eiect', I.50) would more truthfully describe Cinna's state, the poems suggest, while Leda is building on this false security to lead her to 'Sathan' (I.80). The flagrant deception of the 'precise Taylor' (I.40), which plays so sharply on the meaning of 'precise' (puritanical and legalistic), made this poem immensely popular in the period. England is shown to be full of atheists, characterized by Dante as 'Elephants' (I.70), and the country is suffering from heavy rain because 'sinn doth raigne on earth' (I.60). England's troubles reach their climax at the end of the book as Alciati's 'offensive emblem' combines with Harington's own allegorical use of *stercus* (excrement) to characterize the corruption afflicting Elizabethan society (I.90). A sequence of poems that begins with I.85 and runs to the end of the 'first booke' draws on Alciati's emblem *Aduersus naturam peccantes* and his own *A New Discourse*. This suggests a dating of the composition of the end of this book around 1596–97. The climax of the sequence is the carefully crafted final poem (I.100), where Harington links the 'rents' taken from church property with schism, and ends, under a heading 'Against Churchrobbers', with a scathing view of the Elizabethan court devouring 'fryers' and delivering 'souldiers'. The 'Favorites and courtly Minions' (made to rhyme with 'Lutheran opinions') swallow up the church and 'Voyd forts and Castles in their excrements'(the last word of Book I). May, while highlighting the irony of this attack from one whose family fortune was founded on church lands seized during the dissolution, suggests that several of the epigrams indicate that he entertained nostalgic ideals of a national church as wealthy, prosperous, and doctrinally united as he supposed the pre-Reformation church to have been.[2]

At the start of Book II, Harington appropriately invokes the radical spirit of the More circle by citing 'Old Haywood' (II.1) as his 'soule laments', in the decades that follow, a church ruined by schism, 'venereous' clergy, the hypocrisy produced by the doctrine of 'prædestination', and the consequent collapse of values in society. The first (II.10), disarmingly dressed as personal advice to his wife, 'Mine own', on the right use of images, actually addresses one of the central battlegrounds of the Reformation. Harington's position is traditional: to 'keepe the mean between the two extreams' of iconoclasm ('Do not deface such pictures') and idolatry ('do not thinke in them there is devinity'). The second (II.20) returns to the the seizure of church property by a word-play on 'Rents', which skilfully links financial depredation with ecclesiastical schism. As so often, Harington begins by a self-deprecating disclaimer ('after my wanton fashion'), only to make a more serious charge: 'fauorites' do not 'consume the Churches Rents' or income, as he said before (I.100); rather they 'increase the Churches Rents', the divisions threatening the church. Clerical marriage, and the spurious reasons given for it, form the target of the next decade (II.30). The reader here is forced by the rhyme to supply the missing word in the empty parenthesis ([arse]), and made to link the decline in Latin among the clergy with their failure to turn down wives or 'declyne vxores in the gendring cases'. II.40 is a complement to I.60: there is 'dearth' on 'earth' because men need help from heaven. The atheism of Paulus (Sir Walter Ralegh), outlined in II.50, is one reason for this parlous state of affairs, along with the doctrine that Harington ridicules in II.60: 'prædestination'. In a witty refutation that prefigures the style of Dr Johnson, Harington argues that he, 'no Doctor at this disputation', can prove that the 'foollish fellow' preaching this doctrine does it because he 'list' (likes), just as Harington can 'list' not to believe him. The book concludes with three decades that move from the empty 'brabling' (II.70) and 'mooneshine' (II.90) of Puritan preachers, whose 'disputes' have produced such 'slender fruits', to a climactic sonnet that contains a bravura display of rhyming in Harington's advice to the archetype of predestination, 'Cinna a Brownist' (II.100). The triple rhyme that characterizes the falsity of an 'election' that offers 'sure protection' where 'faults are free from all correction' is confronted by Harington's irrefutable argument borne of his 'affection', to which there is no 'obiection', proving 'wicked mans subiection'. In the middle of all these rhyming 'disputes' Harington offers the only hopeful image (II.80) of a better kind of theological debate, a symposium where 'Lawyer' and 'devyne' resolve their question over dinner in 'lafter'. This epigram, for all its light tone, is serious in purpose; as he wrote to Tobie Matthew in 1602 in his plea for 'a peaceble parley' (now entitled *A Tract on the Succession*), 'I wishe as I said all rancour laid away on all sides'.[3]

Book III balances the encouragement given to 'Maister Bastard' to continue writing epigrams like a 'prophet' (III.1), with one that politely regrets that 'men of such holy function' should marry (III.10), and another (III.20) that compares the clergy of his day, building genealogical families, with the pre-Reformation clergy who left behind a dynasty of 'Colledges' and 'Abbeys well endow'd and Churches sumptuous'. An attack on the self-indulgence of the period, 'In defence of Lent' (III.30), leads to images of the clergyman as disguised 'Mountbank' (III.60) who would 'fall to preache | but patching Sermons with a sorry shift'; the attempt of the clergy to blame 'Symony' on 'the tyme' (III.80); and finally the lamentable fact that 'in theise days', in a reversal of the church before the Reformation, 'The Cleargie men are fat their lyvings leane' (III.90). There is more satire of those who are better at controversy than charity, who can 'cyte Saint Paule' but 'haue not God the worde', (III.50) and of the Family of Love (III.100) who are busy living up to their name (see below).[4] The worst criticism of this book, however, is reserved for the royalty and the court. In a stunning use of Heywood's aphorism 'where no receiuors are there be no theeues' (III.80), Harington implicates the establishment in the corruption of 'Symony', a charge made explicit in an epigram (III.70) that is so savage in its criticism of Elizabeth's reign that one wonders how this godson of the Queen dared to circulate it, even in manuscript. Her 'forty yeares' have not been of 'sweet peace and restfull dayes' but rather 'abounding with abhomination':

> For law with lust and rule with rape is yoaked,
> And zeale with schisme and Symony is choaked.

No wonder that after Sir Thomas Tresham had this transcribed, it was hidden in the walls of Rushton Hall (see Chapter 4).[5] Even more devastatingly, an apparently innocent decade on King David's adultery (III.40) is set within a group of epigrams that, endlessly playing on the words 'head' and 'woman', suggests contemporary parallels. Henry VIII desired both the 'body' and 'head' of his wives, and the Queen is as much 'a headles woman' as the Queen of Scots she had executed.

Harington's concern for the church is so closely bound up with his concern for the state of the nation that it is hard to separate the two. This is at its most obvious in the great sequence of Book IV, which ends with an attack on the fruits of 'Symony' and begins with a plea for national reform. England is 'bank'rout' (IV.1) because it has been plundered by 'Treasorers . . . Iudges, Councellors'. Even worse (IV.10), a man is forced to make an absurd choice, if he wishes 'to keepe his soule and body both in saf'ty', between those who follow 'Geneua late reformed' and 'that old Catholicque' church. The revisions (mostly by overwriting) Harington made to the last line for Prince Henry, from 'liue in the new, dy if you can in th'old' to '*die* in the new, *live* if you *list* in th'old', suggest that Harington intends the Prince to read both radical alternatives. What Harington does to the text in the last line – late *re-forming* the letters – is a literary equivalent of the Reformation: over-writing, causing confusion on matters of the soul's eternal safety. The last line, for all its appearance of tremulous uncertainty and textual fluidity, after flying kites above the line in autograph revisions, allows the weight of the original text to come to rest on 'th'old'. As Harington wrote to Tobie Matthew: 'It is possible both of them may be wronge, but it is impossible both can be righte.'[6]

In the same typology as III.60, the 'zealous preacher' of IV.20 is a failed physician, whose theology is worse than his medicine, so Harington prays to be kept 'free from his phisick, far from his devinity'. 'Against swearing' (IV.30) became so popular because it clearly touched a nerve in the national consciousness (Chapter 4). Here the image of 'wayghty matters' sliding downhill, embodied in the physical term 'mas', runs through this careful linking of moral decline with the loss of ancient rituals, and culminates in what seems more like a peroration than the final line of an epigram: 'hauing lost Mass, crosse, fayth, they find damnacion.' This is the first in a sequence of three poems that paint a picture of a nation in moral and spiritual decline which reach their climax in the centre of Book IV. The next two show the seamless 'cote' of 'our saviours' church torn by greed and on the brink of 'schisme' (IV.40), thanks to the greedy unconcern of the 'great Prelats of the state' now dividing the spoils of a 'Church with Schisme turmoyled' (IV.50). Church 'buildings and revenews' have fallen into the hands of the false 'Harlot' in the judgement of Solomon story, while 'the lawfull mother', the 'Catholick', is left 'Lamenting' the final performative utterance: 'Dividatur'.

These 'Prelates', IV.60 implies, are too busy with the 'apron stringes' of their wives to be 'pontificall' (priestly), so Harington damns them as 'babes' of the arch-impostor of the early church, Simon Magus, whose headlong plunge to hell was an ancient emblem of heresy and its infernal end.[7] Harington passes, in IV.70, straight from Simon Magus to Luther, whose central theological tenet leaves out 'grace, loue feare and hope', and seeks to 'foyst vnto our faith a word exclusiue'. In a final devastating rhyme (*one* then being pronounced *own*), Harington, taking on the mantle of Erasmus, argues that Luther's 'fayth saveth onely' is 'one lye'.

Indeed the word 'Preacher' runs through the theological sequence at the climax of Book IV. These Preachers are too interested in another kind of 'Pulpitt' (IV.80), and their 'earnest disputation' has left the 'chappell voyde' (IV.90). Benefices are being indirectly bought, and it is no accident that the last in the sequence (IV.100) ends in a devastating play on 'Symony'; there may be no open sale, but one can 'indirectly' (a 'direct ly') 'see money in yt'. Word-play goes to the heart of Harington's 'catholic' (universal) theology, as it does in his rejection of 'factions' and their divisive names of 'Papist, and Hugonot, | Brownist, and Zuinglian' (III.45). 'Of Christs Cote' (IV.40), which uses the biblical image of the church as Christ's seamless garment for 'Saint Peeters tottring bote', shows Harington's concern for the unity of the church and the primacy of Peter, threatened by this 'devision so extreame'. To the question 'Who stird such waues in this still running stream', there can be only one answer: Luther. The final couplet, however, holds out a gleam of hope: the garment is not yet torn, just worn:

Ist not a schisme? no say not so beware,
But we haue almost worne the coate threebare.

Yet the pleasure of the complete collection of *Epigrams* is the counterpoint between the tightly controlled structure of four books and the variety, apparent spontaneity and anarchic humour of individual poems. For the decade that follows the epigram on the 'Parsons part'(III.94) is immediately subverted by the inclusion of two riotous poems about Bath (99*bis* and 99*ter*) as if Harington is forced to disrupt the orderly sequence because he cannot resist a good digression about a lady who's come to Bath to find a cure for her sterility, having already travelled to 'Oxford to the vniversity' for similarly dubious therapy (III.99*ter*). The appearance of spontaneous disorder, however, is deceptive. When the final epigram of Book III comes, it is a devastating combination of Harington's festively 'wanton' Muse and his serious purpose. In the extreme Puritan sect, the Family of Love, the 'sister' and 'saynt' are busy getting a 'Prophitt' (III.100) because, as IV.80 makes clear, this kind of Preacher 'stands' erect in only one kind of 'Pulpitt'. The attentive reader remembers that Book III began with Harington reminding Mr Bastard (a Minister who 'wrate a pleasant booke of English Epigrams') of his prophetic role. For all its appearance of *copia* (overflowing abundance), the book's frame reminds the reader why Harington is using verse epigrams to castigate abuses in the church and state: because the preachers are busy elsewhere.

Indeed, Harington's most insistent theme is embodied in the word-play (lost in all printed editions) on 'Pillers of the Church' (as in pillage) that is at the heart of two linked epigrams. In the first, II.71, 'Christes fayr feild' used to have 'true and paynfull tillers', where now it only has those who would rob it of all its wealth. The visual image of the despoiled monasteries, like the ruined Bath Priory Harington did so much to repair, seems to inform this invective against the predatory materialism of his age. In its central line, 'but where are now the men of that Society?', the poem seems about to break out of the confines of the epigram into the *Ubi sunt?* trope of early English poetry, only to be pulled back into the biting satire of the final line: 'gods feild hath harrowers still, his church hath pillers'. In the second, III.63, the Purbeck marble 'pillers' of Salisbury Cathedral – one for every hour, it is said – have become, by the change of that one letter, the hourly 'pillers'. Men like Sir Walter Ralegh, who took possession of the lands of Sherborne Abbey (part of the Salisbury Cathedral estate), have transformed the meaning of the ancient *vsum Sarum* (Sarum Rite) from a pattern of liturgical service to a national prescription for daylight robbery of church property.

A zealous searcher of eternall truthe

Into this tapestry of prophetic satire and theological irony, Harington skilfully weaves a clear picture of his own stance. It comes in his answer (II.64) to the question so frequently asked, even today, as to why he succeeded so little in advancing his career at court.[8] He concedes that, among the attributes recommended by his friends is hidden 'the reason':

> And chiefly that he hath bene from his youth,
> A zealous searcher of eternall truthe./

This epigram is immediately followed by one about how easy it is to conform in matters of religion; it can be done 'in less then ten dayes warning' (II.65). This last, ostensibly a story about 'king Henry the eights time', is transcribed in *C* under the autograph title, *Another to the Queen*: the choice is the same under Queen Elizabeth: pursue 'eternall truthe' or 'conforme'. These two epigrams give a clear picture of Harington's confessional stance and profound political pragmatism.

For the two central strands in Harington's poetry, the wanton and the ecclesiastically didactic, turn out to be intricately and subtly woven into a single garment. Harington may protest (IV.43) that his Muse is like 'king Edwards Concubine' who 'duly did each day to church resort, | saue if she weare int*y*s't to Venus sport'. In fact, wantonness becomes the agent of his prophetic satire on ecclesiastical abuses, as well as the clever disguise in which he clothes his serious purpose. As May argues,

> More than a dozen epigrams attack radical reformers in the established church under such epithets as "pure," "precise," and Brownist. Numbers 374 [III.100] and 413 [IV.80] ridicule the Family of Love, an extreme Protestant sect imported from the Low Countries. The absence of any similar degree of contempt for Catholics is quite noticeable.[9]

In one poem Harington answers the charge (said to be put by Lynus) of 'papistry' (III.45). Specifically avoiding 'deniall' he twice asserts that he is a 'christian Catholicque', in terms that contain no self-deprecating irony and assert his right to live his life as he means to die. As the term 'catholic' was claimed by reformers, it was safe for Harington to use it, but his choice is accurate in a more profound etymological sense: universal. In another (IV.51), Harington ostensibly advises his wife 'against women Recusants'. The story of the Jewish Esther, who married King Assuerus and won pardon for the Jews in Persia, is used to show that subtle guile (indeed sleeping with the enemy) achieves more than the open refusal of Vasti, her predecessor as Queen. This poem (which Harington does not include in *C*, the gift volume to his wife and Lady Rogers) is perhaps more of an *apologia* for Harington's own policy: acting as Esther did with King Assuerus. It is, after all, what he does as a courtier of Queen Elizabeth, and later of King James and Prince Henry: gain admission to the royal presence, and try to influence the ruler.

And yet, sweet foole, I loue thee

On the title page of the gift book presented to Lady Rogers and Mary (Plate 8), his wife, Harington has written in his own hand, above the coloured engraving, *Non sic Petrarcha Lauram* (not in this way did Petrarch celebrate Laura). The epigraph covers not only the book as a gift, but the fifty-two poems lovingly transcribed on the fifteen leaves added to the volume and then lavishly bound together with the translation. To the selection of forty-one domestic epigrams Harington has appended eleven politically subversive poems ('some, that I durst never show any Ladie') and asks the two women to 'lay vp this booke safe in your Chest'.[10] The self-deprecating dedication of 'manie of the toyes I haue formerly written to you and your daughter, as I could collect out of my scatterd papers' is intended to disguise the political – and reinforce the domestic – feel of this collection. The painted title page, the gilt-edged Lebé paper and fine binding all indicate a more serious purpose.[11] These are not fanciful Petrarchan sonnets, but they are love poems: a profound celebration of the marriage – children, dogs, maids, arguments, reconciliations, love-making and griefs – of an Elizabethan courtier and the political context in which that marriage was lived. The poems on Elizabeth, Henry VIII and the execution of Mary, Queen of Scots, are included not because 'there was spare room', but because the happiness and wealth of Harington's family has been defined by its relationship to the monarch. On *19 December 1600*, the date of the autograph dedication (the half-birthday of James VI, and still some fifty days before the Essex rebellion), Harington could be thankful that he was not caught up in Essex's disgrace. To be in the margins of court life, in the last years of Elizabeth's reign, was certainly safer.

These domestic poems I see not as a bid for his inheritance or a 'struggle for mastery', but as a carefully staged colloquy in which the readers – whether the named recipients or the outsiders who read the poems in the larger collections – are asked to participate.[12] As part of the larger collection, these domestic poems place Harington outside the tradition of Martial, and alongside that of Heywood, More and Erasmus. The inclusion of eleven politically sensitive poems in the conjugal gift shows the way Harington's concern for truth is linked to his choice of epigram and avoidance of the idealizing Petrarchan sonnet. The honesty of the domestic poems helps ground the criticism of ecclesiastical and political 'abuse', while the political poems form the backcloth to Harington's domestic life.

Many of these domestic poems start in mid-conversation, with a little incident: 'Your little dog that barkt as I came by' (I.37), or 'Last night you layd it Madam in our dishe' (I.52). The situations are recalled not, like Donne's, re-enacted, as in the poem of remembered farewell, 'When I from thee my deare, last daie departed' (III.28). The studied bathos of the contrasts in this poem of parting for war serve to create loving humour. Mall is like Lucrece only in her fidelity but not, of course, in the tragic 'ruin'. More encouraging is the comparison with Penelope, whose husband 'fayned madnes': Odysseus did come home, and Penelope remained faithful. The message of this fondly ironic poem is that rulers have always been arbitrary, and that wars have always been more about the personal ambitions of the leaders than justice. At first sight, the intimate affection of the last line (even more in his own punctuation of *C*: 'And yet (Sweet foole) I loue thee thou beleeuest') is disarming. The absoluteness of the verb allows us to read the phrase several different ways, all complimentary to Mall: she believes in her husband and (despite the affectionate parenthetic 'Sweet foole') in his love for her. The incident may be in the past, but the conclusion is as immediate as any line in Donne: the present tense spans the time from the moment of the remembered parting to the moment when his wife and Lady Rogers read this again. The reader shares in the sense of marital completeness that the last line enacts. The hyperbole of the classical allusions serves to make ridiculous not their love, but the grandiose ideas that lead men to wars, while the self-deprecating irony of the last line only reinforces the realism of this honest love and the implied embrace.

This concern for rooting the poems in the real world is exemplified in the autograph additions (in both *F* and *C*) made to the title of a gloriously funny poem (I.78), 'Of an accident of saying grace at the Lady Rogers; who vsed to dyne exceeding late. Written to his Wife; *from Bathe.*/' At first sight, the addition *from Bathe* seems superfluous, but it locates this story firmly in the geographical reality of their lives, and humorously hints that Mall is to blame for being away from 'this place'. Addressed to 'his wife', and opening 'My Mall', it ends again in 'a kiss', but the projected reconciliation is with Lady Rogers (one intended recipient of the poem). This triangular structure may owe something to Sir Thomas More's Ep. 249, where he apologizes for failing to notice a noble lady standing by while he was talking to a prominent cleric. For this too asks the prelate to effect a reconciliation with a grand lady on the grounds that it was the prelate's charm that was responsible for More's lapse of manners:

> *Dedecus hoc lepidae quoniam peperere fabellae*
> *(Quum dominae et mihi me surripuere) tuae,*
> *Dedecus hoc lepidae debent purgare fabellae*
> *Meque meae dominae conciliare tuae.*
> [Since your gift of charming speech (which made me forget myself and ignore the lady) has imposed upon me this embarrassment, your gift of charming speech ought to relieve me of this embarrassment and restore me to my lady's good graces.] [13]

Harington's version is more endearing, in the familial intimacy of including the dialogue of son, grandson and grandmother, in the realism of the shared theatrical space of a domestic dining table, and in the humour of the *grande dame* dismissal of a concern with time as belonging to clowns (rustics like Harington), self-mockingly confirmed by Harington's earthy rhyme of 'cocks' with 'clocks'.

The boundary between public and domestic life is again crossed in the ironic poem 'To his wife in prayse of the war of Ireland' (III.38). Erasmus's famous essay (*Adages* IV.i.1) on *Dulce bellum inexpertis*, 'warr is sweet to them that haue not tride it', was printed separately in fifteen different editions between 1515 and 1540.[14] We know that Edward VI wrote an exercise based on it, dated 28 July 1549.[15] Harington transforms this into something more idiomatic, homely and ironic. Harington draws on Erasmus's description of the physical hardships 'those idiots of soldiers put up with':

> food at which a Cyprian ox would turn up its nose, sleeping quarters that would be scorned by a dung-beetle, few hours of sleep and those not of their own choosing, a tent that lets in the wind from every direction, or no tent at all. They have to endure an open-air life, sleep on the ground, stand in their arms, bear hunger, cold, heat, dust, rain.[16]

As so often, what Harington omits, the role of rulers in waging unnecessary wars and Erasmus's vivid depiction of the suffering of the innocent, is as important as what he includes. Harington's ironic emphasis on trivial domestic details allows him to outline the grotesque unnaturalness of war, while giving the reader vivid glimpses of home life, including interrupted sleep ('if a childe but cry') or the exotic wines in his cellar ('At home Canary wines and Greeke grew lothesome').

The most affecting strand in these poems is the intimate celebration of their love-making, its fruits in nine children, and the shared lament for the loss of two of those children. 'To his wife after they had been married 14 yeares' (III.11) humorously ends with Harington describing himself as getting worse and worse 'in th'occupation'. The sexual pun on the word 'occupy' seems wholly appropriate to the tender tone of the poem, coming as it does after the honest opening, which starts with the notion of an apprenticeship being seven years:

> Two prentiships with thee, now haue I been,
> mad times, sad times, glad times, our life hath seen,
> Soules we haue wrought four payre, since our first meeting
> Of which two souls, sweet souls, were to *too* fleeting.

Harington's own revision to *too* of 'bee' in *F* and 'be' in *C* confirms how much personal emotion there is in this poem. The loss of these two children is referred to in at least two other poems in Book III: 'To Mall to comfort her for losse of a Childe' (III.80*bis*) and 'To my Wife' (III.91). In the last poem, Harington 'in loues defence alledges' the 'Nine organ pipes our loues assured pledges', but in the gift copy to his wife he has deleted nine and written '*Seavn*' above, expressing in private the mutual sense of loss here (see also Chapter 1).[17]

The honest representation of conjugal love is especially striking in 'To my Lady Rogers that she loved not him: yet she loved his wife' (IV.28), where the last line is 'your daughters place is not aboue but vnder.' Immediately following this (IV.29) is a poem discussing how much lust is necessary to his love for Mall, and how much her looking 'chast babies in my wanton eyes' makes his 'loue wantonise'. The last intimate poem selected for Lady Rogers and Mall is 'To his wife a rule for Church house and bed' (IV.85). In *F*, two lines included by the scribe in the gift selection (*C*) have been added in Harington's own hand:

> But when thou see'st my hart to mirthe inclyne
> the tongue, witt, bloud, warme with good cheere and wyne,
>   {*and that by lawful fansy I ame led*
>   {*to clym my nest thyne vndefiled bed.*
>   then of sweet sport let no occasion skape
>   but bee as wanton toying as an Ape./

This is certainly not how Petrarch serenaded Laura, but it is a celebration of mutual, married love that is unequalled in its honesty, humour and charm. As Scott-Warren observes, 'The frankness with which the conjugal situation is unmasked by these epigrams, in all its tender coerciveness, can disarm even the modern reader.'[18] There is nothing like this in Martial, or even in More; while Erasmus and Heywood provide models, the combination of homely learning, intimacy, politics, humour and pathos is wholly original. On their own, in the gift copy to his wife and Lady Rogers, these poems are a moving portrayal of a marriage; as part of the larger collection of *Epigrams* they offer the reader an intimacy unmatched by any of Harington's contemporaries, and provide the illusion for the reader of joining the household: sharing its remembered sayings, its jokes, its maids – and its dogs.

Table talk

It is not only in the familial poems that Harington creates an impression of allowing the reader to enter a shared convivial space. Whereas Saturnalian obscenity and outrageous abuse is the default mode in Martial, Harington cultivates the impression that we are joining the 'Table talk' of a group of people who have, like Samuel Daniel, all earned the title 'good frend'. It is surely of Martial that Ben Jonson is thinking when he declares his intention, at the start of his *Epigrammes*, not to satisfy the expectation the title might suggest, of 'Wormewood, and sulphure, sharpe, and tooth'd withall'. So, Jonson's '*Epigrammes*' blend caricatures of 'Don Surly' (28) and 'Sir Lucklesse Woo-All' (46) with tributes to royalty, noble men and women, and friends. In the sad elegies for his lost children (22 and 45) and in the convivial charm of 'Inviting a Friend to Supper' (101) we approach something like the normal mode in Harington's poetry. In the poetry of Martial, the poet is the solitary, cynical gadfly, exposing by his bitter wit the numerous weaknesses of his fellow human beings. As Humez argues, 'Slightly more than half of Martial's 1,200 epigrams are critical treatments of fictionally named characters.'[19]

This is not true of Harington. In addition to the forty-six poems dealing with the family circle, another thirty-six deal in a convivial way with friends who are fellow poets, neighbours or courtiers. The poets included in this welcoming circle are 'my good frend M^r. Samuell Danyell' (II.56), Charles Fitzgeffrey in return 'for a booke he gaue me' (IV.36), 'Old pleasant Haywood' (III.27), 'My deare frend Davis' (IV.25), 'Maister Bastard a Minister that wrate a pleasant booke of English Epigrams' (III.1), Sir Philip Sidney whose 'works in fames bookes are enrolld' (III.64), Sidney's sister, Mary, Countess of Pembroke, one of two Maries 'that merit endles prayse by dew desart' (IV.47), Henry Constable and Edmund Spenser, too good (along with 'Sydney, Daniell') to be praised by Lynus (III.55).

Neighbours and fellow courtiers are also included. As May argues, 'Many of Harington's epigrams were specifically used to entertain and communicate with his fellow courtiers.'[20] Harington's neighbour, Sir Hugh Portman, is the recipient of several warm – and profound – epigrams (I.3, 25, 62; II.29; III.52), the two 'wylde' sons of John Heywood, as we have seen, of two more (III.57 and III.60*bis*). The sayings of Dr John Sherwood of Bath, like family jokes, are lovingly and humorously recounted (I.14, III.18, IV.3), as is Bishop Bonner's witty retort (I.57) to someone greeting him 'good morrow bishop quondam' (sometime bishop): 'Adew knave semper' (farewell forever knave).

The combined effect of these evocations of family and friendship is to create, at the centre of the *Epigrams*, an alternative collegiate society with its own more enduring values. Just as in the last part of *A New Discourse*, 'An Apologie', Harington empanels a jury of twelve good friends, officially to pass judgement on 'The Metamorphosis of Aiax' but actually to acquit his two slandered relatives (Thomas Markham and Ralph Sheldon) from the charge that they are *Mal-contents*, so, in the *Epigrams*, Harington casually creates a virtual bench of friends, family, neighbours and fellow poets. From the safety and security of these 'men of worth' (IV.12, 59), who are solidly united with the 'reverent elders' (IV.40) of the past, judgements can be made of those currently, and temporarily, in power. This is epitomized in the five poems addressed to Sir Hugh Portman, who is not only the tenth juror in 'An Apologie' (and therefore placed next to Sheldon and Markham) but given the task of passing judgement at the end, both on the 'pamphlet' ('The Metamorphosis of Aiax') and also on Harington's religion.[21] The fourth of the five epigrams dedicated to him, on the forbidden topic of the 'Succession' (II.29), rebuffs 'My good frend Lynus' in his attempts to get Harington to reveal his loyalties, but makes clear in the last line what they are: 'no Enfant, nor no Queene, whom then? a King'. The fifth poem, simply entitled 'Of the growth of trees to Sir Hughe Portman' (III.52), ends with an indictment, added in autograph to *F*, of the materialistic culture of his day:

> *which made my muse so wood she sayd in rage*
> *that thirst of gold makes this an Iron age.*

Mr John Ashley is the recipient of a fine epitaph (IV.23), and his son of a poem that constitutes an ironic apologia by Harington for his 'Muse' (IV.43).

The most striking case where political and familial seem to combine is in the group of poems (discussed in the previous chapter) addressed to 'old Haywood' and his 'sonns': I.56; II.1; III.27, 57, 60*bis*; IV.25. The effect of these epigrams is not only to align Harington's poetic form (English epigrams in 'hundreds') with that of John Heywood, but to show a detailed and sympathetic understanding of the predicament of these members of Heywood's family, and in particular of his Jesuit sons. Harington seems to identify himself with the family circle of More and Heywood, their oppositional and, frequently, imprisoned stance.

Finally, the most famous of the named characters that is treated sympathetically may serve as introduction to Harington's larger concern with justice. The sequence dealing with the Earl of Essex (apparently in temporal order) is at first neutral, then critical, and finally compassionate. The first (I.55) seems to reflect an innocent time before Essex's fall from favour when Harington could talk about his own poetry. The second, apparently contemporary with the 'Irish action' (III.95), advises Essex to obey his Sovereign and go 'Northe'. The third (III.97), by using the subtle analogy of Charles V, implies of Essex that likewise 'an endles thirst he had to raigne'; his 'retyred' life is portrayed as merely a pause in a life of restless political ambition.[22] The politically correct tone of these critical epigrams is replaced in the final epigram (IV.59) by an account of the execution in which Harington characteristically appeals to the judgement of a 'man of worth' by quoting the general response: 'Ys't not great pitty thinke you?' Although Essex is the focus of this epigram, the presence in the poem of others that he knew, Blunt and Charles Danvers, 'such braue souldiers', makes the deaths more poignant, both for Harington and for the reader. The idiomatic phrase is ironically reversed to give a harsh verdict on the Queen's decision: the last words on Essex are 'little pitty'.[23]

Men of worth and the state of the realm

In addition to the eighty or so theological poems that look at the way the seamless 'cote' of Christ's church is being plundered and torn apart, there are over fifty poems concerned with the realm: with injustice and the corruption of power. The whole collection is framed by royal dedications. The collection begins with a prose dedication to Prince Henry, a verse dedication to King James, and an autograph date of *1602*. It ends with 'the Lanterne' emblematic of the King's role, and the inscription *Post Crucem lucem*. The King is to bring light to the kingdom after the suffering of the previous regime. A thirty-six line 'Elegie of the Lanterne', in both Latin and English, explicates the emblem, and the autograph gloss on *sapiens stulti simulator* (wise pretender of foolery) casts Harington in the role of (Lucius Junius) *Brutus*. After the Cross, James, as the Sun, will usher in a new 'golden age'. After fifteen 'disticks' (couplets) on the Rosary, in Latin and English, an engraving of the same, linked to the account of a King of Scots who knew 'This Storie at his fingers ends', the book passes to a 'gratulatory Elegie' for King James's entry at 'Burleighe' in 1603, and an 'Elegie written at the same time for the welcome of Queene Ann into England'. The central theme of the final poem is that, after the King's accession, the time when it was necessary to use disguise is over:

> *Iam dabitur veras audire ac reddere voces*
>   *Nostra sat est pietas dissimulata diu.*
> [Now we may tell playn truth to all that ask,
>   Our love may walke bare-faste without a mask.]

The framing of the *Epigrams* within royal elegies precisely follows, as we saw (Chapter 2 above), the pattern set by Sir Thomas More, but by 1605 they also contain an implicit criticism: a challenge to live up to the high expectations aroused (and not, so far, fulfilled) by James's accession.[24]

Harington's *Epigrams* show a profound concern with the role of the King in establishing justice within the kingdom. Striking proof of this comes with the epigram (IV.1) Harington placed at the end of his 'plea for a peaceble parley', as 'An Epigram shewing how England might be reformed', less than a month before he presented his 'ydle Epigrams' to James VI.[25] Whereas each of the first three books begins by discussing the role of the epigrammatist, Book IV begins with 'How England may be reformed' whose final line ('Yes, one good Stewart might set all in order') echoes the last line of the dedicatory epigram. ''Tis you great Prince that one day must correct them'. The language of this poem is harsh indeed; England 'late is bank'rout grown'. The 'cause vnknown' is all too obvious, rank corruption among the highest ministers of the Crown:

> Rich Treasorers 'tath had, and wary keepers,
> Fat Iudges, Councellors in gayn no sleepers.

In More's *Epigrammata*, the poems concerned with kingship (distinguishing kings from tyrants, the fragility of power and the King's dependence on the will of the people) tend to come in sequences. So too in Harington, but the emphasis has shifted from reminding a king that he is mortal to reminding him that he is the guardian of justice. Some contain echoes of More, like the poem to Lynus (III.53) who is slandering Harington for making fun of 'king Henries marriadge'. The very topic resonates with More's great stand, but the phrase, 'play with a dead Lions bearde', echoes More's advice to a courtier (*Ad Aulicum*, 144) that trusting the favour of a king is as dangerous as 'playing with tamed lions' (*inter domitos . . . leones*); the King may turn, and suddenly what was a game becomes death (*Et subito mors est, qui modo ludus erat*). Another poem (III.72) is only clear, as we saw in Chapter 2, if one understands its allusion to More's savage attack, in *Utopia*, on the greed of 'noblemen, gentlemen, and even some abbots' who are displacing the poor to enclose more land for their wool trade.[26] Harington's 'Of Sheepe whose sheapheards are Wolues' not only alludes to More's tirade in the title and in the last line, 'of Cotsold Lions first to England came', but widens the charge to indicate that the greed has got worse, 'since this age in habit, and in act | excells the sins of ev'ry former age.'

One of the most powerful political sequences in the *Epigrams* runs from III.38 to 44. It begins with the ironic version (already discussed) of Erasmus's essay, *Dulce bellum inexpertis*. It continues with a poem that is apparently 'Against excesse in weomens Apparell', but actually focuses on 'Priests wiues' (III.39*bis*), the recent product of 'Of king Henry the 8. his Woing', the subject of the next grimly ironic poem (III.39), which suggests how quickly beheading follows bedding and, in its proximity to III.40, links Henry's adultery and executions with King David's weakness of the flesh before 'blynd buzzard Cupids *h*ookes', his worst crime being the result of his lust for Bathsheba. The next (III.42) effortlessly moves from beheaded wives to argue that the greatest monster is 'a headles woman' (a woman without a husband). Subtly, Queen Elizabeth has been woven into this Tudor sequence, and the paternal inheritance is made clear in the next two poems: 'Of treason' (III.43) and 'A tragicall Epigram' (III.44). In the trial and execution of Mary, Queen of Scots, they 'found (oh straunge) without allegeance treason', and showed there was more 'remorse in Hangmen'. The prelude to this harsh verdict is Harington's epigram, 'Of treason' (III.43), now endlessly anthologized and recycled by political commentators. Both manuscripts make the opening phrase a question to the reader, 'Treason doth neuer prosper?', a nuance lost in all the printed versions. Witty as the epigram is on its own, its position in the sequence serves to raise a fundamental question about the legality of power. Harington comes close here to his favourite 'Snt Awgustin', whose *City of God* succinctly asks: *Remota itaque justitia, quid sunt regna nisi magna latrocinia?* (Therefore, if you take away the rule of law, what are kingdoms but large groups of bandits?).[27] His own commentary on 'A tragicall Epigram', which he included in the treatise he sent to Tobie Matthew, links his indignation at the execution of Mary, Queen of Scots with the plight of Catholics, and makes clear how dangerous he thought this poem was, and why it circulated among Catholic recusants:

> I confesse for my part that meditating of what I had heard of the manner of her arraignement & execution, I made this epigrammaticall Epitaphe, and tould it to some good freindes bothe English and Scottish, but now, having ventured upon more daungerous matter in this booke, I will adventure also to sett it downe herewith.[28]

As Alison Shell argues, 'Though Harington refrains from voicing the conclusion that Elizabeth was wrong to issue the warrant for Mary's execution, he compels the reader to observe his reluctant act of refraining.'[29] Placed together, this sequence of seven poems implicates the Queen in her father's arbitrary cruelty, and portrays Mary, Queen of Scots as 'a Queene annoynted'. In a word-play that links her beheading with Elizabeth's lack of a husband (and by implication, heirs), he prays that 'in this noble yle a Queene | without an head, maie neuer more be seene./'[30] Three of these poems are transcribed in the Cambridge gift copy for Lady Rogers and Mall. One (III.40) is given a more pointed title: 'Of king David written to the queene'. The network of allusions in this sequence is as subtle as in an ode of Horace.

The sequence at the end of 'the first booke' uses the imagery of *A New Discourse*, damning the corruption practised by 'Favorites and courtly Minions' who devour 'whole churches and their rents' and 'Voyd forts and Castles in their excrements'. The allusion is more learned than scatological, since Alciati's most famous emblem lies behind the last word of Book I (see above). Here Alciati's classical learning is being used for a moral purpose, not for empty display. The opposite is true of the learning of the new churchmen. From I.12 to I.20 the word 'nothing' (sometimes 'nought') recurs in varying forms. What looks at first like innocent banter ('Sith you do nothing aske I nothing graunt yee', I.17), turns, with an autograph revision, into an indictment of nepotistic simony ('thou sau'st ten pound *to buy thy sonne a lyving*', I.19), and a climactic demolition of a lecture by 'Bellarmins Corrector' (Dr John Reynolds), where Harington concludes, in a poem that plays twelve times on the word 'learning', that he has 'learned nothing at the schooles' (I.20). Winding its way through a sequence of twenty poems at the end of Book III is a subtle conjugation of the word 'Symony' with 'venereous action': when church and university are so corrupt, the poet must take 'the Parsons Part'.

These poems are very different in tone from anything by Martial or Jonson as one can see in I.76, 'Against Promoters' (professional informers). Harington had translated the Martial epigram on which this is based in his lengthy denunciation of informers in his notes on Book XVII of *Orlando Furioso*. Before quoting in full 'a verse of that pleasant Poete *Marciall*, written above 1500 yeares since' celebrating the banishment of 'promooters' from Rome, he there argued:

> how hurtfull a thing it is in a common wealth when a magistrate (and specialy a Prince) shall here such a Martanist as *Martano* or such a Gille as *Origilla* was, wisper them in their eares, and geve malicious and vntrue (though probable) information against well deseruing men . . . And even so these doggs, these bloodhounds, nay bloodyhounds that byte in their barking . . . if their neckes were broken, the Realme should (I thinke) have a faire riddaunce of them.[31]

Harington's own version splutters with savage indignation at what these spies are doing to society now, and transforms Martial's *Turba grauis paci* into a sibilantly plosive apostrophe: 'Base spies disturbers of the publicque rest'.[32] There is nothing like this in Martial's complacent retrospect, or the quietly laconic wit of Ben Jonson's epigram on the same subject, 'Spies':

> Spies, you are lights in state, but of base stuffe,
> Who when you'have burnt your selues downe to the snuffe,
> Stinke, and are thrown away. End faire enough.[33]

Jonson provides an interesting parallel. 'The poet, wrote Jonson in *Discoveries* (1045-48), is one who "can feign a commonwealth . . . can govern it with counsels, strengthen it with laws, correct it with judgements, inform it with religion and morals."[34] So Jonson feigned a commonwealth that is composed of 'subjects presented not as individuals, but as types of virtue: as exemplars of the good poet, historian, soldier, statesman, judge or friend, and as models of feminine grace or chastity.'[35] Harington's 'men of worth', by contrast, are friends and neighbours, shown at table, visiting a new house, talking to Queen Mary, surveying their orchard or muttering in the city about Essex's death. Harington creates a series of everyday colloquies that nevertheless show contemporary abuses and corruption to be aberrations from the lasting ethics of 'auncient custome'. When Harington appeals to 'scripture' and 'the Creede', and adopts the title 'christian Catholicque' (III.45) he is appealing to a higher authority than the passing divisions of his own time. While 'Promoters' like Lynus are 'disturbers of the 'publicque rest' (I.76) and preachers like Lalus 'trouble ours and *all* our neighbor Reames./' (IV.90), while the kingdom is threatened by the likes of Justice Young, the only stance is with those who, like More and Erasmus, had used their wit, and the disguise of folly, as a defence in 'times abounding with abhomination'.

Whereas Martial's work was essentially inspired by satirical contempt, Harington, like Jonson, creates a benign impression of a common-weal. Only those who – by spying, hypocrisy or injustice – place themselves outside the circle of family, friends and fellow poets, attract Harington's passionate scorn. Harington's familial colloquies provide the framework for the judgement of humanity on those temporally in power, and his chosen position on the margins of the court gives him the freedom to appeal to another court: the shared views of 'men of worth'.

Our verse hath some Acumen

May was the first person to point to the variety and originality of Harington's stanza forms.[36] That so few of the poems are in forms popular in his day – *ottava rima*, the six-line stanza of *Venus and Adonis* and *Lucrece*, the Petrarchan and English sonnet – suggests that Harington is expressing both 'his deliberate independence' and his immense versatility.[37] As May points out, while 'thirty-two of the epigrams have fourteen lines, there is only one Petrarchan sonnet (I.55) and four English ones among them' (I.26, II.99, III.68 and 97).[38] He uses rhyme royal in four poems (I.4, 97; III.12; IV.35). III.60 is a tour de force: it runs two rhymes only for fifteen lines, mingling Petrarchan with English patterns, and then runs (mainly) Petrarchan quatrains in the second half of thirty-one lines, but finishes with a flourish of two rhyming couplets. This is combining *sprezzatura* with panache. Harington introduces his discussion of literary debt into a poem (IV.25) that immediately follows a translation by the Earl of Surrey of Martial, and pins his own colours to the mast of Surrey and 'worthy Wyatt'. This is more complex than it looks. Sir Thomas Wyatt had introduced the sonnet into English, and Henry Howard, Earl of Surrey, in 1557, blank verse, with his translation of the *Fourth Boke of Virgill*, so Harington is allying himself with 'honorable theeues': with poets whose imitations are creative adaptations. Wyatt's poetry, collected by Harington's father in three different manuscripts, 'assumes that his readers are part of a small group who will be able to unpick the often cryptic allusions to personal and public events which it contains.'[39] Harington, it seems, learnt more than skills of transcription from these paternal manuscripts. He followed Wyatt in bringing Italian forms into English, in translating the Psalms and in experimenting in many genres. Harington only emulated Surrey's epic translation (but in *ottava rima*) in the early years of James I's reign, with his translation of *Aeneid* VI. Harington learnt a great deal from Wyatt and Surrey, not least that it was safer to remain in the margins with comic epigrams than be a serious poet at the heart of the court. John Heywood, after all, only 'scaped hanging with his mirth'.[40]

Harington experimented with an immense variety of stanza forms. While epigrams in couplets are represented, Harington stretches the length for his seven narratives (I.29; II.2 and 78; III.54 and 60; IV.13 and 33) as far as sixty lines; these 'tales' have all the vigour and economy of 'Chaucerian fabliaux'.[41] They often hilariously show poetic justice being done, as in the case of the lady who sacrifices modesty to save her jewelled 'borders' (IV.33). An increasing proportion of epigrams in Books III and IV have an odd number of lines (7, 9, 11, 13 or 15). As May says: 'Among the courtier poets, only Sir Philip Sidney and the Countess of Pembroke made efforts comparable to Harington's toward introducing a variety of new forms into their poetry.'[42] In contrast to their metrical variety, however, Harington stays with the iambic pentameter as his staple metre. Variety of stanza forms is combined, however, with an extraordinarily assured command of rhyme, which allows the stress at the end of the line, or the end of the poem, to punch out the ironic message. Repeated feminine (and Latinate) endings are often devastatingly used to suggest woolly theology or political obfuscation (as in II.30, II.100 or III.44), while the poet beats out the return to reality with sharp Anglo-Saxon rhymes, like 'scarse | ([arse])' (II.30), 'pelfe | selfe' (II.100), 'steele | feele' (III.44). The variety of rhyme and stanza reinforces the originality and universality of the *Epigrams*, and reveals Harington's enormously versatile poetics.

Bath

Sixteen poems use Harington's home town as a setting. Most of these appear, at first sight, to be light-hearted references to 'the Bathe', like the two epigrams that appear to have forced themselves into Harington's tight numerical scheme at the end of Book III. (III.99*bis* and 99*ter*). Yet even these reveal Bath to be full of 'bowlling, carding, dycing' and Oxford (there may be an ironic Cambridge bias here) to be full of amorously willing 'young Phisitians' and 'toward sprites'. One of the most amusing Bath poems (II.85) concerns the 'Sarzens head' tavern (still in business) where the drunken Sextus has lost his 'pantaffles' (overshoes) on two drunken evenings; 'greeu'd both with the mocke and with the cost' he goes thereafter 'in his pumps' (slippers). Although Harington's defence of his calling 'our Bathes the pilgrimage of Saynts' (III.88) looks innocent, the debasement of the concept of both 'pilgrimage' and 'Saynts' is just beneath the surface of the humour. Politicians are no better, since the fact that 'fayr Ladies come in pilgrimage' also brings great statesmen 'faster thether' (IV.3). Another (II.45) ironically suggests that Bath vintners solve a difficult theological question and 'for pure zeale mix with water all our wines'. Three poems, as we have seen, recount amusing dialogues with Harington's friend, the Bath physician, Dr John Sherwood. Several reply to the Mayor's concerns that Harington's epigrams will stem the flow of visitors. Harington has compared Bath to Purgatory (II.6), so he consoles the Mayor by overwriting it in a second epigram as '*Paradice*' because 'men in Bathe goe naked not ashamed' (II.17). Another (II.7) ironically refutes the charge that ladies come to Bath 'to see and to bee seene' by claiming that they 'chiefly came to feele, and to be fealt'. Two poems use going to 'the Bath' to make fun of Galla and Lesbia (II.51 and IV.65). Finally, two show how Harington uses this local setting to launch attacks on maladies that afflict the whole nation. In an epigram addressed 'To the learned bishop of Bath and Wells' (I.70), Harington uses Dante's comparison of atheists with elephants to complain that England 'breedes enow such Elephants'. In III.70, as we have seen, Harington is stirred by 'an extreame flatterer that preached at Bathe' in 1598 to his sharpest prophetic denunciation of the injustices of Elizabeth's reign.[43] He tells the Bath preacher that, instead of praising the 'forty yeares sweet peace and restfull dayes' he should rather have 'words of Commination, | for times abounding with abhomination', and imagine God saying: 'I forty yeares haue dur'd this generation'. The Latinate rhymes, here suggesting scriptural *gravitas*, reach a rhetorical climax in the multiple alliteration and hissing sibilance of the final lines, which end, characteristically, on a savage Anglo-Saxon rhyme: 'yoaked | choaked'. It is not surprising that this poem did not find its way into any of the early printed editions, but instead was hidden in the secret cavities of a recusant wall (see Chapter 4). The Bath poems show Harington characteristically rooting his epigrams in amusing local stories and characters, and from behind that attractive base, launching a critique of the faith of the nation and the state of its morals that seems all the more grounded in the real world.

The secret drift of mine intent

In the poem he entitled in his own hand *The last Epigram* (IV.106), Harington has defended his right to maintain 'the secret drift of mine intent'. Whereas Martial's epigrams hurl their satirical darts at a wide range of minor characters, 'eight . . . major characters account for one hundred epigrams in Harington'.[44] May has added considerably to our enjoyment of these four books by collating the work that has been done in identifying some of these.

One of the largest groups of poems focuses on 'Paulus', whose characteristics fit Sir Walter Ralegh, the target of Sir John Davies's epigram 'In Paulum' (Ep. 41).[45] He has robbed 'Spaniards' through a 'writt of Mart' (II.56), is accused of atheism (II.50), sells tobacco (II.69) and denies he has a wife (IV.69).[46] The poems definitely show a progression from approval to moral disgust. In I.22 'my frend Paulus' is invoked to join Harington in disapproval of Lynus. Thereafter the tone becomes more and more critical. May thinks that once Essex had arrived in court in 1586, Harington attacked Ralegh as a consequence of his adherence to the Earl's circle at court. In I.41 he criticizes Ralegh for his servility and moral cowardice, and in III.63 for his taking church lands. In II.12 he is one 'whom I haue thought my frend sometimes'. IV.22 mocks his party invitation, 'for all of both the Sexes' as inviting Hermaphrodites, and IV.62 derides his liaison with 'Galla'.

Galla can probably be identified as Lady Mary Baker, 'a woman of high rank and low reputation', who remarried, in 1595, the Bishop of London, Richard Fletcher.[47] Sir John Davies has five epigrams devoted to a marriage that caused widespread scandal. Harington's 'Of Galla and Paulus' (IV.62) is more allusively witty. Galla's wish is stated ('fayn she would of him bee rid') only to be ruthlessly parodied in a climactic word-play, where Faustus (a third figure brought in to reinforce society's disapproval) is credited with reporting that 'Paulus rode that night and was not booted./'

Lady Penelope Rich is probably the 'great rich Lady' of III.73 (and perhaps of II.88) especially as her very public affair with Charles Blount, Lord Mountjoy, seems to have had the acquiescence of her husband, Lord Rich, for some eight years before her first child by him in 1597. Given Penelope Rich's long discussions with the Jesuit John Gerard, her rescue of John Bolt from torture after he was arrested for carrying poems by the Jesuit poets, Robert Southwell and Henry Walpole, her closeness to Jane Wiseman and her friendship with her neighbour William Byrd, it seems possible that the word 'Roman' in the title refers to her Catholic sympathies: 'Of an Horoycall [whorish] answer of a great Romain Ladie to her husband./'[48]

Lelia, in the ribald 'Lælias Count=es ship' (IV.16), can almost certainly be identified as Anne Vavasour, a gentlewoman of the bedchamber, whose affair with the Earl of Oxford, in 1580, led to the scandalous birth of an illegitimate son in March 1581, banishment from court, imprisonment for both the Earl and herself, and several years of duels and brawls between Oxford and Anne's Knyvet relatives. This libidinous earl may be the Caius of II.84, whose 'first loue and meeting' was in 'Aiax' (a jakes). Lelius was the pseudonym given by Sidney (in *Arcadia*, Book 2) to Sir Henry Lee, who took Anne Vavasour as his mistress, sometime around 1590, and openly proclaimed her as such at tournaments, with 'A.V. Lelia' engraved on his armour.[49]

Another group of poems treats the poet Lynus, 'A Coyner, a Promoter, and a Bawde | A Spie a practiser in ev'ry frawd' (III.66), with more scorn than anyone else. As well as being a bad poet and untrustworthy borrower, 'promoting Lynus' is 'one who attempts to win preferment by deliberately misrepresenting Harington's innocent jests as political criticism (III.53), and by trying to make the poet's religious orthodoxy suspect (III.45).'[50] The language of the debate in III.45 is worth close attention. The epigram begins: 'Pure Lynus papistry layes to my chardge'. The terms are very close to the end of 'An Apologie' (the third part of *A New Discourse*) where 'a couple of formall fellowes in blacke cloaks' lay the charge that 'they supposed me to be in hart a Papist'.[51] There Harington asserts that he is 'neither *Papist*, *Protestant*, nor *Puritan*' but instead 'a *protesting Catholicke Puritan*', and defends this harmonizing statement by referring to *S. Iustus Epistle* (The 'Epistle of St James', dismissed by Luther): 'Pure Religion and vndefiled before God, even the father, is this, to visite orphanes and widowes in their afflictions, and to keepe your self vndefiled from the world.'[52] The epigram is as serious in its open proclamation of faith. Combining the life and death gravity of IV.10 with scholarly reference to 'scripture' and the 'Creede', Harington reclaims the words *pure* and *protest* and stakes his faith on the unity of the ancient, universal ('Catholicque') Church, not the recent divisions:

Euen in my purest thoughts protest do I
A christian Catholicque to liue and dy./

It is not an accident that faith and slander are linked in this poem, as they are in *A New Discourse* where the second of two autograph glosses identifies *Iustice young a promooter* as *stercus* (excrement).[53] Young was a master of the rack, but it was his use of slander that was befouling the realm and turning a man's religion into a divisive matter. The last poem to deal with Lynus (IV.78) deals with his 'sclaunder' of Lesbia. The other twelve poems that condemn Lynus twice mention that 'men of worth' will not read him (I.22 and IV.12). Harington holds the unidentified Lynus, Don Pedro, Lesbia and their kind before the invoked and invisible jury of 'men of worth' which lies behind the whole enterprise of these epigrams. What gives the 'men of worth', named and unnamed, their power is their link with the 'reverent elders' (IV.40) and 'aucient custome' in an 'elder time'(IV.30), just as surely as More and Erasmus summon a host of classical authorities to condemn the shocking destruction of war or the rampant robbery of enclosures. At the opening of More's *Vtopia* in the 1518 Froben edition (p. 25) is an engraving by Hans Holbein showing More, Peter Giles, John Clements and the fictional Hythlodaeus engaged in a Platonic dialogue in an Italian setting. The reader is invited to join in this dialogue that crosses from fact to fiction in an idealized Renaissance setting. In the same way, Harington creates the illusion of an ongoing dialogue of real men and women of worth – wife, neighbours, friends, fellow poets – whose ideals derive from a classical and biblical authority.

To the great Ladies of the Courte

Robert Markham, writing to Harington to warn him of the dangers all around him on the Essex expedition, reveals how close *A New Discourse* had been to bringing him to the Star Chamber (a fact confirmed by the epigram omitted from *F*, and deleted in *BL*, I.87) and shows how effective has been Harington's chosen disguise as entertainer of ladies:

> The Queen is minded to take you to her favour, but she sweareth that she believes you will make epigrams and write *misacmos* again on her and all the courte; she hath been heard to say, "that merry poet, her godson, must not come to Greenwich, till he hath grown sober, and leaveth the ladies sportes and frolicks."[54]

The Queen and ladies of the court are central to the most famous anecdote about Harington, now found in Thomas Park's *Nugae Antiquae*:

> Being well versed in the Italian language, he translated a tale out of Ariosto's "Orlando Furioso," which was highly pleasing to the ladies; but the Queen, who was not unacquainted with what passed around her, soon got a sight of her god-son's poetry, and, thinking it proper to affect indignation at some indelicate passages, forbad our author the court, till he had translated the entire work. This he accomplished, and dedicated to herself, in 1591.[55]

If this was the occasion of the translation of *Orlando Furioso*, it also seems to have become the preferred persona of the poet. In 'An Apologie' he steers the issue away from political satire, and imagines the charge against him that in his 'Ariosto' he has 'wronged not only Ladies of the Court, but all womens sex', and answers that 'The whole work being enioyned me as a penance by that saint, nay rather goddesse, whose seruice I am only deuoted vnto'.[56] Harington's notorious Canto XXVIII of *Orlando Furioso* is addressed to 'Ladyes, & yee that Ladies hold in prise'.[57] Harington begins an epigram, 'To the great Ladies of the Courte' (III.74), with four lines that remind us of the social circulation of these poems, and of the role Harington clearly enjoyed, of entertaining 'noble courtly Dames' with traditional debates of polite gender warfare:

> I haue been told most noble courtly Dames,
> that ye commend some of mine Epigrames,
>> but yet I heare againe which makes me pensiue,
>> some are of them to some of you offensiue.

One of the gift collections, as we have seen, is to Lady Rogers and Mary, his wife, and many of the poems are headed to 'the Queene' or 'To a great Lady'.

In at least one case (IV.105), Harington seems to have received the intended response from Lady Cheke, a close and intimate Lady of the Privy Chamber for the whole of Elizabeth's reign, and widow of Sir John Cheke, a good friend of Harington's father. May has located seven different manuscript collections that contain her reply, and I have found at least one other, in Folger MS V.a.345. In two of these the reply is attributed to Lady Cheke. Harington's original succeeds in striking several targets: the preacher with no Latin, the morals of his own time where no man's word can be relied on and, finally, a witty use of scripture to engage in mild anti-feminist provocation. Lady Cheke turns the preacher's ignorance – and her knowledge – of the Bible to her own advantage. Citing four instances of a 'certain woman' in the Bible, she retorts in the last two lines that

> Yet for his comfort one true note he made
> when there is now (no certaine man) he sayd.[58]

Even where we have no answer, it is clear that the poems were transcribed and circulated in such a way as to stir what May calls 'friendly sparring in the war between the sexes'.[59] This explains one reason for the popularity of IV.57, 'Of a Lady that left open her Cabinet', where the wife's retort in the original is extended in several versions by four further lines of the husband's wanton response.[60]

Many poems, especially towards the end of the collection, are addressed to, or focus on, named 'great ladies': Lady Leigh, the wife of Sir John Leigh, whose hands rush to protect her jewellery rather than her honour (IV.13), the Countess of Derby (IV.74), Lady Kildare (IV.87 and 91) and the Queen herself (I.85, 94; II.64; IV.88 and 94). How different these are from the elevated language of Jonson's

Epigrammes can be seen by comparing Jonson's poems on Sidney's niece, Mary, Lady Wroth (103 and 105), with Harington's on 'two Maries' (IV.47). Jonson who claims his 'praise is plaine', sees Lady Wroth as a 'template from which ancient virtue might be recovered'.[61] His second epigram ends heroically:

> So you are *Natures Index*, and restore
> I'your selfe, all treasure lost of th'age before.[62]

Harington's poem (IV.47), in paying tribute to Sidney's sister, Mary, Countess of Pembroke, and Mary, Countess of Shrewsbury (who had funded a new court at St John's College, Cambridge), locates his admiration for these noble women below that of the Virgin Mary ('My soule one only Mary doth adore') and Mary, his wife ('onely one Mary doth injoy my hart'). He does so with ostentatious simplicity:

> Their learned payn I prayse, heer costly Alms
> A Colledge this translates, the tother Psalms.

Even with the Queen, Harington uses a simple style. In his last epigram addressed to the Queen (IV.88) he emphasizes her capacity to inspire fear – 'For euer deare for ever dreaded Prince' – and the plain ending contains an ironic plea, revised in his own hand: 'To leaue to read my vearse, *and* reade my fortune./'

Harington has chosen to portray himself as circulating poetry among 'Ladyes & yee that Ladies hold in prise', because that allowed him, like his translation of *Orlando Furioso*, to move in the realm of *commedia*, to ground his critique of the Elizabethan court, church and nation in the domestic, to disguise this profound moral critique as 'the fruictles fruits of ydle houres' (III.74). Harington has yoked Martial's studied impression of anarchic spontaneity to the moral seriousness of the Greek Anthology and a structure of forty theological decades. Situating himself as a 'wise fool' in the tradition of Erasmus, Thomas More and Heywood, and using images from Alciati, he has woven his own colloquies into a completely original collection of *Epigrams*. These poems, ostensibly for circulating among 'noble courtly Dames' (III.74), are made to sound like a continuing conversation among ladies, neighbours, friends and family. Safe from the corridors of power, he is yet able to create a poetic tapestry in which the powerful are placed and judged. Harington follows Italian models – Ariosto and 'the pleasant learnd Italian Poet Dant' (I.70) – in choosing *commedia* as his chosen medium for serious instruction.[63] Being a 'pleasant learnd' courtier poet himself, he writes with *sprezzatura* on the state of the nation and its church: 'a farre greater matter'.[64]

Notes

[1]   Steven W. May, *The Elizabethan Courtier Poets: The Poems and Their Contexts* (Columbia: University of Missouri Press, 1991), p. 143.

[2] Ibid.

[3] York MS XVI.L.6, p. 244 (*A Tract on the Succession*, p. 109).

[4] The numbering of III.50 (like that of III.70) is from *BL*, marked in Table of Contents as one of the 'decades'; III.50*bis* (*BL* III.49) is also marked with a cross in the adjoining column. Harington has left both numbers uncorrected in *F*.

[5] BL Add. MS 39829, fol. 93r.

[6] York MS XVI.L.6, p. 249 (*A Tract on the Succession*, p. 113, wrongly transcribed).

[7] Campion sees him as a prototype of Luther, see my *Edmund Campion*, p. 166, l. 423.

[8] McClure, *Letters and Epigrams*, p. 18, 'He lacked those qualities essential to success in Elizabeth's court'. Scott-Warren, *Sir John Harington*, p. 240: 'Was it something about him – his indiscretion, his neediness, or his lack of requisite talents? . . . explanation of Harington's failure is now probably out of the question.'

[9] May, *Elizabethan Courtier Poets*, p. 151.

[10] CUL, Adv. b.8.1, fol. 204v; p. 1 of manuscript section.

[11] For full details of all these, see Chapter 4.

[12] Scott-Warren, *Sir John Harington*, pp. 103–34 argues a different view.

[13] *Latin Epigrams*, Bradner and Lynch, pp. 110–12 (trans., pp. 232–3)

[14] After the essay first appeared in 1515, Erasmus returned again and again to the folly of war in *Querela Pacis, Enchiridion Militis Christiani* and *Moriae Encomium*. See John Mulryan, 'Erasmus and War: The *Adages* and Beyond', *Moreana* XXIII, 89 (Feb. 1986), 15–28.

[15] *CWE*, vol. 35, *Adages*, III.iv.1 to IV.ii.100, trans. Denis L. Drysdall (Toronto: University of Toronto Press, 2005), p. 415. For the royal exercise, see Baldwin, *Small Latine and Lesse Greeke*, p. 23.

[16] *Adages*, *CWE*, vol. 35, p. 415.

[17] These changes may have been made after the death of Lady Rogers, on 19 January 1602.

[18] Scott-Warren, *Sir John Harington*, p. 112.

[19] Humez, p. 167.

[20] May, *Elizabethan Courtier Poets*, p. 148.

[21] *A New Discourse*, sigs O3v-4r (ed. Donno, pp. 236–8).

[22] Rick Bowers, 'Sir John Harington and the Earl of Essex: The Joker as Spy', *Cahiers Élizabéthains*, 69 (2006), 13–20, sees Harington as sent to keep an eye on Essex in Ireland.

[23] Ibid., p. 18: 'Harington's further epigram on the Earl of Essex's demise remains playfully, deviously, even somewhat scandalously, ambiguous.' Bowers bases this mistaken verdict on the printed text's 'man of sense' (not 'man of worth').

[24] *Epigrammata Clarissimi Disertissimique uiri Thomas Mori* (Basel: Froben, 1520), pp. 16–27; *Latin Epigrams*, Bradner and Lynch, pp. 16–24 (trans. pp. 138–45).

[25] York MS XVI.L.6, p. 261 (*A Tract on the Succession*, p. 123)

[26] *Works of St. Thomas More*, vol. 4, *Utopia*, Surtz and Hexter, pp. 65–7.

[27] Augustine of Hippo, *City of God*, IV.4, trans. William M. Green, 2 vols (London/Cambridge MA: Harvard University Press, 1963), vol. 2, p. 16.

[28] York MS XVI.L.6, pp. 256*bis*–257*bis* (*A Tract on the Succession*, p. 119–20).

[29] Alison Shell, *Catholicism, Controversy and the English Literary Imagination, 1558–1660* (Cambridge: University Press, 1999), p. 120. See also p. 161, on Esther (IV.51).

[30] Harington suggests elsewhere that she may have had 'in body some indisposition to the act of marriage', York MS XVI.L.6, p. 50 (*A Tract on the Succession*, p. 40).

[31] *Orlando Furioso*, p. 135 (ed. McNulty, p. 196).

32 Ibid. For original, see Martial, *Epigrams*, pp. 16–17; *De Spectaculis*, 4. Harington's reading is *Tradita*. Aldus Manutius (Venice: 1517) has *Traducta*, sig. A2v, but like Harington, keeps the six lines as one poem.

33 Beniamin Ionson, *The Workes* (London: W. Stansby, 1616), *Epigrammes*, LIX, p. 784.

34 Ian Donaldson, 'Jonson's poetry', in *Cambridge Companion to Ben Jonson*, eds Richard Harp and Stanley Steward (Cambridge: University Press, 2000), pp. 119–39 (p. 125).

35 W. David Kay, *Ben Jonson: A Literary Life* (New York: St Martin's Press, 1995), p. 126.

36 May, *Elizabethan Courtier Poets*, pp. 154–5.

37 Ibid., p. 154.

38 Ibid., p. 155.

39 *ODNB*, 'Sir Thomas Wyatt', by Colin Burrow, p. 10. The three Harington manuscripts of Wyatt are: BL Egerton 2711, the Arundel Harington MS and BL Add. MS 36529.

40 *A New Discourse*, p. 27 (ed. Donno, p. 102).

41 May, *Elizabethan Courtier Poets*, p. 156.

42 Ibid., p. 155. A few years later George Herbert was to use 111 different stanza forms in 174 poems.

43 Compare the treatment of the Bath preacher, glossed as 'Mr Richard Meredith', in *A New Discourse*, pp. 81–3 (ed. Donno, pp. 148–51).

44 Humez, pp. 168–9.

45 Robert Kreuger, ed., *The Poems of Sir John Davies* (Oxford: Clarendon Press, 1975), p. 387, citing Carolyn Bishop, 'Raleigh Satirized by Harington and Davies' (*R.E.S.*, xxiii (1972), 52–6. Ralegh's secret marriage to Elizabeth Throckmorton led to his imprisonment, and the payment to the Queen of a 'ransom' of £80,000 from his Spanish prize money.

46 May, *Elizabethan Courtier Poets*, pp. 145–6.

47 Kreuger, *The Poems of Sir John Davies*, pp. 398–9.

48 For Penelope Rich's secret sympathies, see my 'Scribal Coincidences: Campion, Byrd, Harington and the Sidney Circle', in *Sidney Journal*, 22 (2004), 73–89 (pp. 73–86).

49 Hughey, *Arundel Harington Manuscript,* vol. 1, pp. 215–16; vol. 2, pp. 259–61.

50 Humez, p. 169.

51 *A New Discourse*, sig. P7r-v (ed. Donno, pp. 261–2).

52 Ibid., sigs P8v-Q1r (ed. Donno, pp. 261–4).

53 Ibid., sig. O6r-v (ed. Donno, pp. 243–4).

54 *Nugae Antiquae*, vol. 1, p. 240.

55 Ibid., vol. 1, pp. x-xi. Park's footnote elaborates on the source and the story.

56 *A New Discourse*, sigs P3v-4v (ed. Donno pp. 255–6). Lord Lumley's copy (and all presentation copies) contain nine triply scored lines at this point.

57 *Orlando Furioso*, p. 225 (ed. McNulty, p. 313), an exact translation of Ariosto's 'Donne, e voi che le donne havete in pregio', see McNulty, p. xx.

58 Folger MS V.a.345, p. '245' (271). See May, *Elizabethan Courtier Poets*, pp. 246–7, for transcription, collation and a list of the other manuscript sources.

59 May, *Elizabethan Courtier Poets*, p. 149.

60 As in Folger MS V.a.339, fol. 282r. See Chapter 4 for a full discussion of this version.

61 Donaldson, 'Jonson's poetry', p. 127.

62 Ionson, *Workes* (1616), p. 802.

63 Cf. 'that excellent Italian poet Dant', in *Orlando Furioso*, sig. ¶6v (ed. McNulty, p. 10).

64 Castiglione, *The Courtyer* (1561), sig. M3; *The Courtier* (1588), sig. L1r-v (Italian).

Chapter 4

The Texts and Early Modern Readers

The Manuscripts

Folger Shakespeare Library Manuscript V.a.249 (F)

This complete collection of 406 'Epigrams' in four 'bookes' was designed for presentation to Henry, Prince of Wales. The letter of dedication is dated, in Harington's hand, *19 June 1605*, the birthday of King James. We know Prince Henry received the book (this copy or one very like it) from Harington's own comment in *A Supplie or Addicion to the Catalogue of Bishops to the Yeare 1608*: 'I cannot say so for your Highnes knows I haue written otherwise in a booke of mine I gaue you. lib: 3. Num. 80.'[1] The hand of the *Epigrams* is not the 'author's holograph', as originally thought, but that of Harington's Scribe A, as identified by P. J. Croft and R. H. Miller, with autograph revisions, and is combined with a painted and, in part, gilded emblem of 'the Lanterne' (Plate 5), painted manicules (Plate 6) and an engraving of the Rosary tipped in (Plate 9).[2]

The book was bound in gold-tooled calf, possibly by John Bateman, the Royal Bookbinder, with tools linked to the shop of the McDurnan Gospels Binder, with a single and double gilt fillet bordering a semé of quatrefoils, a central arabesque cartouche and gilt corners of a floral horn figure on hatched ground (dust jacket).[3] It has gilt-edged pages measuring 200 by 150 mm, with a spacious text, on twenty-four ruled lines to a page of 150 by 105 mm, within double red-ruled margins. The 136 leaves, including two free endpapers, are numbered by the scribe (with two numbers doubled) as 266 pages, and made up of seventeen gatherings in eights, the first eleven of which, pp. 1–172, have the watermark of Hans Durr (basilisk on top of crozier and cross in letter *V* encircled by letter *C*), who owned the Upper Schliefe Mill in the St Albantal complex, Basel, from 1604 to 1635.[4] The paper changes during 'The third booke', and the last six gatherings, pp. 173–266, have the watermark of Nicolas Lebé of Troyes: the letter *B* within an elaborate scroll, akin to Briquet 8079. This is the watermark of all the surviving large-paper copies of *A New Discourse*; only those given to Lord Lumley and Thomas Markham are complete.[5] Two of the most important manuscripts of Sir Philip Sidney's *Old Arcadia* (the Helmingham Hall Manuscript, now BL Add. MS 61821, and the Queen's College, Oxford, MS 301), and a newly discovered fragment of the *Old Arcadia*, identified by Henry Woudhuysen as coming from the Huddleston family of Sawston, are also on paper made by Lebé.[6] Finally, Harington used Lebé's paper for the selected epigrams he gave to Lady Rogers and Mary, his wife (*C*).

Harington's autograph revisions, easily identifiable because the ink of his slightly tremulous hand has dried a grey-black colour (as opposed to the brown of the scribe), are frequent. Most of the variable and idiosyncratic punctuation has been added by him. The numbering of eleven of the decennial poems (decades) from II.80 to IV.20 has slipped by one in *F*, while *BL* has the correct numbering. Harington has made easily identifiable autograph changes to nine of the eleven, sometimes altering nearby numbers and sometimes not. At the end of Book II, the scribe has left a blank page (116), perhaps uncertain whether Harington might want to include some personal poems, which are at this point in *BL* (see below).

The epigrams themselves were clearly written over an extended period of time. Jason Scott-Warren cites Humez as the first to notice the temporal sequence, that

> dateable events appeared in the manuscript in the order in which they occurred; poems about the Ariosto translation appear before those concerning the *New Discourse*; poems on Harington's journey to Ireland in 1599 appear later on, in the third book; and poems anticipating the Stuart succession cluster in book IV.[7]

Since we can observe a movement from his completed translation of Ariosto (I.48) and the birth of his daughter 'of nine years old' (I.51) to the group of poems reflecting both the imagery and content of *A New Discourse* at the end of Book I, the poems criticizing Elizabeth's reign and the political exclusion of Essex at the end of Book III (70, 95 and 97), and the poem lamenting his execution at IV.59, we can see the poems growing over a period from 1590 to 1602. There is also, from the end of 'The second booke', a greater sense of theological and political urgency.

The four books, each of a hundred epigrams, are framed by a letter and poem of dedication 'To James the sixt' at the beginning and, at the end, the painting of 'the Lanterne' emblematic of his kingship, five 'Elegies' dedicated to the King and 'Queene Ann', and the engraving of the fifteen decades of the Rosary, together with accompanying 'disticks'. In 'the Lanterne', the crown, sun, moon, stars and candle have all been gilded. In this illustrated and elegant transcription, intended for presentation to a Prince on the birthday of the King, the conspicuous frame of royal instruction is intended to guide one's reading. Echoing the *Epigrammata* of Sir Thomas More given to an earlier Prince (later, King) Henry, this collection of poems spells out for Henry, Prince of Wales, and his father, their royal role in bringing justice and religious harmony to the whole nation, and highlights ecclesiastical abuses that threaten both the church and the peace of the country.

The book was owned in the eighteenth century by 'Eliz. Hoyle' (whose name occurs in the margin of the dedication, fol.1ᵛ), and then, in the nineteenth century, by 'R. Joyner Emmerson' of 'Sandwich' whose name is on the first free endpaper. The manuscript was offered for sale by Dobell's Antiquarian Bookstore (then under the control of Percy Dobell) for £165, and bought by the Folger Shakespeare Library, in 1935. If this book was the one given to the Prince, it must have long since passed out of royal ownership.

British Library Add. MS 12049 (BL)

This manuscript, with minor variations, contains the same collection of 'Epigrams' with their attendant dedications and 'Elegies' as *F*, and in the same order. It includes, with deletion marks, three poems at the end of 'The first booke', (I.86, 87 and 93) omitted from *F*, presumably because they were thought too politically dangerous. These are the only three poems I have restored from *BL* (creating a total of 409 epigrams), since gaps were left in both the numbering and the sequence of fifteen poems related to *A New Discourse* and the poems form part of the textual tradition (John Budge printed them in 1618). At the end of Book II, there is a page (86) containing four intimate poems in Latin, addressed to his wife, Mary, and to Lady Rogers, written in Harington's own hand, both secretary and italic. There are other deleted poems not in *F*, a number of additional Latin poems and a prefatory poem on the death of Lady Rogers (all in the Appendix below).

The manuscript, in an unidentified secretary hand, has 251 numbered pages, each measuring 190 by 145 mm, of thirty lines within a ruled frame measuring 165 by 115 mm. The watermark is a bunch of grapes akin to Briquet 13213, originating in central France between 1593 and 1612. There are 218 numbered pages of epigrams, sometimes heavily corrected, followed by an index of first lines (219–34), and a table of first lines in order (235–50). This indexed scribal collection may have become an authoritative text from which copies of individual poems could easily be made. Harington's revision of the text and autograph marginal annotations of the table of contents, mostly indicating *latin* or *lat* versions of the poems, support this interpretation. Six (of some fifty-six noted) of these Latin translations survive, of which five are only in *BL* (in the Appendix below). Harington chose, perhaps, to continue working with his scribes to supply friends and colleagues with copies, in Latin or English. There are two columns of marginal crosses in the index next to the theological poems: one for every tenth poem and another for poems not on the decade (See First-line Index). Many things suggest this book is a working copy: the more common paper, the secretary hand, the intimate poems, frequent revisions and large number of deletions. Equally, since the emblem and engraving are missing, *BL* could be a copy intended for a printer, a view supported by the instruction on p. 206 that: *Mr Swizzer in Sho lane must graue in wood, the lantern.*

That Harington added a first-line index and table of contents to this manuscript, and that he took so much trouble to correct the numbering in *F*, suggests that he regarded the collection of *Epigrams* as having an authoritative order and shape. The relationship between the two complete manuscripts, *F* and *BL*, is both intricate and complex. *BL* seems to have started as the draft in the hand of a third Harington scribe (neither Scribe A nor Scribe B but close to the scribe of the Index to Godwin's *Catalogue of the Bishops of England*, pp. 280–302 of BL Royal MS 17. B.XXII). At some point, perhaps after *F* was given to Prince Henry, it became Harington's principal copy, since it has autograph revisions, especially in Book IV, that appear to be later than *F*. It is less easy to distinguish Harington's hand from that of his scribe, because the smaller page contains thirty closely written lines of secretary hand, and his revisions, over a longer period, are in different inks, and sometimes lead. Nevertheless, distinctive features remain.

The manuscript remained in the Harington family until it was sold in 1825 to Joseph Haslewood, who notes on a flyleaf:

> Memo. 1825 Nov. 22^d. Purchased this manuscript of Lieut: Harington of Charmouth, near Bridport, who stated himself to be of the family of Dr H. of Bath and to whom this MS. had belonged. I paid for same, with part of the printer's copy of the Orl. Fur., the sum of 50£ by check on Morland & Co.

Haslewood annotated Harington's first-line index, cross-referencing the poems to John Budge's 1618 edition; he may be responsible for many of the later marginal numbers and annotations in the manuscript. Haslewood purchased the MS together with a defective copy of *Orlando Furioso*, and used it to collate the numbering of the poems with the 1633 edition of the *Epigrams*. Haslewood's notes and annotations probably constitute the first attempt to make sense of the relationship between the manuscript (which he thought was autograph) and the printed editions.[8] He noted that the poems were 'divided into four books of 100 Epigrams each'.[9] This manuscript was bought at a Haslewood sale, apparently by 'Mr. S. Butler', and added to the manuscripts of the British Library in 1841.

Cambridge University Library Adv. b.8.1 (C)

The second presentation copy, made for Lady Rogers, Harington's mother-in-law, and his wife, Mary, contains a selection of fifty-two epigrams (Table 2), again transcribed by Scribe A, on fifteen leaves of paper manufactured by Nicolas Lebé, which measure 275 by 200 mm. The ruled pages are bound together with Harington's own translation of *Orlando Furioso*, printed in 1591 by Richard Field. This composite volume has pages that are gilt-edged and framed throughout by lines ruled in red ink; the use of handwritten rules to combine print and manuscript (framing thirty-two lines to a page) is also found in the presentation copy of Harington's *A Supplie or Addicion to the Catalogue of the Bishops of England to the Yeare 1608*, BL Royal MS 17.B.XXII.

This gift-book, like *F*, is bound in gold-tooled brown calf with tools from the shop of the McDurnan Gospels Binder, possibly by John Bateman.[10] A double gilt fillet border frames a semé of gold daisies among which are the name of 'IANE ROGERS' tooled in gold on the upper cover, and that of 'MARY HARYNGTON' on the lower cover (Plate 7). At the centre of both covers is an arabesque strapwork cartouche, echoed in the four gilt corner pieces (also found on bindings for James I and Prince Henry) and enclosing a semé of cinquefoils. The title page, engraved by Thomas Coxon, has been painted, possibly by Thomas Combe, and at its head is an ironic autograph inscription in ink: *Non sic Petrarcha Lauram* (Plate 8). Petrarch certainly did not celebrate Laura in this way, but Harington's gift is fit for a Prince (transcribed, painted and bound in the same way as his royal gift five years later) and his epigrams are celebrations of a married love vibrantly lived in a political context. The suggestion that the poems were found among his 'scatterd papers' may be another allusion to the *rime sparse* (scattered verses) of Petrarch.

The book is both intimate and political, carefully dated six months from King James's birthday. On the verso of the colophon of Richard Field, where printed book meets manuscript, is the following dedication in the scribe's hand, with the date and signature in Harington's own hand:

> To the right vertuous and his kynde Mother
> in law, the Ladie Jane Rogers.

Madame I haue sent you my long promisd Orlando, and that it maie properly belonge to you and your heire femall, I haue added to it as manie of the toyes I haue formerly written to you and your daughter, as I could collect out of my scatterd papers; supposing (though you haue seene some of them long since) yet now to revew them againe, and remember the kynde, and sometime the vnkynde occasions, on which some of them were written, will not be vnpleasant, and because there was spare roome, I haue added a few others that were showd to our Soueraigne Lady, and some, that I durst neuer show any Ladie, but you two. And so wishing you to lock me vp as safe in your loue, as I know you will lay vp this booke safe in your Chest. I commend me to you.

19 December   Your sonne in law and in Loue
1600.

Iohn Haryngton.[11]

Lady Rogers died thirteen months later, so some of the revisions (especially those marking the loss of children) may have been made solely for 'Mary Haryngton'. Harington's description of the forty-one domestic poems as 'toyes' from his 'scatterd papers', and his claim that he included the eleven political poems 'because there was spare roome' is pure *sprezzatura*. Since the domestic poems occur in the same order as in *F* and *BL*, we can deduce that, by this date, the shape of the four books of *Epigrams* had already become fixed, and remained so. This is confirmed by Harington's referring Prince Henry in 1608 to 'lib: 3. Num 80', the same number in both extant collections. One can note that he was already adopting the artifice of presenting his 'toyes' as a transcript of earlier work: a device he employs in both subsequent presentation copies for Prince Henry (the translation of *Aeneid* VI and *A Supplie or Addicion*).

The bookplate, now on the front pastedown, and originally on the title page verso, makes it clear that this book came to the University of Cambridge in 1715 as part of the bequest by George I of the library of John Moore (1646–1714). Moore had been bishop, first of Norwich, and then of Ely. The shelfmark on the title page, *Y.7.50*, confirms that the book was catalogued by Cambridge University Library in the eighteenth century.

The scribal workshop and Thomas Combe

All three manuscripts show a close affinity to each other. The hand of two, *F* and *C*, is the same (Scribe A), and identical autograph revision is often made to all three (III.33.7, III.40.12, III.49.6, for example). Sometimes two are revised, bringing all three in line (see II.66.15; IV.29.5). Conversely, the original text of poems heavily revised in *BL* is the same as in *F* (III.7; IV.8, 13 and 86). Apart from the more politically explicit titles (Table 2), variants in *C* are extremely rare and usually personal (referring to the deaths of his children in III.11, III.91, or the length of marriage in IV.9). Either *C* and *F* were transcribed from *BL*, or from a single common source (*q*). The revision and punctuation of *F* seems to have been done as each gathering was finished.[12] Analysis of the ink colour suggests that much of the revision and most of the punctuation is Harington's own; commas and ambiguously placed apostrophes look as if Harington added them while moving rapidly down the page. The slightly tremulous hand, the longer ascenders and descenders combine with the different ink to provide graphic evidence of Harington at work with his scribe, especially on *F* and *C*. While there is even more extensive autograph revision in *BL*, especially in Book IV, much of this appears to be later than *F*.

The hand of *F* and *C* appears to be the same as that in four other Harington manuscripts. Two of these are transcriptions of Edmund Campion's poem on the early history of the church, *Sancta salutiferi nascentia semina verbi*: Holkham MS 437 (*H*) and Bodleian MS Rawlinson D. 289 (*R*). Both of these are in the distinctive italic hand of Scribe A, both are on paper from the St Albantal complex of paper mills, Basel, and share the same ruled borders. *H* has the watermark of Niklaus Heusler, who owned the Zunziger Mill between 1586 and 1613, and shares many textual similarities with another Harington manuscript of Campion's poem, BL Add. MS 36529.[13] *R*, which has only recently come to light, has the same watermark as the first eleven quires of *F*: that of Hans Durr.[14] This indicates that the transcription was made sometime after 1604 and before Harington's death in 1612. It is significant that between 1586 and 1612, some forty years after the poem's composition around 1568, Harington was involved in making at least two presentation copies (*H* and *R*) of Campion's poem on the early history of the church. We would know whether there were more, if we could find or identify the copy sold by Sotheby's on 24 May 1825.[15] The watermark of *R* is identical to that of Folger MS V.a.421, the manuscript of *Two Letters and Short Rules of a Good Life* by Robert Southwell, S.J.[16] The third manuscript in the same hand is Trumbull Additional MS 23, a presentation copy of Harington's translation of 'that vj booke of Eneyds' (Virgil's *Aeneid* VI), 'done fyrst for the benefyt of myne own chylde, and now commented on and amplyfyed for the use of the Peerles Prince', Henry.[17] The fourth is the presentation copy for Prince Henry of *A Supplie or Addicion to the Catalogue of Bishops to the Yeare 1608*, that now forms Royal MS 17.B.XXII. Here Harington's autograph marginal annotations to Godwin's text are followed by a table of contents for the printed text in secretary hand, and the distinctive italic hand of Scribe A for Harington's index ('table Alphabeticall') and the text of his *A Supplie or Addicion.* All six manuscripts share the same distinctive capital letters (including two kinds of capital *E*), long ascenders and descenders, and a very idiosyncratic *v*. While a final swirling flourish on an *e* at the end of a line is rare in *C*, it is quite common in *F* (see Plate 6), where Scribe A also frequently gives an elegant ligature to his double *s*.

Clearly, Harington's scribes belonged to a household circle, and may have included his brother, Francis (see the Appendix). Since all the elegant, and often coloured, presentation copies, even the dangerous Campion texts, were entrusted to Scribe A, there is much to suggest that he is Thomas Combe, whom we have already seen entrusted with carrying Harington's Petrarch (and possibly secret correspondence), and drawing the 'devise' at the centre of *A New Discourse.* 'An Anatomie of the Metamorphosed Aiax' is written and drawn by 'T. C. Traveller' who describes himself as 'a dealer in Emblems'.[18] The printer's copy (BL Add. MS 46368) states clearly that it is 'by Thomas Combe travaller'.[19] Combe is the author of *The Theater of Fine Devices*, a creative transformation of Guillaume de la Perrière's *Le Théâtre des bons engins* (1539).[20] Since Richard Field registered Combe's translation with the Stationers on 9 May 1593, one can assume that this rare book (only two copies survive) was first published near that date.[21] One of the earliest English emblem books, it exerted considerable influence at the time and, by 1598, Francis Meres was including Combe among notable emblematists in his *Palladis Tamia*:

> As the Latines haue these *Emblematists, Andreas Alciatus, Reusnerus*, and *Sambucus*: so we haue these, *Geffrey Whitney, Andrew Willet* and *Thomas Combe*.[22]

Scribe A seems also to have been a limner. His painting of the engraved title page of *C* for Lady Rogers and Lady Harington transforms it into a colourful work of art; *F* is similarly transformed by his illuminated lantern and marginal manicules. A reversed engraving of the Mysteries of the Rosary has been tipped in (Plate 9) and re-numbered in brown ink.[23] Combe is a 'Professor of paynting', as the title page for 'An Anatomie' describes him, who can 'paint prettily'.[24] The combination of an elegant italic hand with painting skills would have been reason enough for Harington to choose Combe for all six of his presentation texts from 19 December 1600 to 18 February 1608. In his dedication to 'An Anatomie', Combe makes it clear he is no ordinary servant and that he has spent time in Oxford:

> Though I neuer troubled the schooles of Oxford, with any disputes or degrees yet I carried there a good schollers bookes after him.[25]

Harington's many references to 'my servant Thomas' suggest close collaboration and complete trust. I suggest tentatively, therefore, that there is a strong, but not proven, case for identifying Scribe A as Thomas Combe, painter, emblematist and Harington's most trusted servant.[26]

Lay vp this booke safe in your Chest

Harington had published in print his *Orlando Furioso* in 1591 and *A New Discourse* in 1596. On both volumes he had worked closely with Richard Field to produce a special edition for named recipients, on large paper, to be ruled, annotated, and sometimes coloured, by hand (see Chapter 1). Harington's decision not to see his 'ydle Epigrams' through the printing press may owe more to his lifelong interest in providing individual texts for particular readers than to fear of censorship.

Nevertheless, the highly sophisticated printing of *A New Discourse of a Stale Subiect, called the Metamorphosis of Aiax*, where the margins leave space for subversive glosses, only added in Harington's hand in the large-paper copies, did attract hostility at court, to which several of the epigrams refer. The modern assumption has often been that the hostility was to the scatological nature of the work, but it is clear that, even if the allusions were too vague for a charge in the Star Chamber (see I.87), many at the court understood very well how to 'allegorise the homely subject'.[27] Harington may have preferred not to risk disfavour again, especially after the near execution of his cousin, Sir Griffin Markham, in the Bye Plot. In addition, there was an official ban on epigrams and satires in 1599 that would have been worth taking seriously in the dangerous time between 25 February 1601, the death of Essex, and the death of the Queen on 24 March 1603. Finally, during the period from his New Year's gift of 1602 to 19 June 1605, Harington was using the *Epigrams* to try to influence the new King, and then his heir to the throne, Prince Henry, to restore peace, religious harmony and justice to a country divided and oppressed. By November 1605, the long-feared outrage, the 'Powder Treason', was nearly put into practice, and Harington must have watched with horror as the country slid from an atmosphere of suspicion and denunciation into one of Manichean struggle with infernal malcontents. The moment had passed when his *Epigrams* might influence Prince and people towards moderation.

When other books of epigrams were being published in print by Sir John Davies (1594–96), John Weever (1599), Charles Fitzjeffrey (1601), John Owen (1606–07), Sir John Stradling (1607) and John Davies of Hereford (1610), Harington had at least three manuscripts transcribed for named readers. We know, therefore, that the *Epigrams* were read during his lifetime solely in manuscript, and continued to circulate in manuscript for seventy years after his death. The popularity of the 'wanton' poems, especially those that involve sparring between the sexes, suggests that, among courtly readers, their appeal lay largely in their wit and conversational format. While we can only speculate on what a printed edition, supervised by him, would have done for the subsequent reputation of the *Epigrams*, we can conclude that it may not be an accident that the named readers – King James, Prince Henry, Lady Rogers, Mary Harington and Lucy, Countess of Bedford – were the only ones able to appreciate 'the secret drift of mine intent' (IV.106): the complex, learned and politically radical art that lay just beneath the carefully contrived 'Collection or rather confusion of all my ydle Epigrams'.

Sir John Harington, most learned Knight

So how was Harington read in his own time, and in the seventy years following his death? The four earliest published tributes to the *Epigrams* come long before any poems were printed. One of the four also supplies the earliest known date for the circulation of the poems. Sir John Stradling, in his *Epigrammatum Libri Quatuor* (1607), dedicates a discerning epigram to *D. Io. Harington Equ. doctiss.* (Sir J. Harington, most learned Knight), who 'sent' some epigrams *dono missis 1590* (as a gift about 1590):

> *Svnt, qui derident epigrammata: Forte quod ipsos,*
>   *Et mores stimulet falsè epigramma suos.*
> *Dant multi ridenda merè: Tu qualia sensum*
>   *Lectori infundant, iudiciumque tuo.*

[There are those who deride epigrams; perhaps the people whom the epigram falsely arouses because of their morals. Many produce epigrams that simply make for laughter, your epigrams flood the reader with a deeper meaning and force him to admire the judgement of the writer.][28]

In 1601, the *Affaniae sive Epigrammatum Libri tres* of Charles Fitzjeffrey were published.[29] In Book 3 is an epigram to Sir John Harington, *Equitem Auratum, Poetam vere aureum* (Gilded Knight, truly golden Poet). This speaks of Harington, *bleso argutum te patere ore cani* (singing sharp-witted poetry in a lisping voice), notes that he has both British and Latin models (*sive Britanna iuvent sive Latina magis*) and praises him for being on a level with Martial, and surpassing 'the likes of Heywood and Davies' (*Illis Heywodos Daviosque praeis*). The Latin adjective *blaesus* (lisping or mispronouncing) connects Harington's genius (and perhaps his word-play) with Martial, but the deliberate echo of Martial's touching elegy on the death of a six-year old Erotion (*et nomen blaeso garriat ore meum*, V.34.8) may be drawing attention to the more intimate side of Harington. Certainly Fitzjeffrey goes on to praise Harington for taming *Orlandi furias* (the furies of *Orlando*) and *Angelicam Angelica vel cecinisse tuba* (having sung an *Angelic* song on an *Angelic* trumpet), perhaps indicating that his translations of the Psalms were already known. In a deliberate challenge to popular opinion, Fitzjeffrey puts Harington ahead of Heywood and the man who claimed to have upstaged him, Davies. In his *Palladis Tamia* (1598), Francis Meres, although praising 'mellifluous and hony-tongued *Shakespeare*' for 'his sugred Sonnets among his priuate friends', and Harington 'for his translation of *Orlando Furioso*', makes no mention of Harington in his survey of 'Epigrammatists'.

> These and many other Epigrammatists the Latin tongue hath, *Q. Catulus, Porcius Licinius, Quintus Cornificius, Martial, Cn. Getulicus*, and wittie sir *Thomas Moore*; so in English we have these *Heywood, Drãte, Kendal, Bastard, Davies*.[30]

This may be because, while Shakespeare's sonnets circulated outside the court, Harington's epigrams were circulating only in courtly circles to which Meres had no access.

In 1606–07, at the same time as Stradling's *Epigrammatum Libri Quatuor*, John Owen published three editions of his *Epigrammatum Ioannis Owen Cambro-Britanni Libri Tres*.[31] This contains two tributes to Harington. The first, II.5, is addressed *Ad D. I. H. Poetam ingeniosissimum* (To Sir J. H., the most brilliant poet), and praises Harington as *egregius* (exceptional). The second, II.34, *Ad D. Ioann. Harington, equitem doctissimum* (most learned knight) implies that, in Owen's view, his poems have not won the acclaim they deserve:

> *Carmina non sine re tua sunt, sine nomine quamquam*:
> *Scriptores alij, re sine, nomen habent.*
> [Your poems do not lack substance even if they lack fame; other writers lack substance but have the fame.]

The tributes of Fitzjeffrey, Stradling and Owen suggest that Harington's reputation as a learned epigrammatist was widely accepted before any printed edition had appeared: concealing his serious side under a word-playing exterior and, in the eyes of the discriminating Fitzjeffrey, outshining Heywood and John Davies.

'My deare frend Davis' as Harington calls him (IV.25), who had achieved a place alongside Heywood (as Meres testifies), pays tribute in his *envoi* not only to Harington but to the inclusion of his dog, Bungey, in the title page of his *Orlando Furioso*. Many of the *Epigrammes* of Sir John Davies were composed before 1594 (as Robert Krueger argues), so this poem, 'Ad Musam. 48', probably belongs to that period:

> Yet Bankes his horse is better knowne then he,
> So are the Cammels and the westerne hog,
> And so is Lepidus his printed dogge:
> Why doth not Ponticus their fames envie?[32]

Harington wittily returns the compliment in 'Against Momus in praise of his dog Bunguy./' (III.77), and uses Davies's praise against an unknown opponent, writing 'of Lepidus, and of his famous dog'. For this interchange to be enjoyed, the epigrams of Harington and Davies, as well as the dog, had to be sufficiently 'famous'. In his letter to Prince Henry of 14 June 1608, Harington mentions this epigram: 'The verses above spoken of, are in my book of Epigrams in praise of my dogge Bungey to Momus.'[33] Harington's earliest self-presentation, on the title page of *Orlando Furioso*, uses his dog to subvert the classical pretensions of a title page; seventeen years later he is still wittily using Bungey to present himself as an unthreatening and avuncular figure to the Prince.

The printed texts and their readers

The first printed miscellany to contain epigrams of Sir John Harington appeared in the year after his death. This was *ALCILIA: Philoparthens louing Folly. WHEREVNTO IS ADDED Pigmalions Image With The Loue of Amos and Laura And also Epigrammes by Sir I. H. and others* (London: Richard Hawkins, 1613). Unlike Harington's manuscript collections, this contained seventeen randomly selected epigrams (see Table 4), including the poem that became the most popular in manuscript collections (IV.57).

The first dedicated edition of *EPIGRAMS Both PLEASANT AND SERIOVS Written by that All-Worthy Knight SIR IOHN HARRINGTON and neuer before Printed* was published in 1615 by John Budge in an elegant, but slight, quarto text of only thirty leaves, with 116 epigrams numbered continuously. The selection and subsequent ordering seems haphazard rather than deliberate.[34] There is a marked absence of theological poems; only eight of the 116 epigrams come from the theological decades. From each of the first three books Budge printed just over twenty poems, and from Book IV, over thirty poems. He also included eleven poems not found in the three authorial manuscripts (see Table 1). The even distribution suggests Budge may have been working from a complete manuscript, but it is also possible he was printing a selection transcribed by someone else. Only two of the theological poems of Book IV (30 and 100) find their way into the collection (the latter in both English and Latin), which does suggest at least some censorship. Surprisingly, perhaps, several of the most political poems are included: three poems, for example, from the sequence that focused on Mary, Queen of Scots are included, without the theological poem on King David (III.40) or the poem 'On Monsters' (III.42), but they lose much of their power by being separated (as numbers 5, 13 and 97).

Three years later, in 1618, Budge published an octavo volume, *THE MOST ELEGANT AND WITTY EPIGRAMS OF Sir Iohn Harrington, Knight, Digested into Foure Bookes, Three whereof neuer before published*, containing 346 epigrams. Many of the theological decades, and several bawdy poems are omitted. None of the *Foure bookes* resemble the 'bookes' Harington planned so carefully. The new poems make up the first three books, and the poems of the 1615 edition are taken to form what now becomes the fourth book. The order of Harington's epigrams has been completely lost, and the poems have now been twice scrambled. There are two places where there is double numbering (1.84 and 3.30–32) so four has to be added to the apparent total of 342. In the 1618 edition, Budge roughly follows the order of the manuscripts in Books I, II and III, but only includes a further twenty poems from Book IV. The result is that, of the 106 poems in the manuscript Book IV, only half are included; excluded are all but two of the theological decades. It seems possible that Budge had acquired a much better manuscript of the first three books, so he decided to create three books of his own that bear some relation to the scheme of the manuscripts. When he reached Books III and IV, he realized that, in order to keep his first edition as the current Book IV, he would have to squeeze the manuscript's Books III and IV into his new Book III. The result is that the most theologically and politically dense part of Harington's work suffered the most: from the early part of Book III to the end of Book IV. Thirteen of the twenty theological poems are missing from this section of the epigrams; it is also the most dismembered, since Book IV is now spread chaotically between Budge's Book III and his Book IV. The pattern of omissions is particularly puzzling. From Book I of *F* there is only one omission, while there are nine from Book II, nineteen from Book III, and fifty-three from Book IV. The poems omitted from the first three books certainly look as if they are censored, mostly for religious reasons, but occasionally for lewdness. Once we reach Book IV, the situation looks much more like fragmentary copy than censorship.[35]

Omitted also were the emblem of 'the Lanterne' and its accompanying poem, the poems of dedication and elegies addressed to King James and Queen Ann, which enclosed the whole collection and echoed the collection of Thomas More's *Epigrammata*, together with the 'disticks' (couplets) on the Rosary and their accompanying engraving. In 1804, Park printed most, but not all, of these poems separately in his *Nugae Antiquae* (I:325–35), the loss of context depriving them of their real significance. The dedications and emblems with which Harington so carefully framed his collection have never before been printed with the *Epigrams*.

Included in the 1618 edition are twelve mediocre poems that are not in the authorial manuscripts, and are therefore of doubtful authority (see Table 1).[36] It looks as if the printer has used them to fill up space in a defective text of Book IV. The attractive hypothesis that the printer had an early manuscript dating from, say, 1599 is ruled out by the fact that IV.59 (which is included) refers to the death of Essex. The most likely hypothesis is that the printer was working from genuinely 'scattered papers'. Most of the poems which reach the 1618 edition from the original Book IV seem to do so because they are also in the 1615 edition, suggesting that the printer was working from the same limited manuscript of Book IV as he was using in 1615.

At one end of the scale, readers lost the popular 'A vertuous lady sitting in a Muse' (IV.57), presumably because it was thought too bawdy; at the other, 'Men say that England late is bank'rout grown' (IV.1), one of the most profound analyses of contemporary social and political corruption. What is left is a confused collection of 346 poems without their original spelling and word-play or theological backbone. It is a mystery how two such carefully supervised manuscript texts, ordered, revised and punctuated by the author, came to be so disregarded and dismembered by the printer. The poems were certainly subject to a progressive process in which they were both disordered and trivialized.

Those purchasing the printed edition read something very different from the author's annotated and indexed manuscript. Sir Edward Dering notes in his 'Booke of Expences' in '1619 3d qter' that he paid '6d' for 'Sir Iohn Harringtons booke of epigramms' (presumably the 1618 edition). This was the same price as he paid for a quart of white wine, mending his spurs or slaughtering a boar (compared to the '8s 6d' he spent at the same time on Aquinas's *Catanea aurea* and the '9s' on '27 playbookes').[37] While individual epigrams became popular in miscellanies in the succeeding century, the *Epigrams* were not, and could not, be seen as a whole. The 1618 edition became the fixed text, which Budge repeated in 1625, though he now mercifully omitted the spurious last epigram *In Romam* (only re-introduced by McClure in 1930). George Miller followed this for his 1633 edition, correcting one but repeating two of the numerical muddles of the third book, and adding a new one. First published separately, this edition was appended to the third edition of *Orlando Furioso*, published by Miller in 1634. It seems unlikely that either Budge or Miller had access to any authorial manuscript.

Norman Egbert McClure, who did have access to *BL*, still chose to follow the printed text of 1618, both in his first edition of 1926 and his 1930 compilation of *The Letters and Epigrams of Sir John Harington*, and to append most of the eighty or so additional poems he found in *BL* as addenda, adding a third confusion to the two earlier muddles. While editorial theory in the 1930s advised editors to use printed exemplars where possible, W. W. Greg 'could have provided McClure with a sound justification for observing the textual integrity of the manuscript tradition' especially 'where all the editions are posthumous'.[38] Harington's didactic frame of dedication and elegies was dispersed, and McClure compounded the defects of earlier editions by silently omitting the description of the lantern in *BL*, its accompanying 'Elegie', the Latin and English couplets on the fifteen mysteries of the Rosary (there was a space for the engraving in *BL*) and, bizarrely, five poems, he apparently considered too bawdy (Table 1). It is not surprising that T. S. Eliot, reviewing McClure's edition in 1927, thought the epigrams "illustrate well the mentality of a cultivated and wholly uninspired country gentleman of the time".[39] He was echoing Thomas Park who, when editing the *Nugae Antiquae* in 1804, had noted, 'That the epigrams were popular in their day . . . but they have little now to recommend them, unless for the purpose of contemporary illustration.'[40]

McClure's greatest service to scholarship was to cloak his strange amalgam of earlier editions with a unified system of numbering that has been an easy scheme of reference for eighty years, but he also gave permanence to the pejorative estimate of Harington with this chiastic coda to his introduction:

> No one will contend that Harington's epigrams have any great literary merit; that they are extremely interesting for the light that they throw upon the customs and manners of the time, no one can deny.[41]

Fortunately, in 1971, Jean McMahon Humez breathed new life into the study of Harington's *Epigrams* with her dissertation on 'The Manners of Epigram'.[42] She drew attention to the shape of the work, the theological decades, the importance of More and Heywood, and used the order of the *Epigrams* in the manuscripts to reveal deliberate sequences. In a seminal article in 1984, R. H. Miller argued:

> A new edition of all the epigrams, based on the Folger manuscript, would be an improvement over McClure's, although probably not feasible at this time. In lieu of one

I have tried to provide texts of these hitherto unpublished poems, drawn in cases where texts exist in it, from *F*, and in the remaining cases from *BL*.[43]

Miller here began an important work of reconstruction. His courteous description of the 'limitations' of McClure's edition is a masterpiece of understatement, especially as he notes that 'McClure's annotations of textual variants are erratic and unreliable'.[44] P. J. Croft identified three secretary hands, Harington's own and two scribes, A and B, in Sir John Harington's manuscript of Sir Philip Sidney's *Arcadia*; three years later, Miller, building on Croft's work, identified the same three hands in 'Sir John Harington's Manuscripts in Italic'.[45] It is now possible, thanks to Croft and Miller, to identify Harington's more tremulous italic in the revisions and glosses in all three manuscripts of the *Epigrams*. We can begin to form a clear impression of Harington at work, even on the table of contents and first-line index which, remarkably, no earlier edition has carried.

Following the lead of Humez, D. H. Craig, in 1985, provided an informed and sympathetic reading of the *Epigrams* in his biographical study, although he ends by saying that 'they belong to a backwater of literary history'.[46] In 1991, Steven W. May, in his *Elizabethan Courtier Poets*, provided an authoritative survey of the range of subjects, historical characters and verse forms in the Epigrams.[47] Finally, in 2001, Scott-Warren devoted two scholarly sections to the manuscripts of the *Epigrams* in his *Sir John Harington and the Book as Gift*.[48]

Early readers in manuscript

The only surviving manuscript copies of the *Epigrams* that can definitely be dated to the Elizabethan period were collections put together by Harington himself.

From the reign of Elizabeth is the gift manuscript (*C*) to Lady Rogers and Lady Harington, already described in full (see Table 2 for the contents and structure of this manuscript). Here the mixture of highly subversive poems with domestic poems shows us how complex are Harington's intentions even when the binding suggests that this is an elaborate matrimonial album. The question of whether (or when) children were allowed to read these tender and amorous verses provides a sharp focus on Harington's control of his readership. We can only speculate on whether readers included the wider family and close friends like Ralph and Edward Sheldon, Thomas Markham, Henry Babington, or Sir Matthew and Thomas Arundell.

A second selection was dedicated, with the same *sprezzatura*, to his (remoter) cousin, Lucy, Countess of Bedford – 'I have presumed to fill-up the emptie paper with som shallowe meditations of myne owne' – and given the same date '19 December 1600'; twenty leaves of this book survive, now incorporated in a composite volume of state papers.[49] In the original order Harington has followed the Countess of Pembroke's translation of three Psalms (51, 104 and 137) and Petrarch's *Il Trionfo del Morte* with ten carefully selected epigrams (Table 3).

Harington's own selection, significantly, is of eight theological epigrams and two poems concerning Elizabeth (I.69, 'Of Soothsaying' and IV.88, 'To hir Maiestie').[50] While the eight theological poems are from the decades, the selection has none of the intimate or subversive feel of its contemporary gift, *C*.[51] The poems, while deploring a general decline in religion and morals (I.60 and I.10), focus more sharply on matters of doctrine: use of images (II.10), salvation by faith alone (I.80), the hypocrisy of many who know the Bible but do not practise it (III.50), and the damnation that will follow Paulus's denial of the Creed (II.50). One poem uses Dante's comparison of atheists with Elephants to hint at the decline of faith in England (I.70). The first poem, III.40, a meditation on King David, perfectly blends with the tone of the preceding penitential Psalms and subtly hints at royal sinners. That IV.88 is given to Lucy, Countess of Bedford, but not included in the selection for Lady Rogers and his wife, might suggest that Harington cultivates the pose of the luckless courtier only as a public mask.

Confirmation of Harington's statement that he sent the poems as a 'Newyeares guift' to King James VI in *1602* (6 January 1603) exists in the form of three letters in a contemporary hand, tipped into 'A Miscellaneous Chronicle of the Family of the Haringtons' by Dr Henry Harington, the great, great grandson.[52] The first is dated '3rd. of Aprill. 1603' by 'Will. Hunter' from 'the court at Hallyruid house', who writes that 'his Maiestie excepted your Embleme Lanterne and letters now last exceiding kyndely'.[53] The second is by Sir Thomas Erskine (1560–1639) to 'the honorable kny[t.] my trustie freind S. Iohn Harington': 'All you sent to M[r]. Hunter is . . . sa weill accepted of his Ma[tie.]'.[54] Finally, there is a reply from King James I, dated 'April the Thyrde, 1603', just after his accession, saying, 'We have raissavit your Lanterne, with the poesie ye send us be our Servand William hunter', which has also been copied, in a later hand (fol. 1[r]), into *F*.[55]

Among the papers wrapped in a white sheet, sealed and immured on 28 November 1605 at Rushton Hall, the house of the well-known recusant, Sir Thomas Tresham, was a single leaf in a manuscript, which remained hidden till a workman knocked down the wall in 1828.[56] This has a transcription, probably Elizabethan, of three highly subversive epigrams.[57] The first is 'A tragicall Epigram' on the execution of Mary Queen of Scots (III.44). The second is III.70, 'Against an extreame flatterer that preached at Bathe', a devastating critique of the forty years of Elizabeth's reign. The third is 'How England may be reformed' (IV.1). That Tresham had these three epigrams transcribed and hidden among his papers shows how closely Harington was being read in Catholic recusant circles, and how interleaved were the friends of these two men. The first and the third of these poems were also included by Harington in the prose treatise he sent to Tobie Matthew, later Archbishop of York, on 18 December 1602.[58] Yet, in Tresham's papers, immediately preceding the poems, are two letters to Tobie Matthew, referring to their common experience as students at Christ Church, Oxford.[59] Immediately following is a letter of Tresham to Lord Henry Howard on the Bye Plot of 1603, which he calls 'An atheisticall Anthonie Babington complottment'; both Babington and Sir Griffin Markham, implicated in this plot, were first cousins of Harington.[60] Tresham had been interrogated, in 1594, by Justice Young, who is named, in two autograph glosses, as the target of Harington's *A New Discourse* in Lord Lumley's copy.[61]

The manuscript transmission during the next eighty years shows the *Epigrams* quickly being reduced to a small number of popular poems passed from book to book. About 120 miscellanies survive from 1603 to 1680 that contain transcriptions of between one and eighteen Harington epigrams each.[62] This is almost exactly half the number of known manuscript collections containing transcriptions of the most popular poet of the century, John Donne, but in a much smaller quantity. Having examined over forty of these, I shall discuss a representative sample of ten manuscripts. In one of the earliest, Rosenbach MS 1083/15, copied before 1630, are poems by three contemporary epigrammatists referred to by Harington: Sir John Davies, given a large group of forty-seven poems, followed by groups of poems by Thomas Bastard (4) and John Heywood (20). Yet only four of Harington's own epigrams are copied (I.65, II.94, III.3, IV.85), and these are dispersed throughout the miscellany.

The impression of random selection and dispersal is confirmed by a second quarto miscellany, Rosenbach MS 1083/16, where, unusually, we know the name of the compiler, Robert Bishop, who wrote a title page and dated it '1630', and organized the poems. Of the fifteen Harington poems (including two found only in the printed editions) seven are copied in the section headed 'Women' (pp. 14–60). Harington's 'Of a certayn man' (IV.105), now headed 'A certaine woman' (p. 16), includes Lady Cheke's response (here unattributed). Here too (p. 19) is the most transcribed poem (copied 37 times) among surviving manuscripts, 'Of a Lady that left open her Cabinet' (IV.57). This poem was never printed by Budge, but had appeared in *Alcilia*, in 1613 (Table 4). Another popular poem, 'Of a pregnant pure Sister' (IV.80), copied twenty-six times, is here (p. 29), as is the other anti-Puritan epigram, II.94 ('Of certaine puritan wenches', p. 17), found in ten miscellanies. Since neither had ever been printed, their popularity must derive solely from manuscript circulation. Elsewhere (pp. 186–7) is another anti-Puritan poem, 'Of a precise Taylor' (I.40), found in twenty-five miscellanies, though this had been printed in 1618. Anti-Puritan bawdy would account for most of the poems included here, but the tales have often lost their narrative opening. Now simply entitled, 'Of a Bayliffe distrayning for rent', II.2 no longer begins, 'I heard a pleasant tale at Cannington'; the leisurely fifty lines have been reduced to thirty-six (pp. 187–8). Even IV.80 has lost its opening, 'I learnd a tale more fitt to be forgotten': the thirteen lines, as often in miscellanies, reduced to a blunter ten (p. 29). The poem 'Against swearing' (IV.30), found in twenty-five miscellanies, is transcribed (p. 119) after the section of 'Epitaphs', its lament for a loss of morals in the nation sitting rather oddly in this collection. 'Of Treason' (III.43), found in seventeen miscellanies (and printed 1615), valued today for its brevity and wit, is transcribed, under the same heading, below Fulke Greville's couplet 'On treason' (p. 146).

In a third mid-seventeenth century quarto miscellany, Rosenbach MS 239/18, the process of diminishing dislocation is complete. This compiler helpfully provides evidence of how these poems were transcribed, since he notes that he has copied the only two Harington poems here: the popular IV.57 and the anti-Puritan IV.80, both bawdy, from the book of a friend, 'Libr. Hilton' (fol. 45^{r-v}).

An unusually coherent selection is found in a fourth miscellany from about 1630, belonging to Margaret Bellasys (BL Add. MS 10309), and transcribed in a neat, italic hand. The four Harington epigrams selected contain a strongly political and anti-Puritan sentiment that accords with what we know of the Catholic sympathies of the Bellasys family. We have already seen two of the poems here in Tresham's papers and Harington's own *A Tract on the Succession*: 'England (men say) of late is Bankrupt growne' (IV.1), never printed but found in eleven other miscellanies, and 'A tragicall Epigram' (III.44), found in thirteen other miscellanies (fols 120^{r} and 148^{v}). Completely concordant with the mood of these (fol. 62^{v}), is 'In elder times an ancient custome t'was' (IV.30). The fourth poem is 'Sixe of the weakest sexe but purest sect' (fol. 148^{r}), significantly under the title 'Verses on Puritan Women' (II.94).[63]

A fifth miscellany, neatly transcribed on 103 leaves, is BL Add. MS 15227, from after 1630. Amidst poems on both universities, some anti-Catholic poems and several poems on the Duke of Buckingham (whose death was in 1628) are eight epigrams by Harington (I.10, 30, 40; IV.30, 57, 80, 88, 105), five of which are theological, only one of which is wanton (the ever-popular IV.57, which is entitled 'Sir John Harrington on his wife') and one of which, 'For euer deare for euer dreaded Prince' (IV.88), concerns the Queen's failure to grant Harington preferment. On one page (fol. 16^{r}) are transcribed both 'There was not certaine when a Certaine Teacher' (IV.105), together with one of eight surviving copies of the witty retort by Lady Cheke, here attributed: 'That noe man yet could in the Bible find | A certaine woman, argues men are blind'.[64]

A sixth miscellany from after 1630, Folger MS V.a.345, has poems inscribed on all but the last two of 160 leaves. The last poem in the collection is a savage epigram on the Duke of Buckingham, and there is a libel that Robert Cecil died of the 'pox' (after affairs with Lady Walsingham and the Countess of Suffolk).[65] Yet there are also poems by Thomas Bastard, George Herbert, Ben Jonson, Shakespeare, and eight Harington epigrams, mostly attributed. Three of the same poems occur as in BL 15227: IV.57, 80 and 105, in combination with two that occur in the Bellasys collection: II.94 and III.44. 'On the Q: of Scots Execution' is here placed (p. 103) among several elegies and epitaphs, and attributed in the margin to 'Harington'. The first line here reads, 'when doom of death by iudgment for=appointed', while 'Ah was remorse' replaces 'Ah, is remorse'. Yet the dominant mode of the miscellany is ribald, and the inclusion of IV.57, 82 and III.99*ter*, perhaps suggesting a university origin for the miscellany, fits the pattern of wanton verse. This is one of the few miscellanies that shows any indication of possible influence by the printed versions, since IV.82 and IV.105, that follow each other in the 1615 (22, 23) and 1618 editions (IV.22, 23), are copied together and attributed to Harington (p. 171). The title of the first, 'Of a saucy Cater' might be derived from the printed text, but the second poem, copied with an autograph gloss referring to 'An answere erat quidam homo' on 'page 245' (but without attribution to Lady Cheke), suggests the popularity of response poems. Indeed the sense of continuing debate, both in the wanton verse and in the religious and political poems, is the most striking feature of these handwritten miscellanies.

A seventh miscellany of 291 leaves, Folger MS V.a.339, dates from 1630–50.[66] In this are to be found, among several poems on the subject, the epigram on tobacco (I.89) as well as, without title, IV.57, complete with the marginal gloss: 'A couplet or two fastened to Sir Io: Harrington his Epigram to doe his Ladies knight yeomans service'. After what is the last line in *F* and *BL* we find:

> But he might have replide; good wife you mock:
> my key can open but not shut the lock.
> Sith tis a spring; & kayes in general
> will do't if so it open ly to all. (fol. 282^r)

The marginal gloss and additional couplets – found in other versions – suggest that even when the poem was being transcribed with its addition, the difference between Harington's text and its more wanton accretion was acknowledged. As late as 1674–84, William Jordan, a schoolmaster, was transcribing this poem, in Folger MS V.a.276 (fol. 50^v), this time without accretion or attribution.

An eighth miscellany, Folger MS V.a.262, also from 1630–50, has 172 octavo pages compiled by someone from an Inn of Court with Oxford connections. Amidst a large collection of famous epitaphs ('Underneath this sable herse', p. 53), and several poems by Donne and Henry King, are six Harington epigrams. 'Upon one that would not marry a learned wife' (I.7) occurs with the variant last line most common in miscellanies: 'The learned scholar, not the learned wife' (p. 69). 'Upon a Knight and his Lady', IV.57, is included (p. 80), but without elaboration, and III.84, here entitled 'To a paynted Lady' (p. 102), found in twenty-four surviving anthologies. The bawdy 'Of a Catour' (IV.82) is here (p. 103), and so are IV.30 'Of Swearing' (p. 83) and the coarser ten-line version of IV.80, 'Vpon a Holy Sister' (p. 147). This last, popular epigram here fits into an eclectic mix of a solemn epitaph on Prince Henry and a scurrilous one on Lady Rich (pp. 146–7).

Folger MS V.a.162, a quarto miscellany from about 1650, with an Oxford, perhaps Christ Church, connection, has been compiled by at least two different hands, on ninety-seven leaves. It includes an 'An Epigram of Cardinall Pooles Picture' (fol. 11^v) and sonnets by Shakespeare and George Herbert. On the verso of the torn first sheet is IV.39, 'A vertuous Dame that sawe a lawyer Rome'; a different hand has copied the next four Harington poems. I.7 (fol. 32^v) has the same variant last line (popular in universities), 'The learned Scholler, not the learned wife', while one page (fol. 34^r) contains I.30, entitled 'An honest vicar', and the epigram on Heywood and the book as cheese (II.1). 'On Treason' (III.43) is here, again coupled with Fulke Greville's couplet (fol. 35^v), but next to an anonymous poem comparing women to 'Epigrams': 'Once prest, common to all'. Finally comes, without title, I.10, 'A curate & a cobler longe disputed' (fol. 65^v). In this collection, lewd poems jostle with epitaphs on Queen Ann and 'an infant that dyed' (fol. 86ᵛ). Another octavo miscellany, V.a.97, a collection, in a small, tidy hand, of poems by Donne and Jonson and several epitaphs on the Countess of Pembroke and Prince Henry, contains only one Harington epigram, I.30, here (p. 54) called 'On a Vicar'.

The final miscellany, from about 1627, BL Sloane 1489, has three poems all on one leaf (fol. 10ʳ⁻ᵛ). The first (1615 edn: 63) is a poem with its source in Martial that is in none of the authorial manuscripts. The other two are: 'In elder time, an ancient custome was' (IV.30) and 'Heywood affirms and proves in some degrees' (II.1). Although all had been in print since 1615, neither the text nor order of these last two poems conforms to Budge's printed texts.

Although Harington himself had transcribed and circulated individual poems in the 1590s, he had, sometime before 1600, carefully arranged his *Epigrams* in four 'bookes', and given a special place to the political and theological epigrams. Early modern readers, however, continued to transcribe, quite freely, an eclectic mix of wanton and anti-Puritan verse. The artistic, political and theological coherence of the four 'bookes' of *Epigrams* was lost very early in the transmission. A small number of very popular poems continued to circulate in manuscript for over seventy years, though the printed texts may have had an influence on the popularity of certain poems (IV.30, 57 and 105, for example). The bawdy anti-Puritan tone of these miscellanies largely determined the choice of epigrams; only in rare instances, like the Tresham papers, the Bellasys collection or Harington's own selections, does one find political and theological poems on their own.

Editorial Conventions

I have transcribed Folger MS V.a.249 (*F*), treating this manuscript, clearly dated by Harington himself, *19 June 1605*, as a moment in the history of the text, but I have collated it fully with *BL* and *C*. For reasons outlined above, I have treated these three manuscripts as a closely related family, and made no emendation from any source outside this group. I have imported variants from *BL* or *C* only to replace obvious transcription errors (usually eyeskip) by Scribe A or, in the one case already noted, to fill the gap left by the omission of three poems (I.86, 87 and 93). All these changes and variants are noted in the Critical Apparatus.

Although the entire text is in Scribe A's elegant italic script, it was not possible adequately to represent this typographically, and I have therefore converted the entire text into Roman type. This allows Harington's autograph revisions (apparent in *F* both because the ink is darker and because his own italic hand is quite distinctive) to be represented by italics, so that they are visible but not distracting.[67] For this purpose I have eliminated from the text, Apparatus and Appendix all other italics (except for running heads, sigla, *bis* and *ter*). Readers, alerted by the italics in the text, can see what has been deleted (or overwritten) in the Apparatus (indicated by a single strikethrough). In the text, linear italics are used to represent marginal and interlinear revision. In the Apparatus, superscript and subscript are used to represent interlinear revision; I have not reproduced Harington's own very light carets, since these seemed more obtrusive, and superfluous, in type. Only in the Apparatus, sadly, can one enjoy those cases where Harington used overwriting to allow readers to see both the 'wanton' or daring original and its respectable, or politically acceptable, covering (I.47, II.17 and IV.10).

In *F*, Scribe A has used every available space on the page, so poems are sometimes separated from their titles by the page break. Although it was not possible to preserve the pagination of *F*, I have punctiliously recorded the page numbers, their autograph corrections and variable 'pointing' in the right-hand margin, omitting only the catchwords. I have followed meticulously the line breaks (preserving the archaic '=' for divided words) but, for the modern reader, I have tried to make the ends of most poems coincide with the page break. I have also left a space between title and poem, as the scribe does in *C*, and Harington himself always does. Scribe A made elegant schemes of indentation (though they are often ambiguous, and he sometimes forgets them on a page break) which I have scrupulously tried to interpret and represent. I have preserved the overall layout, where each 'booke' begins on a new page and has its own scribal running heads. Every letter of the text is Harington's; the space is, necessarily, an approximation.

In the Apparatus, I have ignored scribal *currente calamo* corrections and insignificant variations in spelling (mute *e* or *i/y* variation, for example) to enable Harington's interventions to stand out. In the text itself, I have silently expanded abbreviations (except for titles like M^r and $M^{tie.}$), but preserved the original spelling (including the scribal *i/j* and *u/v* graph), since Harington's word-play often depends on slight changes of spelling ('hoeroycall' or 'pillers', for example). I have retained Harington's punctuation of *F*, even though it was clearly done at speed. The position of the apostrophe required discernment, and forty-two poems lacked any terminal punctuation. Most of this I was able to supply from *BL*, but I had to add closure to eight poems and to two parentheses (all listed at the end of the Apparatus). Aware that there are already three sets of numbers on each page, I have added line-numbering (in square brackets) only every ten lines. Biblical quotations in the sacred poems at the end of the text were written in bold Roman by Scribe A, a graph I have represented similarly by a bold font.

Since Harington's carefully ordered manuscript collection of *Epigrams* has never been printed in full, I have omitted nothing that is in these three manuscripts, including in the text the copy of a letter from King James that has been added in a much later hand at the beginning of *F* (fol. 1^r), as this is authenticated by contemporary copies (discussed earlier in this chapter). All other additional material in *BL* I have placed in the Appendix. Apart from the letter to Lady Rogers, printed above, there is no additional material in *C*, and variants in the titles are recorded in Table 2 and in the Apparatus.

Harington went to considerable lengths to make sure that his four hundreds contained four decades of theological poems, where every tenth poem was on a theological theme. Harington emphasized his concern for the scheme of four decades by the changes he made in his own hand to the numbering. I have therefore recorded these changes and variations in the Apparatus, preserving Harington's numbering and his changes for the reader to see, while giving every poem its own number for ease of reference. In the two cases where I have been able to replace an incorrect number, III. 50 and 70, with the correct number from *BL*, I have done so, noting the change in the Apparatus. In nine cases, largely in Book III, I have been forced by Harington's autograph revision of the decennial numbers (represented in italics) to distinguish two identical numbers, and have had to use *bis* (and once *ter*) for the original, superseded, number. This does allow the reader to see how much attention Harington gave to the correct numbering of the theological decades, even at the expense of the numerical sequence. Only once, at III.90, did Harington decisively solve the problem by renumbering the preceding poem, III.91 (which I have followed). *BL* contains a table of contents that Harington himself has annotated. Every tenth poem (with two exceptions at the end of 'The first booke') is marked with a large cross to the immediate left. Other theological poems, not decades, are marked with a smaller cross in a different column, and Harington has also placed *Latin*, *lat* or *H* in the margin. I have transcribed these in the Table of Contents, and used them as corroborating evidence of Harington's numerological intentions. I have also transcribed the First-line Index from Harington's untitled index in *BL*. The spelling and numbering of both index and table are, of course, adapted to correspond to this edition.

Erasmus perfectly expresses the ideal of the editor:

> A labour indeed worthy of Hercules, fit for the spirit of a king, to give back the dead, to repair what is mutilated, to correct what is corrupted in so many ways . . . He who restores a literature in ruins (almost a harder task than to create one) is engaged on a thing sacred and immortal.[68]

Yet 'Between the idea and the reality', as Eliot warns, 'Falls the Shadow.'[69] Harington's habit of creating different texts, in manuscript and in print, for individual readers, poses special problems, and heroic failure has crowned several editions of Harington. Each editorial decision (on font, margin, space or numbering) makes one confront the impossibility of reproducing a scribal text. Randall McCleod, after deconstructing another edition of Harington, argued that 'photography has killed editing', and concluded, 'Indeed, what rationale can there be for editing?'[70] My hope, however, is that this edition will enable the common reader, for the first time in four hundred years, to enjoy all the *Epigrams*, in their frame of elegies and emblems, in the creative spelling, and in the form and order that Harington so elaborately designed and so lovingly revised with his own hand.

Notes

[1]   *A Supplie or Addicion*, p. 20 (ed. R. H. Miller, p. 52).

2 P. J. Croft, 'Sir John Harington's Manuscript of Sir Philip Sidney's Arcadia', in Stephen Parks and Croft, *Literary Autographs* (Los Angeles, University of California, 1983), pp. 39–75. 'Harington's scribes, while they were not required to be slavish imitators, were evidently expected in a general way to model their handwriting on their master's excellent example.' (p. 47); R. H. Miller, 'Sir John Harington's Manuscripts in Italic', *Studies in Bibliography* (40), 1987, 101–6.

3 'Tools that link with this shop are found well into the seventeenth century', Howard M. Nixon and Mirjam M. Foot, *The History of Decorated Bookbinding in England* (Oxford: Clarendon Press, 1992), pp. 38–41 (p. 39).

4 C. M. Briquet, *Les Filigranes*, 4 vols (Amsterdam: Paper Publications Society, 1968), vol. 3, no. 1380. W. F. Tschudin, *The Ancient Paper-Mills of Basle and Their Marks, Monumoenta Chartae Papyraceae Historiam Illustrantia, VII* (Hilversum: Paper Publications Society, 1958), no. 300.

5 Cambridge University Library Adv. b.8.1 (*C*). STC 12779: Lord Lumley's copy, and the original parts of Robert Nares's copy are in the Folger; Thomas Markham's is in the Robert H. Taylor Collection, Princeton University Library. Other mutilated copies are in Sheffield University Library, shelfmark *827.32 and University of Texas at Austin, shelfmark Wh./H244/1596n. All are annotated in individual ways.

6 H. R. Woudhuysen, *Sir Philip Sidney and the Circulation of Manuscripts, 1558–1640* (Oxford: Clarendon Press, 1996), p. 394, and H. R. Woudhuysen, 'A New Fragment of Sidney's *Old Arcadia*: The Huddleston Manuscript', in *English Manuscript Studies 1100–1700*, vol. 11: *Manuscripts and Their Makers in the English Renaissance*, ed. Peter Beal and Grace Ioppolo (London: British Library, 2002), pp. 52–69 (pp. 55–6).

7 Jason Scott-Warren, *Sir John Harington and the Book as Gift* (Oxford: University Press, 2001), p. 198.

8 This made-up volume is now in the British Library, shelfmark 638 K. 17.

9 In a gathering inserted between *Orlando Furioso* and the *Epigrams*.

10 Mirjam M. Foot, *The Henry Davis Gift: A Collection of Bookbindings*, 2 vols (London: The British Library, 1978), vol. 1, pp. 36–43 (corners I.3.B and C) and vol. 2, plate 53.

11 CUL Adv. b.8.1, fol. 204v, p. 1; and Scott-Warren, *Sir John Harington*, Fig. 8, p. 105.

12 Scott-Warren deduces this from the fact that pp. 45–48 and 161–63 contain minimal revision and punctuation. His detailed analysis of the ink colour, in handwritten notes passed to me, helped to corroborate all attributions of Harington's autograph in *F*.

13 For this text, see my *Edmund Campion*, pp. 150–53. York MS XVI.L.6 is in the secretary hand of Scribe A, and has the watermark of Clevia During, who acquired the Stegreif mill in 1587; this is between the mills of Durr and Heusler, St Albantal, Basel.

14 See Chapter 1, note 11. The eighteen leaves have been bound in limp vellum, and the work appears unfinished (see the gap at a textual crux of Campion's poem: l. 712).

15 'A Catalogue of the Entire Library of the late James Boswell, Esq. . . . Item 3190: Certain Psalms of David, translated into English Verse by the Countess of Pembroke and Sir Philip Sidney; prefixed is a Latin Poem, entitled "*Nascentis Ecclesiae generatio prima*".' None of the surviving copies of the catalogue that I have examined indicate who purchased this manuscript.

16 Robert Southwell, S.J., *Two Letters and Short Rules of a Good Life*, ed. Nancy Pollard Brown (Charlottesville: University of Virginia, 1973), p. xlv.

17 Harington, *Aeneid VI*, ed. Cauchi, p. 2.

18 *A New Discourse*, sig. L8r (ed. Donno, p. 204). Bp. Matthew glosses Henry Constable as 'the traueilour', York MS XVI.L.6, p. 81 (*A Tract on the Succession*, p. 64).

19   BL Add. MS 46368, fol. 45r. Donno argues strongly for accepting Combe's authorship of 'An Anatomie', in her *A New Discourse*, pp. 12–13.

20   Thomas Combe, *The Theater of Fine Devices* (London: Richard Field, 1593), STC 15230. Field also published *Venus and Adonis* (1593) and *The Rape of Lucrece* (1594).

21   A modern facsimile of the Glasgow copy (which lacks a title page but is assumed to be of 1593) of *The Theater of Fine Devices* has been edited by Mary V. Silcox (Aldershot: Scolar Press, 1990), while the Huntington Library produced, in 1983, a facsimile of its own complete copy, published by Richard Field in 1614.

22   Francis Meres, *Palladis Tamia: Wits Treasury Being the Second part of Wits Commonwealth* (London: Burbie, 1598), STC 17834, fol. 285v.

23   The provenance of the (certainly Catholic, probably Continental) engraving remains puzzling. Erin. C. Blake, Curator of Art and Special Collections at the Folger, writes, 'The printed image appears with both the design and the numbering in reverse . . . perhaps because it was copied directly onto the printing plate from an existing image by a non-professional . . . The correct-reading numbers in the image have been added in manuscript. Under 100x magnification, the ink is clearly browner, reflects light differently, and in places can be seen to lie on top of the blacker printing ink.' I suggest, after consulting Dom Geoffrey Scott, that Harington asked Combe to copy the engraving by making a plate from a tracing, and then to re-number the reversed image.

24   *A New Discourse*, sigs L1r and A3r (ed. Donno, p. 187 and p. 57). See Michael Bath, '"Dirtie Devises": Thomas Combe and the *Metamorphosis of Ajax*', in *Emblematic Perceptions: Essays in Honor of William S. Heckscher*, eds Peter M. Daly and Daniel S. Russell (*Saecula Spiritalia* 36, Verlag Valentin Koerner), 9–23.

25   *A New Discourse*, sig. L2v (ed. Donno, p. 190). Donno suggests that Francis Harington, who received his B.A. at Corpus Christi College in 1581, may be the 'good scholler'.

26   See Donno, p. 13, on the marriage of George Harington and Mary Combe of Lincombe.

27   *A New Discourse*, p. 127 (ed. Donno, p. 185).

28   Sir John Stradling, *Epigrammatum Libri Quatuor* (London: Bishop and Norton, 1607), STC 23354, pp. 32–3.

29   Chalres Fitzjeffrey, *Affaniae sive Epigrammatum Libri tres* (Oxford: Joseph Barnes, 1601) STC 10934, H6v.

30   Meres, *Palladis Tamia,* fol. 284r. See fols 281v-282r for Shakespeare; for *Orlando Furioso* and Thomas Combe among *Emblematists*, see fol. 285v.

31   John Owen, *Epigrammatum Libri Tres* (London: John Windet, 1606), STC 18984.5/7; the enlarged *Editio Tertia* was published by Humfrey Lownes in 1607, STC 18986, from which these quotations come.

32   Sir John Davies, *The Poems*, ed. R. Krueger (Oxford: Clarendon Press, 1975), p. 151.

33   *Nugae Antiquae*, I.390–84 [compositor's error for 380–84].

34   See Table 1 for evidence of this.

35   As Scott-Warren argues (in a personal communication) after an exhaustive examination of the migration of poems from the manuscripts to the printed texts.

36   Book IV (1618): 25, 30, 47, 54, 55, 56, 58, 61, 68, 73, 88, 92. McClure adds a further five poems that were on a leaf that was missing from *BL* but present in *F*.

37   'Sir Edward Dering . . . and his "Booke of Expences" 1617–1628', ed. Laetitia Yeandle, www.kentarchaeology.ac, p. 16.

38   R. H. Miller, 'Unpublished Poems by Sir John Harington', *ELR*, 84 (1984), 148–58 (p. 148).

39   T. S. Eliot, 'Epigrams of an Elizabethan Courtier', *TLS*, 17 February 1927, p. 104.

[40] *Nugae Antiquae*, vol. 1, p. xxiii.

[41] McClure, *Letters and Epigrams*, p. 52.

[42] Humez, pp. 119–253.

[43] Miller, 'Unpublished Poems by Sir John Harington', pp. 151–2.

[44] Ibid., p. 149. Miller notes also that the 'accumulation of letters' is incomplete, and that 'The Prayse of Private Life', which McClure includes, is 'not by Harington'.

[45] Croft, 'Sir John Harington's Manuscript of Sir Philip Sidney's Arcadia', pp. 39–75; Miller, 'Sir John Harington's Manuscripts in Italic', 101–6.

[46] Craig, *Sir John Harington*, pp. 84–102 (pp. 101–2).

[47] May, *The Elizabethan Courtier Poets*, pp. 140–56, pp. 245–7 and pp. 326–37.

[48] Scott-Warren, *Sir John Harington*, pp. 99–122 and pp. 135–153.

[49] Inner Temple Petyt MS 538, vol. 43, fols 284–303. Though this selection was separated from its original binding and disordered, Scott-Warren, in notes passed to me, has conjectured the original order of the leaves, so we can now see how these epigrams formed the last section of the gift. See also his, *Sir John Harington*, p. 151, note 32.

[50] The catchword, 'Of my readers', at the foot of fol. 290v, suggests one or more epigrams followed.

[51] The most interesting variants are the titles (Table 3). The scribe uses the apostrophe and hyphen in eccentric ways, and first-line variants (the commonest) often suppress the rhythm. There is no evidence of authorial revision, so I have not collated this.

[52] BL Add. MS 46381, a handwritten collection, presumably made c. 1769.

[53] Ibid., fol. 138r (letter tipped in).

[54] Ibid., fol. 141r (letter tipped in).

[55] Ibid., fol. 145r (letter tipped in). Only the Scottish spelling varies slightly.

[56] BL Add. MS 39829, fol. 93r. While the buried papers fill eleven BL vols, much of this volume charts building work, some internal: 'the particion wall in the gallerie' and 'seeling the gallerie closett', fols 52v and 71v.

[57] Included in May, *Elizabethan Poetry*: EV 5754, EV 29301, EV 32425. Another copy of III.70 exists in the hand of John Stowe, Harl. MS 367, fol. 144, dated by May, c. 1600.

[58] York MS XVI.L.6, pp. 257*bis* and 261 (*A Tract on the Succession*, pp. 119–20 & 123).

[59] BL Add. MS 39829, fols 81^r- 83^v.

[60] BL Add. MS 39829, fol. 105r.

[61] *HMCR*, 55, III, pp. xiv-xv; Lord Lumley's copy of *A New Discourse*, sig. O6r-v.

[62] Scott Warren's list of manuscripts (personal communication) reconstructed from Beal.

[63] For details, see the listings in Beal and in May.

[64] See May, *Elizabethan Courtier Poets*, pp. 246–7, for transcription and collation.

[65] For a full account of the 'salacious gossip' in Folger MS V.a.345, see *Breaking News: Renaissance Journalism and the Birth of the Newspaper*, eds Chris R. Kyle and Jason Peacey (Washington, DC: Folger Shakespeare Library, 2008), p. 32.

[66] There were originally 300 leaves; nine leaves have been taken out. J. Payne Collier inserted eighty-three ballads, a forgery discussed by Giles E. Dawson, 'John Payne Collier's Great Forgery', in *Studies in Bibliography*, 24 (1971), 1–26 (pp. 1–3).

[67] Scott-Warren's close examination of the ink led him to distinguish between the very light punctuation of the scribe and Harington's more detailed punctuation and revision.

[68] *CWE*, 33, *Adages*, II.i.1, trans. Sir Roger Mynors, pp. 9–10.

[69] *Collected Poems: 1909–1962* (London: Faber and Faber, 1963), p. 92.

[70] Random Cloud, 'from *Tranceformations in the Text of "Orlando Furioso"'*, *Library Chronicle of the University of Texas at Austin*, 20 (1990), 60–85 (p. 72 and p. 76).

PART 2
The Epigrams

A Letter from King James the 1st.
to Sir John Harrington, in the Original
Spelling

To our Trusty & Well-belovede Sir John
Harrington Knight. by which it appears
Sir John was the Author and writer of
this Book:

Ryhte trustie and welbelovite Frinde
we greete yow heartily weill. We have raissavit
yowr lanterne, with the poesie yow sende us bei
owr Sirvande Williame Hunter, gevinge yow
hairtie thankes; as lykewayse for yowr laste
letter, quharin we persaife the continuance of
yowr loyall affectione to us and yowr servyce;
we shall not be unmyndefule to Extende owr
princelie favoure heirafter to yow and yowr
perticulers at all guid occasions.
We committe yow to God.

James Rex.

From our Cowrte at
Hallyruid Howse
april the Thyrde, 1603.

To the most gratious and noble [fol. 1v]
Prince Henry ≈ ≈ ≈
≈ ≈ ≈ ≈ ≈
≈

Right Gracious, and inestimably Deare Prince.
For your pleasures sake and my promise, I present
your Highnes, this Collection, or rather confusion
of all my ydle Epigrams; some of which, some guilty
mindes might perhaps take in some despyte, but
(Candidi et Cordati Lectores,) Cleere mynded and
Worthie Readers, I know will pervse with good disport.
The common lycence, or rather lycensiousnes of Poets
may bee my excuse, if not my Warrant, as well for
[10]   some sharpe reprehensions, as for some broade phrases
in them. For I haue indevored so to sawse the
matters, that though your Highnes, and all noble
mindes, maie finde some Delectacion in the vearse,
yet it shall breede rather detestacion of the vice
reprooued in the verse./
I subscribe it thus with this picture rather then
my name, bycause so light and inglorious a worke was [fol. 2r]
fitter for those younge yeares, and the barbatula, or
french Pecque Devaunt, then for, questas barbas, (as
[20]   the Spaniards call yt) that should bring, with gray
hayrs, more graue thoughts./ Which thoughts
shall thinke their Maister no longer worthie of life
then he remaynes

Most faithfully Devoted
to your Highnes.

19 Iune.
1605.

To Iames the sixt, king of Scotland   page. 1.
The dedication of the coppie
sent by Captayn Hunter
1602.

O Ioy to present hope of future ages,
    bright northren starre, whose orient light infused
In south, and west, stayes minds that stood amused;
accept a present heer, of skribled pages./
    A worke, whose method ys, to bee confused,
A worke, in which my pen it self ingages
    to vse them right, that haue the world abused./
Yf I, where sin is wrought, pay shame for wages,
let your rich grace hold my poore zeale excused,
Enormous acts, moue modest minds to rages,   [10]
Which straight a tart reproofe well giv'n asswages,
    And duly giv'n yt cannot bee refused./
      We do but poynt out vices and detect them
      'Tis you great Prince, that one day must correct them./

The Epistle to all Readers how   .2.
Epigrams must be read atten=
tively. That legere et non intelli=
gere est negligere.

1   When in your hand you had this Pamphlet caught
      Your purpose was to post yt ouer speedy:
      but chaunge your minde, and feed not over greedy
Till in what sort to feed you first be taught.
Suppose that first and second course is donne,
      No goose, Porke, Capon, snytes, nor such as theese,
      But looke for fruite, as nutts and Parma Cheese
Comfetts, Conserus, and Raysons of the Sonne
Tast but a few at once, feed not too fickle,
      so shall you finde some coole, some warme, some byting,   [10]
      some sweet in tast, some sharp, all so delighting
As may your inward tast and fancy tickle.
But though I wish *the* Readers stomacks full,
Yet fast, or come not yf your witts bee dull,
      For I had *rather you sate* still and whistle
      as reading not to reade./ So ends th'Epistle./

Against Momus. That his Poetry
shalbe no fictions but truths.

2.   Skant wrate I sixteen lynes, but I had newse   3.
How Momus found one fault past all excuse,
that of Epistle, I the name *abews*,
    No gentle Momus, that is none abuse,
Without I call that gospell that ensews,
    But read to carp, as still hath been thine vse,
       Frett out thine hart, to search, seeke, sift and pry,
       thy hart shall hardly giue my pen the ly./

To Sir Hughe Portman of
Table frends.

3.   Thinke you his fayth is firme, his frendship stable
Whose first acquaintance, grew but at your table
    He loues your venson, snytes, larkes, quayles not you
    make him such fare, take Paulus frendship too./

Against Sextus a scorner
of Wryters

4.   Of wryters all, Sextus a known dispyser,
    sayth that vpon our wrytings oft he lookes,
And yet confesseth he growes near the wyser
    but Sextus, where's the fault, ys't in our bookes?
no sure, 'tis in your self (I'le tell you why sir)
Bookes giue not wisedome, where was none before,   .4
    but where some is, there reding makes it more./

Of one that vowd to disinherit his
sonne and giue his goodes to
the poore./

5.   A Cittizen that dwelt near Temple barre
by hap one day fell with his sonne at Iarr
    whom for *his* evill life and lewd demerit
    he oft affirmed he would quite disherit,
And vowd his goods and lands all to the poore,
His sonne, what with his play, what with his whore,

was so consumd at last, as he did lack
meat for his mouth, and clothing for his back.
    Oh crafty pouerty, his father now
    may giue him all he hath yet keep his vow./

            Against Lesbia both for hir
                patience and impatience

6.   Lesbia, I heard how ear yt came to passe,
        that when old Peleus calld th*y* lord an *A*sse
            You did but smyle, but when he calld him oxe,
            Straightwayes you curst him with all plages and pox
                There is some secret cause why you alow   5.
                a man to scorne his brayn, but not his brow./

                Of women learned in
                    the languages.

7.   You wisht me to a wife fayr, rich and young,
        that had her latten, french and spanish tounge,
            I thankt and told you I desir'd none such,
            I feard one language may be tongue to much./
                Then loue not I the learnd? yes as my life
                A learned mistris; not a learned wife./

                An Elegie of a poynted Diamond
                    giuen by the Aucthor to his
                        wife at the byrth of his
                            eldest sonne.

8.   Dear, I to thee this Diamond commend,
        in which a modell of thy self I send,
            How iust vnto thy Ioynt this Circlett sitteth,
            So iust thy face and shape my fancy fitteth./
        The touch will try this Ring of purest gold,
        my touch tryes thee as pure, but softer mold,
        that metall pretious ys, the stone is true,
        As true, and then how much more pretious you.   .6.
        The gemme is cleer, and hath nor needs no foyle,
        Thy face, nay more, thy fame is free from foyle,   [10]
            You'l deem this deere, bycause of me you haue yt,

I deem your faith more deer bycause you gaue yt.
This poynted Diamond cutts glasse and steele,
Your loves like force in my firm hart I feele.
      But this, as all things els, tyme wasts with wearing,
      Where you my Iewills multiply with bearing./

Of Quintus Alms

9.   When Quintus walketh out into the street,
     as soone as with some beggar he doth meet,
       Ear that poore soule to aske his Alms hath leasure
       he first doth chafe and sweare beyond all measure
     And for the Beadle all about he sends
     to beare him to Brydewell, so he pretends,
     The beggar quickly out of sight doth goe,
     Glad in his hart that he hath skaped so.
       Then Quintus laughs, and thinks it is less charges,
       to swear an oth or two, then giue a larges./   [10]

Of a Precyse Cobler and
an ignorant Curat.

10.   A Cobler and a Curat once disputed   7.
     afore a Iudge about the Queenes Iniunctions,
       And sith that still the Curat was confuted
     One sayd t'was fitt they two had chaunged functions,
       Nay sayd the Iudge, that mocion much I lothe,
       But if you will, we'el make them Coblers both./

Against wryters that carp at
other mens bookes.

11.   The Readers, and the hearers lyke my bookes
       but yet some wryters cannot them disgest,
     But what care I? for when I make a feast,
       I would my guests should prayse yt, not the Cookes./

Of Sextus a bad husband

12.   Had I good Sextus, well considerd first
      and better thought on Phrases of civillity,
When I sayd you of husbands were the worst,
      I should haue said, excepting the nobillity./
Well now to speake more mannerly and trew,
      the nobles and great states men all foreprised
An husband worse then you I neuer knew,
      then mend, yet thus, in mending be advised.
          Bee no good husband, for as some haue thought   .8.
          Husbands that wilbe good make huswifes nought.   [10]

Of a young Gallant

13   You boast that noble men still take you vp
      that when they bowle or sh*oo*te or hauke or hunt
      in Coache, in Bardge on horse, thou still art wont
To runn, ryde, row with them to dyne or supp,
      this makes you skorne them of the meaner sort,
      and thinke your credit doth so far surmount,
      When as indeed of you they make no count
but as they do of Hawks or doggs, for sport./
          Then vaunt not vnto vs this vayn renowne,
          least we both take you vp, and take you downe.   [10]

To my Ladie Rogers the Authors
wiues mother, how Doctor
Sherwood commended
her house in Bath./

14.   I newly had your little house erected
      in which I thought I had made good convayance
      to vse each ease, and to shun all anoyance,
And prayd a frend of Iudgment not neglected
To view the roomes and let me know the faults,   9.
      he hauing viewd the lodgings stayrs and vaults
Said all was exc'lent well, saue here and there,
You think he praysd your house? no I do sweare
          He hath disgras't yt cleane, the case is cleare,
          for evry roome is eyther there or heare./   [10]

Of Lesbia a great Lady

15.   Lesbia doth laugh to heare Sellers and buyers
cald by this name substantiall Occupiers,
    Lesbia the word was good, while good folks vs'd yt,
    You mard yt, that with Chaucers Ieast abus'd yt,
      But good or bad how ere the word be made,
      Lesbia is loath perhaps to leaue the trade./

Of Lynus poetry

16.   When Lynus thinks that he and I are frends,
then all his Poems vnto me he sends,
    His Disticks, Satyrs, sonnets and Examiters,
    His Epigrams, his Liricks, his Pentamiters,
then I must censure them, I must correct them
then onely I must order and direct them./
    I read some three or fowr and pass the rest
    And when for answer I by him am prest   .10.
I say that all of them some prayse deserue
for certayn vses I could make them serue   [10]
    But yet his Ryme is harsh, vnev'n his number,
    the manner much, the matter more doth cumber,
His words too straung, his meanings are too mistick,
but at one worde I best indure his distick./
    And if I might perswade him to mine humor,
    not to affect vayn prayse of common rumor
      Then should he wryte of nothing: for indeed
      gladly of nothing, I his vearse could reed.

Of one that begged nothing and
had his sute graunted.

17.   When thou dost beg, as none beggs more importunate,
and art denyde, as none speedes more infortunate,
    With one quaynt phrase, thou dost enforce thy begging
    My minde vnto thy sute in this sort egging./
Alas Sir this? 'tis nothing; once deny me not,
Wel then for once content, hencforth bely me not./
    Your words so wisely plaste do so enchaunt me,
    Sith you do nothing aske I nothing graunt yee.

Another of asking nothing   11.

18.   Some thinke thee Lynus of a Fryre begotten
for still you beg, where nothing can be gotten.
     Yet oft you say, for so you haue bene taught,
     Sir graunt me this, 'tis but a thing of naught.
And when 'tis so indeed, and I beleeue yt
as nought; and to a thing of nought I giue yt./
     Thus with your begging you but get a mocke,
     and yet with begging little mend your stock.
       Leaue begging Lynus for such poore rewards,
       Else some will beg thee in the Court of Wardes./   [10]

Of Liberality in giuing nothing.

19.   I heare some say, and some beleeue yt too,
that Craft is found ev'n in the clowted shoo
     Sure I haue found yt, with the loss of pence
     my Tennants haue both craft and eloquence.
For when one hath a sute, before he aske yt
his Oratour pleads for him in a Baskyt.
     Well Tenant well, he was your frend that taught you
     this learnd exordium. Maister heer cha brought you.
For with one Courtsy, and two Capons giuing,
thou sau'st ten pound *to buy thy sonne a lyving.*   [10]
     Which makes me say that haue obserud this quallity   12.
     Clowns when they nothing giue, vse liberallity.

Of learning nothing at a lecture, vpon occasion of Doctor Renalds reading at Oxford afore my Lord of Essex and diuers Lords, at the Queenes last being there, on theise wordes. *1592.* Hoc scimus quia Idolum nihil est.

20.   While I at Oxford stayd a few months since
only to see and serue our gratious Prince,
     Where gratiously her grace did see and show
     the choysest fruits that learning could bestow./
I went one day to heare a learned lecture,
read as some sayd by Bellarmins Corrector.
     And sundry Courtiers more, then present were,

that vnderstood him well, saue here and there./
Among the rest one whom yt least concearned,
Askt me what I had at this Lecture learned,   [10]
   I, that his ignorannce might soone beguile
   sayd, I had learned nothing all the while.
Yet did the Reader teach with much facillity
And I was wont to learne with some docillity .
What learned you Sir quoth he in swearing moode   .13.
nothing I learnd for nought I vnderstood.
I thanke my parents they when I was young
barrd me to learne this popish Roman toung,
And yet it seemes to me if you say true,
I without learning learnd the same that you.   [20]
    most true sayd I, yet few dare call vs fooles,
    that this day learned nothing at the schooles./

A Paradox of Doomes day.

21.   Some Doctors deeme, the day of Doome drawes near
    but I can proue the contrary most cleere,
      For at that day our Lord and sauiour sayth,
      that he on earth shall skant finde any faith,
    But in theise dayes it cannot bee denyde,
    All boast of only faith, and nought beside,
      But if you seeke the fruite thereof by works,
      You shall finde many better with the Turks./

Against a foollish Satyrist
called Lynus./

22.   Help frends I feele my credit lyes a bleeding
    for Lynus who to me beares hate exceeding
    I heare against me is ev'n now a breeding   14.
    A bitter Satir all of gall proceeding.
    Now sweet Apollos Iudge to bee his speeding,
    Nor what he wrytes I take no care nor heeding,
    For none of worth will thinke them worth the reeding.
      So my frend Paulus censures them, *who* swears
      That Lynus vearse sutes best with Midas ears./

Of one that seekes to be stellified
being no Pithagorian./

23.   An vse there was among some Pithagorians
if we giue credit to the best Historians,
    How they that would study the course of starrs,
    to purge the vapours that our cleer sight barrs,
And bring the Brayn vnto a setled quiet,
did keep a wondrous strict and sparing dyet,
    Drink water from the purest heads of springs,
    eat hearbs and flowers, not tast of lyving things,
And then to this skant fare their bookes applying
they calld this sparing dyet stellyfying,   [10]
    Then thinkest thou, scholler of Epicure
    that neuer couldest vertuous paynes indure,
That eatst fat venson, bowzest clarret wyne
Dost play till twelue, and sleepe till after nyne,   15.
    And in a coach like Vulcans sonne dost ryde,
    that thou art worthy to bee stellifyde?

Of a fayr woman translated
out of Casineus Catalogus
gloriæ mundi.

24.   Theise thirty things that Hellens fame did rayse,
a dame should haue that seekes for bewties prayse.
    Three bright, three black, three red, three short, three tall.
    Three thick, three thin, three close, three wide, three small
Her skin, hayr, teeth, must be cleer, bright and neat,
Her browes, eyes, privy parts, as black as Ieat,
    Her cheekes, lips, nayles, must haue vermillian hew,
    Her hands, hayr, height, must haue good length to view,
Her teeth, foot, ears, all short no length allowes,
Large brest, large hips, large space betweene the brows,   [10]
    A narrow mouth, small waste, strayght privy member,
    her fingers, hayr and lips, but thin and slender,
Thighs, belly necke, should be full smooth and rownd,
Nose head and teats, the least that can be found.
    Sith few or none perfection such attayn
    But few or none are fayr, the case is playne./

To Sir Hugh Portman 16.

25 You prayse all Ladies, well let you alone
Who speaks so well of all, thinks well of none.

Of Peleus freindship.

26. When Peleus is brought vp to London streets
by Process forst, to answer waighty sutes,
Oh what kynde words he speakes to all he meets
how frendly by their names he them salutes?
Then one shall haue a horse of his best race,
another getts a Warrant for a Bucke,
Some deeper brib'd, according to their place
ys like to serue to worke or wish good luck.
But when his troubles all to end are *brought*
by time, or frendly payns on his behalfe [10]
Then straight, as if he set vs all at naught,
he doth not shew himself so kynd by halfe./
Sith then his sutes in law his frendship doubles,
I for his frendship sake, do wishe him troubles.

To my Lady Rogers of
Cannington, the Authors
wiues mother.

27 Frow'rd and yet fortunate; if fortune knew yt, 17.
Beleeue me Madam, she might make you rew yt./

Of a toothles Shrew
calld Ellen.

28. Old Ellen had foure teeth since I remember,
She cought out two of them the last December,
And this shrewd rewm in her raignd so vnruly,
She *c*ought out t'other two before 'twas Iuly./
Now may she cough her hart out for in sooth
this same shrewd cough hath left her near a tooth,
But her curst tongue, wanting this common curbe
may more than earst our houshold all disturbe./

Of a houshold fray frendly
ended. To his wife

29.   A man and wife straue erst, who should be masters
            and hauing chaungd between them houshold speeches
        The man in wrath, brought fourth a pair of wasters,
            and sware those two should proue who ware the breeches.
        She that could breake his head and giue him plasters
            accepts the challendge, yet withall beseeches
            that she as weakest may at him strike first
        And let him warde, and after do his wurst,   .18.
        He sware yt should be so as god should bl*i*ss him
            and close he layes him to the surest lock   [10]
        She flourishing, as though she would not miss him
            layd down her Cudgell and with witty mock,
        Told him that for his kyndnes she would kiss him
            that now was sworne neuer to giue her knock.
            You sware said she, I should the first blow giue
            and I sware Ile nere strike you while I liue./
        A flattring slut said he, thou darst not fight,
            I am no Larke quoth she, man do not dare me,
        Let me poynt time and place, as 'tis my right
            by law of Challenge, and then neuer spare me.   [20]
        Agreed said he; then rest quoth she to night,
            to morrow at Cuckolds hav'n I will prepare me
                Peace wife quoth he wee'le cease all rage & rancor
                Ear in that harbor I will ryde at Ancor.

Of blessing without a Cross.

30.   A Priest that earst was ryding on the way,
        not knowing better how to pass the day,
            was singing with himself Geneua psalms,
            a blynd man hearing him straight begd an alms.
        Man said the Priest, from Coyn I cannot part,   19.
        but I pray god bless thee with all my hart,
                Ah sayd the man, the poore may liue with loss,
                Now Priests haue learnd, to bless without a cross.

To Cayus of one that is
his wiues Proctor.

31. What curld pate youth is he, that sitteth there
so near your wife, and whispers in her ear
And takes her hand in his, and soft *doth* wring her
And slydes *her* ring still vp and down *her* finger?
Sir, tis a Proctor seene in both the laws,
retaynd by her in some important cause,
Prompt and discreet both in his speach and action
and doth her busines with great satisfaction./
And thinkst thou so? a horne plague on thy headd
art thou so like a foole and Wittoll leadd   [10]
To thinke he doth the busines of thy wife,
he doth thy busines, I dare lay my life./

Against Momus

32   Momus that loues mens lynes and liues to skan
sayd once by chaunce I was an honest man
But yet one fault of mine he strayght rehearses   .20.
which is I am so full of toyes and vearses.
Momus tis trew, that is my fault I graunt,
Yet when thou shalt thy chiefest vertue vaunt,
I know some worthy sprytes one might entyce
to leaue that greatest vertue, for this vice./

Of Faustus Esquior.

33. Faustus for keeping of a wrong possession
taken by force was bound vnto the Session
The Cryer the Recognizannce doth call
Faustus Esquior come forth into the hall
Fy said the Iustice of all foollish cryers,
Diuells are Carpenters, where such are squyers.

Of Lesbia.

34. Lesbia with study found a means in th'end
In presence of her Lord, to kiss her frend./
Each of them kist by turns a little whelp,

transporting kisses thus by puppies help,
   And thus the good old Lord they did beguile,
   Was not my Lord a Puppy all the while./

        Of Galla and her tawny   21.
          fanne.

35.   When Galla and my self do talk together
      her face she shrowds with fann of tawny fether,
         And while my thought some cause hereof deviseth,
         a double doubt within my minde aryseth.
      First if her skin, or that darke fan be brighter,
      and secondly whether her lookes be lighter
         then that same plume wherewith her lookes are hidden,
         but if I cleer theise doubts, I should be chidden./

        Of wryting with a double meaning

36.   A certayn man was to a Iudge complayning,
      how one had wrytten with a double meanyng,
         Foole sayd the Iudge no man deserueth trouble
         for double meaning, so he deale not double./

        To his wife of stryking
         her Dogge.

37   Your little dog that barkt as I came by,
      I strake by hap so hard I made him cry,
      And straight you put your finger in your ey
      And lowring sate, and askt the reason why
      Loue me and loue my dog thou didst reply   .22.
      Loue as both should be lou'd, I will sayd I
      And seald yt with a kiss, there by and by
      Cleerd were the clouds of thy fayr frowning sky,
      thus small events great masteries may try.
         For I by this do at their meaning guess   [10]
         that beat a whelp before a Lioness./

Against Cosmus a
great Bryber./

38. This wicked age of ours complayns of brybing
the want of Iustice most to that ascrybing
When Iudges who should heare both with equallity
brybed by one side, to that shew partiallity.
But Cosmus in this case doth well provide,
for euer he takes brybes of euery side
Wherefore of him complayn, can no man rightly
But that he still may sentence giue vprightly
First I could chuse one that all brybes doth loath
next I could vse him that takes bribes of boath. [10]

Of a woman Cooke

39. Pure Cinna getts his wife a mayden Cooke,
With yellow locks, red Cheekes, and cheerfull looke   23.
What might he meane hereby? I hold my life
she dresseth flesh for him, not for his wife./

Of a precise Taylor.

40. A Tailor thought a man of vpright dealling,
Trew but for lying, honest but for stealling,
Did fall one day extreamly sick by chaunce,
and on the sodaine was in wondrous traunce:
The fends of hell mustring in fearfull manner,
Of sundry coullord silks displayd a banner
Which he had stoln, and wisht as they did tell,
that one day he might finde yt all in hell.
The man affrighted with this apparicion,
Vpon recovery grew a great Precision,   [10]
He bought a bible of the new translation,
and in his life he showd great reformation,
He walked mannerly, he talked meekly,
He heard three lectures and two sermons weekly,
He vowd to shun all companies vnruly,
and in his speach, he vsd no oath but truly./
And zealously to keep the Saboths rest
his meat for that day on the Eve was drest.
And least the custome that he had to steale   .24.

might cause him sometime to forget his zeale,   [20]
he giues his Iourny man a speciall chardge,
that if the stuffs allowannce being lardge
he found his fingers wear to filtch enclyn'd,
bid him but haue the banner in his minde./
This done, I skant can tell the rest for lafter.
A Captain of a Ship came three dayes after
and brought three yards of vellet and three quarters
to make venetians down below the garters.
He that precisely knew what was enuff,
soone slipt aside three quarters of the stuff.   [30]
His man espying it, sayd in derision,
Master remember how you saw the vision.
    Peace knave, quoth he, I did not see one ragge
    Of such a coullord silke in all the flagge./

            Of one Paulus a great man
            that expected to be followed.

41.   Proud Paulus late advaunc't to high degree,
        expectes that I should now his follower bee.
        Glad I could be to follow ones direction,
        by whom mine honest suits might haue protection.
        But I sew Don Fernandos heir for land,   25.
        against so great a Peere he dare not stand./
        A Bishop sews me for my tithes, that's worse,
        he dares not venture on a Bishops curse.
        Sergeant Erifilus beares me old grudges,
        Yea, but saith Paulus, Sergeants may be Iudges./   [10]
        Pure Cinna ore my head would beg my Lease
        Who? my Lord *keepers* man, oh hold your peace.
        Rich Widow Lesbia for a sclaunder sews me,
        Tush for a womans cause he must refuse me.
        then farewell frost, Paulus henceforth excuse me,
            For you, that are yourself thrall to so many,
            Shall near be my good Lord. Yf I haue any./

Against a Wittoll broker that
set his wife to sale./

42.　I see thee sell swords, Pistols, Cloakes and gowns,
Dubletts and slops; and they that paie thee Crowns,
Do, as 'tis reason beare away the ware
Which to supplie is thy continuall care
But thy wiues Ware far better rate doth hold,
Which vnto sundry chapmen daylie sold,
　　Her fayr lasts all the yeare and doth not finishe
　　Nor doth her Ware ought lessen or diminishe.　　26.

Of a terrible temporall
non resident.

43.　Old Cosmus hath of late got one lewd quallity,
　　to rayle at some that haue the cure of souls,
　　and his pure sprite their avarice controuls,
That in their lyvings is such inequallity
that some that can do keepe no hospitally*ty*
　　and some that would, (whose fortune he condoles)
want meanes, which comes he *sais* in generallity,
bycause of theise same Totquots, and plurallyty,
　　affirming as a sentence full discust,
　　one Cleargie man haue but one lyving must./　　[10]
But he, besides his sundry civill offices,
　　hath bought in fee fiue fat Impropriacions
　　twelue Patronages rights, or Presentacions./
All which he keeps, yet preaches *not* nor Prophecies,
Well Cosmus hold thy tongue, els some will scoff at this
For make vs thinke a Priest should haue but one,
Wee'l thinke, nay say, nay sweare, thou shouldst haue none.
　　Yll suits it thee to blame them for non Residents
　　That giu'st thereof so fowle, and shamefull Presidents.

Of a gentleman too full　　27.
Of Courtesie

44　A Courtier kind in speach, curst in condicion,
　　finding his faults could be no longer hidden,
Came to his frend to cleer his hard suspicion
　　and doubting least he might be more then chidden,

Fell to a flattring and most base submission,
   and vowd to kiss his foot, if he were bidden./
      My foote quoth he, nay that were too submisse
      but three foote higher, you deserue to kisse./

          A tale of a rosted horse

45.   Two Lords, four Squyers, three knights, and me the least
      my kynd frend Marcus bad vnto his feast,
      Whear was both fish and flesh, and all acates
      that men are wont to haue that feast great states.
      To paie for which next day he sold a Nag,
      Of whose pace, coullor, rayn, he vsd to brag./
         Well I'le near care for red, or fallow Deere,
         Yf so a horse thus cookt, can make *soche* cheere.

          Of Madam Dondrages with
            her fayr brest.

46.   A favourite of Charls late king of Fraunce   28.
      disporting with the king one day by chaunce
      Madam Dondrages came among the rest
      All naked as she vsed all her brest,
      The king would needes haue notice of his minion
      Of this free dame what was his franke opinion,
      I say and dare affirme my Liege quoth he
      that if the Croupper like the pattrell be,
         None but a king I worthy can account
         vpon so braue a trapped beast to mount.   [10]

          The Aucthor to his wife of
            a womans eloquence.

47.   My Mall I marke that when you mean to proue me
        to buy a vellet gown or some rich border
      thou callst me good sweet hart, swear'st thou dost loue me
        thy locks, thy lookes, thy lips speake all in order
      thou thinkst, and right thou thinkst, that theise do moue me
        that all theise seuerally thy sute do furder
         But shall I tell what most thy sute advaunces
         thy faire smooth words? no, no, thy fayr smooth *b*ʳaunches./

Of his translation of Ariosto

48.   I spent some yeares, and months, and weekes, and dayes   29.
        In englishing th'Italian Ariost.
    And straight some offred Elegies in prayse
        of that my thankles paynes, and fruitles cost,
    But while this offer did my spirits rayse,
        and that I told my frend thereof in bost,
    He disaproou'd the purpose many wayes,
        and with this prouerbe prooud it labour lost,
    You know said he how th'auncient Adage sayes,
        Good wine doth need no signe, good ale no bushe,   [10]
        good verse of praysers neede not passe a rushe./

Of Peleus ill fortune in
burying his frends.

49.   Old Peleus playnes his fortune and ill chaunce
        that still he brings his frends vnto their graue,
    good Peleus I would thou haddst lead the daunce
        and I had poynted thee what frends to haue./

Of Cinnas election

50.   Pure Cinna makes no question he is elect,
        yet lewdly liues, I might beleeue him better,
        Yf he would chaunge his life or chaunge one letter
        And say that he is sure he is eiect.   .30
        An holy trew, and long preserued purity
        may hap, and but perhap breed such security./

The Author to a daughter
of nine yeare old.

51.   Though pride in damsells ys an hatefull vice
        Yet could I like a noble mynded girle,
    that would demaunde me things of costly price,
        rich vellet gowns, pendents and chayns of pearle
    Carknetts of Aggat cut with rare devise.
    not that heerby she should my minde entice
        to buy such things, against both wit and proffit
        but I like well, she should be worthy of yt.

To my Lady Rogers of breaking
her bitches legg./

52.   Last night you layd it Madam in our dishe,
            how that a mayde of ours, whom we must check
        had broke your bitches leg, I strayght did wishe
            the baggage rather broken had her necke./
        You tooke mine aunswer well, and all was whish,
                but take me right, I meant in that I sayd,
                Your baggage Bitche and not our baggage Mayd./   31.

Of Paying

53.   A Captayne late ariv'd from loss of Sluse,
        hearing some frend of mine did him abuse,
                Vowd he would paie him when he met him next,
                my frend with theise great threats no whit perplext,
                prayd that the promise faild not of fulfilling,
                for three yeares past he lent him forty shilling./

Of Cayus barren land
and fruitfull wife.

54.   While Caius doth remayne beyond the seas
                to follow there some great important sute,
        his land beares neither wheat, nor oats, nor peas,
                but yet his wife bare fayr and full grown frute.
        Now what thinke you, doth cause his lands sterrillity,
                and his wiues fruitfullnes and great fertillity,
                His lands want occupiers to manure them,
                but she hath store, and knowes how to procure them.

To the Earle of Essex of an envious
Censurer of Ariosto translated.

55   My noble Lord, some men haue thought me proud   .32
                bycause my Furioso is so spredd
                and that your Lordship hath yt seene and redd
        And haue my vayne and payn therein allowd,
        no sure I say, and long time since haue vowd,
                my fancy shall not with such bayts be fed,

nor am I framd so light in foote or head,
That I should daunce at sounde of Prayses Crowde.
Yet Ile confess this pleasd me when I heard yt,
   how one that euer carps at others wrytings,   [10]
   Yet seldom shewes any his own Endytings,
With much a doo gaue vp *t*his hungrie verdit
      Twas well he sayd, but twas but a translation
      Ist not some ramme that butts of such a fashion?

    The Author of his own fortune

56.   Take fortune as it falls, so one adviseth,
      Yet Haywood bids me take yt as yt ryseth,
         and while I think to do as both do teache,
         yt falls and ryses quyte beside my reache./

    Two Answers of Bonner
    Bishop of London.

57.   Fat Bonner late that Bishop was of London,   33.
      was bid by one good morrow bishop quondam,
         he with the scoff no whitt put out of temper,
         replyde incontinent, Adew knave semper.
One other in such kynde of scoffing speeches,
Would beg his tippet needes, to lyne his breeches,
      Not so quoth he, but it may bee thy hap,
      to haue a foollish head to lyne thy cap./

    Of a speachles woman
    To his wife.

58.   A curst wife of hir husbands dealling doubting,
      at his home comming scilent was and mute,
      and when with kyndnes he did her salute,
She held her peace, and lowring sate and pouting,
Which humor thus he thought to check with flouting,
He causd one secretly to raise a brute,
      that she lay speachles: strayght the bell doth tole,
      and men devoutly giv'n, prayd for her soule,
Then some kynd gossips made a spetiall sute
To visit her, her hard case to condole,   [10]

She wondred at the cause, but when she knew't
From that time forward, so her toung did role
That her goodman did wish he had beene breechles   .34.
When first he gaue it forth, that she was speechles.
    Well then my Mall, least my mishap bee such
    bee neuer dumbe, yet neuer speake too much.

Of a Dunne horse

59.   When you and I Paulus on Hackneys hyred
rode late to Rochester my Hackney tyred
You that will loose a frend, to win a Ieast
playd thus on me and my poore tyrye beast,
Marke in Misacmos horse a wondrous chaunge,
a sodaine Metamorphosis most straunge./
    His horse was bay at rysing of the sonne,
and now you playn may see his horse is donne.
Well Paulus thus you please with me to sport,
but thus againe your scoffe I can retort,   [10]
    Your hayre was blacke, and therein was your glory,
    but in two yeares it grew all gray and hory.
Now like my hackney worne with two much travell
myr'd in the clay, or tyred in the grauell,
    While two yeares more skant ore your head are run
    Your hayr is neither black nor gray, 'tis donne.

Of the cause of Dearth.   35.

60.   I heare our country neighbours oft complayn,
their fruits are still distroyd with too much rayn,
Some guess by skill of Starrs and Science vayn,
some watry Plannets in the heav'ns doth raigne.
No; sinn doth raigne on earth, the cause is playn,
Which if we would repent and then refrayn,
the skyes would quickly keep their course agayn.
    Now that with lewdnes we be lulld a sleepe
    the heave'ns to see our wicked *acts* doth weepe./

A rule for gamsters

61. Lay downe your stake at play, laye downe your passions
        a greedy gamster still hath some mishap,
     to chafe at luck proceedes of foollish fashions,
        no man throwes still the dyce in fortunes lap.

                To Sir Hughe Portman of supping
                  alone in too much company.

62. When you bad forty guests to me vnknowne,
        I came not, though you twise for me did send,
     for which you blame me as a sullen frend,
        Sir Pardon me, I list not sup alone./

                To one that beggs his booke   .36.

63. My frend you presse me very hard
        my bookes of me you craue
     I haue none, but in Pauls churchyard
        at Nortons you maie haue.
     What should you then your coyne bestow
        (say you) such toyes to buy
     You are not such a foole you trow
        forsooth, no more am I.

                Of Don Pedros pennyworth in
                  a rich sute of hanginges

64. Don Pedro bought within three hundred pound
     a sute of Arras hanging passing ritch
     Larded with gold and silke in euery stitch.
     a merv'lous pennyworth doubtles he hath found
     Why? were they worth yt? was their goodnes such
     no nothing lyke, nor hardly half so much
        Yet was the pennworth great, then thus I reed yt
        he neuer payes for that he takes on credit./

Of wryting with double poynting
as. It is said that king Edward
of Carnaruan lying at Berkly Castle Prisoner,   37.
a Cardinall wrate to his keeper. Edouar=
dum occidere noli, timere, bonum est,
which being read with the poynt
at timere, yt cost the king his
life. Here ensews as doubtfull
a poynt, but I trust not
so daungerous.

Dames are indewd with vertues excellent./
What man is he can proue that they offend?
Dayly they serue the lorde with good entent.
Seelde they displease their husbands to their end.
allwayse to please them well they do entend,
neuer in them one shall finde Shrewdnes much.
   Such are their humors and their grace is such.

To my Lady Rogers

65   Good Madam in this vearse obserue one poynt
that though it seemes the wryter did appoynt
With smoothest oyle of prayse your ears to noynt,
Yet one his purpose soone may disapoynt,
For in this vearse displacing but a poynte,
Will put the *senc*e so clearly out of Ioynt
That all this prayse will skant be worth a poynt./

To hir daughter vpon   38.
the same poynt
Reading the same vearse with
another poynt.

Dames are indewd with vertues excellent?
What man is he can proue that? they offend
Daylie: they serue the lord with good entent
Seeld: they displease their husbands to theyr end
allwayes: to please them well they do entend
neuer: In them one shall fynd Shrewdnes much.
Such are their humors, and their graces such.

66.　My Mall the former verses this may teach you
　　　that some deceaue, some are deceau'd by showes
　　　For this verse in your prayse so smooth that goes　　　　　[10]
　　　　　with one false poynt and stop did ouerreache you.
　　　and turne the prayse to scorne, the ryme to prose,
　　　by which you might be sclaundered all as shrowes,
　　　　　and some perhap may saie and speake no treason,
　　　　　the vearses had more ryme: the proase more Reason./

　　　　　　　Of Leda that playd at Tables
　　　　　　　　With her husband.

67.　Yf tales are told of Leda bee not fables　　　　　　　　39.
　　　thou with thine husband dost play false at tables.
　　　First thou so cunningly a Dye canst slurre
　　　to strike an ace so dead yt shall not sturre,
　　　Then play thou for a pounde, or for a Pin
　　　Highe men or low men still are foysted in./
　　　Thirdly, though for free entrance ys no fearing,
　　　Yet thou dost overreache him still at bearing,
　　　Yf poore alms ase, or sinns haue beene the cast,
　　　thou beares too many men, thou bearst too fast.　　　　　[10]
　　　Well Leda, heare my Councell, vse it not,
　　　Else your fayr game may haue so foule a blott,
　　　　　that he to loose, or leaue will *rather* venter
　　　　　then in so shamefull open poynts to enter./

　　　　　　　Comparisons of the Sonnet
　　　　　　　　and the Epigram.

68.　Once by mishap two Poetts fell at squaring
　　　the sonnet, and our Epigram comparing.
　　　And Faustus having long demurd vpon yt
　　　Yet at the last, gaue sentence for the Sonnet.
　　　Now for such censure, this his chief defence ys
　　　their sugred tast best lykes his lickres sensys.
　　　　　Well though I graunt sugar may please the taste　　　40.
　　　　　Yet let my verse haue salt to make yt last.

Of Southsaying. to the
Queens Matie.

69.   Might Queenes shunn future mischief by foretelling
        then among Soothsayers 'twear exc'lent dwelling.
        but if there be no meanes such harmes expelling,
        the knowledge makes the griefe the more excelling.
            Well yet deer Liege, my soule this comfort dooth
            that of theise soothsay'ers very few say sooth.

To the learned bishop of
Bath and Wells.

70.   The pleasant learnd Italian Poet Dant
        hearing an Atheist at the scripture Ieast,
        askt him in sport which was the greatest beast,
        he simplie sayd, he thought an Elephant.
        Then Elephant sayd Dant, it were commodious
        that thou wouldst hold thy tongue, or get thee hence
        that breedes our conscience scandall and offence,
        with thy blasphemous speach prophane and odious.
            Oh Italy, thou breedst but few such Dants
            But England breedes enow such Elephants.   [10]

How an Asse may proue   41.
an Elephant.

71.   It hath bene sayd to giue *young* spirits hope,
        A knight maie proue a king; a Clarcke, a Pope.
        But our young sprytes disdayning all old rules,
        Compar'd by holie writt to horse and Mules,
        tis vayn with auncient Prouerbes to provoke
        to vertuous course, with theise such beare no stroke
            then their old pride let my new proverb daunt,
            an Asse may one day prooue an Elephant./

Of a precise Lawier.

72.   A Lawier calld vnto the barre but lately,
        Yet one that loftie bare his lookes and stately,
        and howsoear his minde was in sincerity,

his speach and manners shewd a great austerity.
This Lawier hapt, to bee a bidden guest
With divers others to a gossips feast.
Where though that many did by entercourse,
exchaunge sometimes from this to that discourse,
Yet one bent brow, and frown of his was able
to gouerne all the talke was at the table./ [10]
His manner was perhaps to help disgestion.
Still to Devinitie to draw each question 42.
in which his tongue extravagant would raunge
and he pronounced Maximes very straunge.
First he affirm'd it was a passing folly
to thinke one day more then an other holly.
If one said Michaelmas, strayt he would chyde
and tell them they must call yt Michells tyde.
If one had sneezd to saie (as is the fashion)
Christ help: 'twas witchcraft, and deseru'd Damnation. [20]
Now whyle he talked thus you must suppose
the gossips cup came often from his nose.
And were yt the warme spice, or the warme wether,
at last he sneezed twice or thrice together./
A pleasant guest that kept his words in minde,
and heard him sneeze, in skorne, said kiss behynde.
at which the Lawier taking great offence,
said Sir you might haue vs'd saue reuerence.
    I would (quoth t'other) saue I feard least you
    would then haue calld saue reverence witchcraft to.

A Prophecy when Asses
shall grow Elephants

73.1   When making harmfull gunns, vnfruitfull glasses.
      Shall quite consume our statelie oakes and ashes. 43.
2   When law fills all the land with blotts and dashes.
3   When land long quiet held concealed passes./
4   When warr and trewce plaie passes and repasses,
5   When Monopoles are giv'n of toys and trashes,
6   When Courtiers mar good cloths with cutts and slashes,
7   When Priests haue got free leaue to ly with lasses,
8   When cleargie roomes to buy, sell, none abashes,
9   When foule skins are made fayr with new found washes, [10]
10   When new found speach to tydes hath turned masses.
11   When Prints are sett on worke with Greens & Nashes,

12   When Letchers learn to stir vp lust with lashes,
13   When playnness vanishes, vaynnes surpasses,
          Some shall grow Elephants, were known but Asses./

                    To my Lady Rogers of her
                         Servant Payne.

74.   Your servant Payn for Legasies hath sude
           seav'n yeare; I ask him how his matter passes
           he tells how his testator left not Assets
       by which plea him th'excec'tor would elude;
       I in this Lawyers french but dull and rude
           Replyde, the plea my learning far surpasses.
       Yet when reports of each side I had viewd   44.
       In forma paper, thus I did conclude
       He was left Payn, and all his councell Asses./
           Yet you would giue an hundred crowns or twayn   [10]
           that you could cleere discharge your seruant Payn./

                    Of one that is vnwilling
                         to lend.

75.   When I but buy two sutes of ritch Apparrell
       or some fayr ready horse against the running
       Rich Quintus that same Miser sly and cunning,
       Yet my great frend, begins to pick a quarrell,
       to tell me how his credit is in perrill.
       How some great Lord, whose name maie not be spoken,
       With him for twenty thousand crowns hath broken.
       Then with a fained sighe and show of sorrow,
       Swearing he thinks theise Lords will quite vndo him
       he calls his servant Oliuer vnto him,   [10]
       And sends him to th'exchange to take on vse.
       One thousand Pounds must needes be payd to morrow.
       Thus would he blynd mine eyes with this abuse.
       and thinks though he were sure I came to borrow
       that now I needes must shut my mouth for shame.
       Fy Quintus fy, then when I speake deny me   45.
           But to deny me thus before I try thee
           blush and confess that you bee too too blame./

Against Promoters

76.   Base spies disturbers of the publicque rest
        With forged wrongs the true mans right that wrest
        Pack hence exilde to desert lands and waste
        and drynke the cup that you made others taste
            But yet that prince to yow doth bountie show
            that doth your very liues on you bestow./

Against too much trust.

77.   If you will shrowd you safe from all mishaps
        and shun the cause of many after claps
            Put not in any one too much beleefe
            Your Ioy will be the less, so will your greefe.

Of an accident of saying grace at the
        Lady Rogers; who vsed to dyne exceeding
        late. Written to his Wife; *from Bathe./*

78   My Mall in your short absence from this place
            my selfe here dyning at your mothers boorde
        Your little sonn did thus begin his grace   46.
            The eyes of all thinges looke on thee o lord
        And thou their foode dost giue them in dew season.
            Peace boy quoth I not more of this a worde
        For in this place, this grace hath little reason
            When as we speake to god, we must speake trew
        And though the meat be good in taste and season
            this season for a dinner ys not dew   [10]
        Then peace I say, to ly to god is treason.
            Say on my Boy saith she your father mocks
        Clowns and not Courtiers vse to go by clocks
        Courtiers by clocks sayd I and Clowns by cocks
            Now if your mother chide with me for this
            then you must reconcyle vs with a kiss.

Of daungerous reconcyling

79   Dick sayth beware a reconciled foe
      for though he soothe your words he seeks your woe
         But I would haue my frend late reconcyled
         Beware thee Dick, least he be worse beguiled./

Of Læda that sayes she ys
sure to bee saued.

80.   Since Leda knew that sure she was elected   47.
      She buyes rich cloathes, fares well and makes her bost
      her corps the temple of the holy ghost
      must be more cherished, and more respected
      but Leda liueth still to sin subiected.
         Tell Leda that her frend Misacmos feares
      that till she get a minde of more submission
      and purge that corps with Isope of contricion
      and washe that sinfull soule with saltish tears
      though Quayles she eat, though gold and Pearle she wears   [10]
         Yet sure she doth with damned Core and Dathan
         but feed and clad a Sinagogue of Sathan.

Of Don Pedro and
his Poetry

81.   Sir, I shall tell you newes, except you know yt
      our noble frend Don Pedro is a Poet.
      His vearses all abroade are read and showne
      and he himself doth swear they are his owne
      his owne? 'tis trew for he for them hath payd
      two Crowns a Sonnet as I heard yt sayd
      So Ellen hath fayr teeth, that in her purse
      she keepes all night, and she sleeps near the worse
      So widow Lesbia with her paynted hyde   48
      seem'd for the tyme, to make a handsome bryde   [10]
         Yf Pedro bee for this a Poet calld
         So you may call one hayry that ys balld./

A comfort for poore poetts.

82. Henceforth for Pencions Poets need not care
   Who call you beggars you maie call them lyers
For vearses grow such merchantable ware
   That now for Sonnets sellers are and buyers.

    Against a foollish
    Satyrist.

83. I read that Satyre thou entitlest first
   and layd aside the rest and ouerpast
And sware I thought that Author was accurst
   that that first Satyr had not been his last.

    In commendacion of George
    Turberuill a learned gen=
    tleman. an Epitaphe.

84. When rymes were yet but rude thy pen indevored
   to pollish barbarisme with purest style
When tymes were grown most lewd thy hart perseuered
   godlie and iust vnstaynd with guifts or guile
Now liues thy soule though from thy corps disseuered
   there, in high bliss, here in cleer fame the while.
    To which I paie this debt of dew thanks giuing
    My pen doth praise thee dead, thine grac't me liuing./

    49.

    To the Queenes Matie. when she found
    fault with some particuler
    matters in Misacmos
    Metamorphosis.

85. Dread Soueraigne take this trew though poor excuse
of all the errors of Misacmos Muse
a hounde that of a whelp, my self had bred,
and at my hands and table taught and fed,
When other Currs did fawn, and flatter coldly,
did spring and leap, and play with me too boldly./
    For which although my Pages check and rate him
    Yet still my self do much more loue then hate him./

To the Ladyes of the Queens privye
Chamber at the making of their perfumde
privy at Ritchmond the book hangd
in chayns saith thus./

86   ffayr Dames yf any took in skorn and spyte
me that Misacmos Muse in myrth did write
to satisfy the sinn lo heer in chaynes
for ay to hang my master me ordaynes
yet deem the deed to him no derogacion
but deign to this devise new commendacion
sith heer you see, feele, smell that his convayance
hath freed this noysom place from all annoyance
Now Iudge yow that the work mock envy tawnt
whose service in this place may I make most vawnt   [10]
    yf vs or yow to prayse it wear moste meet
    yow that made sower, or vs that made it sweet.

To Mr Cooke the Queens attorny that
was incited to call Misacmos into the star
chamber but refused it saying he that
could geue another a venew had a
sewr ward for himselfe./

87   Those that of dayntie fare make deer provision
yf som bad Cookes marr it with dressing evill
are wont to say in Iest but iust derision
the meat from good the Cookes came from the devill
But yf this dish though drass in apparition
wear made thus sawst a service not vncivill.
    Say ye that taste and not digest the booke
    the deele go with the meate God with the Cooke./

Against Lynus a wryter that
found fault with the
Metamorphosis.

88.   Lynus to giue me a spightfull fromp,   50.
sayd that my wrytings savord of the Pompe,
and that my Muse for want of matter, takes
An Argument to write of from the Iakes,
Well Lynus, speake each reader as he thinks,
though thou of Scepters wrat'st, and I of Sinks,
    Yet some will saie, comparing both together
    my witt brings matter thence, thine matter thether.

Of Garlick. To my
Ladie Rogers

89.   Yf Leeke*s* you leeke, and do the smell disleeke
eat Onions and you shall not smell the Leeke
Yf you of onyons would the sent expell
eat garlick that will drown the onions smell.
    But sure gainst garlick savour at one worde
    I know but one receipt, what's that? *Tobacco.*

A dishe of daynties for
the Deuill.

90.   A godlie father, sitting on a draught
to do as need and nature hath vs taught,
    Mumbled as was his manner certayn prayers,
    And vnto him the Deuill straight repayres,   51.
And boldly to reuile him he begins,
Alledging that such prayres were deadly sins,
    And that yt proou'd he was devoyde of grace,
    to speake to God from so vnfitt a place./
      The reuerent man, though at the first dismayd,
      Yet stronge in faith, thus to the Deu'll he sayd.   [10]
Thou damned Spirite, wicked false and lying,
dispayring thine own good, and ours envying
each take his dew, and me thou canst not hurt
to god my prayre I meant, to thee the durt./
    Pure prayr ascends to him that high doth sitt,
    Down falls the filth for fiends of hell more fitt./

Of Don Pedro his sweet
breath.

91   How is't Don Pedro's breath is still perfumed,
            and that he neuer like himself doth smell,
        I like it not for still it is presumed,
            Who smelleth euer well, smells neuer well.

Misacmos against his
booke

92.   The writer and the matter well maie meet   52.
            Were he as eloquent as it is sweet.

Of Cloacina and Ster
quitius./

93   The Romans ever cownted supersticious
        adored with high titles of Devinity
        Dame Cloacina with the lord Stercutius
        two persons in their state of great affinity
        but we that skorn opynions so pernicious
        are taught by trueth well tryde t'adore the trynity
            And who so care of trew religion takes
            will thinck soch saynts well shryned in Aiax./

To the Queene when she was
pacified, and sent Misac=
mos thankes for the
Invention.

94.   A Poet once of Traian begd a Lease
        Traian terror of War, Mirror of peace,
        And doubting how his wrytings were accepted,
        gainst which he heard some Courtiers had excepted
        He came to him and with all due submission
        Deliuerd this short vearse with his peticion.
            Dread Soueraigne, if you like not of my wrytings
        graunt this sweet Cordiall to a spirit daunted,
        But if you read and like my poor endytings,
        then for reward let this small sute be graunted,   [10]
            Of which short vearse I finde ensewd such frute
            The Poet of the Prince obtaynd his sute./

A poets priviledge.

95. Paynters and Poets clayme by old enrollment
a Charter to dare all without controllment.

To Faustus   53

96. Faustus fyndes fault my Epigrams are short
bycause to read them, he doth make some sport
  I thanke thee Faustus, though thou iudgest wronge,
  Ear long Ile make thee swear they bee too long./

To the Lady Rogers of her
vnprofitable sparing

97. When I to you sometimes make frendly mocion,
    to spend vp your superfluous provision,
Or sell the same for coyne: or for devotion
    to make thereof among the poore devision,
Straight way you answer me half in derision,
    and bid me speake against your course no more,
    for plenty you do loue, store is no sore.
But ah such store is enemie to plenty,
    you wast for feare to want I dare assume yt,
For while to sell, spend, giue, you make such daynty,   [10]
    keepe Corne and cloth, till Ratt and rot consume yt,
    let meate so mould, that Muske cannot perfume yt,
And by this sparing think to mende your store,
    Sore is such store, and God offending sore./

Against Faustus   54.

98. What is the cause Faustus that in dislike
proude Paulus still doth touch thee with a pyke
    It breedeth in my minde a great confusion
    to thinke *w*hat he should meane by such allusion.
Trow'st thou he meanes that thou mightst make a Pykeman
that cannot bee for that, thou art no like man
    thy crased bones cannot endure the shock
    besides his manner is to speake in mocke.
Or ist because the Pyke a greedy fish,

Devours as thou dost manie a daynty dish   [10]
   and in another sort and more vnkinde,
    wilt byte and spoyle those of thy proper kynde?
Or doth he meane thou art a Quarrell pyker
that amongst men weart neuer thought a stryker?
   In this he sayes, thou art a christen brother
    that stricken on one eare, thou turnest t'other.
Or doth he mean that thou wouldst pike a thanke,
no sure, for of that fault I count thee franke.
How can thy tale to anie man be gratefull?
Whose person face and manners are so hatefull.   [20]
    Then Faustus I suspect yet one thing wurse,
    thou hast pickt somwhat els: what's that? a Purse./

      To his wife of the .12. signes   55.
        how they rule.

99   Marke heer my Mall how in a dozen lynes
        thus placed are the twelue celestiall signes
1   First the' horned Ram doth rule in head and face
2   the stiffe neckt bull in necke doth hold his place,
3   The twinns mine Arms and hands do both imbrace,
4   Heer Cancer keepes the small ribbs and the brest,
5   There Leo backe and hart hath ay possest,
6   Then virgo claymes our entrayles and the Paunch,
7   The navell Libra raynes and eyther haunch,
8   Scorpio pretends power in the privie parts,   [10]
9   Both thighs are pierct by Sagittaries darts,
10   Then Capricorn to knees his force doth send,
11   Aquarius doth to leggs his vertue bend,
12   Pisces beneath vnto the feet discend.
        Thus each part is possest: now tell me Mall
        Where lyes thy part, in which of theis? In all./
        In all? content: yet sure thou art more Ielowse
        Of Leos part and Scorpios then their fellows.

Against Churchrobbers vpon
a picture that hangs
where it is worthye.   56.

100   The Germans haue a byword at this hower,
          by Luther taught, by paynters skill exprest,
       How Sathan dayly fryers doth devour,
          Whom in short space he doth so well disgest,
       that passing down through his posterior parts,
          tall souldiers thence he to the world deliuers:
       And out they fly all armd with pykes and darts,
          with Halberds and with musketts and Callivers.
       According to theise Lutheran opinions
          they that devour whole churches and their rents   [10]
       I mean our Favorites and courtly Minions,
          Voyd forts and Castles in their excrements./

The Second booke of   57.
Epigrams.

A comparison of a booke
and a Cheese.

1.   Old Haywood wrytes and proues in some degrees
       that one maie well compare a booke with Cheese,
           At euerie market some buy cheese to feede on,
           at euery Mart some men buy bookes to reede on,
       All sorts eat cheese, but how? there is the question,
       the poore for foode, the rich for good disgestion,
           All sorts reed bookes: but why? will you discearne?
           the foole to laughe, the wyser sort to learn.
       The sight, tast, sent of cheese to some is hatefull,
       The sight, tast, sence of bookes, to som's vngratefull.   [10]
               No Cheese there is, that ever pleasd all feeders,
               No booke there is that ever pleasd all Reeders.

A tale of a Baylie distrayning
for rent.

2   I heard a pleasant tale at Cannington
       there where my Ladie dwelt, calld the fair Nonne.
           How one that by his office was Deceavor,   58
           (my tongue oft trips) I should haue said Receavor.
       Or to speake plaine and true an arrant Baylie,
       such as about the contry trauell daylie./
           that when the quarter day was two dayes past
           went presently to gather rents in hast,
       And if (as oft it hapt) he brake good manner,
       he straight would plead the custome of the mannor   [10]
           swearing he might distrayn all goods and chattell,
           were it in moueables, or els quick cattell./
       This Baylie comming to a tenement
       in th'tennants absence, straynd his wife for rent,
           in which the beast so pliable he found,
           he neuer needes to driue her to the pound./
       The tennant by intelligence did guesse
       the Baylie taken had a wronge distress,
           and to the Baylies wife he went complayning
           of this her husbands vsage in distrayning,   [20]
       Requesting her like courtesies to render,

and to accept such rent as he would tender.
  She whether moued with some straunge compassion
  or that his tale did put her in new passion,
Accepts his paiment like a gentle wenche,
All coyne was currant, English, Spanish, french./   59.
  And when she taken had his sory pittance,
  I think that with a kiss she seald the Quittance./
When next theise husbands met, they chaft, they curst,
happie was he, that could cry Cuckold furst.   [30]
  From spightfull words they fell to daggers drawing
  and after each to tother threatned lawing,
Each party seekes to make him strong by faction,
in seuerall Courts, they enter seuerall action.
  Actions of Battry, actions in the case,
  with Riotts Routs, disturbed all the place./
Much bloud, much money had bene spilt and spent,
about this foollish strayning for the Rent,
  Saue that a gentle Iustice of the Peace,
  willing to cause such foollish quarrells cease,   [40]
Prevayld so with the parties by intreaty,
of concord both agreed to haue a Treaty,
  and both referrd the matter to the Iustice,
  who having well obserued what a Iest, tis:
To thinke two Cuckolds were so fairly parted,
each hauing tane the blow that neuer smarted,
  He charged each of them shake hands with other,
  and when they met to say good morrow brother
Thus each quit other all old debts and dribletts   60.
And set th'Hares head against the gooses gibletts./   [50]

       Of casting out Spiritts by
       fasting without prayre./

3.   A vertuous dame that for her state and quallity
     did euer loue to keepe great hospitallity,
Mr Pen.   Her name I must not name in playn recyting,
mother to S   But thus the chiefest instrument of wryting./
Michel   Was by Duke Humphreys guests so boldly haunted
Hix and   that her good minde thereby was shrewdly daunted.
S Baptist*   She sighing said one day t'a careles Iester,
Hix.   theise ill bred guests my boord and house so pester
     that I praie God oft times with all my hart,
     that they would leaue this haunt and hence depart,   [10]

he, that by his own humour hap'ly guest,
    what manner sprite, these smell feasts had possest
        Told her the surest way such sprites outcasting
        Was to leaue prayre a while, and fall to fasting.

A Riddle translated out of Italian.

[4]   I saw two stand with bellyes ioyning nye
            to which sweet sight, diuers theyr eye did cast
            And I did wryte the matter as it past,   61.
        What great delight each party tooke thereby
        One thrust raw flesh in tothers hollow place,
            and on his hinder parts her hand she stayd,
            Wherewith the t'one was pleasd, but tother sayd,
        Still still my deare, and still they did imbrace,
        the flesh that in the place forenam'd had been,
            cast forth a Iuice of coullor white indeed,   [10]
            of which you Ladies oft haue stood in need,
        A nobler iuice, no doubt was neuer seen
            holesome in men, and vnto women dew,
            Yf this iuice faild, the world the want might rew,
                and this I saw, in prose and vearse tis trew,   *this was*
                the tone was pleasd the tothers belly grew./   *a child sucking*
                                                                  his nours.

Of misconceauing

5.   You Ladies blame my vearses of scurrillity
            While with the double sence you were deceaued,
        Now you confess them free from incivillity,
            take heede henceforth, you bee not misconceaued./

How the Bath is like
Purgatory.

6.   Whether it bee a fable or a Story   62.
        that Beda and others write of Purgatory
        I know no place that more resemblance hath
        with that same purgatory, then the Bath,
        Men there with paines do purge their passed sinns,
        many with paynes purge here, their patched skinns
        Frying and freezing are the paynes there told,

heer the chief payn consists in heat and cold.
Confused cryes, vapor, and smoake and stinke,
are certayn here, that there they are some think.   [10]
There fire burnes Lords and louts without respect,
our water for his force works like effect./
thence none can be deliuered but with praying,
hence no man ys deliuered but with paying,
    But once escaped thence haue *seure* saluation,
    But these go hence still feare recidivation./

Of going to the Bath

7.   A common phrase long vsed here hath been
    and by præscription now some credit hath
    that diuers ladies comming to the Bath,
Come chiefly but to see, and to bee seene,
But if I should declare my conscience briefly,
I cannot thinke that is their Arrant chiefly,   63.
    For as I heare that most of them haue dealt,
    they chiefly came to feele, and to be fealt./

Of playn dealling

8.   My wrytings oft displease you, what's the matter
You loue not to heare truthe, nor I to flatter.

Of trusting a
Captayne.

9.   An Alderman one of the better sort
    a worthy member of our worthiest citty
Vnto whose table diuers did resort
    himself of stomack bold, in answers witty
Was once requested by a table frend
    to lend an vnknown Captain forty pound
Which that he might to him the rather lend,
    he said the man in Statute *should* be bound
Whose band said he you maie be bold to take,
    for hee's a man of late grown in good credit,   [10]
And went about the world with Captayn Drake,
    out (quoth the Alderman) that ere you sed yt

For forty pounds, no nor for forty pence
    His single bond I count not worth a chip,   64
I say to you (take not hereat offence)
      he that hath three whole yeares dwelt in a ship
         In famin, plagues, in stench, and stormes so rife
         Cares not to ly in Ludgate all his life.

        To my dearest a Rule for
            praying.

10.   Mine own when in your closet for deuotion
      you kneele to pray vpon some godly motion,
        I do not saie tis sinne, your eye to fixe
        on some Saints Picture, or the Crucifix./
      Such Images may serue thee, as a booke,
      on which thou maist with godly reuerence looke,
        And thereby thy remembrannce to acquainte,
        with life or death or vertues of the saynt,
      Thus, bee it wood, or stone, or glass, or mettle
      yt serueth in thy minde good thoughts to settle.   [10]
        But though I do allow thou kneele before yt,
        Yet would I in no wise, you should adore yt,
      For as such things well vs'd are cleane and holly,
      So superstition soone maie make it folly.
        I keepe thy picture in a golden shryne,
        And I esteeme it well bycause tis thyne,   65.
      But let me vse thy Picture nere so kyndly
      'twear little worth if I vs'd thee vnkyndly.
        All images are skornd, and quite dishonored,
        Yf the Prototipos, bee not more honored./   [20]
      Sith then my Deare, our heavenly lord aboue,
      Vouchsafeth vnto ours, to like his loue,
        So let vs vse his pictures that therein
        against himself, we do commit no sin
      But pray our harts by faiths eyes be made able,
      to see that mortall eyes see on a table.
        Leaue then old weomens tales, young womens dreams
        and keepe the mean between the two extreams.
      Do not deface such pictures, nor deride them
      like fooles, whose zeale mistaught, cannot abide them,   [30]
        nor do not thinke in them there is devinity
        for with great fondnes that hath much affinity
      Would you not thinke one did deserue a mocke

Shoulde say o heavn'ly father to a stocke?
    Such a one were a stocke, I straight would gather
    that would confess a stock to bee his father./

      To Cinna of lying at Kew
        near Richmond.

11.   Aske you what profitt Kew doth to me yeild   66.
    this, Cinna there I shall see thee but seild,
      for as good neighbors make a cottage gratefull
      so such as thou may make a Pallace hatefull./

      Against Paulus

12   Because in theise so malcontented times
      I please my self with priuate recreation,
      in reeding or in sweetest contemplation
    Or wryting sometimes prose, *oft* pleasant rymes,
    Paulus, whom I haue thought my frend somtimes,
      seekes all he maie to taint my reputation
    Not with complaints, or any haynous crymes,
      but onely saying in his scoffing fashion,
    Theise wryters that still sauour of the schooles,
    frame to themselus a paradice of fooles:/   [10]
      But while he skorns our mirth and playne simplicity,
      himself doth saile to Affricke and to Inde,
    and seekes with hellish paynes, yet doth not finde
    that blisse in which he frames his wise felicity./
      Now which of twayn is best some wise man tell
      our Paradice, or els wise Paulus hell?/

      Against Itis a Poet.   67

13   Itis with leadden sword doth wounde my Muse,
    Itis whose Muse in vncouth tearmes doth swagger,
      What should I wish Itis for this abuse
      but to his Leadden sworde, a wodden dagger./

        Of Caius hurts in
        the Warrs.

14.   Caius of late returnd from flemmish warrs,
       of certayn little scratches bears the skarrs,
            and for that most of them, are in his face
            with, tant plus beau, he shews them for his grace
       Yet came they not by dint of Pyke or Dart,
       But with a pot, a pynte, or els a quart,
            But he near makes his boast how, and by whom
            he hath receau'd a greater blow at home./

        Of two welshe gentlemen.

15   I heard among some other pleasant tales
       how once there were, two gentlemen of Wales,
            Noble in bloud, discended of his house
            that from our Ladies gown did take a lowse
       Theise two (thus goes the tale) vpon a day
       hapned to travaile vpon London way   68.
            And for 'twas combersome to weare a Boote
            for their more ease, they needes would walk on foote
       Their fare was dainty, and of no small cost
       for euery meale they calld for bakt and rost,   [10]
            And least they should their best apparrell lack
            each of them bare his Wardrop at his back
       Their Arrant was, but sore against their Wills
       to Westminster to speake with Maister Mills.
            Nor mervaile men of such sumptuous dyott
            Were brought vnto Starrchamber for a ryott./
       Theise Squyres one night arriued at a town,
       to looke their Lodgins, when the sonne was downe,
            and for the Inkeeper his gates had locked,
            in hast like men of some account, they knocked.   [20]
       The drowsie Chamberlayn asketh, who's theare,
       they told that gentlemen of Wales they weare,
            how many quoth the man, is there of you
            quoth they: Heer's Iohn ap rice ap Iones ap Hew
       And Nicholas ap Steev'n ap Iyles ap Davy,
       then gentlemen adew quoth he, God saue yee,
            Your worships might haue had a bed or twayn,
            but how can that suffize so great a trayn./

Of Gallas gallantry.

16.   Know yee the cause our Galla is so gallant
       like ship in fayrest winde top and top gallant,
           Hath she not late been courted by some gallant?
           no sure, how then? Galla hath quaft a galland./

               To Mr. Maior of Bathe, that
               Bathe is like P*aradice.*

17   Sir if you either angrie were, or sory,
       that I haue likened Bath to Purgatory,
           Lo to regaine your fauour in a trice,
           Ile proue it much more like to Paradice,
       Man was at first in Paradice created,
       manie men still in Bathe are procreated,
           Man liued there in state of innocence,
           Heer manie liue in wit like Innocents.
       There sprange the heads of four most noble streams
       from hence flow springs, not matcht in many Reams   [10]
       Those springs and frutes brought help for each disease
       thease vnto many Malladies bring ease
           Man there was moneyles, naked, and poore,
           Many goe begging here from dore to dore.
       Man there did tast the tree, he was forbidden
       Heer many men tast fruts make them be chidden./   70
           Angells dwell there in pure and shyning habit,
           Angellike faces som this place inhabit./
       Angells let in all are admitted thither,
       Angells keepe in all are admitted hither.   [20]
           Yf Himmes were there by Adam sung and Heua
           Heer knights and Ladies psalms sing of Geneua./
       Many are said to go to heav'n from thence,
       Many are sent to heav'n or hell from hence./
           But in this one thing likenes most is framed
           that men in Bathe goe naked not ashamed./

Of Don Pedros debts

18.   Don Pedro's out of debt be bold to say it
        for they are said to owe, that meane to pay it./

Of a Wittoll

19   Caius none reckned of thy wife a poynt
        While each man might without all let or cumber
        But since a Watch o're her thou didst appoynt,
        Of Customers she hath no little number,
            Well let them laugh hereat, that list and scoffe yt,
            but thou dost finde, what makes most for thy proffit.

That Fauorites help the Church   71

20.   Of late I wrate after my wanton fashion
            that fauorites consume the Churches Rents,
        But mou'd in conscience to this retractation,
            Ile shew how sure that rashnes me repents,
        For noting in my priuate obseruation,
            What rents and scismes among vs daylie grow,
        No hope appeares of Reconciliation,
            by help of such as can or such as know,
                My Muse must sing, although my soule laments
                that fauorites increase the Churches Rents.   [10]

Of the bishopprick of
Landaffe.

21.   A learned Prelate late disposd to laffe
        Hearing me name the Bishop of Landaffe,
            You should said he, advising well heeron
            Call him Lord Affe, for all the land is gone./

Of Don Pedros dyet drinke

22.   Don Pedro drinks to no man at the boord
        nor once a tast doth of his cup affoord
        Some thinke it pride in him, but see their blyndnes
        I know therein his Lordship doth vs kyndnes./   72.

Of Leda and Balbus

23 Leda was Balbus queane yet might she haue denyde yt
    She weds him: now what means hath Leda left to hyde yt./

Of Cinnas goships cup

24 Cinna when I with thee do dyne or sup
    thou still dost offer me thy goships cup,
        And though it sauour well, and bee well spiced
        Yet I to tast thereof, am not intyced./
    Now sith you needes will haue my cause alledge,
    Why I strayn Curtsie in that cup to pledge,
        One said thou madst that cup so hot of spice,
        that it hath made thee now, a widdower thrice./
            I will not say tis so, nor that I thinke yt,
            but good Sir pardon me, I cannot drinke yt./   [10]

Of Ledas Religion

25. My louely Leda some at thee repyning
    Aske me vnto what sect thou art enclyning
    Which doubte shall I resolue among so many
    Whether to none to one to all to any.
    Surely one should be deemd a false accusant,   73
    that would appeach Leda for a Recusant,
        Her fault according to her former vsing,
        was noted more in taking then refusing,
    For Lent or fasts she hath no superstition,
    for if she haue not chaungd her old condition,   [10]
        Bee it by night in bed, by day in dish,
        flesh vnto her more welcome ys then fishe./
    Thou art no Protestant, thy falshood saith
    thou canst not hope to saue thy self, by faith,
        Well Leda, yet to shew my good affection
        Ile saie thy sect is of a double section,
            A Brownist louely browne, thy face and brest,
            the famelies of loue, in all the rest./

To my Ladie Rogers the
Authors wiues mother

26. If I but speake words of vnpleasing sound
    Yea though the same be but in sport and play,
You bid me peace, or els a thousand pound,
    such words shall worke forth of my childrens way.
    When you saie thus, I haue no word to say
Thus without Obligacion I stand bounde,
Thus wealth makes you commaunde, hope me obay   74
but let me finde this true another day
els when your body shalbe brought to grounde
    Your soule to blessed Abrams Bosome, I   [10]
    maie with good manner, giue your soule the ly./

Of Cinnas courage

27. Pure Cinna saith and proudly doth profess
    that if the quarrell he maintaines bee good
    no man more valient is to spend his blood
No man can dread of death or daunger lesse,
but if the cause be bad, he doth confess,
    his hart is colde and cowardly his moode.
    Well Cinna yet this cannot bee withstood,
thou hast but euill luck I shrewdly guess,
    that byding where as brauls are bred most ryfe,
    thou near hadst yet good quarrell all thy life./   [10]

Of a Lawyer that deseru'd his fee.

28. Sextus retaynd a Sergeant at the Lawes
With one good foe in an ill favored Cawse,
    the matter bad, the Iudge, nor Iury plient,
    the verdit clearly past against the Client,
With which he chaft and sware, he was betrayd   75.
bycause for him, the Sergeant little said,
    And of the fee, he would haue barrd him halfe,
    Whereat the Sergeant wroth, said Dizzard calfe,
thou wouldst, if thou hadst wit or sence to see,
    Confesse I had deserud a double fee,   [10]
    that stoode and blushed there on thy behalfe./

To my good frend Sir Hughe
Portman of Succession

29. My good frend Lynus still is vndermyning,
    to know my minde in matter of succession.
    and though by law it is a flat transgression,
to tell which way affection is inclyning,
    he saith such law of conscience was oppression,
    that all franke minds of whatsoear profession,
Against this law haue shown a flatt repyning.
I thus reply I never vse devining,
    As for the Prince that pleadeth now possession,
My soule hath euer blest without disguising.   [10]
Wherefore to speake of any sonne arysing,
    I hold it vayn while our dear sonne is shyning
And had I Powr I should be enterprysing,
    To stay this Sonne with Iosua from declyning   76.
But sith the fates are stayd by no devising
When her liues thred shall faile with long vntwyning
    I wishe the future age with peace may bring
    no Enfant, nor no Queene, whom then? a King./

Of one that had gotten a Benefice
and after sought for a
Bellypeece.

30.   A Contrie Preacher aged toward fifty
       In all his life nor wanton nor vnthrifty,
            came once to me, and made an earnest motion
            to haue a widdow thought, at my devotion,
       By mean her liuing, lying in my Mannor,
       was held by Widdows state as is the manner.
            He told me first a learned tale of Marriadge
            saue I perhaps haue lost some in the Carriadge
       But this he prou'd by manie learned Clauses,
       how Marriadge is allowd men for two Causes,   [10]
            As namely first, for honest procreation,
            next to avoyde dishonest fornication,
       And that late wryters, men of passing pietie
       haue found a third cause, mutuall societie.
       This said, he told how he this sute attempted   77.
       not that to carnall lust he was much tempted
       nor that he should by this inrich his purse
       but that his yeares required now a nurse
       A nurse said I, oh head of wisedome scarse
       thou seekst a Nurse but thou wouldst haue (an   )   [20]
            Cannot great Clarks that hold such ghostly places
            Declyne vxores in the gendring cases.

            Of Don Pedro.

31.   A Slaue thou wert by byrth, of this I gather
       for euermore thou sayes*t*, my Lord my father./

            Against Lynus a Wryter

32   I heare that Lynus growes in wondrous choller
       because I said he wrote but like a scholler
            Yf I haue said so Lynus, I must graunt yt
            Yet to regaine thy loue, thus I recant yt.
       What ear I speake, thy schollership concearning,
       I neuer thought or meant, that thou hadst learning,
            but that hereof maie grow no more recitall,
            Ile teache thee how to make me full requitall
       Say thou to breed my equall spite and doller   78
       Misacmos neuer wrytes but like a scholler./   [10]

Of Don Pedros Bonds.

33.   Don Pedro cares not in what bonds he enter
        then I to trust Don Pedro soone should venter
            for no man can of Bands stand more secure
            then he that meanes to keepe his payment sure.

                Against Caius that skornd
                my Metamorphosis./

34.   Last day thy Mistris Caius being present,
        one hapt to name to purpose not vnpleasant,
            the tytle of my misconceaued booke,
            at which you spet as though you could not brooke
        So grosse a worde? but shall I tell the matter.
        Why if one name Aiax, your lipps do water./
            there was the place of your first loue and meeting,
            there first you gaue your mistris such a greeting
        As bred her skorne your shame and others lafter,
        and made her feele yt twenty fortnights after.   [10]
            then thanke their witt that make the place so sweet
            that for your Hymen you thought place so meete.
            But meete not maydes at Madam Cloacina   79.
            least they cry nine months after: help Lucina./

                Against an Atheist

35.   That heav'ns are voyd and that no gods there are
        Rich Paulus saith, and all his proofe is this
            that while such blasphemies pronounce he dare
            he liueth here in ease and earthly bliss.

                Of Cosmus heyre

36.   When all men thought, old Cosmus lay a dying
            and had by will giv'n thee much goods and lands
        Oh how the little Cosmus fell a crying
            oh how he beate his brests and wrung his hands
        How fervently for Cosmus health he prayd
            what worthy alms he vowd on that condicion,
        But when his panges a little were allayd,

and health seemd hoped by the learnd Phisicion,
    Then though his lipps all loue and kyndnes vaunted,
    his hart did pray his prayr might not be graunted./   [10]

        Of a drunken tobacco
        taker.

37   When Marcus hath carrowst March beere and sacke   80.
      and feeles his head grow dizzie therewithall
then of Tobacco he a pipe doth lack
    of Trinidade, of Cane, in leafe or ball
Which tane, a little he doth spet and smacke
    then layes him on his bed for feare to fall
    and on Tobacco layes the blame of all
    But that same pipe that Marcus brayne did lade
    was of Medera, not of Trinidade./

        Of Faustus a Stealler
        of Vearses.

38   I heare that Faustus oftentimes rehearses
to his chast mistris certaine of my vearses,
    In which with vse so perfitt he is grown,
    that she, poore foole, now thinks they are his own,
I would esteeme it (trust me) grace not shame,
Yf Dauis, or if Daniell did the same,
    for would I thank or would I quarrell pike,
    I, when I list could do to them the like./
But who can wish a man a fowler spite
then haue a blindman take away his light   [10]
    A begging theefe is daungerous to my purse,   81.
    A baggage poet to my vearse is wurse.

        Misacmos of himself

39.   Muse you Misacmos failes in some endevor,
Alas an honest man's a Nouice euer
    Fy but a mans disgrac't noted a Nouice,
    Yea but a man is grac't, noted of no vice./

Of the corne that rayned

40. I handled, tasted, saw it with mine eyes
the graine that lately fell down from the skies,
Yet what it tokned could I not devise,
and many doubts did in my minde arise,
At last I thus resolu'd, it signifies,
that this *ys* our sole mean to mend this dearth,
to ask from heauen, what we *do* lack on earth.

To his wife at the birth
of his sixt child./

41. The poet Martiall made a speciall sute
vnto his prince to graunt him vnder seale
Right of three Children, which they did impute,
a kind of honour in their common weale
But for such sute my self I neede not trouble,   82.
for thou dost seale to me this Pattent double./

Against Feasting

42. Kind Marcus me to supper lately bad
and to declare how well to vs he wishes
the Rome was strowd with Roses not with Rushes
And all the cheare was got that could be had,
Now in the midst of all our dainty dishes,
me thinke said he to me you looke but sad,
alas said I 'tis to see thee so mad,
To spoyle the sky of fowles, the seas of fishes,
the land of beasts, and bee at so much cost,
for that which in one howr will all be lost.   [10]
That entertaynment that makes me most glad,
Ys not the store of stewd boyld bakt or rost,
but sweet discourse, mean fare, and then beleeue me
to make to thee like cheer shall neuer greeue me:/

To Sextus an yll Reader.

43 The vearses Sextus thou didst reade are mine,
But with bad reeding, thou maist make them thine./

Against Cosmus covetousnes./

44   Cosmus when I among thyne other vices   83
      that are in nature fowle, in number meny
Aske thee what is the reason thee entices,
      to be so basely pinching for thy penny.
Dost thou not call vpon thy selfe a curse
      not to enioy the wealth that thou hast wonne.
But saue, as if thy soule, were in thy purse.
      Thou strayght replyest I saue all for my sonne,
        Alas this reconfirms what I said rather,
        Cosmus hath euer bene a penny father./   [10]

Against Vintners of Bath

45   If men ought those of duty to commend
that questions of religion seeke to end,
then I to praise our Vintners do intend;
      For question is twixt wryters old and latter,
      Yf wine alone, or if wine mixt with water,
      should of the blessed Sacrament be matter,
Some auncient wryters wish it should be mingled,
but latter men with much more zeale inkyndled,
will haue wine cleare, and pure from water singled.
      Our zealous Vintners here grown great Devines,   [10]
      to find which way antiquity enclynes.
For pure zeale mix with water all our wines,   84
      Well plainly to tell true and not to flatter,
      I find our wines are much the worse for water./

To pacifie his wiues mother
when she was angry

46.   Madame I read to you a little since
      the storie of a knight that had encurr'd
the deepe displeasure of a mighty Prince,
      for feare of which long time he neuer sturrd,
Till watching once the king that came from Chapple
      his little sonn fast by him with his guardon,
Entis't that enfant to him with an Apple
      so caught him in his Arms and su'de for pardon,
        then you should turne your angrie frown to lafter
        as oft as in mine armes you see your dafter./   [10]

To his wife, of Poppeas
Sabinas fayr hayr.

47   Mall once I did but do not now envy
      Fierce Neroe's bliss, of fayr Poppeas rayes,
that in his lap, coaming her locks would ly,
      each hayre of hers a vearse of his would prayes.
But that praisd bewtie fruteles spent her dayes.   85.
No young Augustus euer calld him Dad,
      no small Poppeas with their pretty playes,
Did melt their harts, and melting make them glad,
      but thou in this dost pass his fayr Sabina
      that hast seav'n times bene succord by Lucina./   [10]
Thy wombe in braunches seav'n it self displayes,
        Then leaue I Nero with Poppeas hayres,
        To ioy, and to enioy thee, and thine heyres./

Against Lalus an ill
Preacher.

48.   Young Lalus tooke a text of exc'lent matter,
and did the same expound but near the latter,
his tongue so vainly did and idely clatter,
the people naught but hem and cough and spatter,
then said a knight not vs'd to ly or flatter,
      Such Ministers do bring the devills blessing,
      that mar vs so good meate, with so bad dressing./

Against Marcus drunken
Feast.

49.   When Marcus makes as oft he doth a feast
The wine still costs him more then all the rest,   86
      Were water in this town as dear as hay,
      his horses should not long at Liuery stay.
But tell me ist not a most foollish trick,
to drink to others health till thou be sick,
      Yet such the fashion is of Bacchus Crew,
      to quaffe and bouze vntill they belch and spew,
        Well leaue yt Marcus els thy drinking health,
        will proue an eating of thy wit and wealth./   [10]

Against Paulus an Atheist
denying the Resurrection

50.   Lewd Paulus led by Saduces infection,
        doth not beleeue the bodies resurrection,
            and holds them all in skorne and deepe derision,
            that tell of Saints or Angells apparision,
        And sweares such things are fables all and fansies,
        Of Lunaticques or folks possest with fransies.
        I haue (saith he) traveld both near and far,
        by sea, by land in tymes of peace and war,
            Yet neuer met I spryte or ghost or elfe,
            or ought (as is the phrase) worse then my self.   [10]
        Well Paulus, this I now beleeue indeed,/
        For who in *all or* part denyes his Creede,   87
            Went he to sea, land, hell, I would agree,
            a fend worse then himself should neuer see./

                    Of Galla going to the
                    Bath./

51.   When Galla for her health goes to the Bath,
            she carefully doth hyde, as is most meete
            with aprons of fine linnen, or a sheet,
        Those parts that modestie concealled hath,
        Nor onely those but ev'n her brest and necke,
        that might be seene and shown without all check.
            But yet one foule and vnbeseeming place
            she leaues vncovered still: what's that? her face./

                    A Paradox to Cinna the
                    Brownist./

52.   Pure Cinna deemes I hold a Paradox,
        not to be proov'd , but vnto stones and stox,
            That Brownists are vnto the Papists neerer
            then Protestants: 'tis cleer, there's nothing cleerer.
        First Cinna: often haue I heard thee graunt
        The Popes chief opposit's a Protestannt.
        Now then to try the distannce trew compare   88
        and make religion either round or square.
            Yf it bee round, as in theise careles dayes

Yt runneth rounde (more pitty) many wayes   [10]
Place Protestannts and Papists east and west
and place the Brownist where he list to rest
    except that he the circle quite will miss
    hee nearer still vnto the Papist is.
If square it be, as sure, as now tis faring,
about religion neuer was more squaring,
    nor farder out of square I think 'twas neuer,
    nor few'r that to bring't in square endeuer,
Place th'opposites at two points most opposed,
and then againe, this secret is disclosed,   [20]
    for either they bee quite beside all square
    or nearer to the Papists still they are.
But bee they near so neer, they neede beware,
    Both sides will daunger them except they turne them
    the Protestants will hange, the Papists burne them.

To one that had meat
yll drest.

53.   King Mithridate to poysons so envr'd him
    As deadly poysons damage none procur'd him   89.
        So you to stale vnsavery food and durty
        are so invr'd as famin near can hurt yee./

Of giuing much creditt.

54.   Of all this town old Codros giues most credit
    who hee? poore soule, alas that ear you sed it
        How can he credit much and is so poore,
        hee's blynde, yet makes he loue to euery whore./

Of a Mart by two that gat
Letters of a Marte.

55.   Young Titus sold a wench to buy a Barke,
    old Caius sold the Ship, to buy the Slutt,
        Who makes the better Mart, now let vs marke,
        t'one goes to roue, the tother goes to rutt./

                    Of honest theft to my good
                    frend M^r· Samuell Danyell:

56.   Proud Paulus late my secresies revealling,
         hath told I got some good conceyts by stealling,
                 But where got he those double Pistoletts
                 with which good cloaths, good fare, good land he getts
         Tush those he saith, came by a man of war   90.
         that brought a prize of price, from contry far./
                 Then fellow theife, lett's shake togither hands
                 Sith both our wares are filtcht from forren lands
                     You spoyle the Spaniards by your writt of Mart
                     And I the Romans rob by witt and art./   [10]

                    Against Faustus./

57.   In skorne of wryters Faustus still doth hold
         nought is now said, but hath bene said of old
                 Well Faustus say my witts are gross and dull
                 if for that worde I giue not thee a gull.
         Thus then I proue thou holdst a false position,
         I saie thou art a man of faire condicion.
                 A man true of thine word, tall of thyne hands,
                 of high discent, and left good store of lands.
         Thou with false dice and cards hast neuer playd,
         corrupted neuer widdow wife nor mayde,   [10]
                 and as for swearing, none in all the Reame,
                 doth seldomer in speach curse or blaspheme.
         In fyne your vertues are so rare and ample
         for all our sonns thou maist be made a sample.
                 This I dare swear none euer said before   91
                 this I may swear, none euer will saie more./

                    To Caius of his
                    Chaste wife.

58.   A Thais? no Diana thou didst wed
         for she hath giv'n to thee Acteons head.

Of cursing Cuckolds

59   A gallant talking late in way of skorne
of some that ware invisibly the horne
    Sware he could wish and did as for his part
    all Cuckolds in the Temms with all his hart
      but straight a pleasant knight reply'de to him
      I hope Sir gallant you haue learnd to swim./

Of free will

60   I know a foollish fellow hath a fashion
to proue that all is by prædestination,
    and teach nor man nor spirit hath free will,
    In doing, no nor thinking, good or ill.
I am no Doctor at this disputation,
    nor are deepe questions fitt for shallow skill
Yet Ile renounce with learnd men reputacion   92.
    if I disproue not this by demonstration./
Ile proue so plaine as none can yt resist,
that in some things three things do what them list.   [10]
    The wynde saith scripture, where yt list doth blow,
    his tongue talks what it list, his speaches show,
    My hart beleeues him as it list, I know./

Of a devout Damosell

61.   A neighbour mine, an honest learned Curate
    preaching one day according to his function
said that their harts were hard and too obdurate
    that in their conscience neuer feele compunction,
Of which to make some plainer explanation,
    with varied phrase (as schollers haue the trick)
He vs'd some words of like signification,
    a feelling, a remorse, a sting, a pricke,
A zealous maide heard him with great attention,
    and being pregnant of conceyt and *quick*   [10]
Calld oft to minde the words, he last did mention,
    which most as seem'd did in her conscience stick.
All melancholy from the church she went,
    and comming home she layd her on her bed,
And vnto those that were to see her sent   93.

and asked what did ayle her thus she sedd,
    The sermon in my conscience made me sick
    to heare our parson preaching of a (compunction)./

      Of Don Pedro./

62.   Don Pedro neuer dynes without red Deare
    Yf read Deere be his guests, grass is his cheer
      tush I do meane, he hath it in his dishe
      oh: so haue I oft that I do not wishe./

      Of a drunken Paraclesian

63.   When Philo other trades of thrift had mist
    he then profest to be an Alchimist
      That's all to much, Chimist you might him call,
      and so I thinke 'twere trew, and leaue out all./
    He takes vpon him he can make a mixture
    of which he can extract the true Elixar,
      Tincture of Pearle and Currall he doth draw,
      and quintescence the best that ere you saw,
    He hath the rare receyte Aquæ mirabilis,
    onely he wants some drams Auri potabilis,   [10]
      He doth of nature so the secrets ferit.
      that he of ev'ry thing can draw the sperit   94.
    Speritts of wines, sperits of stones and hearbs
    Whose names can skant be told with nowns and vearbs
      But of all sprites, my spirit doth devine
      his spirit best doth loue spirit of wyne./

      Of Misacmos his success
        in a sute./

64.   Misacmos hath long time a sutor beene
    to serue in some neer place about the Queene
      in which his frends to worke his better speed
      do tell her highnes as 'tis true indeed,
    That hee's a man well borne and better bred,
    In humain studies seen, in Stories redd,
      adding vnto an industry not small,
      pleasant conceyts and memory with all,

And chiefly that he hath bene from his youth,
a zealous searcher of eternall truthe./ [10]
    Now neuer wonder he his sute doth miss
    for I haue told you what the reason ys.

A Groome of the Chambers Religion
in king Henry the eights time

65.   One of king Henries favorites began   95.
to moue the king one day to take a man
    whom of his chamber he might make a Groome
    Soft said the king, before I graunt that roome
It is a question not to be neglected
how he in his religion stands affected?
    for his religion aunswerd then the minion
    I do not certaine know what's his opinion,
        But sure he may talking with men of Learning
        Conforme himself in less then ten dayes warning./ [10]

To his wife of womens
vertues./

66.   A well learnd man in rules of life no Stoyke,
    Yet one that careless Epicures deryded,
    of womens vertues talking, *them* devided
In three, the private, civill and heroyke.
And what he said of thease to tell you briefly,
    he first began discoursing of the private,
    which each plaine contry huswife may ariue at,
as homely, and that home concearneth chiefly
the fruite, mault, hops, to tend, to dry, to vtter,
    to beat strip, spin, the hemp, the woll, the flax, [10]
    Breede poultry, gather honney, try the wax,   96.
And more then all, to haue good cheese and butter./
Then next a step, but yet a large step higher,
    was civill vertue fitter for the Citty,
    with modest *looks*, good *cloaths* and answer witty
Those baser things not done but guided by her
Her ydle times and ydle coyne she spends
    on needle works and when the season serues,
    in making dainty Iunketts and conservs.
To welcome in kynde sort his dearest frends./ [20]

But far above them all he most extolled
   the stately Heroyns whose noble minde,
   It self to those poore orders cannot bynde,
Anomelons that still liue vncontrolled.
Theis entertayn great Princes, theise haue learned
The tongue, toyes, tricks, of Rome, of Spaine, of Fraunce
   theis can Currentos, and Lavoltas daunce,
And though they foote it false, 'tis nere discearned.
The vertues of theis dames are so transcendent
   themselus are learn'd, and their heroyck sperit   [30]
   can make disgrace an honor, sin a merit,
All pens, all praysers are on them dependent./
Well gentle wife thou knowst I am not Stoycall
Yet would I wish take not the wishe in evill   97
You knew the private vertue, kept the civill
But in no sort aspire to that hoeroycall./

To Doctor Harvy of Cambridge

67   The proverb saith who fights with durty foes
    must needs be soyld, admitt they win or lose;
       then thinke it doth a Doctors credit dash,
       to make himself antagonist to Nashe.

An infallible rule, to
rule a Wife.

68   Concerning wiues hold this a certaine rule,
       that if at first you let them haue the rule,
    Your self at last with them shall haue no rule,
       except you let them evermore to rule./

Why Paulus takes so
much Tobacco.

69   When our good Irish neighbors make repaire
    With Lenton stuffe, vnto Bridgwater fayre
       At euery booth, and Alehouse, that they come,
       they call for herring; still, they must haue some.
    Hostish I pree dee haist tee any heerring?   98.
    Yea Sir, o passing meat, o happy heerring.

Heerring they ask, they praise, they eate, they buy,
   No prise of heerring can be helld to hye.
But when among them it is closely mutterd,
those herrings, that they brought to sell, are vtterd   [10]
   then giue them herring: Poh away with theese,
   Pree thee good hostish, gev's some english cheese.
Hence I haue learnd the cause, and see yt cleerly
Why Paulus takes Tobacco, buyes it deerly.
   At tabling houses where he eats and drinks
   that ev'ry roome, strayt of Tobacco stinks.
He swears 'tis salue for all diseases bred;
It strengthens ones weake back, comforts ones head
   Yt breeds fresh appetite, 'tis cordiall, durable
   It cures that ill that some haue thought incurable./   [20]
Thus while proud *Paulus* hath Tobacco praysed
the price of ev'ry pownd, a pound is raysed.
   And why's all this? bycause he loues it well?
   No: but bycause himself hath store to sell
   But hauing sold all his, he will pronounce
   The best of Cane, not worth a groat an ounce./

Of a formall Minister   99.

70.   A Minister affecting singularity,
   and preaching in the Pulpit of his theam,
   borne with the current of the common stream,
Extoll*ed* faith and hope, forgetting charity;
   for while he was most busie in his text
   he spide a woman talking with her next;
And straight he cryde to her, Dame leaue your babling,
   Wherewith the good poor woman shrowdly vext;
   could hold no longer but fell flat to brabling,
      Beshrew his naked hart she doth reply   [10]
      that bableth in this place most thou or I./

Of Pillers of the Church./

71.   In old time they were calld the Churches pillers
               that did excell in learning, and in piety,
               and were to youth examples of sobriety,
           Of Christes fayr feild the true and paynfull tillers,
               but where are now the men of that Society?
           Are all those tillers dead, those pillers broken?
           No god forbid such blasphemy be spoken.
               I saie to stop the mouths of all ill willers
               gods feild hath harrowers still, his church hath pillers.

Of a lawfull wife./   100.

72.   At end of three yeares law and sute and strife
               When Cannon Lawes and common both commaund her
               Cis marred thee, now sue them for a sclaunder
               that dare deny she is thy lawfull wife./

Against Zoylus and all
envious Readers

73   Who reed our lynes with visage sowr and grim,
               I wish him envy me, none envy him.

Against Feasting

74.   Last daie I was vnto your house envited
               and on the boord were forty diuers dishes,
               of salletts and of flesh, of fowls, and fishes,
           With which god knowes I little am delighted,
               Before I came I tooke it you did bid me
               But now I rather thinke you did forbid me./

Against Lynus that said the
Nobillity were decayd./

75.   You Lynus saie that most of our Nobillity
         are much decayd in vallor and in witt:
      Though some of them haue wealth and good abillity   101.
         Yet verie few for government are fitt./
      Foole see'st thou not, that in our stately buildings
         plaine massie stones the substannce do sustayn,
      Yet coullors wreath'd and carvd set out with guildings
         must in high ranke for ornament remayn.
            So men of noble birth the state adorne
            but by the wise, stout, learnd, the sway is borne./   [10]

To Itis, aliasse Ioyner, an
vncleanly token convaid
in cleanly tearms./

76.   Torquato Tasso, for one little fault
         that did perhaps merrit some small rebuke,
         was by h*is* sharpe and most vngratefull duke,
      Shut vp close prisoner in a loathsome vault.
      Where wanting pen and ynke by Princes order
         his witt that walls of Adamant could pearse
         found meanes to write his minde in exclent vearse
      for want of pen and yncke in piss and ordure.
      But thy dull witt damnd by Apollos crew
         to Dungeon of disgrace, though free thy boddy   [10]
         with pen nay print doth publish like a noddy./
      Base taunts that turned vpon thy self are trew,   102.
      And wanting salt thy wallowish stile to season,
         and being of vncouth tearms a senceles Coyner,
         thou callst thy self vnproperly a Ioyner,
      Whose vearse hath quite disseverd ryme from reason
            Deserving for such raylling, and such bodging,
            for this, Torquatos ynck, for that, his lodging./

To his Wife./

77.   When I to thee, my letters superscribe
        thus: To mine owne; Leda there'at do gibe.
              and aske her why: she saith, bycause I flatter.
              but let her thinke so still, it makes no matter.
        If I doe flatter onely thou canst try,
        suffizeth me, I thinke I do not ly./
                  But let her husband wryte so: for my life
                  he flattreth himself more then his wife./

                  Sir Iohn Raynsfords
                  Confession./

78.   Rainsford a knight fitt to haue seru'd king Arthur,
        And in Queene Maries time a Demie Martir
              for though both then, before, and since, he turned
              Yet sure, per ignem hanc, he might be burned.   103
        This knight agreed with those of that profession,
        and went as others did, to make confession
              Among some Peccadilios, he confest
              that same sweet sin that some but deeme a Iest./
        And told how by good help of bauds and Varletts,
        Within twelue months, he had six times twelue harletts,   [10]
              The Priest that at the table was half astonished,
              with graue and ghostly councell him admonished.
        To fast and pray, to driue away that Devill,
        That was to him causer of so great evill,
              That the lewd sprite of Letchery no question,
              Stird vp this lust with many a lewd suggestion,
        A filthy fend sayd he, most fowle and odious,
        nam'd as appears in holy writt Asmodious./
              Thus with some pennance that was nere performed,
              away went that same knight, smally reformed./   [20]
        Soone after this, insewd Religions chaunge
        that in the Church bred alteration straunge.
              And Rainsford with the rest followd the streame
              the Priest went roving round about the Reame,
        This Priest himselfe in clothes disguisd did hyde,
        Yet Rainsford three yeares after him had spyde.
              And layd vnto his charge, and sorly prest him,   104
              to tell if 'twere not he, that had confest him,
        The priest (though this knights words him sore did daunt)

Yet what he could not well deny, did graunt, [30]
    And pray him not to punishe or controule,
    that he had done for safty of his soule./
No knaue (quoth he) I will no harme procure thee,
vpon my worship, here I do assure thee
    I onely needes must laughe at thy great folly,
    that wouldst perswade with me to be so holly,
To chastice mine owne fleshe, to fast and pray,
to driue the sprite of Letchery away./
    Swounds foollish knaue, I fasted not nor prayd
    yet is that sprite quite gone from me he sayd. [40]
If thou couldst help me to that sprite againe,
thou shouldst an hundred pownds haue for thy payn.
      That lusty lord of Letchery, Asmodius,
      that thou callst odious, I would count commodious./

      A pretty question of Lazarus
      soule, well answeared./

80   Once on ocasion two good frends of mine
    did meet at meat a Lawyer and devyne
      Both hauing eat'n well to help disgestion   105.
      to this Devine, the Lawyer put this question
    When Lazarus foure dayes, in graue did stay
    Where was his soule in heav'n or hell I pray?
      Was yt in hell? thence no redemption is
      and if in heav'n, would Christ abate his bliss./
    Sir said the Preacher for a short digression,
    first answer me one poynt of your profession,   [10]
      If so his heyres and he, had faln to strife
      Whose was the Land when he return'd to life.
        This latter question mou'd them all to lafter,
        and so they drunke one to another after./

      Against long Sutes
      in Law.

80.bis   In Court of Wards, kings Bench and Common place
    thou follow'd hast a sute this seav'n yeares space,
      Ah wretched man in mothers wombe accurst,
      that couldst not rather loose thy sute at first./

Of an importunate prater out of Martiall

81.   He that is hoarse, yet still to prate doth prease,
       proues he can neither speake nor hold his peace./

Against Iealowsie. to my frend   106.

82.   Right terrible are wynds on waters great
          most horrible are tempests on the sea
       Fier merciless that all consumes with heat
          plagues monstrous are, that citties cleane decay
       War cruell ys, ánd pinching famin curst
          Yet of all ills the iealouse wife is wurst./

Against Quintus that being poore
and prodigall, became rich
and miserable./

83.   Skant was thy liuing Quintus ten pound cleere,
          when thou didst keepe such fare so good a table,
          that we thy frends prayd god thou mightst be able
       to spend at least one hundred pownds a yeare.
          behold our boone god did benignly heare,
       thou gottst so much by fortune favourable,
          and foure frends deaths to thee both kinde and deare
       But sodenly thou grewst so miserable,
          We thy old frends to thee vnwelcome are,
       Poor Iohn and Applepies is all our fare,   [10]
          No Salmon, Sturgeon, Oysters, Crab nor Cunger,
       What should we wishe thee now for such demerit.
          I would thou mightst one thousand pounds inherit   107
          then without question, thou wouldst starue for hunger./

To my Lady Rogers./

84.   Madam with speeches kynde and promise fayr
          that from my wife you would not giue a ragg,
       But she should be Exector sole and heir
          I was (the more foole I) so proud and brag,
       I sent to you against Saint Iames his fayr,
          a tearse of Clarret wine, a great fat Stag,

You straight to all your neighbors made a feast,
    each man I meete hath filled vp his paunche
With my red Dear, onely I was no guest
    nor euer since did tast of side or haunch./   [10]
Well Madam you maie bid me hope the best,
    that of your promise you be sound and staunch,
      Els I might doubt I should your land inherit,
      that of my Stag did not one morsell merit./

Of Sextus mishap comming
from a Taverne.

85.   Now Sextus twise hath supt at Sarzens head,
    and both times homwards comming drunk to bed,
      he by the way his pantaffles hath lost,
    And greeu'd both with the mocke and with the cost   108.
      to saue such charges, and to shun such frumps
      he goes now to the tavern in his pumps./

How Sextus layd clayme
to an Epigram./

86.   When Sextus heard my ryme of Raynsford reeding
    with lafter lowd he cryes, and voyce exceeding,
      that Epigram was mine, who euer made it,
      I told him that conceyt: from me he had yt;
    Ah barbarisme, the blynder still the bolder,
    will Sextus near grow wiser, growing older./
      When Phidias framed had in marble pure
      Ioues goodly picture, would a man indure,
    A Pioner to challenge half the prayse
    that from the Quarr, the ragged stone did rayse   [10]
      Or should a Carman boast of his desart
      bycause he did vnlode it from the Cart
    I think that Sextus self would neuer say't
    So in like manner Sextus: that conceyt
      was like a ragged stone dig'd from thy foollish head
      now tis a statue carv'd by vs, and pullished./

Of an Alborne Rabbett.   109.

87.   Late comming from the Pallace of the best
      the Center of the men of better sence,
      my purse grown low in ebb through long expence,
And going for supplies into the West,
Mine host to whom I was a welcome guest
      makes me great chear, but when I parted thence,
      my trusty servannt William tooke offence
(Though now God wot it was too late to spare)
that in the shott, things, to high prised are
      And namely for two Rabbetts twenty pence.   [10]
The Tapster well envr'd to prate and face
      told they were white, and young, and fatt and sweet,
New killd, and newly come from Alborne chase,
      that for good fare, good paiment is most meet.
I willing to make short, their long debate,
      bad my man paie the reckning at his rate:
          Adding I knew a Miser of his money,
          giue more then ten pence for an Alborne Coney./

Of a fayr Shrow./

88.   Faire rich and young how rare is thy perfection
Were it not mard with one most fowle infection./
      I mean so proud a hart, so curst a tonge   110.
      as makes thee seeme nor fayr, nor rich, nor young./

Of hearing Masse

89.   Men talking as oft times it comes to pass,
how daungerous 'tis now to heare a Mass,
      A valient knight sware for a thousand pound
      he would not present at a Mass be found,
A noble Lord stood by, and hearing yt
said Sir, I then should much condemne your wit,
          for were you founde and followd near so nearly,
          you gaine nine hundred pownds, and vpwards clearly.

Of a Preacher that sings Placebo./

90.   A smooth tong'd preacher that did much affect
to be reputed of the purest sect,
    Vnto theise times great prayses did afford
    that brought he said the sunnshine of the worde?/
The sunshine of the word this he extold?
this sunshine of the word this still he told?/
    But I that well obseru'd how slender fruits,
    haue grown of all their preachings and disputes,
Pray God they bring vs not, when all is donne
Out of Gods blessing into this warme sonne: [10]   111.
    For sure as some of them haue vsd the mater
    their sunshine is, but mooneshine in the water./

Of the naked Image that was to
stand in my Lord Chamberlains gallery.

91   Acteon guiltles vnawares espying
    Naked Diana bathing in her bower
    Was plagu'd with horns his dogs did him devowr./
Wherefore take heed *least for your* curious prying
    With some such forked plague you bee not smitten,
    and in your forhead so, your faults bee written./

Of the same to the Ladies./

92.   Her face vnmaskt, I saw her corps vnclad,
    no vaile, no couer, her and me between,
No ornament was hid that bewty had,
    I blusht that saw, she blusht not that was seen,
    With that I vowd neuer to care a rushe
    for such a bewtie, as doth neuer blushe

Of Don Pedros threats./

93   Don Pedro thinks I skorn him in my ryme
            and vowes if he can proue I vse detraction   112.
            of the greate scandall he will haue an action,
        I that desir'd to cleere me of the cryme
        When I was askt, said no my Lord I ha'not
        Then swear said he, not so my Lord I cannot./
                Since that I neuer heard newes of this Action,
                Wherefore I think, he hath his satisfaction./

Of certaine puritan wenches./

94.   Six of the weakest sex and purest sect,
        had conference one day to this effect,
                to chaunge that old and popish name of preaching.
                And first the first would haue yt called teaching./
        The second such a vulgar tearme, dispysing,
        said it were better call yt catechising.
                The third not full so learn'd, yet foole as wise,
                told that her husband calld it exercise./
        The fourth a great Magnificents corrector,
        said she allowd them best, that calld it Lector./   [10]
                Nay said the fift, our brethren as I heere
                do call it speaking in Northampton sheere,
        Tush sayd the sixt, then standing were more fitt
        Sith Preachers seldome in the Pulpit sit.
                Now though this word was worst, yet notwithstanding   113.
                I know not why, but all likt best of standing./

Against Brauery./

95.   When Roman Mutius had in contries quarrell
                the servant killed to the maisters terror
        What time his eye deceaud with rich Apparrell
                did cause his hand commit that happie error
        The king amaz'd at so rare resolution
                both for his safe'ty and his reputation
        Remou'd the fyre, and stayd that execution
                and for his sake made peace with all his nation
                        Perhaps it is from hence the custome springs
                        that oft in courts, knaues goe as braue as kings./   [10]

Of Ledas vnkindnes./

96. Faire Leda, late to me is grown malitious
    at all my works in prose or vearse repyning.
Bicause my words she saith, make men suspicious,
    that she is to the Puritans enclyning./
      Leda what ear I said, I did suspect
      thou art not pure ynough, in one respect./

A distick of frends

97. New frends are no frends how can that bee trew   .114.
the oldest frends that are, were sometimes new./

Of a Zealous Ladie./

98 Two Aldermen, three Lawiers, five Phisitions
seav'n Captaines, with nine Poets, ten Musitions
woo'd all one wench, she waying all conditions
    By which she might attayn to most promotion
    married a Prieste at last for pure devotion.

Of an Abbot that had been
a good fellow./

99. An Abbot, that had led a wanton life
    and cyted now by deaths sharp Somner sicknes
felt in his soule great agony and strife
    his sinns appearing in most hideous likenes.
The Monkes that saw their Abbot so dismayd,
    and knew no less his life had bene lascivious,
Yet for his finall comfort thus they sayd,
    think not deer Sir, we wilbe so obliuious
But that with fasting and with sacred ringing
    and prayer, we will for you such grace attayne,   [10]
That after Requiem and such Dirges singing   115.
You shalbe freed from Purgatories payn.
      Ah thanks my sonns said he, but all my feare
      ys onely this, that I shall near come theare.

Against Cinna a Brownist that
saith he ys sure to be saved./

100.   Yf thou remaine so sure of thine election,
            as thou saidst Cinna when we last disputed,
            that to thy soule no sin can be imputed,
         that thy strong faith hath gott so sure protection,
         that all thy faults are free from all correction./
            Heere then my councell to thy state well suted,
         It comes from one, that beares thee kind affection,
         Tis so infallible that no obiection
            there is by which it may be well confuted./
         Leaue Cinna this base earth with sin polluted   [10]
         and to be free from wicked mans subiection
         and that the saynts may bee by thee saluted.
               Forsake, wife, lands, goods, and worldly pelfe
               and gett an halter quickly, and hange thy selfe./

                    The end of the second booke./

[Blank page: see Appendix for '*Certayn epigrams*' at this point in *BL*]   116.

The third booke of   117.
Epigrams.

To Maister Bastard a Minister that
wrate a pleasant booke of
English Epigrams.

1.   Though dusky witts of this vngratefull time
            carp at th*y* booke of Epigrams and scof it,
            Yet wise men know, to mix the sweet with proffit,
        Ys worthy prayse, not onely voyd of cryme,
        then let not envy stop th*y* vayn of Rime,
            nor let thy function make thee shamed of it,
            a Poet is one step vnto a prophet;
        And such a step as 'tis no shame to clyme,
        you must in Pulpet treat of matters serious,
            as best beseemes the Person and the place,   [10]
            there preach of fayth, repentannce, hope, and grace
        Of Sacraments, and such hy things misterious
        But *they* are too severe, and too imperious
            that vnto honest sports will graunt no space,
            for theis our myndes refresh, when those do weary vs.
            And spurr our dulled sprite to swifter pace,   118
        The holsom'st meats that are will breed satiety,
        except we should admitt of some variety,
            in musicque notes must be some high, some base./
        And this I note your vearses haue en*tend*ement   [20]
            still kept within the lists of good sobriety,
        to worke in mens ill manners good amendement,
        Wherefore if any thinke such vearse vnseasonable
            their Stoick myndes are foes to good society,
        and men of reason, maie thinke them vnreasonable
            It is an act of vertue and of piety,
                to warne vs of our sinns in any sort,
                in prose, in vearse, in earnest, or in sport./

Of an vnkynde *kynde*
Husband.

2.   A rich old Lord did wed a fayr young Lady,
            of good complexion, and of goodly stature,
            and, for he was of kynde and noble nature,
        he lou'd to see her goe so braue as may bee:

A pleasant knight one day was so presumptuous,
to tell this Lord in way of playn simplicity,
   'tis you my Lord that haue this worlds felicity:
That haue a dame so young, so sweet, so sumptuous,   119.
Tush sayd the Lord, but theis same costly gownes,
   with kirtles, karknetts, plague me in such sort,   [10]
   that everie time I tast of Venus sport,
I wilbe sworne costs me one hundred Crownes./
Now fy Sir said his wife where ys your sence,
though 'tis too trew, yet saie not so for shame,
   for I would wish to cleare me of the blame,
   that each time cost you but an hundred pence./

     Of Gallas goodly Perrywig

3.   Yow see yon goodly hayr that Galla weares,
   tis certayn her own hayr, would one haue thought it./
She sweares it is her own, and true she sweares,
   for hard by Temple bar last day she bought it
     so fayr a hayr, vpon so fowle a forhead,
     augments disgrace, and showes the grace is borrowd.

     Of Maister Iohn Davis booke
     of dauncing. to himself./

4.   While you the Plannetts all do set to dauncing,
beware such haps, as to the fryre was chauncing,
   Who preaching in a Pulpet old and rotten,
   among some notes most fitt to be forgotten,   120.
Vnto his Auditory, thus he vaunts,
to make all Saynts after his pipe to daunce,
   in speaking which as he himself advaunces
   to act his speache with gestures; lo it chaunces,
Down falls the Pulpit, sore the man is brused,
Neuer was fryer, nor pulpit more abused.   [10]
   Then beare with me, though yet to you a straunger
   to warne you of a like, nay greater daunger,
for though none feare the falling of those sparks,
(and when they fall 'twill be good catching larks.)
   Yet this may fall: that while you daunce and skip
   With femall plannets, so your foote may trip
     that in your lofty Caprioll and turne,
     their motion may, make your demension burne./

To Paulus

5.   To loue you Paulus I was well enclyn'd,
      but euer since you honor did requyre
      I honord you, because 'twas your desire,
    but now to loue you, I do neuer minde./

Of table talke

6.   I had this day carrowst the thirtenth cup,   121.
      and was both slipper tongu'd, and ydle braynd,
    And said by chaunce that you with me should sup,
      You thought hereby a supper cleerly gaind,
    And in your tables strayght you cote it vp,
      Vncivill guest, that hath been so ill traynd,
        Worthy thou art hence supperles to walke,
        that tak'st advauntage of our table talke./

Of the commodities that Priests
haue by their marriadge./

7.   A fine young Priest of kin to Fryer Frappert,
    prompt of his tongue, of person, neat, and dappert,
      not deeplie reade, yet were he put vnto it
      one that could saie his service, and would do it./
    His marks and hayr showd him of exc'lent harriadge,
    this Priest one daie hapned to talke of Marriadge,
      and prou'd not onely that 'tis honorable,
      but that the ioyes thereof are admirable,
    He told the tale to me and other frends
    and straight I learn'd yt at my fingers ends/   [10]
      which ioyes that you maie better vnderstand,
      Ile place one on each finger of my hand
    Foure ioyes he said on marrid priests be cast   122.
A wyfe   a wife, and frends, and coyn, and children last;
frends   And first the wife, see how at bed and boord
Mony   What comfort and what ioyes she doth affoord,
children Then for her frends, what ioye can be more deare
    then loving freinds, dwell they far of, or near./
      A third ioy then it is to haue the portion,
      Well got, and voyde of strife, frawd or extortion   [20]
    And fouthly those sweet babes that call one Dad,

oh how they ioy the soule and make it glad./
    But now Sir there remaines one Obseruation,
    that well deserus your dew consideration,
Marke then againe I say, for so 'twere meete,
Which of theis Ioyes are firme and which do fleet.
    First for the wife, sure no man can deny it,
    that for most part she sticks most surely by it,
But for the frends, when they should most avayle you,
by death or fortunes chaunge oft tyme they fayle you,   [30]
    Then for the Portion without more forecast,
    While charge increaseth money fails as fast,
And last the children most of them outliue you,
but ill brought vp, perhaps they liue to greiue you;
Wyfe   Now marke vpon the fingers who remayn,
Chyldren   The children, and the wife, onely theise twayn./

        To Marcus that would borrow   123.

8.   You sent to me Marcus for twenty marke
    but to that sute I would by no meanes harke.
        But straight next day you sent your man in post,
        to tell *me* how a Lord with you would host,
And I must lend to entertaine this state,
Some Basons, Ewres, and some such other plate.
    Are you a foole, or thinke you me a foole,
    that I should now be sett againe to Schoole.
        Were not my wisedome worthy to be wondred,
        Denying twenty marks, to lend one hundred.   [10]

        In prayse of a booke calld the gentle
        Craft, written by a Shoomaker

9.   I past this other day through Pauls Churchyard,
        and saw some reade a booke, and reading laft,
        the tytle of that booke was gentle craft,
The project was, as by their speach I hard,
    to proue among some less important things,
    that Shoomakers and Sowters had beene kings./
But as I markt the matter with regard,
    a new spronge braunch it in my mynde did graft.
And this I sayd, Sirs scorne not him that writt yt
    A guilded blade hath oft a Dudgeon haft   [10]   124.

and sure I see this wryter roues a shaft
Neer fayrest marke though haply hath not hit yt.
   for neuer was the like booke sold in Powls,
Yf so with gentle craft it could perswade,
     great Princes *in* their Pomps to learne a trade
     Once in their liues to worke to mend their sowls./

       To Maister Bastard the Minister
       That wrytes the pleasant Epigrams./

10.   Had you bene knowne to me ear you were maryd,
     I should haue wisht that single you had tarryd.
       Yet of your sprite, my spirit is so awfull,
       I dare not say such marriadge is vnlawfull./
     Nor dare I say men of such holy function,
     should castrat quite themselus from such coniunction.
       Nor dare I much, our Saviours speaches scan,
       To whom 'twas spoken, take yt they that can.
     Nor dare I say, the worde would worke more good,
     Yf preachers wallowd less in flesh and blood.   [10]
       Nor dare I say such lyvings were provided,
       With Crosier staues, not distaues to be guided.
       Yet least I might bee deemd among the Dastards,
       I dare say this, thy Children shalbe Bastards./

       To his Wife after they had   125.
       been married fourteen
       Yeares./

11.   Two prentiships with thee, now haue I been,
     mad times, sad times, glad times, our life hath seen,
     Soules we haue wrought four payre, since our first meeting,
     of which two souls, sweet souls, were to *too* fleeting.
     My workemanship so well doth please thee still,
     thou wouldst not graunt me freedome by thy Will,
     and Ile confess such vsage I haue founde,
     Mine hart yet ne're desir'd to be vnbound./
     But though my self am thus thy Prentice vow'd
     my deerest Mall, yet thereof bee not prowd.   [10]
     nor clayme no rule thereby, there's no such cause,
     For Plowden who was father of the Lawes
     which yet are read and rul'd by his endytings

Doth name himself Apprentice in his wrytings
And I, if you should challenge vndew place,
could learne of him to alter so the case.
I playn would proue I still keepe dew priority,
and that good wiues are still in their minority.
But far from thee my Deare be such audacity
I doubt more thou dost blame my dull capacity   [20]
  That though I travayle true in my vocation   126.
  I grow still worse and worse in th'occupation.

    Of a Bequest without a Legasie

12. In hope some Lease or Legasie to gayne
  You gaue old Titus yearly ten pound pension.
  Now he is dead, I heare, thou dost complayne
    that in his Will of thee he made no mention:
  Cease this complaynt, that showes thy base intention
    He left thee more, then some he lou'd more dearely
    for he hath left thee ten pound pention yearely./

    Of one that lent money
     on sure Bonde.

13. When Lynus litle store of Coyne is spent
  and no supply of office or of Rent,
    He comes to Titus known a wary spender
    of pleasant witt, but no great money lender
  And prest him very hard for twenty pounde,
  for which small kyndnes he were surely bound
    And least (quoth he) you deeme it my presumption
    if I should offer you my bare Assumption
  I swear Allhallows, I will make repaiment
  Yea though I pawn mine Armor, and mine Rayment.   [10]   127.
    And for your more assurance you shall haue
    what obligation you yourself will craue
  Or Bill or Bond your paiment to performe
  Recognizannce, or Statute, any Forme.
    Now Titus by report so well did know him
    that he might skant trust him so far as throw him./
  And said he should haue so much at his hands
  forthwith if he might poynt the forme and bands./
    Agreed quoth Lynus straight, and doth him thanke

But Titus brings a fourme of foure inch planke [20]
Two of the Guard might skantly well it lift,
and e're that Lynus well perceiu'd the drift,
    Fast to that fourme he bound him hands and feete
    then brought the money fourth, and let him see't,
        And sware till he his fashions did reforme,
        None other Bands could serue nor other forme./

Of light Merchandize

14   In Rome a Cryer had a Wench to sell
such as in common Stewes are wont to dwell
her name nor his I shall not neede to tell
    but hauing helld her long at little prise
    And thinking thus some Chapman to entise   128.
    he clipt her in his arms as nothing nice
and so he kist her more then once or twice
What might he gayn thinke you by this devise
    One that before had offred fifty shilling
    to giue one fift part, seemd now vnwilling./   [10]

Of father Peleus stable./

15.   Old Peleus burnd a stable to the ground,
which new to build doth cost three hundred pownd,
    that's but one Iennets price with him: no forse,
    a Stable? no. he did but loose a horse./

Of a Censurer of english
Wryters./

16.   That English men haue small or no invention
    Old Guillam saith, and all our works are barren,
    but for the stuffe we get from Authors forren,
Why Guillam, that same gold thou takes in pension,
Which makes thee loue our Realm more then your owne
    and follow still our englishe Court and Campe,
    now that it hath our dearest Soue'raigns stamp,
Ys english coyn though once 'tweare Indian growne./
    Except not then gainst english witts I pray,   129.
    You that accept so well of English pay.   [10]

The third booke

Of Titus boasting

17   A kind companion Titus all his dayes
      and till his last, a pleasant witt and tonge,
If he had heard a man his own *strength* prayse
      Would tell what he would do when he was younge.
And hauing first with oaths his speeches bound,
      thus would he speake. I would at twelue score pricks
Haue shott all daie an arrow of a pounde,
      haue shot the flight full forty score and six,
I would haue ouerlifted all the Guarde,
      out thrown them at the barr, the sledge the stone   [10]
And he that is in wrastling held most hard,
      I would in open playn haue overthrown./
Now say some by, was Titus e're so strong?
      Who he? the weakest man hundreds among.
Why tells he then such lyes in serious sort
What he would do? nay sure 'twas true, though sport
      He said not, he could doe, that were a fable
      He said he would haue done, had he bene able./

To Doctor Sherwood how
    Sack makes one leane

130.

18.   I mervaild much last day what you might meane
to saie that drinking Sacke would make one leane
but now I see I then mistooke you cleane
For my good neighbour Marcus who I troe
feares fatnes much, this drynke hath plyed so
that now except he leane he cannot goe./
    Ha gentle Doctor now I see your meaning
    Sacke will not leaue one leane, 'twill leaue him leaning./

Of swearing first between the
    wife and the husband./

19.   Cys, by that candle in my sleepe me thought
one told me of thy body thou art nought,
    good husband he that told you ly'de she sedd,
    and swearing layd her hand vpon the bredd.
Then eat the bread (quoth he) that I maie deeme,
that fancy false, that trew to me did seeme
    Nay Sir said she, the matter right to handle
    sith you sware first, you first must eat the candle.

To his Wife

20.*bis*   Because I once in Vearse did hap to call   131.
       thee by this louing name, my dearest Mall,
           thou thinkst thy self assured by the same,
           in future ages I haue giu'n thee fame
       But if thou merit not such name in verity,
       I mean not so to misinforme posterity,
              For I can thus enterpret if I will,
              My dearest Mall, that is my costliest ill./

That the Cleargie bee greate
builders now as well as of old

20.   Was *that* a pride in Priests, or was it piety?
        had those more zeale, or were they more presumptuous,
     to build such Colledges for their society,
        With Abbeys well endow'd and Churches sumptuous./
     If that were pride haue ours to much humillity?
        Yf theire's weare zeale, haue ours no godly motion?
     Yes: I can proue that ours both haue abillity
        and that they build much, and with more devotion
     With stone, yea with free stones, they rear of building
        Worlds, pretty Microcosmous, little ones: [10]
     With temples timber'd well, and some haue guilding,
        Shrines not of dead mens, but of liuely bones./
     Theise buildings walke, oh works worth admiration,   132.
        and each beares surname of their Architector;
     And as it ought Loue laid the first foundation,
        but Loue, read in Saint Luke, with Ouid's lector.
           Well, sith this building from those old ones varies,
           Some men could wish such builders had no Quarries./

To a prating Epicure

22.   If thou loue dainty fare at others tables
        thou must their humours and their howrs indure
     Leaue Arguments, controllings, thwarts, and brabbles
        such freedome sutes not with an Epicure./

Of Don Pedro.

23.   The wise Vlisses, loathing forrain Iarrs
        fayn'd himself mad, to keepe him from the wars
        But our Don Pedro sees our Martiall schooles
        prefer before wise Cowards *valient* fooles,
            And fearing fayning mad will not suffise
            to staie him from the Warrs, faynes himself wise./

                    The censure of a Ladie in Ireland
                    of the ouerthrow at Blackwater./

24.   Two Dames of two beleifs, the old and later   133.
        talkt of the loss late taken at Blackwater,
            the Catholicque affirm'd she could not know
            the hidden cause of that curst overthrow./
        The t'other that professed greater purity,
        said that the cause was hid in no obscurity.
            For God said she strength'ned the Rebells Arme
            bycause the Papists in our Camp do swarme,
        Whose erring faith and great abhomination,
        Ys cause no doubt of our great desolation./   [10]
            Oh witty reason t'other straight reply'de,
            Were they not all Papists on t'other side?/

                    To Maister Bastard, taxing
                    him of flattery.

25.   It was a saying vs'd a great while since
        the subiects euer imitate the Prince
            A vertuous maister, makes a good Disciple
            Religious Prelates, breed a godly peeple,
        And euermore the Rulers inclynation
        works in the time, the chaunge and alteration,
            Then what's the reason Bastard why thy rymes
            magnifie Magistrates, yet taunt the tymes?/
                I think that he to taunt the time that spares not   134.
                Would touch the Magistrate, saue that he dares not.   [10]

Ovids confession translated into
English for Generall Norrice
1593.

26.   To liue in lust I make not my profession
      nor in my vearse my vices to defend,
    But rather by a true and plaine confession
      to make men know, my meaning is to mend./
    I hate, and am my selfe that most I hate,
      I loade my selfe yet striue to be dischardged,
    Like steerlesse Ship vnstaid runns mine estate,
      bound by my self I sew to be enlarged./
    No certaine shape my fancies doth enflame,
      a hundred causes kindell mine affection,   [10]
    Yf sober lookes do show a modest shame,
      straight to those eyes my soule is in subiection./
    A wanton looke no less mine hart doth pierce,
      bycause it shews a pleasant enclynation,
    Yf she be coy, like Sabynes sharpe and fierce,
      I thinke such coyness deepe dissimulation./
    Yf she be learned, I honor guifts so rare
      Yf ignorant I loue a myld simplicitie,   135
    Yf she do prayse my wrytings and compare
      them with the best: in her I take felicitie;   [20]
    If she dispraise my vearses and their maker,
      to winn her lyking I my Loue would lend her./
    goes she well grac't? her gate would make me take her
      Yf ill, perhaps to touche a man would mend her.
    Is she with well tun'd voyce a learned singer
      to snatch a kiss ev'n then I feele a Will,
    Playes she on Lute with sweet and learned finger,
      what hart can hate a hand so full of Skill?
    But if she know with art hir armes to moue,
      and daunce *Cu*rrentoes, with a comly grace,   [30]
    T'omit my self that quickly fall in loue
      Hippolitus would *ha*ue Priapus place
    Like th'auncient Heroynes, I count the tall
      me thinks the*y fill* a braue roome in the bed,
    Yet comlier sports are founde in statures small,
      thus long and short haue ay my lyking bred./
    Yf she goe playn, then what a piece were this,
      Were she attyrd? Yf braue, I like her bravery,
    Fayr, nutbrown, sallow, none do looke amiss,
      My wanton lust is thralld in so great slavery   [40]

If heyr like iett, her neck like Ivory cover,   136
    Lædas was black and that was Ledas glory;
With yeallow locks Aurora pleasd her louer,
    Lo thus my fancie sutes to every story.
The Matron graue, the green young girle and pritty
    I like for age or manners vnsuspitious,
        In fine to all, in contry, court, or citty,
        my Loue doth press to proue it self ambitious./

A wittie speache of Haywood
to Queene Mary./

27.   When good Queene Marie, with much paine and anguish
    did on deaths bed by lingring sicknes languishe,
        Old pleasant Haywood came her grace to visit,
        for mirth to such doth oft more good than phisick,
    Whom when the gracious Princesse had espide,
    Ah Haywood heer they kill me vp she cryde,
        for *being* smoothered quite with too much heate,
        Yet my Phisitions proue to make me sweate,
    But it doth proue so painfull to procure yt,
    that first Ile dy, before I will indure yt./   [10]
        Haywood with cheerfull face, but cherelesse soule
        thus her bad resolution did controule,
            Sweet Ladie you must sweat, or els I sweare yt   137
            We shall all sweat for it, if you forbeare yt./

To mine own from Chester.

28.   When I from thee my deare, last daie departed,
        Summond by honor to this Irish action,
    thy tender eyes shed teares, but I hard harted
        took from those teares a Ioy and satisfaction,
    Such for her spowse (thought I) was Lucres sadnes,
        Whom to his ruin tyrant Tarquin tempted.
    So mourn*e*d she, whose husband fayned madnes,
        thereby from Troian warrs to stand exempted,
            Thus then I do reioyce, in that thou greeuest,
            and yet sweet foole, I loue thee, thou beleeuest./   [10]

Pl. 1& 2   *Orlando Furioso*: title-page of large-paper edition, 1591 and *The Workes of Beniamin Ionson*: title-page of First Folio, 1616. *By permission of the Folger Shakespeare Library.*

Pl 3   Sir John Harington of Kelston (1560–1612) by Hieronimo Custodis, 1590. *By kind permission of the Abbot and Community of Ampleforth Abbey.*

Pl. 4   Mary, Lady Harington (d. 1634) by Marcus Gheeraerts the Younger, 1592. *By kind permission of the Trustees of Tate Britain*

Pl.5   Emblematic Lantern for King James IV: Folger MS V.a.249, p. 256.
By permission of the Folger Shakespeare Library.

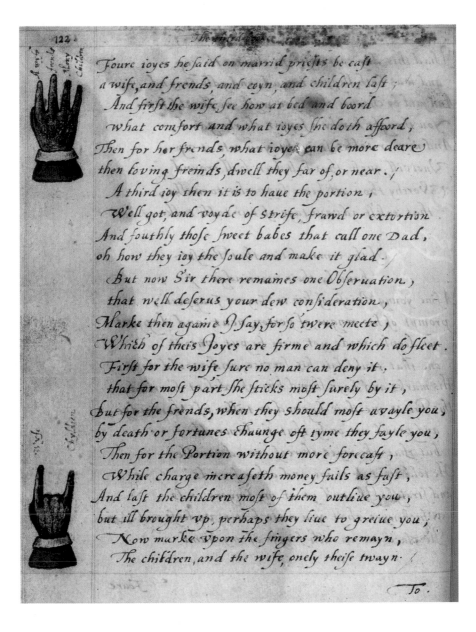

122

The ...

marrs friends
Many Children

Foure ioyes he said on marrid priests be cast
a wife, and frends, and coyn, and children last;
And first the wife see how at bed and boord
what comfort and what ioyes she doth afford,
Then for her frends what ioyes can be more deare
then loving freinds, dwell they far of, or near.;
A third ioy then it is to haue the portion,
Well got, and voyde of strife, frawd or extortion.
And southly those sweet babes that call one Dad,
oh how they ioy the soule and make it glad.
But now Sir there remaines one Obseruation,
that well deserus your dew consideration,
Marke then againe I say, for so 'twere meete;
Which of theis Ioyes are firme and which do fleet.
First for the wife sure no man can deny it,
that for most part she sticks most surely by it,
But for the frends, when they should most avayle you,
by death or fortunes chaunge oft tyme they fayle you,
Then for the Portion without more forecast,
While charge increaseth money fails as fast,
And last the children most of them outliue you,
but ill brought vp perhaps they liue to greiue you;
Now marke vpon the fingers who remayn,
The children, and the wife, onely theise twayn.

To.

Pl. 6   Folger MS V.a.249, p. 122: painted manicules, hand of Scribe
A, autograph annotations and basilisk watermark of Hans Durr.
By permission of the Folger Shakespeare Library.

Pl. 7   McDurnan Gospels Binding of Cambridge University Library
Adv. b.8.1. *By kind permission of Cambridge University Library.*

Pl. 8   Coloured title-page of Cambridge University Library Adv. b.8.1.
By kind permission of Cambridge University Library.

P. 9   Folger MS V.a.249, p. 261: Engraving of Mysteries of the Rosary.
By permission of the Folger Shakespeare Library.

Against lying Lynus

29.*bis*   I wonder Lynus what thy tongue doth ayle
that though I flatter thee thou still dost rayle,
Thou thinkst I lie perhaps, thou thinkst most trew,
Yet to so gentle lyes pardon is dew,
    A ly well told to some tasts *ys* restority,
    beside we Poetts ly by good aucthority./
    But were all lying Poetry I know yt
    Lynus would *quickly* proue a passing poet./

Of lending money on privie seals.   138

29   A frend of mine to me made mickle mone
about some moneys lending in the lone,
    Alleaging that to lend were little greife,
    Yf of repaiment men haue firm beleife,
But other mens examples make vs dredd
to speed as some in other times haue spedd.
    For if one fayle, who then will care for vs
    now I to comfort him replyed thus,
        While God preserus the Prince, ne're be dismayd
        But if she faile be sure, we shalbe payd./   [10]

In defence of Lent./

30.   Our belly gods dispraise the Lenton fast,
    and blame the lingring dayes and tedious time,
And sweare this abstinence too long doth last,
    Whose folly I refute in this my ryme.
Methusalem nine hundred yeares was fed
    With naught but hearbs and berryes of the field,
Iohn Baptist thirty yeares his life had led
    With locusts and wylde honey woods did yeild.
He that the Iseralites from Ægipt brought,
    Where they in slavish thraldome long did dwell.   [10]
He whom to heav'n the fiery Charret raught,   139
    Yea Christ himself (that saues vs all from hell)./
Theis three as holie scriptures do repeate,
in forty dayes did neither drinke nor eate.
Why then should we against this Law repine,
    that are permitted ev'ry kind of fishe,

Are not forbid the tast of costly wyne,
    are not debarrd of many a daynty dishe,
Both sugar, ginger, pepper, Cloues and mace
    And Synamon, and spice of ev'ry kynde,   [20]
And Raysons, figgs, and Almonds in like case,
    to please the taste, and satisfie the mynde.
        And yet forsooth, we thinke we shalbe mard,
        Yf we from flesh, but forty dayes be bard.

        Malum bene positum ne moveas.

32.   A Iudge to one well studied in the laws
    that was too earnest in his clients cawse
        Sayd stirr't no more, for as the cause doth sinke
        into my sence, yt seemeth like a sinke./

        Of Moyses

33.   Most worthy Prophet that by inspiration
    Didst tell of heav'n and earth and seas creation,   140.
        That first deseru'dst the name of sacred poet,
        Now so prophan'd, that fooles on fooles bestow it.
    Thou for thy peopl's libertie and good,
    didst scorne the tytle of the Royall blood
        thou that by grace obtayned from thy God
        from rocks derivedst rivers by thy rod,
    And in that Rod's true reall alteration,
    didst show vndoubted transubstantiation./   [10]
        thou that didst plague all Egipt with their prince
        that ten such plagues were ne're before nor since;
    Thou that didst by thy makers speciall grace,
    Speake with him in the mountayne face to face,
        and there receaudst of him ten hy Behests,
        in stony bookes, for our more stony brests./
    Thou that twise forty dayes, tookst no repast,
    and gau'st two samples, of one Lenton fast,
        thou that in zeale revenge didst take so sore,
        vpon that damned crew Dathan and Core   [20]
    And at another time in rightfull yre,
    consumedst some with sword, and some with fyre
        Obtayn my pardon, if (vntoward Scholler)
        I proue in nothing like thee, but in choller.

And now giue leaue vnto my awfull Muse,   141.
to tell one fault of thine in mine excuse,
    For though I needes must graunt my foollish wrath,
    those lawes to breake sometimes me caused hath.
      I breake but one and one, none for the nonce,
      thou in thy wrath, didst breake them all at once./   [30]

      Against Leda for carping./

34   Last daie dame Leda reading in my ryme
    how Moyses in his anger brake the tables,
      What; haue we byble stories ioyn'd with bables,
Oh Sacriledge, vnexcusable cryme,
And oh (saith she) the manners, oh the time
    that feares not to confound our faith with fables./
Now fy, for shame on wryters so prophane.
but fly from shame, pure Leda is mistane,
    for he that me to speake, and write enables,
Knowes that mine humble hart my Muse acquaints   [10]
With none but reuerent thoughts of all his Saints,
    Who though on earth they subiect were to passion,
    in heav'n they feele no passion, but compassion.
Wherefore surcease Leda thy vayne complaints,
not Saynts but shrowes are subiect vnto skorns.
For sample Leda, now Ile saie but this,   142
thy Husband like to Moyses picture is,
    for Moyses euer painted is with hornes./

      Of a Crow

35   A Baron and a knight, one day were walking,
    on Richmond green, and as they were in talking,
      A Crow that lighted on the rayle by fortune
      Stood becking *and* cryde kaw, with noyse importune.
This byrd (the Baron said) doth you salute,
Sir knight, as if to you, he had some sute;
      Not vnto me, (answerd the knight in pleasance)
      'tis to some Lord, he makes such low obeysance./

Of Divorse

36. A fonde young cowple, making hast to marry
    without their parents, kin, or frends consent
    ere manie yeares were past, did both repent
And spake vnto the Bishops Ordinary,
that they together, may no longer tary
    Sith all their Coyne, and meane, to liue is spent
    they sued to bee devorst incontinent.
And that theyr act so indiscreetly done
Might by his more discretion, be vndone.   143.
Alass said he, this sute no sence doth carry,   [10]
    knotts to vndoe that are so surely ty'ed,
But to teache others witt, by thee my sonne
Parte of your sute shall not bee *you* denide,
    For though the marriadge firm must still abide,
    Yet I will graunt you two, shalbe vndone./

Of Bedas opinion
of Purgatory.

37. Pure Cinna saith, that Beda is a lyer,
    because he writes there is a purging place
    in which men after death must stay a space,
And so bee sau'd yet as it were by fyer./
This question is too deepe for our decision,
    but yet to chardge a wryter with a fable,
    whom all our elders helld so venerable
I thynke such person worthy of derision.
But Cinna that twixt vs bee no devision,
    Thus far I think we might agree togither,   [10]
    these that beleeue it not, shall ne're goe thither./

To his wife in prayse of the warre
of Ireland./

38.   I praisd the speach but cannot now abide it   144
      that warr is sweet to them that haue not tride it.
        For I do prooue it now, and plainly see't
        Yt is so sweet, it maketh all things sweet.
      At home Canary wines and Greeke grew lothesome
      here milke is nectar, water tasteth toothsome.
        At home in silken sparvers, beds of Down
        we skant can rest, but still toss vp and down
      Here I can sleepe, a saddle to my pillow,
      an hedge the curtayn, Cannopie a willow.   [10]
        There if a childe but cry, oh what a spight
        here we can brooke three Larums in a night.
      There without bak't, rost, boyld, yt is no cheere
      Biskett we like, and bonny clabbo heere.
        There I'le complaine of one reer rosted chick,
        here no vile meate, worse cookt, doth make me sick./
      There from each little storme, we shrinke like pulletts,
      here we stand fast, against a storme of bulletts.
        There homely roomes must be perfum'd with roses,
        here match and powder, ne're offends our noses./   [20]
      Lo then how greatly their opinions erre
      that thinke there is not great delight in warre.
        Yet I for this sweet war, am most thy detter,
        I shall for euer loue my home the better.

Against excesse in weomens   145.
Apparrell: to my Lady Rogers.

39.*bis*   Our zealous preachers that would pride repress
      complaine against Apparrells great excess,
      For though the lawes against it are express,
      each Ladie like a Queene her self doth dress,
      A Merchannts wife like to a Barroness,
      but yet Priests wives, if I aright do guess,
      offend no lawes herein, nor more nor less.
        For why no written law proclaim'd or printed
        hath our Priests wiues, for their apparrell stinted./

Of king Henry the 8. his
Woing./

39   Vnto some stately great outlandish Dame
a messenger from our king Henry came,
      That Henry of famous memory the eight
      to treate with her in matters of great weight./
As namely how the king did seeke her marriadge,
because of her great vertues and good carriadge
But she, that heard the king lov'd chaunge of paster,
Reply'de, I greatly thanke the king your master,
      And would (such loue in me his fame hath bred)
      My body venture so: but not my head./   [10]

To King David   146.

40   To princes Prophett, and of Prophetts king
      grown from poore Pastoralls and Sheppards fold
      to chaunge the Sheephooke to a Mace of gold
Subdewing sword and speare, with staffe and sling./
Thou that didst quell the dreadfull beare, and Lion
      With courage vnapalld, and actiue limms
      thou that didst prayse in yet induring himnes
With poetry devine, the god of Sion,
Thou sonne in law to king and prince appointed,
      Yet when that king by wronge did seeke thy harme,   [10]
      didst help him with thy harpe and sacred charm.
And taught'st, no*t once* to touch the lords anoynted.
thou thou great Prince with so rare guifts replenished
      couldst not eschew blynd buzzard Cupids *h*ookes
      lapt in the bayt of Bersabees sweet lookes,
With which one fault thy faultles life was blemished./
Yet hence we learne a document most ample
      that falne by fraylty, we may rise by faith,
      and that the sin forgiv'n, the pennance stay'th
Of grace and Iustice both a sweet example.   [20]
Let no man then himself to sin imbolden
      by thee, but thy sharp pennance, bitter teares.
      May strike into our hartes such godly feares,   147
As we may bee thereby from sin withholden.
      Since we for ours, no iust excuse can bring,
      thou hadst one great excuse, thou weart a king./

Of Monsters, to my Lady Rogers./

42.   Straunge headed monsters painters haue discribed,
to which the Poetts strange parts haue ascribed,
    As Ianus first two faces had assignd him,
    Of which one lookt before, t'other behinde him,
So men maie yet be founde in manie places,
that vnderneath one hood can beare two faces,
    Thre headed Cerberus porter of Hell
    Ys fayn'd with Pluto god of wealth to dwell,
So still with greatest States and men of might,
Dogs dwell that do both barke, and fawne, and bite,   [10]
    Like Hidras heads that multiply with wounds,
    ys multitude that mutinie confounds.
On that seav'n headed beast, the Strumpet sitts
that weares the skarlet, poseth many witts,
    Whether seav'n sins be meant, or els seav'n hills,
    Yt is a question fitt for higher skills.
    But of all theis, if you can rightly conster
    a headles woman is a greater monster.

Of treason   148

43.   Treason doth neuer prosper? What's the Reason?
    for if it prosper none dare call it treason./

A tragicall Epigram.

44.   When doome of peeres and Iudges fore appointed
    by strayning lawes beyond all reach of reason,
Had vnto death condemn'd a Queene annoynted
    and found (oh straunge) without allegeance treason.
That Axe that should haue done that execution,
    Shun'd to cut of a head that had bene crowned,
Our hangman lost his wonted resolution,
    to quell a Queene of noblenes so renowned./
Ah is remorse in Hangmen, and in steele,
When Peeres and Iudges no remorse can feele,   [10]
    Graunt Lord that in this noble yle a Queene
    without an head, maie neuer more be seene./

Of the name Papist Brownist
and Zuinglian./

45.   Pure Lynus papistry layes to my chardge,
                and that my vearse bewrayes my thoughts he saith
        I by deniall could my self dischardge
                Yet least some thinke that I denyde my faithe,   149.
        Euen in my purest thoughts protest do I
        A christian Catholicque to liue and dy./
        As for theis names Papist, and Hugonot,
                Brownist and Zuinglian, that but factions feede,
        I skorne, but christian Catholicque I note,
                that in the scripture nam'd, this in the Creede./   [10]
                But Lynus either I my marke haue mist,
                Or thou of theis may yet choose wh*ich* thou list./

                Of a pleasant Broker

46.   A Broker that was hyr'd to sell a farme
        whose seat was very sound fruitefull and warme
                thinking to grace the sales man with his tale
                said thus: Freinds, Marius sett's this land to sale.
        But thinke not 'tis for debt, or need to sell,
        for as for money he is sto*ar*'d so well
                He hath at all times readie in his Chest,
                and some beside he hath at interest./
        Then were the Chapmen earnestly in hand
        to question of the title of the Land.   [10]
                Why should one sell say they, that letts to vse
                the Broaker driven to seeke some sodayne 'scuse.
        Did study first, and smyling thus replyde,   150.
        His worships sheepe and beasts and hyndes there dyde
        Since which he neuer could the place abyde./
        now though in this, the foolish Broker ly'de,
                Yet th*is* report hereof, did so much harme
                that now poore Marius cannot sell his farme./

To the Lady Rogers

47. To praise my wife your daughter (so I gather)
    your men saie, she resembleth most her father
        And I no less to prayse your sonne her brother
        affirm that he is to much like his mother
            I know not, if we iudge aright or erre
            but let him be like you, so I like her./

To his wife in excuse he had
calld her foole in his wryting./

48. A man in show that skorns, in deed envies
        thy fervent loue, and seekes the same to coole,
        findes fault that in a vearse I calld thee foole,
    And that it could be kyndly tane denyes./
    But thou didst kyndly take yt, then he lyes,
    Well therefore I wish him a wife most wise.
        Noble discended from great De la poole,   151.
        So learn'd to set her husband still to schoole,
    So faire to draw to her all amorous eyes,
        Let flattring tongues protest she doth deserue,   [10]
        that great commaunders her should sew to serue./
    Then let him walke, and with Acteons luck
    Amid the hearde, say welcome fellow bucke,
        Meane while my Mall, think thou 'tis honorable
        to bee my foole, and I to be thy bable./

Against Pius quintus that excomu=
nicated the Queene./

49. Are kings your fosterfathers, Queenes your Nurses
        Oh Romain Church? then why did Pius quintus
        with Basan bulls, like one not Pius intus,
    Laie on our sacred prince, vnhallowe'd Curses,
    'tis not the health of soules, but wealth of purses
        You seeke by such your hell denouncing threats
        oppugning with your Chayres our princes seats,
    Disturbing our sweet peace, and that which worse is,
    You suck out bloud, and byte your Nurses teats.
        Learne, learne, to aske your milke, for if you snatch yt   [10]
        the Nurse must send your babes pap with a Hatchitt.

Of Cinnas studies   152.

50.*bis*   Fiue yeares hath Cinna studied Genesis
            and knowes not yet what in Principio is,
                And greiu'd that he is graueld, thus he skips
                o're all the Byble to th'Apocalips./

                    Of reading Scripture: to his
                        wiues mother./

50   The sacred scripture treasure great affords
                to all of seuerall tongues of sundry Reames
            For weake and lowly sprites in shallow fords
            for highe and curious witts in deeper streames.
                the sondry parts, to sev'rall vse so made
                an Elephant may swim, a mouse may wade./
            Not that all should with barbarous audacity
                reade what them list, and how them list expound
            But by aduise sewting our weake capacity
                for many great scripturians may be founde   [10]
                    that cyte Saint Paule at evry bench and borde
                    and haue Gods word; but haue not God the worde./

                    Of the growth of trees to
                        Sir Hughe Portman.

52.   At your rich Orchard, you to me did show,   153.
            how swift the trees were planted there did grow,
                Namely an Elme, that in no longe abode
                did of a twig grow vp to bee a lode.
            But you would quite condemne your trees of slothe,
            compar'd to our trees admirable grothe,
                Our Planters haue found out such secret skills,
                with Pipe and barrell Staues, and yron Mills.
            That oakes for which, none ten yeares since was willing
            to giue ten groats, are grown worthe thirty shilling./   [10]
                which made my muse so wood she sayd in rage
                that thirst of gold makes this an Iron age.

Against promoting Lynus

53.   Thou Lynus that loues still to be promoting,
           bycause I sport about king Henries marriadge,
           thinkst this will proue a matter worth the carriadg,
       Let it alone Lynus, it is no booting./
       While Princes liue who speakes or writes or teaches
           against their faults, may pay for speach & wryting,
           but being dead, dead men they say leaue byting,/
       Their eyes are seal'd, their arms haue little reaches
           Children they are and fooles that are affeard
           to pull and play, with a dead Lions bearde./   [10]

                   The Story of Marcus life   154
                       at Primero.

54.   Fond Marcus euer at Primero playes
       long winter nights, and as long sommer dayes.
           And I heard once to ydle talke intending
           the storie of his times and coyns mispending.
       As first he thought himself half waie to heave'n
       Yf in his hand he had but got a seav'n.
           His fathers death set him so high on floate
           all rests went vp, vpon a seav'n and coate
       But while he drawes for theis gay coats and gowns
       the gamsters from his purse, draw all his crownes.   [10]
           And he ne're ceast to venter all on prime
           till of his age quite was consum'd the prime./
       Then he more warily his Rest regards
       and setts with certainties vpon two Cards
           on six and thirty, or on seav'n and nine
           if any set his rest, he saith and mine,
       But seeld with this he either gaines or saues
       for either Faustus prime is with three knaves
           or Marcus neuer can encounter right
           Yet drew two Ases, and for further spight   [20]
       Had coullor for yt with a hopefull draught
       But not incountred it avayld him naught,   155.
           Well sith encountring he so fayre doth misse,
           he setts not till he nine and forty is
       And thinking now his rest would sure be doubled,
       He lost yt by the hand, with which sore troubled,
           He ioyns now all his stocke vnto his stake

that of his fortune, he full proofe maie make.
At length both eldest hand, and five and fifty
he thinketh now or neuer (thriue vnthrifty)   [30]
    Now for the greatest rest he hath the pushe,
    But Crassus stopt a club, and so was flushe.
And thus what with the stop, and with the packe,
poore Marcus and his rest goes still to wracke,
    Now must he seeke new sooyle to set his rest,
    for here his seedes turne weedes, his rest vnrest.
His land his plate he pawns, he sells his Leases,
to patch to borrow shift he neuer ceases,
    Till at the last, two Catchpoles him incounter,
    And by Arrest they bear him to the Counter,   [40]
        Now Marcus maie set vp all rests securely
        for now hee's sure to be incountred surely./

        Lesbias rule of prayse.

55.   Lesbia whom some haue thought a louely creature   156.
doth sometime praise some other weomens feature
    Yet this I do obserue that none she prayses
    whom worthie fame, by bewties meritts rayses
But onely of their seemely parts she tells
whom she doth sure beleeue her self excells
    So Lynus prayses Churchyard in his censure
    not Sydney, Daniell, Constable, nor Spensure./

        A wary aunswer

56.   Among some table talke of little waight
    a frend of mine was askt by one great Lady
What sonns he had (my wife (saith he) hath eight)
    Now fy said she, 'tis an ill vse as may bee
I would you men would leaue theis fond conditions
t'envre on vertuous wiues such wronge suspicions
    Tushe said her Lord you giue a causeless blame
The gentleman hath wisely spoke, and well,
    To reckon all his sonns, perhaps 'twere shame,
his wiues sonnes therefore, he doth onely tell   [10]
        Behold how much, it stands a man in steede,
        to haue a frend answer, in tyme of neede./

Of old Haywoods sonne

57. Old Heywoods sonns did wax so wylde and youthfull,
     it made their aged father sad and ruthfull,
         A frend one daie the elder did admonish
         with threats, as did his courage half astonish,
     How that except he would begin to thriue,
     his Syre of all his goods, would him depriue
         for whom, quoth he, ev'n for your younger brother.
         Nay then said he no feare, if't be non other,
     My brother's worse then I, and till he mends
     I know my father, no such wronge intends,   [10]
         Since both are bad to shew so partiall wrath
         to giue his younger vnthrift that he hath./

                 To M^r· Barkley.

58. Your father gaue me once a dorman warrant,
         but sending at Saint Iames tide to the keeper,
     My men came back as from a sleeules Arrant,
         and in a box I layd my warrant sleeper.
             You noble Sir that are his heyr apparant
             Will giue henceforth I hope a waking warrant./

                 Of Faustus the fault finder./

59. Of all my vearses Faustus still complaynes   158
         I wryte them carelesly and why forsooth,
         because he saith they go so plaine and smooth,
     Yt shewes that I for them ne're beat my brayns./
         I that mens errors neuer loue to soothe,
         sayd they, that say so may be thought but noddies
         for sample marke said I your mistris boddies,
     that sit so square, and smooth, down to her raynes,
         that, that fyne waste, thy wealth and wit doth waste,
         thinke you her Taylor wrought it vp in haste,   [10]
     No? aske him and he'ele saie he tooke more paynes
         then with old Ellens double welted frocke,
         that sitts like an old felt, on a new blocke.
     Who cannot wryte, ill iudge of wryters vaynes,
         The worke of Taylors hands, and wryters witts
         was hardest wrought, when as it smoothest sitts./

Young Haywoods answer to
my Lord of Warwicke./

60.*bis*   One neare kin to Haywood by his byrth
and no less near in name and most in myrth
　　Was once for his Religions sake committed
　　Whose case a noble Peere so greatly pittied.
He sent to know what things with him were skannt   159.
and offred frankly to supply his want
　　Thanks to that Lord said he that wills me good
　　for I want all things sauing Hay and wood./

Of an ill Phisition for the body that
became a worse Surgeon for
the Soule./

60   A certaine Mountbank or paltry Leache
　　finding his phisick furdred not his thrift,
　　　　thought with himself to finde some further drift,
And though the skill were far aboue his reache,
he needes would proue a Priest, and fall to preache
　　but patching Sermons with a sorry shift,
As needes they must that e're they learne will teache,
　　at last some foes so nearly doth him sift,
And of such words and deedes did him appeach,
　　As from his lyving quite, they did him lift,   [10]
　　and of the Patron straight they beg'd the guift,
And so the Mountbank did ouer reach.
　　Who when he found he was pursewd so swift,
Gaue place vnto so fierce and sharpe a breache,
Shutting vp all with this shrewd muttring speache./
Well though said he my lyving I haue lost,   160.
Yet manie a good mans life, this losse shall cost.
　　A stander by that would be thought officious,
Strayght as a haynous matter of complainte,
doth with his speach the Iustices acquaint,   [20]
　　Alleadging as it seem'd indeed suspitious,
　　that to the state his meaning was pernitious,
The Leache thus touched with so shrewd a taint,
Yet in his looke, nor action did not faynt
　　protesting that his mynde was not malitious.
　　but if the course that he must take be vitious,
He flatt affirmed yt was curst constraynt,

for of my lyving, hauing lost possession,
I must sayd he turne to my first profession,
  In which I know too well for want of skill, [30]
  my med'cynes many an honest man will kill./

   Of Galla to his wife.

62. Braue Galla late a loftie Prelate wedding
sumptuous at boord, but sumptuous more at bedding
  out of her pride by all men much abhord
  When she will name her husband, saith her lord
Ys this a pryde? 'tis grace I rather guesse,
Sara did saie no more, Galla no less,   161.
Yet when she sayes so next, thus much say I
let Papist none nor Puritan be by,
  For whyle my Lord my husband she doth clatter,
  t'one will deny the first, t'other the latter./ [10]

   A Salisbury tale.

63. Fayr Sarums Church beside the stately tower
  hath manie things in number aptly sorted
answearing the yeare, the monthe, weeke, day and hower,
  but above all, as I haue heard reported
  and to the view doth probably appeare
  a piller for each hower in all the yeare.
Further this Church of Sarum hath bene found
  to keepe in singing seruice so good forme
that most Cathedrall churches haue bene bounde
  themselves to vsum Sarum to conforme. [10]
I am no Cabalist to iudge by number
  Yet that this Church is so with pillers filld
Yt seemes to me to be the lesser wonder
  that Sarums church is ev'ry hower pilld
   And sith the rest are bound to Sarums vse
   What mervaile if they tast of like abuse./

Of Sir Phillip Sidney   162.

64.   Yf that be true the latten prouerb sayes
       Laudari a laudatis is most prayse
            Sidney thy works in fames bookes are enrolld
            by princes penns that haue thy worke extolld
       Whereby thy name shall dure to endles dayes
       But now if rules of contraries should hold
       then I poore I were drownd in deepe disprayse
            Whose worke base wryters haue so much debased
            That Lynus dares pronounce them quite defaced./

                    Of impudent Lynus

65   Not any learning Lynus no god knowes
       but thy brute boldnes makes some to suppose
       that thou mightst haue bene bred in brasen nose
            A murren on thy pate 'twould do thee grace
            So weare thyne head full armd in ev'ry place
            a steeld scull, copper nose and brasen face./

                    Against an vnthrifty
                    Lynus.

66.   Many men mervails Lynus doe's not thriue
       that had more trades than any man aliue.
            As first a Broker, then a Petty fogger   163
            A Traveller a gamster and a Cogger
       A Coyner, a Promoter, and a Bawde
       A Spie a practiser in ev'ry *frawd*
            And missing thrift by theis lewd trades and sinister
            he takes a worse then theis, hee's grown a Minister.

                    Of Faustus

67.   I finde in Faustus such an alteration
       he giues to Paulus wondrous commendation
            is Paulus late to him waxt friendly? no
            but sure poore Faustus fayn would haue it so./

Of a devout vsurer

68.   A Merchannt hearing that great Preacher Smyth
            preach against vsury that art of byting,
        the sermon donne imbrac'd the man forthwith,
            Vnto his borde most frendly him invyting./
        A frend of his hoping some sweet aspertion
            of grace, would move him to some restitution,
        Wisht him in token of his full conversion
            release some dettors held in execution./
        Foole (sayd he) thinke you I will leaue my trade
            No, but I thanke this Preacher learn'd and painfull   [10]   164.
        Because the more he can from it perswade,
            'tis like to proue to me more sweet and gainefull,
                Was euer Iew of Malta or of Millain
                    then this most damned Iew, more Iewish villain.

                Of a reformed
                brother.

69.   In studying scriptures hearing sermons oft,
        thy minde is grown so pliable and soft,
            that though none can attayn to true perfection,
            thy works come neare the words of their direction.
        They councell oft to fast and euer pray,
        thou lovest oft to feast and ever play.
            Sackcloth and Cinders they advise to vse,
            Sack, cloves and sugar thou wouldst haue to chuse.
        They wishe our works and life should shyne like light,
        thy workes, and all thy life is passing light./   [10]
            They bid vs follow still th'Apostles lore
            Apostatas thou follow'st euermore./
        They bid refresh the poore with kinde Almes deeds
        thou ravish dost the poore with all misdeeds.
            They promise ioyes internall neuer wasting.
            You meritt noyse infernall ever lasting./

To his wife   165

70.*bis*   Your mayde Brunetta you with newes acquaints,
                how Leda, whom her husband wanting yssew
           Brought earst to Bath, our pilgrimage of Saints,
                Weares her gown vellet, kirtle cloth of Tissew,
                a fugerd Sattin petticote Carnation,
                With six gold Parchman laces all in fashion.
           Yet neither was Dame Leda nobler borne,
                nor drynks in gossips cup by sov'raigne sent,
           Nor ever was her highnes woman sworne.
                Nor doth her husband much exceede in Rent,   [10]
                Then Mall be proud that you may better weare them,
                and I more proud, you better do forbeare them./

                  Against an extreame flatterer that
                    preached at Bathe on the Queens
                        day the fortith yeare of
                            her Raigne./

70   You that extoll the bliss of this our nation,
                and lade our eares with stale and loathsome prayse
                of forty yeares sweet peace and restfull dayes,
           Which you advaunce with fayned admyration,
           Much better would yt sute your high vocation,
           To beat down that your flattring tongues do rayse,   166.
                And rather seeke some words of Commination,
                for times abounding with abhomination,
           Say that gods wrath against vs is provoked,
                and tell vs 'tis to vs the scripture sayes   [10]
                I forty yeares haue dur'd this generation,
           And sayd theise people haue not known my wayes.
                    For law with lust and rule with rape is yoaked,
                    And zeale with schisme and Symony is choaked./

Of Sheepe whose sheapheards
are Wolues./

72.   When harts obdurate make of sin an habit,
       high frowning Nemesis was wont to send
       Beares, Lions, Wolues, and serpents to this end
to spoyle the coasts where so bad folks inhabit,
Now since this age in habit, and in act
       excells the sins of ev'ry former age,
       no mervayle Nemesis in her iust rage,
Doth like or greater punishment exact,
And for this cause a crewell beast is sent.
       not onely that devours and spoyles the people,   [10]
       but spares not house nor village Church nor steeple
And makes poore widdowes mourne, Orphans lament,   167
You muse perhaps what beasts they bee that keepe
       So beastly rule as seeld was seene before,
       'tis neither beare nor lion, bull nor bore,
But beasts then all theise beasts more harmfull, sheepe./
       Lo then the misterie of whence the name
       Of Cotsold Lions first to England came./

Of an Horoycall answer of a great
Romain Ladie to her
husband./

73.   A graue wise man that had a great rich Lady,
Such as perhaps in theis dayes found there may be,
       Did thinke she playd him false, and more then thinke,
       saue that in wisedome, he thereat did winke./
Howbeit one time dispos'd to sporte and play,
thus to his wife he pleasantly did say.
       Sith straungers lodge their arrows in thy Quiuer,
       Deare dame I pray you yet the cause deliuer
Yf you can tell the cause and not dissemble,
how all our children me so much resemble.   [10]
       The Lady blusht, but yet this answer made
       though I haue vs'd some trafficque in the trade,
And must confess, as you haue toucht before,   168
my barke was sometime steerd with forrayn ore.
       Yet stow'd I no mans stuffe, but first perswaded
       the bottom with your ballast, full was laded./

To the great Ladies of
the Courte

74.   I haue bene told most noble courtly Dames,
that ye commend some of mine Epigrames,
 but yet I heare againe which makes me pensiue,
 some are of them to some of you offensiue,
Those that you like Ile giue and aske no guerdon,
So that you graunt those that mislike you pardon,
  Both are the fruictles fruits of ydle howres,
  theis for my pleasure reade, and those for yours./

Of Lynus borrowing

75.   When Lynus meets me after salutacions,
Curtesies *and* Complements, and gratulacions,
 He presses *mee* ev'n to the third denyall,
 to lend him twenty shillings, or a Ryall.
But of his purpose with his Curtsies failling,
he goes behinde my back cursing and raylling.
  Foole thy kind speaches cost not thee a penny,   169.
  and more foole I, if they should cost mee enny./

Of one M^r. Careless

76   Where dwells Maister Careless? Iesters haue no dwelling,
where lyes he? in his tongue, by most mens telling,
Where bords he? there where feasts are found by smelling,
Where bytes he? all behinde, with all men melling./
Where bydes he man? oh sir I mist your spelling,
 Now I will reade, yet well I do not wott,
 but if that I to him shall poynt his lott,
  In Shottover, at Dogs head in the pott,
  for in that signe, his head's oft overshott./

Against Momus in praise of
his dog Bunguy./

77   Because a witty wryter of this tyme
doth make some mention in a pleasant ryme
    of Lepidus, and of his famous dog,
    thou Momus that dost loue to skoffe and cog,
Prat'st amongst base companions and giu'st out
that vnto me therein is meant some flout.
    Hate makes thee blynde Momus, I dare be sworne
    He meant to me his loue, to thee his skorne,   170
Put on thine envies spectacles and see,
Whom doth he skorne therein? the dog or mee.   [10]
    The dog is grac't compared with gray Banks,
    both beasts right famous for their pretty pranks,
Although in this I graunt the dog was wurse,
he onely fed my pleasures not my purse;
    Yet that same dog (I may say this and bost yt)
    hath found my purse with gold when I haue lost it.
Now for my self some fooles, like thee, may iudge
that at the name of Lepidus I grudge,
    No sure, so far I thinke it from disgrace
    I wishe it cleaue to me and all my race.   [20]
Lepus or Lepos. I in both haue parte,
that in my name I beare, this in mine harte./
    but Momus I perswade my self that no man
    will deign thee such a name English nor Romayn,
        I'le wage a Butt of Sack, the best in Bristo,
        Who calls me Lepido, will count thee Tristo.

Of Faustus

78   Now Faustus sayth long Epigrams are dull
Lowt, *Larks* are loathsome when ones paunch is full
    Yet whom the short do please, the long *not* weary   171.
    I wish them *weary* neuer, euer merry./

Of Summum bonum

79.   While I of summum bonum was disputing
propounding some positions, some confuting
    Old Sextus sayes that we were all deluded

and that not one of vs aright concluded
knowledge saith he is onely true felicity
straight way a straunger askt me in simplicity
   Is Sextus learn'd? quoth I, no by this light.
   then without light, how iudgeth he so right,
      He doth but ayme, as poore men vallew wealth,
      the feeble vallew strength, the sickman healthe./   [10]

        To Mall to comfort her for
        losse of a Childe

80.*bis*   When at the window thou thy doues art feeding,
then thinke I shortly my Doue wilbe breeding,
   Like will loue like, and so my lyking like thee,
   as I to Doues in many things can like thee,
Both of you loue your lodgings dry and warme,
both of you do your neighbours little harme.
   Both loue to feed vpon the fynest grayn,   172
   both for your liuings take but little payn,
Both murmur kyndly, both are often billing,
Yet both to Venus sports will seem vnwilling./   [10]
   Both do delighte to looke your selues in glasses,
   You both loue your own howses as it passes,
Both fruitefull are, but yet the Doue is wiser.
for though she haue no freind that can advise her,
      She patiently can take her younge ones loss,
      thou too impatiently dost beare such cross./

        Of the excuse of Symony.

80   Clerus I heare doth some excuse alleadge
of his and all his fellows sacriledge,
   As namely that 'tis sore against their wills,
   that men are bound to take the less of ills.
that they had rather (no man needes to doubt yt)
take lyvings with the lands, then thus without yt,
   And therefore we must lay this haynous cryme,
   not vnto them forsooth, but to the tyme./
Alas a fault confest were half amended,
but sin is doubled that is thus defended.   [10]
   I know a right wise man sayes, and beleeues,
   where no receiuors are there be no theeues./

In commendation of M^r· Lewkners booke   173
of the discription of Venice, dedicated
to the Lady Warwick.
Febr: 3. 1598.

82   Lo here discrib'd though but in little roome,
　　　faire Venice, like a spouse in Neptunes armes,
for freedom emulous to auncient Roome,
　　　famous for councell much, and much for Armes.
Whose stories written ear'st with Tuskan quill,
　　　lay to our english witts as half concealed,
Till Lewkners learned travaile and his skill,
　　　In well grac'te style and phrase hath yt revealled.
Vennis be proud that thus augments thy fame,
England bee kynde, inricht with such a booke.   [10]
　　　Both giue dew honor to that noble dame,
　　　for whom this taske the wryter vndertooke./

Of one that gaue a Benefice./

83.   A Squyre of good account affirmd he meant
A learn'd man to a lyving to present,
　　　But yet that Squyre in this did breake the square,
　　　he purposed thereof to keepe a share
To sett two sonnes to schoole to make them Clarcks,
He doth reserue each yeare one hundred marks   174
　　　Ah said the Priest, this carde is too too coolling
　　　I set your sonns? nay they set me to schoolling./

Of a Lady that giues
the Cheeke

84.   Ys't for a grace, or is't for some disleeke,
where other kiss with lip, you giue the cheeke,
　　　Some note yt for a pride in your behavor,
　　　but I should rather take yt for a favor,
For I to shew my kindnes and my loue
would leaue both lip and cheeke to kiss your gloue
　　　Now with the cause to make you playn acquainted
　　　Your gloue's perfum'de, your lip, and cheek are painted./

Of Balbus a Poett

85.   Balbus of wryters reckning vp a rabble
         thinks their names are by him made honorable,
             And not vouchsafing me to name at all,
             he thinks that he hath greiv'd me to the gall./
         I galled? Simple soule, no thou art gulled,
         to think I way the prayse of such a dulhead,
         Those that are guilty of defect and blame
         Do neede such testimonialls of their fame,   175.
             Learne then vntaught, learn then you envious Elues,
             books are not prays'd, that do not prayse themselues./   [10]

Of Faustus fishing

86.   With siluer hooke, Faustus for flesh was fishing,
         but that game byting not vnto his wishing,
             He said he did being thus shrewdly matcht,
             fish for a Roache, but had a gudgen catcht.
         Faustus it seemes thy lucke therein was great,
         for sure the gudgen is the better meate.
             Now bayt againe, that game is set so sharpe,
             that to that gudgen thou maist catch a Carpe.

To his frend of the
Booke of Aiax.

87.   You muse to finde in me such alteration,
             that I that maydenly to wryte was wont,
             would now sett to a booke so desperate front
         As I might skant defend by immitation,
         My Muse that time did neede a strong purgation,
             late having tane a bruse, by lewd reports,
         And when the phisick wrought you know the fashion
         Whereto a man in such a case resorts,   176.
             And so my Muse with good decorum spent
             on that base tytled booke her excrement./   [10]

To Leda.

88.　In vearse for want of ryme, I know not how
　　　I calld our Bathes the pilgrimage of Saynts,
　　You Leda much the phrase did disallow,
　　　　and thinke this touch, your pure Religion taynts,
　　　　　good Leda bee not angry, for god knowes
　　　　　though I did wryte of Saynts, I meant of Shrows./

To Sextus an yll Reader

89.　That Epigram that last you did rehearse,
　　　was sharpe, and in the making neat and tearse,
　　　But thou dost read so harshe, poynt so perverse,
　　　Yt seem'd now neither witty, nor a vearse
　　　　For shame poynt better, and pronounce it clearer,
　　　　Or be no reader Sextus, be a hearer./

To my Wife

91.　Your mother layes yt to me as a cryme,
　　　that I so long do stay from you sometime,
　　　And by her fond surmise would make you feare,　　　177.
　　　my loue doth grow more cold, or less sinceare.
　　　　But let no causles doubts make you beleeue,
　　　　that being false, that being true would greeue.
　　　I when I am from thee the farthest distance,
　　　doe in my soule by my true loues Assistance
　　　　in steed of sweet imbracements, douelike kisses,
　　　　send kyndest thoughts, and most indeered wishes./　　　[10]
　　　Then letters, then kynde tokens pass, and then,
　　　my busie Muse imployes my ydle pen.
　　　Then memory in loues defence alledges,
　　　Nine organ pipes our loues assured pledges,
　　　Alas how many liue still with their wiues,
　　　Yet in true kyndnes absent all their liues.
　　　　Absence is true loues sawce, and servs to whet yt,
　　　　they neuer lou'd, whom absence makes forget yt.

Of Cleargie men and their
Livings./

90   In auncient time old men observed that
the Cleargie men were lean, their lyvings fat,
But in theise dayes the case is altred cleane,
The Cleargie men are fat their lyvings leane,
    I searching finde th*is* cause that chaunge to breed   178
    Now they feede fast, then they did fast and feede./

That Misacmos and Lynus
are like.

92.   I mervayle Lynus of thy foollish blyndnes
that of all men, with me wilt haue vnkyndnes
    Whereas we two, (to speake without dissembling)
    in many things are very much resembling./
Thou boasts and truly maiste of some nobillity
I without boast, can boast of true gentillyty,
    I of complexion black, yet somwhat ruddy,
    thou somwhat fayrer, yet perhaps more bluddy./
At Cambridge thou sometimes thy horse hast bayted,
At Cambridge I sometimes in schooles was bayted./   [10]
    Thou often art alone in dumps and Muses,
    And I as oft alone am with the Muses,
I borrow of all I may to mend my sence,
thou borrowst all thou canst for thyne expence,
    I rob some I do reade with prayse for guardon,
    thou robst some thou dost meete in hope of pardon.
Many men will trust me for all they'r worth
any man may trust thee for all th'art worth.
I beare the prime of my witts wealth about me,   179.
thou wearst the pryme of all thy wealth about thee.   [20]
Onely in one conceyt thou dost not like me,
on which I wish I neuer may bee like thee,
    I pray for forrayn peace, thou civile warfare,
    for I haue somwhat, thou hast nought to care for./

Of a Seller of time

93. When of your Lordship I a Lease renewd,
    You promist me before we did conclude,
       to giue me time, namely twice twelumonths day,
       for such a fine as I agreed to pay./
    I bad a hundred pound, 'twas worth no more,
    Your Lordship set it higher by a score.
       Now since I haue by computacion founde,
       that two yeares day, cost me this twenty pound.
          Sir, pardon me to be thus playnly told yt,
          Your Lordship gaue not two years day, you sold yt.   [10]

Of the Parsons Part

94. Whether it were by chaunce, or els by art
       You finde our vearse in number so well couched
    that each tenth Stanze may seeme the Parsons part.
       Marking the matters that therein are touched.   180.
    But sure I am some Parsons are so curst,
       that though tis theirs and I bestow it freely,
    Yet they of all will like that part the wurst,
    Yea thoughe you search from Salisbury to Eely./
       For in all persons this a fault is knowne.
       to lust for others good, and loath their owne./   [10]

Of the Earle of Essex

95. Great Essex now of late encurred hath,
    his mistris indignation and her wrath,
    and that in him she chiefly disallowth,
    She sent him north, he bent him to the South,
       Then what shall Essex do? let him henceforth
       Bend all his witts, his powr and courage Northe./

Of Sextus witt

96. To haue good witt is Sextus thought by many,
    but sure he hides it all, he showes not any.

To the Earle of Essex when he lay
at Grayes and protested to
liue retyred./

97.   Of*t* reading acts admir'd of Charles the fift,   181.
            mine envious mynde and captious in condicion,
        In his liues course discouered hath one drift,
            convincing him of infinite ambicion,
        For having ioyn'd the'imperiall Crowne to Spayn,
            (this grown by byrth, that graunted by election)
        After the conquests great he did attayn,
            getting both Indies vnder his subiection,
        Sicke of ambicion that disease incurable,
            (like Allexander that more worlds would gayn)   [10]
        Fynding his kingdoms great, but nothing durable,
            Yet of an endles thirst he had to raigne,
                Playnly to proue he higher still aspyred,
                he quite renounc't all theise and liu'd retyred./

            Of himself.

98   Because in this my self contenting vayn,
            to wryte so many toyes I borrow leasure,
        Frends sorrow, fearing I take too much payne
            Foes envy swearing I tast too much pleasure
                I smyle at both and wishe to ease their greifs
                that each with other, would but chaunge beleefes.

            Of a Devout Lawier.   182.

99.   I met a Lawier at the Court this lent
        and asking what straunge cause him thither sent
            He said that mou'd with Doctor Androes fame
            to heare him preache onely he thither came
        But straight I wisht him frendly in his eare
        devise some other cause else some will sweare
            Who to the Court come onely for devotion,
            they in the Churche pray onely for promotion.

Of Bathes Cure vpon
Marcus.

99.bis   The fame of Bathe is great and still indures
that oft it worketh admirable cures,
    The barren by their vertue haue conceaved,
    the weake and sick haue health and strength receaued
And many cripples that came thither carried
go sound from thence, when they a whyle haue tarryed.
    But yet one cure on Marcus lately showne,
    my Muse doth thinke most worthy to make known.
For whyle he bathes with Gascoyn wines and Spanish,
thereby old Aches from his limbs to banish,   [10]
    Hunts after youthfull company, entycing
    Them to the sports of bowlling, carding, dycing,   183
    His wantonnes breedes want, his want inforces,
    Marcus by one and one sells all his horses,
        Lo how the Bathe hath searcht his sicknes roote,
        He can, nay more he must goe thence on foote./

Of a Lady that sought remedy
at the Bathe.

[99*ter*]   A lady that no name nor blame none hath,
came the last yeare with others to the Bath,
    Her person comely was, good was her feature,
    in bewty, grace, and speach, a louely creature./
Now as the Ladie in the water stayd,
a playn man fell a talking with her mayd
    that leand vpon the *ray*ll and askt the reason,
    Why that fayr Lady vs'd the bath that season,
Whether 'twere lamenes, or defect of hearing,
or els some inward evill not appearing./   [10]
    No, sayd the mayde to him (beleeue it well,)
    that my fayr mistris sound is as a bell./
But of her comming, this is true occasion,
an old Phisition mou'd her, by perswasion
    Theis bathes haue powr to strengthen that debillity.
    that doth in man *or* woman breed sterrillity.   184
Tush sayd the man with playn and short discourse,
Your mistris might haue tane a better Course,
    Let her to Oxford to the vniversity,
    Where young Phisitions are, and such diversity   [20]

Of toward sprites that in all arts proceede,
much better then the Bathe ys for the deed./
    No, no, that will not serue the mayde replyde,
    for she that phisick hath allready tryde./

    Of two frayle Saynts

100   One of the foollish famely of Loue,
    that of theyr sure election stand so glorious,
    they thinke that ev'n their sins are meritorious,
Did earst a sister to his pleasure moue,
    Alledging sith no sin their souls could taynt,
    they might beget some Prophet or a Saynt./
She graunted or at least she not denyde,
    to giue to his foule lust full satisfaction,
    Yet in the midst of their venereous action,
Rapt in her flesh with zeale of sprite she cryde,   [10]
    How would the wicked and vngodly scoffe yt
    Yf they should fynd vs saynts getting a Prophitt.

    The last Epigram of the frayle   185.
    Saynts, translated into
    latten.

Ex famulis vnus nam sic vocitantur amoris
    Huius at haud parva est Economia dei
Concubitus sacræ fertur petijsse puellæ
    Talibus atque ipsam sollicitasse modis
Cum nullum electis in vita crimen inhæret
    Nec tibi quicquid agas sit dubitanda salus
Quin nos ex sancto generamus semine prolem,
    Exiat ex vtero forte propheta tuo,
Annuit atque ardens meretrix peperisse prophetam,
    Excipit instantem semisupina virum,   [10]
Et tandem medio veneris iam concita motu
    Ediderat tales voce tremente sonos,
Ah quanta reprobi tollent leuitate chachinnos,
    Si sanctam sancto succubuisse sciant./

    The end of the third
    Booke./

The Fourthe booke of   186.
Epigrams.

How England may be reformed

1.   Men say that England late is bank'rout grown
th'effect too manifest, the cause vnknown,
    Rich Treasorers 'tath had, and wary keepers,
    Fat Iudges, Councellors in gayn no sleepers,
Collectors, Auditors, Receavors meny,
Searchers, and Custamers all for the peny,
    As for the Churchmen they both pray and pay,
    Solvat Ecclesia so the Courtiers pray./
      Might some new officer mend old disorder,
      Yes, one good Stewart might set all in order./   [10]

To a great Magistrate in
Re and in Spe

2.   Those that for Princes good do take some payn,
    their good to whom of right all payn we owe,
Seeke some rewarde for service good to gayn,
Which oft their gratious goodnes doth bestow,
    I for my travayle beg not a rewarde,
    I beg less by a Sillable, a Warde./

To Doctor Sherwood the Phisition   187
of Bathe./

3.   Because among some other ydle glaunces,
I of the Bathes say sometimes as yt chaunces
    that this an onely place ys in this age,
    to which fayr Ladies come in pilgrimage,
You feare such wanton gleekes and yll report
may stop great States that thither would resort.
      No neuer feare yt, pray but for fayr weather,
      Such speach as this will bring them faster thether./

Of Marcus Curtesie

4.   When I some little purchase haue in hand
straight Marcus kyndly offers me his band,
    I tell him and he takes it in great snuffe,
    his is a falling band, I weare a Ruffe./
But if you mervayle I his help refuse,
and mean herein some meaner mans to vse,
        The cause is this: I feare within a weeke,
        that he of me like curtesie will seeke./

Of one that had a blacke
heade and a gray beard.

5.   Though manie search, yet few the cause can finde   188.
    Why thy beard gray, thy head continews blacke,
Some thinke thy beard more subiect to the wynde,
    Some thinke that thou dost vse that new found knack,
    Excusable in such as hayre do lacke,
A quaynt Gregorian to thine head to bynde.
Some think that with a Combe of drossy leadd,
    thy silver locks do turne to coullor *darke*,
Some thinke 'tis but the nature of thine head,
    But we thinke most of theise haue mist the marke,   [10]
        For thus thinke we, that thinke we thinke aright,
        thy beard and yeares are graue, thy head is light.

Against an old Letcher

6.   Since thy third curing of the french infection,
Priapus in thee hath found no erection,
    Yet eatst thou Ringos and Potato rootes,
    and Caveare, but it little bootes./
Besides the beds head bottle lately found
of Lycour, that a quarte cost twenty pound,
    For shame, if not more grace, yet shew more wytt,
    Surcease now sin leaues thee to follow yt,
        Some smyle, I sighe to see thy madnes such,
        That that which stands not, stands thee in so much./   [10]

To his wyues mother reprouing   189.
her vnconstancy.

7.   Last yeare while at your house I hapt to tarry
of all your goodes you tooke an Inventary,
    Your Tapistry, your lynnen, bedding, plate,
    Your sheepe, your horse, your cattell you did rate,
And yet one moueable you did forget
More moueable then the*as* therein to sett,
    Your wav'ring mynd I meane, which is so moueable,
    that you for yt, haue euer bene reproueable./

Of a Cuckold that had
a Chast wife./

8.   When those Trivmvirs set that three mans songe
        which stablished in Rome a hellish trynity,
that all the towne, and all the world did wronge,
        killing their frends and kin of their affinity
            By tripertite Indenture parting Rome
            as if the world for them had wanted rome,
    Plotyna, wife of one of that same hundred
        whom Anthony proscrib'd to lose their life,
    for bewty much, for loue to be more wondred,
        sew'd for her spowse and told she was his wife./   [10]
            The Tyrant pleasd to see so *fayr* a Sewtor,   190.
            Doth kiss her and imbrace her, and salute her,
    Then makes nay mocks a loue, too kynd, too cruell,
        She must to saue her husband from proscription,
    Graunt him one night her husbands chiefest Iewell
        and what he meant he shewd by lewd discription./
            Vowing except he might his pleasure haue
            no meanes should serue her husbands life to saue.
    Oh motion moving thoughts, no thoughts but thornes
        either he dyes whom she esteemes most deerly,   [20]
    Or she her self subiects to thowsand skorns,
        both feares to touche a noble Matron neerly./
            Lo yet an act performed by this woman,
            worthy a woman, worthy more a Roman./
    To shew more then her self she lov'd her Spowse,
        she yeilds her body to this execution.
    Come Tyrant come performe thy damned vows
        her single hart hath doubled thy pollution,

thou pollute her? no foole thou art beguiled,
   She in thy filthy lap lyes vndefyled./   [30]
Honour of matrons of all wiues a mirrour,
   Ile swear with thee thy husband weares no horne,
or If this act convince mine oath of errour,
   'Twas a most pretious one an Vnicorne./   191.
     Yf ought I know by hearing, or by reeding,
     this act Lucretias deed is far exceeding./

To his wife of Particion

9.   Some Ladies with their lords devide their states
   and liue so when they list in seuerall rates,
     But Ile indure thee Mall on no condicion,
     to sew with me a writt of such particion,
   Twise seave'n yeares since most solemnly I vowd
   with all my worldly goods I thee indow'd.
     Then house, plate stuffe, not part but all is thyne,
     Yet thus that they and thou and all are myne.
   Wherefore let me go sew my writt of dotage,
   Yf I with thee part house or close or cottage,   [10]
     for where this is my Lords, and that my Ladies,
     there some perhaps thinke likewise of their babies./

Of two Religions./

10.   One by his father kept longe time to schoole
   and prouing not vnlearned nor a foole
     Was er'st by him demaunded on occasion
     which was the sounder Church in his perswasion.
   Yf this Church of Geneua late reformed   192.
   or that old Catholicque that theise haue skorned
     Both do cyte Doctors, Councells both alledge
     both boast the word, truths everlasting pledge./
   Then say my sonne (quoth he) feare no controwle
   Which of the two is safest for my soule./   [10]
     Sure (quoth the sonne) a man had neede be crafty
     to keepe his soule and body both in saf'ty.
     But both to saue, this is best way to hold
     die in the new, *live* if you *list* in th'old./

Of Simpathy

11.   If as some thinke the simpathy of minds,
        is token of sweet loue and kynd accord,
    great Simpathies and in most divers kyndes,
        are between Lesbia and her noble Lord./
    If he to goe from home can take occasion,
        full glad is he, and doth thereat reioyce,
    As glad is she and addeth her perswasion,
        nor would she haue him stay to haue her choyce,
    Sad he returns and seeld but by compulsion,
        for three days fish and guests are thought vnsavery,   [10]
    As glad is shee, her hart feeles great convulsion.
        His presence checks her mirth, her sport, her bravery,   193.
    After he hath a while at home been byding,
        he chafes, he swears nor meat nor drinke is toothsome
    As fast his loving Lady falls to chyding,
        As fast she sweares all cates to her are loothsome./
    He shames sometimes at her new made complections,
        he feares least she should spy his secret sallyings,
    She Shames no lesse at his known imperfections,
        She doubts no less least he discry her dallyings./   [20]
    On hounds and hauks he frankly spends his crowns,
        and horses and such purt'nances of sports.
    As much she spends on kyrtles and on gowns,
        and on some Ruffen that to her resorts./
    Their pray'rs are like, their vows are short and small,
        If so it be with vocall pray're or mentall,
    Each prayes to see t'others funerall,
        but neither greatly cares of Dirge or trentall./
    Thus in their ioy, their sorrow, and their wrath,
        their shame, their feare, their bounty, and their prayre   [30]
    All their whole life so great resemblance hath,
        they make a matchless matche, a peereless payre.
        Sweet Simpathy, I know not who the Devill
        should well agree, if theise agree but evill./

Of Lynus the Wryter   194.

12.   Thou Lynus thinks thy selfe a great endyter
        and now of late thou raisest high thy lookes
        bycause the Stationers do sell thy bookes
    But shall I tell thee true thou art no wryter

thou blottest papers, onely they do wryte
whose wrytings men of worth, reed with delight./

Of a Lady that lookt well to hir
borders. To Sir Iohn Lee./

13.   A lady of high byrth, great reputacion,
       all cloth'd in seemly and most sumptuous fashion
          wearing a border of rich pearle and stone,
          esteemed at a thousand crowns alone,
       To see a certayn Enterlude repayrs,
       through a great press, vp a darke payr of Stayrs.
          Her page did beare a torche that burn'd but dimly,
          two cosning mates *that saw* her deckt so trimly,
       Did place themselus vpon the Stayrs to watch her,
       and thus they layd their plott to conny catch her.   [10]
          One should as 'tweare by chaunce strike out the light
          while t'other that should stand beneath her might
       Attempt (which modesty to suffer lothes)
       Rudely to thrust his hand vnder her clothes,   195.
          that while her hand repelld such gross disorders,
          his mate might quickly slip away her borders./
       Now though this act to her was most vnpleasant,
       Yet being wise (as weomens witts are present)
          straight on her borders both her hands she cast,
          and so with all her force she held them fast.   [20]
       Villayns she cryde, you would my borders haue,
       but I'le saue them, t'other it self can saue.
          this whyle the Page had got more store of light,
          the cosning mates for feare slipt out of sight,
             Thus her good witt, their cunning overmatcht,
             were not thei*s* conny catchers connycatcht?/

Of Thais and Clerus

14   Fayr Thayis skarce had widdow been a weeke
      when Clerus came a match with her to seeke,
         and to set fourth more stately his approache,
         he hyred men and horses and a Coache,
      But as he was dismounting at her gate,
      the Porter told he came one hower too late,
            For she was newly married that fore noone,
            Farewell (quoth Clerus) then I came to soone.

In praise of my Lady *R:*
and her musick.

15.   Vpon an instrument of pleasant sounde   196.
      a lady playd more pleasing to the sight
I being askt in which of theis I found
      greatest content, my sences to delight
          Ravisht in both at once as much as may be
          said sweet was Musick, sweeter was the Lady./

Of Lælias Count=es ship.

16.   When louely Lelia was a tender gerle
she hapt to be defloured by an Earle.
          Alas good wenche, thou wear't to be excused,
          such curtesies oft are offred seeld refused,
Yet bee not proude for she that is no Countis,
and yet lyes with a Count must make account this,
          All Countesses in honor her surmount,
          bycause they haue, she had a noble Count./

How Faustus lost not
his labour.

17.   When you fond Faustus in an ydle sute
had quite consum'd long time *with* little frute./
          Though you confest you had your labour lost   197.
          Yet you gain'd witt thereby, you made your bost
But if you would indeed examin dewly
Your gaynes and loss, and then account them truly,
          Thus to transfer those words it would be fitt,
          You gayn'd the travayle, but you lost the witt./

To his wife in excuse
of his absence.

18.   Mall in mine absence this is still your song,
come home sweet hart you stay from home to long,
          that thou lou'st home my Loue I like yt well,
          Wiues should be like thy Tortes in the shell,
I loue to seeke, to see learn, know, be known,

Men nothing know, know nothing but their owne./
   Yea but you say to me home homely is,
   and comely there vnto, and what of this,
Amonge wisemen they deemed are but Momes,
that allwayes are abyding in their homes,   [10]
     To haue no home, perhaps it is a Curse,
     to be a Prisoner at home 'tis wurse./

       Of a pure preaching Phisition./

20   The zealous preacher Lalus as they tell   198.
    doth practice phisick now: 'tis wondrous well
    for first he taynts souls with erronious spell
    and then his druggs giue quick dispatch to hell.
     God keepe my frends and all of our affinity
     free from his phisick, far from his devinity.

      Of goats milke and Cowes milke between
        a Phisition and a Lady. To my
          Lady Rogers

21   A learned lady of no meane condicion
    question'd one day with a more learn'd Phisition,
     Affirming 'twas but error, or presumption
     that men prescribe to Patients in consumption,
    As they that mark yt, oftentimes shall note,
    sometime an Asses milk, sometimes a gote,
     But I sayd she, for my part do allow
     better then both theis milks that of a cow,
    As hauing sweeter flesh, and finer feeding
    and therefore better bloud and humours breeding.   [10]
     The Learned Leache incombred thus and troubled,
     (for she her words and reasons still redoubled)
      Madam quoth he 'tis not so good by halfe,
      except the patient hap to be a Calfe.

Misacmos of himself that loues   199.
to be worst in the company.

21.*bis*   When I from schooles came to the citty first
my Syre advis'd me warily to chuse
all such as for companions I would vse
So if I could as I might bee the wurst.
For why the grauer and the wiser sort
Men like their chief companions do esteeme
and such they do their inclynation deeme
A*s* their's is known with whom they do consort
Now while I thought I had some prayse deserved
that longe haue sought this rule to haue obserued,   [10]
to daunt my pryde herein I haue bene told,
Faustus as strict as I this course doth hold,
nay more he cannot breake yt if he would./

Of one that kept open house
at Christmas./

22.   This Christmas Paulus for his reputacion
to keepe an open house makes proclamacion
to which (to make it noted) he annexes
theise generall words: for all of both the Sexes
Yf Paulus meaning bee but as he wrytes
he keepes house onely for Hermaphrodites.

An Epitaphe on M^r. Iohn Ashley some=   200.
times M^r. of the Iewills to her Matie.
Sent to his vertuous widdow &
his worthy sonne S^r. Iohn Ashley./

23.   Loe here in Ashes, worthy Ashley lyes
A Iewill to his prince her Iewills master
His corps here shryn'd in Tutch and Allablaster
his soul vntoucht mounts o're the marble skies
Once happie here in Court by Princes eyes,
Eyes whose aspect defends from all disaster
Thrice happie now in heav'nly Hierarchies
Where his soule crownd, sees his all seeing Master
By birth a Squyre, a Barron by his roome,
Now is a kingdome given him by his Toome./   [10]

A translation of the Earle of Surreys
out of Martiall directed by him to
one Maister Warner./

24.   Warner the things for to attayne
            the happie life: are theis I finde./
            the ritches left, not got with payne
                the frutefull feild, the quiet mynde,
            the egall frends, no grudge nor strife
                no chardge of rule, or governance,
        Without disease the healthfull life   201.
            the houshold of continuance
            the meane diet, no delicate fare
            wisedome ioynd with simplicity   [10]
            the night discharged of all care
            Wher wyne maie beare no sov'raignty
            the chaste playne wife without debate
            such sleepe as may beguile the night
            contented with thine own estate
            neither wishe death, nor fear his might.

            To M^r· Iohn Davis./

25.   My deare frend Davis some against vs partiall,
            haue found we steale some good conceyts from Martiall,
                So though they graunt our vearse hath some Acumen,
                Yet make they fooles suspect we skant are true men.
            But Surrey did the same, and worthy Wyatt,
            and they had prayse and reputacion by it,
                And Haywood whom your putting down hath raised,
                did vse the same, and with the same is praysed./
            Wherefore if they had witt that so did trace vs,
            they must againe for their own creditts grace vs,   [10]
                Or els to our more honor and their greiues,
                match vs at least with honorable theeues./

            Of a light huswive.   202.

26.   A wenche but loose of seare not worth the naming
                Went downe a stayr and for she feard to stumble
        In her left hand she held a candle flaming.
                But straight a iolly Mate with her did Iumble

And hotly bent vnto Venereous gaming
   Waxt the more proud, the more he found her humble
But yet when as he did her ruf*l*y handle,
   she cry'de no no, Ile none, then God refuse me,
At last she threats and sweares, now by this Candle
   I'le burne you sir and if you thus misvse me./   [10]
      he blew the candle out to breake her vow
      Yet she perform'd it still, imagin how./

     Of Lynus borrowing.

27.   Lewd Lynus came to me six crowns to borrow
   and sware God damne me Ile repay't to morrow,
     I knew his word as currant as his band,
     and straight I gaue to him three crowns in hand,
       This I to giue, this he to take was willing,
       and thus he gayn'd and I sau'd fifteen shilling./

     To my Lady Rogers that she loved not
     him: yet she loved his wife./

28.   You tell amonge your many auncient Sawes   203.
     which you haue learnd of wryters of renown
     that loue is heavy still discending down
And yet in this your self do breake loues lawes
for still on Mall you fawn on me you frown,
     I feele th'effect, yet cannot fynde the cause.
     Your loue which drawes to her, from me withdrawes
But if your loue be either verbe or nown,
     I'le proue cleare by an vnexpected Clause,
You then should loue me first, nay neuer wonder;   [10]
      for lett the Harrolds set our places down,
       I hope when Mall and I be least asunder,
       your daughters place is not aboue but vnder./

To his wife of loue
without lust./

29.   Thou tellst me Mall and I beleeue it must
that thou canst loue me much with little lust
    but while of this chaste loue thou dost devise
    and lookst chast babies in my wanton eyes,
    thy want of lust makes my loue wantonise,
then thinke but say't no more, for if thou dost
    Trust me I fynd an aptnes to mistrust
    I cannot loue thee long without mee lust./   204.

Against swearing.

30.   In elder time an auncient custome was
to sweare in wayghty matters by the mas
    But when the mass went down, as old men note
    they sware thus, by the Cross of this same grote./
Now when the Crosse likewise was helld in skorne
then by their fayth, the common othe was sworne./
    Last hauing sworne away all faith and troth
    onely God damn me, is the common oth.
Thus custome kept decorum by gradacion
hauing lost Mass, crosse, fayth, they finde damnacion.   [10]

Of a Lenton dinner

31.   I dyn'd by hap at Sextus house this spring
where though himself far'd sumptuous like a king
    With Partridge, Quayles, and Ven'son all in ryot
    there was but little store of Lenton diott./
For fishe of sea or riuer was there none
sauing the king of fishes or poore Iohn./
    Wherewith *content* at last to mend my cheere,
    I call'd to haue a cup of strong marche beere.
It came, and to tell true and not to halt   205.
'twas stronge of hopp and water, not of malt.   [10]
    Y*et* 'twas marche beere indeed, who euer made yt,
    the sunne was but in Taurus when we had yt./
And take this one note more to mend my tale,
though 'twere not stale, yet did yt looke like stale,
    Well let my witt be matcht with a march hare,
    When e're I marche so far for so ill fare.

The Hermaphrodyte translated out of
latten, done formerly by one Kendall,
and after in Albions England:
lib:2. Cap. 10.

32.   When first my mother bare me in her wombe,
        she went to make enquyrie of the Gods,
first of my byrth and after of my tombe,
        all answerd true, yet all their words had ods./
Phœbus affirmd a male chyld should be borne:
        Mars sayd it would be femall, Iuno neither,
But I came forth alas to natures skorne,
        Hermaphrodite, as much as both together./
Then for my death Iuno foretold the sworde
        Phœbus assign'd me drowning for my fate   [10]
Mars threat'ned hanging, each performd his word   206.
        as note how all prou'd trew in severall Rate.
A tree fast by a Brooke I needes must clyme
        my sword slipt out and while no heede I tooke
My side fell on the poynt and at that tyme
        my foote in bowghs, my head hang'd in the brooke
        And I thus borne a male, *a* female, neither,
        Di'de, drown'd, and hangd, and wounded, all together.

Of a Stratagem with a
Tobacco pipe.

33.   Vnto a gentle gentlewomans chamber
        a Pedler came, her husband being thence,
To sell fyne Linnen lawnes, and Muske and amber,
        she franke of favours sparing of expence,
        So bargayn'd with him e're he parted thence,
That for ten ells of Holland, fiue of Lawne,
        to graunt dishonest pleasures she was drawne./
        Next day the man repenting of his cost
        did study meanes to get him restitution,
Or to be payd for that he there had lost.   [10]
        And thus he putts the same in execution,
        he turns to her with setled resolution,
And in her husbands presence vnawares   207.
he asketh fifty shillings for his Wares.
Her husband ignorant what cause had bred yt,
        Why wife sayd he, had you so spent your store?

You must with petty chapmen run on credit,
   now for my honors sake do so no more./
No Sir sayd she I meant it to restore,
   I tooke it of him onely for a triall,   [20]
   and finde yt too highe prized, by a Riall./
Thus neuer chaunging counte'nance she doth ryse
   with outward scilence, inward anger choking,
And going to her closet she espise,
   Tobacco in a pipe, yet newly smoking,
She takes the pipe, her mallice her provoking,
   and lapps it in his linnen comming back,
   and so the pedler putts it in his packe;
 and packs away, and ioyes that with this guile
   he had regain'd his stuffe, yet gayn'd his pleasure,   [30]
But hauing walked skarcely half a mile,
   his packe did smoke and smell so out of measure,
that opening yt vnto his deepe displeasure
   he found by that Tobacco pipe to late
   the fiery force of feoble femall hate.
And seeking then some remedie by lawes   208.
   Vnto a neighbour Iustice he complaynes:
But when the Iustice vnderstood the cause
   in her examinacion taking paynes
And found 'twas but a fetch of womens brayns,   [40]
   the cause dismist, he bids the man beware
   to deale with women, that can burne his ware./

To one of her Maiesties Phisitions in praise of the king of Scotts Phi= sition that was knighted.

34.   To swage some daungerous humors daylie surging
       each spring or fall for feare her health haue harme
    You cause our Queene vse letting bloud and purging
       and many times no great occasions vrging
    Bloud royall spins from scepter bearing Arme,
       But late in North, by treason most contagious
       When Traytors hart his traytrous hands did arme
       With doubled weopon, and with diu'lish charme
    To kill that oryent king with hart outragious,
    And turne his spring to fall (oh brest salvagious)   [10]
       his learn'd Phisition answering that allarme,
    With valient hand, and with an hart couragious,

While letting others bloud his own was spilt 209.
deseru'd and gott the gilded spur and hilt./

Of bag and baggage.

35. A man appointed vpon loss of life
     With bag and baggage at a time assign'd
to part a town: his foule vnweildy wife
     desired him that she might stay behinde./
Nay soft said he Ile neuer be so kynde,
     to hazzard life for such an vgly hag
     as lookes *both* like a baggage and a bag./

To one Mr. Fitzgefferies, with a
     Reward of french crowns for a booke he gaue me

36. You write your purse wasts and consumes your stock
by reason of the crowing of some cocke.
     At which the Lyons whelps take such offence,
     as you suppose that reason driues them thence,
Wherefore to remedy so shrewd abuses
I without Lions send you Flower de luses,
     Thus crost and guarded well with armes of Fraunce
     the Devill in your purse shall neuer daunce./

Of one that praysd his M^{rs.} 210.

37. A scholler once to win his mistris loue
compar'd her with three goddesses aboue,
     And sware she had to giue her due desarts,
     Pallas, and Iunos, and fayr Venus parts./
Pallas was foule and grim so out of measure
as neither gods nor men in her had pleasure.
     Iuno so curst and shrowd was of her tounge
     that all mislyked her both old and younge./
Venus vnchast that she strong Mars intyces
With young Adonis and with old Anchises, [10]
     How thinke you are theis praises few or mean
     compared to a Slutt, a shrow a Quean./

Of a worde in Welch mistaken
in englishe.

38.   An English lad long woo'de a lass of Wales,
and entertayn'd her with such pretty tales,
      as though she vnderstood not yet to try him
      she gaue consent at last to vnderly him./
Both hauing dallyed to their full saciety
the wenche to show some womanly sobriety,
      told in her language she was well apayd
      and degon, degon once or twise she sayd.   211.
Degon in welch doth signifie ynuffe
Which he mistaking answeard thus in snuffe,   [10]
      Dig on that can quoth he, for I so sore
      haue dig'd allready, I can dig no more./

A good Answer of a gentlewoman
to a Lawier.

39.   A vertuous dame that saw a Lawier rome
abroad: reprou'd his stay so long from home,
      and said to him that in his absence thence
      his wife might want his due benevolence./
But he to quit himself of such disgrace
answerd it thus with putting of *a* case.
      One owes one hundred pounds: now tell me whether
      is best: to haue this payment all together,
Or take yt by a shilling and a shilling,
Whereby the bagg should be the longer filling./   [10]
      Sure sayd the Dame I graunt 'twear little loss,
      Yf one receavd such payment all in gross,
          Yet in your absence this might breed your sorrow,
          to heare your wife for want might twelue pence borrow./

Of Christs Cote 212.

40. Our reverent elders had one speciall note
     that trew religion should through out the Reame
be kept like to our saviours wearing cote
     all of one peece, and voyd of any seame
How comes then this devision so extreame
     ready to teare out one anothers throte
Who stird such waues in this still running stream
     able to sinke Saint Peeters tottring bote.
        Ist not a schisme? no say not so beware,
        But we haue almost worne the coate threedbare.   [10]

To his wife when she was
sick of the sullens.

41. Late hauing been a fishing at the ford,
     and bringing home with me my dish of Trowts,
     Your minde that while casting some causles doubts,
When meate was ready set vpon the bord,
I twise sent for you yet you neuer stoord,
     but sullen scilent fed your self with powts,
and at the last you sent me back this word,
     You had but little stomack to your meate,
     Well I feare more, your stomack was to great:

Of Lending money 213.

42. Titus lent Lynus money on his band
But e're that Lynus set thereto his hand
     he was precise in setting down the place,
     for which the Scriv'ner had but left a space./
This done they parte in time the time expires,
Titus at place prefixt his Crowns requyres,
     but all that day of Lynus was no news,
     no letter man, nor freind yt to excuse./
Well *well* quoth Titus with a skornfull frown,
Was this his care to haue his place set down,   [10]
        To bee more sure forsooth to think vpon it?
        Nay nay, but to be sure to keepe him from yt./

Misacmos of his Muse
to Sr. Iohn Ashley.

43.   My Muse is like king Edwards Concubine,
       Whose mynde did to devotion so enclyne
           She duly did each day to church resort,
           saue if she weare int*ys*'t to Venus sport
               So would my Muse wryte grauely, ne're the latter
               She slips sometimes into some wanton matter./

                    Of Lynus   214.

44.   Poore Lynus playnes that I of late forget him
       and sayth hee'l bee my guest if I will let him,
           but I so lyked him last time I met him,
           that Ile be sure do all I can to let him./

                    Of a Lawier that would take
                    a Hare for a
                    fee.

45.   Late to a Lawier rich a Client poore
       came early in the morning to his doore,
           And as he travaild had by breake of day,
           a hare did start, and ran athwart his way.
       Now hauing daunc't attendannce in the place
       at last he gat some councell in the Case./
           With cap and curtsie oft he thus did say,
       I cannot offer fees my states so bare
       But will it please you sir, to take a hare
           He that did still take all, with all his hart   [10]
           sayd yea he would and take it in good part
       Then must you run and that apace sayd hee
       for sure while ear she quite out stripped mee
           Thus he departs, the Hare was neuer taken
           Was not the Lawier taken, or mistaken?/   215.

Of finding a Hare

46.   A Gallant full of life and free of Care
      That lou'd all coursing game, and bought it dearly
      came to his frend earst in a morning early
And sayd come rise let vs goe finde an hare,
Hee that for sleepe more then such sport did care,
      affirm'd that busines toucht him nothing nearly,
        And therefore go sayd he, let me alone
        let them fynde hares that loose them, I lost none./

In prayse of two worthy Transla=
tions, made by two great
Ladies

47.   My soule one only Mary doth adore,
      onely one Mary doth inioy my hart,
yet hath my Muse found out two Maries more,
      that merit endles prayse by dew desart,
Two Maries that translate with diuers art,
      two subiects rude and ruinous before,
      both hauing noblesse great and bewties store,
Nobless and bewty to their works impart./
Both haue ordayn'd against Deaths dreadfull Dart   216.
      a Shield of fame induring euermore   [10]
      both works advaunce the loue of sacred lore,
Both help the souls of sinners to convart./
        Their learned payn I prayse, heer costly Alms
        A Colledge this translates, the tother Psalms./

Against Claudia

48   Claudia to saue a noble Romans bloud
was offred by some frends that wisht *his* good
      a Iewill of inestimable price,
      Which having well pervsed once or twice
        Yet did she take his head; and leaue the Iewell
        Was Claudia now more couetous or crewell./

To the Orient king praying
neuer *to* see him occident, by
any Accydent.

49.   Antiquity distinguisht hath long since
            two sev'rall fashions of Monarchall Raigne,
        A tyrant one, t'other a lawfull Prince,
            Which by theis rules may be discearned playn.
        The lawfull prince his subiects deemes as sonns,
            and toward them myldly himself behaues,   217.
        The tyrant headlong in his fancy runns,
            his will their Law, his subiects counts his slaues./
                Well sayd: yet some I know to serue had rather,
                a gentle master, then a crewell father./   [10]

Of trying Spirits a passage
betweene two Persons of
great calling

50.   A Catholick had conference of late
        With one of our great Prelats of the state,
            Lamenting that the Church with Schisme turmoyled,
            Had eke her buildings and revenews spoyled
        Foole sayd the Prelate why are you molested,
        That ne're are like therein to be revested,
            Yf we retayn a Portion though but small,
            What's that to you, for you haue lost it all.
        Yet said the t'other we do wishe in hart
        That you might keepe it all not spill a part./   [10]
                Now Sollomon be Iudge I wishe none other
                Which is the Harlot, which the lawfull mother./
        This side sayth spare my childe aliue and take yt,
        Let it not perish though I must forsake yt
                She feelling no commorse of grace nor nature   218.
                Sayth neither thine nor mine, but Dividatur.

To his wife againt women
Recusants./

51. The great Assuerus to his royall feast
   envited Vasti his beloued Queene
   but she not then disposed to be seene
Refusd to come, which did him so molest
   that straight, as if this had a treason been,
   Yt was agreed his Lords and Peeres between,
To banishe her for breaking his behest./
For thus resolu'd that Councell sage and wise,
   that though her face was fayr, her portion ample,
   Yet by so daungerous eminent example,   [10]
All Persian Ladies might their Lords dispise./
Wherefore my dearest Mall I thee advise,
       Ensew not Vasties Councell but detest her,
       And rather follow her successor Esther./

Of a fellow iudgd to lose
his Eares./

52. A fellow false and to all fraud envred
   In high Starchamber court was founde periured   219.
       And by iust sentence iudgd to loose his eares
       A Doome most dew to him that falsly swears.
   Now on the pillory as he was pearching,
   the Iaylor for his eares was busie searching./
       But all in vaine for there was not an eare,
       onely their place coverd with locks of heare,
   Thou Cose'ner (sayd the Iaylor seeming wrath)
   thou weart condemned for a falsed oath,   [10]
       But now by right one should of thee complayn
       afore the Lords for Cosonage againe./
           Nay said the man, their order me doth bynde
           to loose mine eares, not you mine eares to finde./

To his wiues mother

53.   When with your daughter (Madam) you be chattring
            I fynde that oft against me you incense her
       And then forsooth my kindnes all is flattring
            my loue is all but lust, this is your censure
            'Tis not my flattring her moues you thereto
            Yt is because I will not flatter you./

Of Lynus and his Mistris.

54.   Chast Linus but as valient as a Gander   220
            came to mee yet in frendly sort as may bee,
       Lamenting that I raisd on him a sclaunder
            namely that he should keepe a gallant Lady./
            Beg me said I, if I proue such a baby,
       to let my tongue so false and ydly wander,
                 Who sayes that you keepe her lyes in his throte,
                 but she keepes you, that all the world doth note./

Of good exhortacion

55   When Faustus is reproued for his folly,
       and warned how such misdeedes draw on damnation
       he vowes in show repentant seeming holly
            not lightly to regard good exhortation./
       But in a trice like to the Bore and Dogg,
            to former filthe and vomit he returns,
       And from his conscience casts all care and clogg,
            still practising some lewd vngratious turnes.
                 Faustus observs his vow, and take him rightly
                 not to regard good exhortation lightly./   [10]

Of sumptuous fare for
        simple guests./

56.   A rich lord had a poore Lowt to his guest,   *221.*
       and hauing costly meat and richly drest,
            Carvd him a winge of one most daynty byrd
            affirming seriously vpon his word,
       That foule was sent him from his loving Cozen,

and were well worthy twenty marke a dozen,
   the man refusd it, yet with much obeysance,
   sayd thus between simplicity and pleasance,
   Ile eate your lordships beefe, pig, goose and Conny,
   but of such fowle giue me my part in monny./ [10]

Of a Lady that left open
her Cabinet.

57   A vertuous Lady sitting in a Muse,
   as many times fayre vertuous ladies vse,
     leaned her elbow on one knee full hard
     the other distant from yt half a yard,
   Her knight to taunt her by a privy token,
   sayd wife awake your Cabbinet stands open,
     She rose and blusht and smyl'd, and softly sayes,
     then locke it if you list you keepe the kayes./

Of Cosmus that will keepe a good
house hereafter.

58   Old Cosmus to his frends this out doth giue   *222.*
   After a while he like a Lord will liue
     after a while hee'le end all troublous sutes,
   After a while retayne some men of quallity,
     after a while of riches reape the fruits,
   After a while keepe house in some formallity.
   After a while finishe his bewteous building,
     after a while leaue of his busy buying,
   Yet all the while he liues but like a hilding,
     his head growes gray, with fresh vexations trying   [10]
   Well Cosmus I beleeue your heire doth smyle,
   to thinke what you must do after a while./
     For sure the prouerbe is more trew then civill,
     blest is the sonne, whose syre goes to the Devill.

Of the Deathe of the Earle
of Essex./

59   When noble Essex, Blunt, and Davers dyed,
One saw them suffer that had heard them tryed,
And sighing sayd when such braue souldiers dy
Ys't not great pitty thinke you? no sayd I.
    There is no man of worth in all the Citty
    will say 'tis great, but rather little pitty.

Of Prelats that they ought to
be more Pontificall.

223.

60   Great Prelates named were in former dayes
    Pontifices, and had revenewes lardge,
Because they built strong Bridges and high wayes,
    and kept them well repaired at their chardge.
But now whyte apron stringes ty vp their purses,
    now Councells those old customes do abrydge,
Symon his babes super entends and nurses,
    scant one among an hundred build a Bridge,
        Yf those were proude, their pride hath had a fall,
        but I would theise were more pontificall./   [10]

Of Repayring Bridges

61.   A Squyre hight Bridges of good reputation,
    gaue in his will near half an hundred pounde,
Onely to keepe a bridge in reparation,
    are not too few such men in our dayes founde?
    too few? no: many so that is our shame,
    for euery man seekes to advaunce his name./

Of Galla and Paulus

62.   Braue Galla much complaynes of her ill fortune
That Paulus euermore doth her importune
    Whom she hath threatned and revilde and chid
    and sweares that fayn she would of him bee rid.
But Galla doth my vnderstanding trouble
her words so doubtfull are, her deedes so double.

224.

For Faustus sayth who marks such matters dewly
and doth not euermore report vntrewly,
that she and Paulus vnder table footed,
and Paulus rode that night and was not booted./ [10]
I know not what he meanes but God forbid,
chaste dames of wanton guests should so be rid./

Of ryding rymes

63. Fayr Leda reedes our poetry sometimes,
but saith she cannot like our ryding rymes,
affirming that the cadens falleth sweeter,
When as a Vearse is plas'te between the meeter./
Well Leda leaue henceforth this quarrell pyking,
and sith that one betweene, is to your lyking,
You shall haue one between, yet some suppose,
Leda hath lou'd both ryding ryme and prose./

Of a Lady early vp.

64 Lesbia that wonted was to sleep till noone   *225.*
this other morning stirring was at fiue,
What did she meane thinke you to ryse so soone,
I doubt we shall not haue her long aliue?
Yes neuer feare yt, there is no such daunger
Yt seemes vnto her course, you bee a straunger
for why at dauncing, banquetting and play,
And at carrowsing many a costly cup
she sate the night before vntill 'twas day.
And by that meane you found her early vp,   [10]
Oh was it so? why then the case is cleere,
that she was early vp and near the neere./

                    Of a Lady that goes priuate
                    to the Bath./

65   Lesbia you seeme a straunge conceyted woman,
          that though thy bed to many one is common,
               Yet priuate still you goe into the Bathe,
               We doubt your bewty some great blemishe hath
          Either your brests hange bagging down your sides
          or els your flesh, which your apparell hydes
               Ys with some vgly morphew fowly tainted
               with which you would not haue vs made acquainted
               Or els your skin is black where 'tis not paynted   *226.*
          Not so, nor so, you say, I much mistake yt   [10]
          and that you shew indeed most louely naked./
                    Then know, thus Doctors saie of Cupids schoole
                    thou hast one greater blemish, th'art a foole./

                    To my Lady Rogers.

66.   Amonge the mortall sinns in number seav'n
          that shut against our souls the gates of heav'n,
               You still do say that letchery is wurst
               most loath'd of saynts, and most of God accurst./
          But Madam eyther you are ill advis'd,
          or in your youth you were ill Cathechis'd,
               For thus learn't I of my good gostly father
               and by his works, as well as words I gather,
          Those sinns are least as all the learned teache,
          Where loue and charity haue smallest breach,   [10]
               those sinns of which wee soonest do repent vs,
               for those a pardon soonest shalbe sent vs./
          Now Letchery as showes the common sentence,
          begins with loue and endeth with repentance./
               Beside all those that take delight therein,
               finde it a liuely, not a deadly sin.
          Then lett this question bee no more disputed,   *227.*
          You see how playn your error is confuted,
               But bee't agreed thus you and me betwix,
               Yt is the greatest sin of seauen, saue six./   [20]

To his wife.

67 My Mall if any fortune to accuse me
    (as to accusing all the world is bent)
that I in lawes of Wedlocke do abuse me
    and secretly do liue incontinent:
Incontinent thus to thy thought excuse me,
    thinke envy doth for spight such lyes invent,
    then note their sex, and guess at their intent,
        Yf they be men, thinke like themselues they take me,
        Yf weomen, thinke that so they fayn would make me./

To his good frend and Schoolfellow
Doctor Sharpe.

68 I late tooke leaue of two right worthy Dames
    and hastend to my wife as I protested,
    but you inforst me stay and thus you iested,
You you maie please your wife with Epigrames,
    Well sayd 'twas doctorlike and sharply spoken
No frendship breakes where Iests so smooth are broken   *228*
    but now you haue new orders tane of late,
Those orders (which as you expounde Saint Paule,)
are equall honorable vnto all
    (I mean of Marriadge the holy state)   [10]
    I hope in Lent when flesh growes out of date,
        You will in steed of t'other recreation
        be glad to please your wife with some collation./

Of Paulus wife and Cayus
Children

69 One sware to me that Paulus hath a wife,
Yet was he neuer married all his life./
    now from this tale the reason plain I gather,
    how Caius getts no barnes yet is a father./

Of onely faith.

70.   Pure Cinna euermore disputing sayth,
        that Christians saued are by onely faith.
            But herein Cinnas speeches are abusiue
            to foyst vnto our faith a word exclusiue,
        For we do finde, marking the scriptures scope,
        Salvation comes by grace, loue feare and hope.
                Wherefore when Cinna speaks fayth saveth onely,   *229*
                tell him Misacmos sayth he speaketh one lye./

                Of Lesbias censure of
                my Vearses./

71.   When some good vertuous strayn my vearse inritches
        Lesbia whose eare for wanton matter itches,
            Straight way findes faults, and sayes it sutes but odly
            to haue a wanton Poet write so godly./
        Thus as Musitians to please some Riggs,
        in sober Lute and Harpe play wanton Iiggs.
            So we that gras'd on high Pernassus Valley
            to please such Dames so long haue vs'd to dalley,
        That if we tuch on goodnes, and on God
        though vearse be ev'n the matter seemeth od.   [10]
                Well Ile be ev'n with them for by their will
                I see they wishe, I would be wanton still./

                Pœnitentia pœnitenda
                of a penitent fryer.

72.   Not very long afore this latter Schisme
            a cuntriman of Luthers and a fryre
        Had got the swelling calld a Priapisme
            That seild is swag'd but with a femall fyre.   *230.*
        The Leach, as oftentimes Phisitions vse,
            to cure the corps, not caryng for the soule,
        Prescribes a cordiall med'cine from the stews,
            which lewd prescript the Patient did controule.
        Howbee't but weake in faythe, and loth to dye,
            and told that such extreams beare dispensation: [10]
        He gaue consent and did the medcine try,
            but being cur'd he made such lamentation,
        That diuers doubting least he might dispayr,

Were not a little in their minds dismayd,
And for his comfort did to him repayr,
   to whom (after long scilence) thus he sayd.
I wayle not that I count my fact so vicious
   nor am I in dispayr no neuer doubt it.
      But feelling femall fleshe is so delicious,
      I wayld to thinke I liud so long without yt:/   [20]

In commendacion of two valient Scottishe
knights, that defended their king from the
Earle Gowry / Sr Thomas Erskin and
Sir Iohn Ramsey./

73   The Persian Monarche who by faithfull spiall
      Was safe preseru'd from slaues intended slaughter,   *231.*
      by him whose Cozen and adopted daughter,
Vn'wares he did endow with Scepter ryall.
      when reading in his bedd a good while after
He founde in trew records that service loyall,
Then with most gratefull mynde to make requitall,
      by lardge edict o're all his chiefest town,
Of so great meritts he doth make recytall,
      and to increase Mardoches great renown,   [10]
Vpon his head such was their vse that season,
      he caused to be set his royall Crown.
         But greater should be your reward in reason,
         he but reveal'd, but you reveng'd a treason./

In praise of the Countess of Darby
marryed to the Lord Keeper.

74   This noble Countess liued many yeares
With Darby one of Englands greatest Peeres
      Fruitefull and fayr, and of so clear a fame
      as all the Brittish yle admyr'd her name.
But this braue Peere extinct by hast'ned fate
She stayd (ah too too long) in Widdows state
      And in that state, tooke so sweet state vpon her
      All eares, eyes, tongues, heard saw and told her honor./   *232.*
      Yet finding this a saying full of Verity
      'tis hard to haue a Pattent of prosperity   [10]
         She found her wisest way and safe to deale
         Was to consort with him that keepes the seale./

Of devout Parents and Children.

75.   A husband and a wife oft disagreeing
        and either weary of the other being,
            In choller great either devoutly prayes
            to God that he will shorten t'others days.
                But more devout then both their sonne and heyre,
                Prayes God that he will graunt them both their praire./

Of neat Galla

76.   The pride of Galla now is grown so great
        She seekes to be surnam'd Galla the *n*eat
            But who their meritts shall and manners skan,
            may thinke the tearme is dew to her goodman?
        Aske you which way me thinks your witts are dull
            my Shoomaker resolue you can at full,
            neats leather is bothe Oxe and Cow and Bull./

Of Reversing an error

77.   I did you wrong, at least you so suppose,   *233.*
        for taxing certaine faults of yours in prose,
            But now I haue the same in ryme rehearst,
            my error, nay your error is revearst./

Of a Sclaunder

78   On *lesbya* Lynus raysed hath a sclaunder
            for which when as she thought to take an action
            Yet by request she tooke this satisfaction,
        that being drunke, his tongue did ydly wander,
            Came this from Viderit vtilitas,
            or els from this in vino veritas./

Of one that tooke thought
for his Wife./

79.   No sooner Cinnas wife was dead and buryed
        but that with mourning much and sorrows wearyed

A mayd a servannt of his wiues he wedded
but after he had bourded her and bedded,
    And in her mistris rome had fully plast her,
    his wiues old servant, waxed his new Master.

Of a pregnant pure Sister

80.   I learnd a tale more fitt to be forgotten,   *234.*
    how that a holy mayd of loues society,
Was by a Preacher late with child begotten,
    and when the birth drew neare in great anxiety,
    amid the pangs she prayd with passing pyety,
That sith a learned man did overreache her,
the child she bare at least might proue a Preacher./
    A child was borne, and when the throes were past,
    She askt what God had sent her at the last.
The Midwife made this answer half in lafter,   [10]
You may said she a Preacher beare hereafter,
    For sure this can be none, God bless the Babye
    but for a Preacher here a Pulpitt may be./

Of Lesbias new loue

81.   Old widdow Lesbia after husbands fiue,
Yet feelleth Cupids flames in her reviue,
    And now she takes a gallant youth and trym
    alas for her? nay nay a lasse for him./

Of a Cator

82.   A Cater had of late some wylde fowle bought,
and when vnto his maister them he brought,
    Forthwith the Master smelling ny the Rumpe   *235.*
    said out thou knaue, theise sauour of the pumpe.
The man that was a rude and sawcy lout,
Swounds sir said he, smell you them thereabout,
    Smell your fayr Lady there, and by your favour
    You fortune may finde but a fulsome savour./

Of good Sawce

83. I went to sup with Cinna t'other night
and to say true, for giue the Devill right,
Though skant of meate we could a morsell gett,
Yet there with store of passing sawce we mett.
  You aske what sauce; where pittance was so small,
  this? is not hunger the best sawce of all./

Of his wiues Py feast, to which he
invyted a knight and a Lady.

84. My wife at other times like other Shrowes
  Yet once a yeare ('tis well 'tis once a year)
Ys kynde to me, and then a feast bestowes
  Of dishes not far fett, nor costing deare,
The chief of which are Pyes, not pyes that chatter
  but pyes of which skant twenty fill a Platter.
Now Sir I you invyte and she your Lady   *236.*
to this same feast of hers, more kind than ample,
Where welcome is best fare, and where it may be
Your Phœnix may of mine take such example   [10]
  As now the weather lowring is inclyned
  it may grow fayre when as they two haue dyned./

To his wife a rule for Church
house and bed.

85. Of late in pleasant company by chaunce
I wisht that you for company would daunce
  Which you refus'd, and sayd your yeares requyre
  now Matron=like both manners and attyre.
Well Mall if needes you wilbe matron=like,
then trust to this I will a Matron like,
  Yet so to thee my Loue may neuer lessen,
  as you for church, house, bedd will learn this lesson./
Sitt in the Church as solemne as a Saynt,
No deed, word, thought your dew devotion taynt./   [10]
Vayle if you will your head, Your soule reveale,
to him that onely wounded soules can heale./
  Bee in my house, as busie as a Bee,
  having a stinge for every one but mee.

Buzzing in ev'ry corner gathering honney   *237*
let nothing waste that costs or yeildeth money./
But when thou see'st my hart to mirthe inclyne
the tongue, witt, bloud, warme with good cheere and wyne,
    {*and that by lawful fansy I ame led*
    {*to clym my nest thyne vndefiled bed.*   [20]
then of sweet sport let no occasion skape
but bee as wanton toying as an Ape./

       Of Gods parte./

86.   One that had farmd a fatt impropriation,
       Vs'd to his neighbors often exhortation,
       to pay to him the tythes and profitts dewly,
       affirming as he might affirme most truly,
       How that the tythe is God allmighties Part
       and therefore they should pay't with all their hart./
          But thus repli'de some one among the rest,
          one that had crost him oft but neuer blest,
            It is gods part indeed, whose goodnes gaue yt,
            but yet sometimes we see the Devill haue yt.   [10]

       Being requested by the Lady Kildare
         to wryte *to wryte an Elegy of a*
           straw this was written and
            showd to the Queen.

87   I vowde to wryte of none but matters serious,   *238.*
       and lawfull vowes to breake is great offence,
     But yet fayr Ladies hests are so imperious,
       that with all vowes all lawes they can dispense./
       then yeilding to such all commaunding law,
       my Muse must tell some honor of a straw.
     Not of Iack Straw with his rebellious crew,
       that set Crowne Realme and Lawes at hab or nab.
     Whom Londons worthy May're so brauely slew
       with dudgen daggers honorable stab,   [10]
Regno   that his successors for his service loyall,
Richardi .1.   haue yet reward with blow of weopon royall./
     Nor can I prayse that fruitles straw or stubble,
       that built vpon most pretious stones foundation
     When fiery trialls come the builders trouble,
       (though our great builders build of such a fashion)

to learned Androes that much better can,
  I leaue that stubble, fyre, and straw to skan.
Nor list I with Philosophers to raunge,
  in searching out though I admyre the reason,   [20]
how simpathizing properties most straunge,
  keepe contraries in straw so longe a season,
Ise, snow, fruits, fish, moyst things and dry and warme
  Are longe preserv'd in straw with little harme./   *239.*
A small thing 'tis but greatly to be wondred,
how one poore straw, doth cherish, beare, sustayn
Of fruitefull graynes oft times aboue an hundred,
  in heat, in storms, in drowth, in wynde, in Rayne,
    breake but that slender stalke and alltogether,
    the corne will straight perish consume and wither. [30]
But let all Poetts my remembrannce wipe
  from of their bookes of fame for euer during,
If I forget to prayse our oaten pipe,
  such musick to the Muses all procuring.
    that some learn'd eares preferr'd it haue before
    both Orpharion, Violl, Lute, Bandore./
Now if we list more curiously examine,
  searching in straw some profitable poynts,
Bread hath bene made of straw in time of famine
  cutting thereof the slender knotted ioynts./   [40]
    but yet remaynes one note of straw to tell
    that all the former notes doth far excell./
That straw, which men, which foule, and beasts, haue skorned,
  hath bene by curious art and hand industrious,
Wrought soe that it hath shadowed, yea adorned
  a face and head of bewty'nd birth illustrious.
    Now prayse I not, I envy now your blisse   240.
    ambitious straw that so highe placed is./
What Architect this worke so straungly matcht,
  an yvory house, dores Rubies, Wyndows tutch.   [50]
A gilded Rou*ffe* with straw all overthatcht
  Where shall Pearles byde, when grace of straw is such?
    Now could I think (alass) I think too much.
    I would be straw, drawn to that liuely tuch./
This lesson yet I learn by this example,
  that vertuous industry their worth can rayse,
Whom sclaunderous tongues tread vnder foote & trample,
  thus told my Muse, and straight she went her wayes,
    Which (Lady) if you seriously allow,
    then 'tis no toy, nor haue I broke my vow./   [60]

To the Queene in prayse of
her reading./

88.   For euer deare for euer dreaded Prince
You read some vearse of mine a little since,
    and so pronounct each word and evry letter,
    your gratious reading, grac't my vearse the better,
Since then your highnes doth by guift exceeding
make that you reade the better in your reeding
      Let my poore Muse your paynes thus far importune   241.
      to leaue to reade my vearse, *and* reade my fortune./

Of a knight that sewed to the
Queene for a reward./

89   A knight and valient servitor of late
playnd to a Lord and Councellor of state,
    that Captaynes in theise dayes were not regarded,
    that onely Carpet knights were well rewarded.
But I sayd he with all theis hurts and maymes
get not the recompence my meritt claymes.
    Good Cozen said the Lord the fault is yours,
    that you impute vnto the higher powrs,
For while you should in Pater noster pray
giue vnto vs our daylie bread to day,   [10]
      Your misdemeanors this peticion needes
      our trespasses forgiue vs and misdeedes./

Of a Preacher and his
hower glasse./

90.   Pure Lalus loues the Church but loaths the Steeple
he speaking on a day vnto the People
    to th'end he might beware how time did pass
    He vs'd as manie doe an hower glass.   242.
He entred to an earnest disputation
to proue that workes are needeles to salvation,
    Saint Iames his doctrine he doth quite deface,
    Of Paule ad Ebrios he brings many a place,
Which while he cytes and sifts with mickle cunning,
outran the glass, but his tongue still was running   [10]
      the people with his tedious tattle cloyde,

shranke one and one, and left the chappell voyde./
Well Lalus least they serue you so hereafter,
run you out first, and let the glass run after.
    But while you make St. Paule fall out with Ieames
    You trouble ours and *all* our neighbor Reames./

        To my Lady Kildare.

91   Fayr noble Lady late I did rehearse
       A story of a straw to you in vearse,
          for which to grace me with our gratious Prince
          my memory I heare you praysed since./
       But Madam I would take you more my frend
       if you would my forgettfullnes commend,
          it is no fault I would not blushe to graunt yt,
          and for 'tis trew, I neede not blushe to vaunt yt
       That thing that lightly is forgot by no man,   243.
       that that bydes firm in mynde of ev'ry woman,   [10]
          Ev'n that I vow I ne're remember longe:
          What's that? if you will guess aright? 'tis wronge./

        Of Sextus Page.

92   Good Sextus think not me to you iniurious,
       to saie that in one choyce, thou art too curious
          in choosing of thy Page, in which election,
          thou specially respectest their complexion./
          Bee not so curious for the fayrest skins
          giue oft occasion to the fowlest sinns./

        Of one that could not abide
          the cross.

93.   You tearme yt superstition fowle and grosse
          to signe a Child in Baptisme with the Cross,
       And say your Iudgment so much doth abhor it,
       that you condemne the Church of England for it.
          I know not Cinna, why you hate that signe
          but that's an evill signe, beware that signe./

A good answer of Doctor Dale
to the Queene.

94   One that was Maister of the Queenes Requests   244.
and wisely could mix serious things with Iests
    Came to her grace one day in winters weather.
    Clad in a Cloake and boots of tanned leather./
The Queen doth checke him in a gratious sport
for comming to her presence in such sort,
    to place of state, of comlines and bravery
    to come in bootes vnsightly and vnsavery.
But he of ready aunswer not to seeke,
answerd her highnes in theis words or like.   [10]
    'tis not my bootes that breedes this iust offence,
    so to displease your highnes dainty sence./
        But 'tis theis Bills that yeild a savour strong,
        that stay vnsigned in my hand so long./

Of a Call of Sergeants./

95   A pleasant Lawier standing at the Barr
the causes done and day not passed far,
    A Iudge to whom he had profest devotion,
    askt him in grace if he would haue a motion,
Yes sir (quoth he) but shorte, and yet not small:
that where of late of Sergeants is a call,
    I wish as most of my profession doe
That there might be a call of Clients to.   245.
        for sure it breedes our sort no little cumber
        to finde of them, there is so little number./   [10]

Of Don Pedro

96   Don Pedro loues not me, I grow so scottishe,
Misacmos loues not him, he growes so sottishe./
    Once he did like me well so he did vow,
    then I was ev'n with him, so am I now./

In commendacion of his right vertuous
Cozen, the Lady Hastings, maried
to M^r· Iustice Kingsmell./

97   Fayr flower of Haringtons renowned race
        Sara, whom Venus envies for her face.
            Trew Saraes kinde, that calld her husband lord
            and liu'd obedient, and in sweete accord.
        A Sara did her husbands age so cheere
        he grew a father at an hundred yeere
            Looke you to do all this? then looke well to it,
            for by your looke, I looke that you should do it./

Vpon a Picture of a Louer in a
Tempest with two in a Boate: of which   246.
he was by commaundement of an Oracle
to drown one. And he himself was
in loue with the one, and the
other was in loue with him.

98   In troublous seas of loue my tender boate
            by fates decrees is still tost vp and down
        readie to sinke and may no longer floate
            except of theis two Damsells one I drowne
                both I would saue, but ah that may not bee
                I loue the t'one, the tother loueth mee./
        Here the Vast waues are ready me to swallow,
            there daunger is to strike vpon the shelfe,
        Doubtfull I swim betweene the deepe and shallow
            to saue th'vngrate, and bee ingrate my selfe,   [10]
        Thus seeme I still by th'eares to hold a Wulfe,
        While fayne I would eschew this gaping gulfe./
        But since loues actions guided are by passion,   }
            and quenching doth augment his burning fewill,   }
        Adew thou nimph deseruing most compassion,   } *a young*
            to merit mercy I must shew me crewill,   }   *mans*
        Aske you me why? oh question out of season,   } *censure*
            Loue neuer leasure hath to render reason.   }

Let soueraigne reason sitting at the Steere   }   247.
    and far remouing all eye blynding passion   }[20]
Censure the due desarts with Iudgement cleere   }
    and saie the crewill meritt no compassion   }   *the old*
Liue then kind Nimphe, and ioy we two together   }   *mans*
farewell th'vnkind, and all vnkind go with her./   }   *censure*

Of the games in the Court that
haue beene in Request.

99   I heard one make a pretty observation
     how games haue in the Court turnd with the fashion.
       The first game was the best, when free from cryme
1.   the Courtly gamsters all were in their pryme./   *Prymero*
2.   The second game was poste, vntill with posting
     they payrd so fast, 'twas time to leaue their boasting./   *Poast & pare*
       Yet oft the Gamsters all haue bene so fayr
       that with one Carde one hath beene set a payr./
3.   Then thirdly followd heaving of the Maw   *Maw*
     a game without civillity or law,   [10]
       An odious play and yet in court oft seene
       a sawcy knaue to trump a king or Queene./
4.   Then was tres Cozes next, a game whose number   *Tres cozes*
     the women gamsters at the first did cumber./
       For at this game a looker on might see   248.
       Yf one made not a payre, yet two made three./
5.   After came Lodam hand to hand, or quarter,   *Lodam*
     at which some maydes so yll did keepe the quarter
       that vnexpected in a short abode,
       they could not cleanly beare away their lode./   [20]
6.   Then Noddy followed next, as well it might   *Noddy*
     although it should haue gone afore of right,
       at which I saw I name not any boddy
       one neuer had the knaue, yet layd for Noddy./
7.   The last game now in vse is Bankerout   *Bankrout*
     which wilbe plaid at still I stand in doubt
       Vntill Lavolta turne the wheele of time
       and make it come about againe to Prime./

Of Lalus Symonicall
horse corsing./

100.   Pure Lalus gat a benefice of late,
        without offence of people, Church or state,
           Yea, but aske eccho how he did come buy it?
           Come buy it? no with othes he doth deny it,
        He nothing gaue, direct, nor indirectly,
        Fy Lalus now you tell vs a direct ly.
           Did not your Patron for an hundred pound   249.
           Sell you a Horse was neither younge nor sound,
        No Turke, no Courser, Barbary nor Gennit?
        Symony? no, but I see money in yt,   [10]
           Well if it were but soe the case is cleare,
           the Benefice was cheap, the Horse was deare./

Of a kind wife a sewtor for her husband
to the Lords./

101   A man that long had liv'd by lewdest shifts,
        brought to that Court that Corne from Cockle sifts,
           Starr chamber that of Iustice is the mirror,
           Was sentens't there, and for the greater terror
        Was iudged first to lie a yeare in fetters,
        then burned in his forhead with two letters.
        And to disfigure him with more disgrace,
        to slitt his nose the figure of his face
           The prisners wife with no dishonest mynd
           to shew her self vnto her husband kynd   [10]
        Sew'd humblie to the Lords and would not cease
        some parte of this sharpe rigor to release,
           He was a man, she sayd had serv'd in warr,
           What mercy would a Souldiers face so marre
        What though he were with some few crymes entangled,   250.
        'twear pitty that a man should be so mangled./
        This much sayd she: but grauely they replyde,
        that that was mercy that he thus was tryde,
           his Crymes deseru'd he should haue lost his life
           and hang in chaynes. alas reply'de the wife,   [20]
        The greif of his disfiguring is such,
        his hanging would not greiue me half so much.
           Yf you disgrace him thus, you quite vndoe him
           good my Lords hange him, pray be good vnto him./

Sir Iohn Raynsfords choyce
of a man.

102   Rainsford whose acts were manie times outragious
had speciall care to haue his men couragious
    A certaine frend of his one day began
    Vnto his service to commend a man./
One well approou'd he said in many iarrs,
Whereof in head, arms, hands, remaind the skarrs.
    The knight the man his marks and manners viewd,
    and flatt refusing him, did thus conclude
        This is no man for me, but I suppose
        hee's a tall man, that gaue him all theis blowes./   [10]

Of a graue Preacher that   251
studied in his bed./

103   A Parson of stayd yeares and honest carriadge,
new ioyned to a modest mayd in marriadge,
    Yet followd still his booke with payn exceeding,
    and oft at night in bed he would be reeding
She though she did not much allow his fashion,
Yet to performe the like in her vocation,
    Calls for her linnen turne vp to her bed,
    one night: and while he reads she spinneth thred./
Which he reprouing, for the noyse and motion
disturbed both his study and devotion./   [10]
    Sure Sir said she, I thinke as much he sinneth,
    that readeth out of time, as she that spinneth,
This speache the matter all to mirth did turne,
    he turns a leafe, she turns away the turne,
    was this a shrewd; no sure a happie turne./

Of the same by a Scottishe gentleman
that was at Bathe
1602.

104   A learned man, lay reeding in his bed
Whois vartuois wife wearied the day befoir
Would faine haue slept yet she her fancy fed   252.
    and vp she sitts (my vartew must be moir
    reach me my Rocke I idlenes abhoir)

And speedily with spindell falls a spinning,
   sings to her self, wha weil their sailfe decoir,
Like vartous wiues must liue vppon their winning.
   Falantidow, this is my Lairds linning.
With that her spindle she twines orethort his nose.   [10]
   How now (quoth he?) what worke is theare beginning
And what he thought, now Sir you shall suppose./
     He kist his wife, she lovingly did looke,
     Doe way thy Rocke, and so shall I my booke./

      Of a certayn man

105.   There was not certaine when, a certaine Preacher
     that neuer learn't, and yet became a teacher
       and having thus in latten read a text,
       of **Erat quidam homo**, much perplext.
     Hee seemd the words with dilligence to skan,
     In english thus. There was a certaine man./
       But no*w* (quoth he) good people note you this,
       He saith there was, he doth not say there is,
     For in this age of ours it is most certayn,
     Of promise, oath, worde deed, no man is certayn   [10]   253
       Yet by my teshe (quoth he) this comes to pass,
       That surely once a certaine man there was,
     But yet I thinke in all the Byble no man
     Can finde this text. **There was a certaine woman.**

      The last Epigram.

106   My Lord thoughe I by you am often prest
     to know the secret drift of mine intent
In theise my pleasant lynes and who are ment
By Cinna, Linus, Lesbia and the rest,
     Yet pardon thoughe I graunt not your request
     tis such as I thereto maie not assent./
What man would aske a woman he possest
     Who was the father of her second daughter
For though she lou'd him, yet so brode a Iest
     Would make her blush to speake a good while after./   [10]
     Theise rymes are Mungrells gotte on witt and lafter
My Muse the Nurse that bred them at her breast,
     the witt asham'd 'twas occupi'de so lewdly

By Riballds: faine would haue their names supprest,
    Saue her young Imps father themselus so shrewdly.
that who gat some of them, may soone be guest./
But as some Irishe dame that false hath playd   254.
    Will not confesse her fact for threats or force
Till death approching makes her soule afrayde
    and toucheth her sick hart with sad remorse./   [20]
Then wishing she the truthe had vttred rather
    She doth her wanton deallings all discover
And makes her children know, and call one father
    that none had earst suspected for her louer.
        So if my Wanton Muse dy penitent
        Perhaps she then may tell you whom she ment.

Finis./

[Blank page; ruled margins but no running heads thereafter]   255.

[Lantern, illuminated, 150 by 90 mm, fills whole page: Plate 5]   256

A Newyeares guift sent to the kings Matie. of
Scotland. Anno. 1602.

A darke lanterne composed of four metalls, gold, silver, brasse,
and Iron.

1. The top of it was a Crowne of pure gold, which also did
    cover a Perfume Pan of silver.
2. In the inside was a plate of silver like a Shield to giue
    a reflexion to the light, grav'd on both sides.
    Next to the light was graved and ymbost, the sunne,
    the Moone and seaven Starrs.

On the other side, the storie of the birth and passion of Christ,
like that which is in Nottingham Castle, graved as is reported,
by a king of Scotts, that was Prisoner in a Vault there, cald
to this day, the king of Scotts Prison./ The word was that of
the good thiefe. **D. M. M. C. V. I. R.** of the other side
Post Crucem lucem.

3. The waxe candle to be removed at pleasure with a loose
    socket of silver to be sett in the top, and make a Candle
    sticke or a lanterne, which you please: the bottome or
    foote brass./
4. The snuffers of steele: and all the outside of the Lanterne
    of Iron and steele Plate./
5. The Perfume had a silver globe in yt fild with Muske
    and Amber, of all which and their Applications
    theise insewing Vearses, were written./

The Elegie of the Lanterne translated
into Englishe.

When that wise Counterfect to Phœbus went,
and would a guift of Prise to him present,
   Hyding a iewell rich in hollow cane,
   No guift was seene, a great guift yet was tane,
And thus devinely taught, he gat his wishes,
And gaue to mother Earth well hastned kisses,/
   Most worthy Prince, and our Apollo rysing,
   accept a Present sent in like disguising,
And thoughe it come in fayned name vnknown,
Yet loue vnfayned maie therein be shown,   [10]
   Pure silver's closd in steele, in darknes light,
   Onely the Crowne apparant stands in sight.
In argent field are sacred stories showne,
Stories to your great Ancestor well knowne,
   Who shutt in Nottingham and kept apart,
   grav'd there this godly monument of Arte,
This Storie at his fingers ends he knew,
For with his fingers ends the same he drew.
   Eke other fancies lurks in this our Present,
   The vse and sence whereof are not vnpleasant: [20]
   Foure mettalls, ages foure resemble doe,   258
   Of which the golden age God send to yow,
Of steele I wish small vse, and little lasting,
Of Brasse, gold silver plenty neuer wasting;
   The sunne, Moone, starrs, and those celestiall fiers,
   Foretell the heave'ns shall prosper your desires.
And as the snuffers quenche the light and snuffe,
So may you quench those take your acts in snuffe.
   The Candle, th'emblen of a vertuous king,
   doth waste it self to others light to bring.   [30]
To your fayr Queene and sweet babes I presume
to liken the sweet savors and Perfume.
   She send sweet breathed loves into your brest,
   She blest with fruitfull yssew make you blest.
Lastly let heav'nly Crownes theise Crowns succeede
Sent sure to both, to neither sent with speed./

254

Cum Phœbum sapiens stulti simulator adiret,   *Brutus.*   257*bis*
    Et dare discuperet munera digna deo,
Ille cava grandem celans in arundine gemmam,
    Visus erat, donans magna, dedisse nihil./
Inde catus, doctore deo, votoque potitus,
    Fert properata tibi basia, magna parens./
Maxime rex, merito nobis et magnus Apollo,
    Talia Misacmi respice dona pij./
Et licet hæc veniant ficto sub nomine dona,
    Non ficti testes forsan amoris erunt,   [10]
Argentum ferro tegitur; lux clauditur vmbra,
    Debita conspicue sola corona patet./
Historia in niveo describitur optima scuto,
    Historia a proavo non male nota tuo,
Namque Notinghamio Brusus reclusus in antro,
    Sculpserat hoc artis tum pietatis opus./
Nec seriem mirum est doctam si novit ad vnguem,
    Vnguibus in muris scalpserat ante suis./
Plura sed invenies nostris latitantia nugis
    Quorum etiam placidus forsitan vsus erit.   [20]
Sæcula bis duo sunt totidem distincta metallis   259.
    Quodque ex his aurum denotat opta tibi,
Sit minimus ferri, vel perbrevis vsus, at auri
    Æris, et argenti, copia quanta voles./
Lucida stellarum lunæque et solis imago,
    Sydera conatis spondet amica tuis./
Extinguet forceps, ceræque superflua scindet
    Extingues hostes sic minuesque feros
Cereus; (ecce pij regisque emblema potentis,)
    Lumina dans alijs liquitur igne suo.   [30]
Fas mihi, quem dulcem laterna expirat odorem,
    Reginæ et natis assimilare tuis.
Illa tibi dulces fœcunda aspiret amores,
    Illaque te multa prole beata beet,
Denique succedens terrestri æterna corona
    Certa, sed ambobus sera venire queat./

Fifteen several disticks on
the fifteen divisions./

Prima salutatam monstrat pictura Mariam,
 Cui Gabriel, fœlix nuncius, inquit ave.
Viserit vt prægnans prægnantem proxima narrat,
 Sensit et haud natus, gaudia nata puer./
Tertia vt illæsa de virgine natus Iesus,
 Veraque iam mater, veraque virgo manet.
Et sequitur iussu tum circumcisio Legis,
 Solus adimplesti hanc, o homo nate deo./
Postea te alloquitur Moses comitatus Elia   262.
 Turbat at hæc sensum visio, Petre, tuum./   [10]
Sancta salutifero sudarunt sanguine membra,
 Cum peccata ingens non sua sensit onus.
Scinditur et flagris, nostri dum flagrat amore,
 Et veneranda tulit verbera dura cutis./
Spinea tum nudo capiti est aptata corona,
 Hostibus ah magis hæc apta corona tuis./
Hinc humeris lignum laceris portare coactus,
 Sustinuit propriæ baiulus esse crucis./
Inque crucem medius, binis latronibus, actus,
 Vni perpetuæ causa salutis erat./   [20]
Morte triumphata triduo, infernoque revixit,
 Inde resurgendum credimus esse pij.
Tum quoque conspicuus cælos ascendit ad altos,
 Vnde reversurus iudicis ora geret./
Denique discipulos paracletum mittit ad omnes,
 Doctaque non notos lingua dat ante sonos.
Creditur et mater cælis assumpta supernis,
 Supra virgineos sola beata choros,   Apocripha.
Da mihi finitæ pater o post tempora vitæ,
 Illi cum sanctis dicere semper Ave./   [30]

256

[Engraving of Mysteries of Rosary, 95 by 85 mm: Plate 9]   261.

Post Crucem Lucem.

The blessed virgins picture first hath place
to whom thus Gabriel saith. **Haile full of grace**.}   The Salutacion.
   Next she her Cosen visitts at whose voyce
   the babe vnborne did sensibly reioyce   }   Visitation.
Thirdly is Christ borne of a mayde vnstayned
and mother trew, a Virgin trew remayned,   }   Nativitie
   Fourthly hee's circumcis'd by lawes decree
   those lawes that no man e're fulfild but hee.}   Circumcision
Moyses Elias, meete him after that   263.
[10]   When Peter ravisht, spake he knew not what}   Transfiguration.
Then follow'd the Agony and bloudy sweat,
the burden of our sins did seeme so great/   }   Bloudy sweate
   Then for base spight, of clothes he was bestripped
   and loving vs, for vs he then was whipped./}   Scourging
On sacred head they clapt a Crowne of thorns,
themselus far fitter obiects for such skorns./ }   Crown of thornes.
   They forced him in sight of lewd beholders
   to carry his own cross on his own sholders.}   Carrying the Crosse.
They hange him, on each side a malefactor,
[20] but he to th'one did proue a benefactor. }   Crucifying
   At three dayes end he brought to full subiection
   both hell and death, and taught vs resurrection./}   Resurrection
Then playn in sight, to heav'n he did ascend
and will returne a Iudge this age to end, }   Ascention
   The comforter to come was then discearned   Comming of the
   and men did speake with tongues they neuer learned}   holy ghost.
And after all theis things it is presumed,   Assumpcion of the
The blessed virgin was to heaven assumed,}   virgin.
   God graunt me, when my life hath run the race
[30]   to say to her with saynts. **Haile full of grace**./}   Glorification.

{A gratulatory Elegie of the peaceable entry of king Iames }
{given to his Matie. at Burleighe. 1603.   }

Come triumphe enter, Church, Courte, citty, town,
 here Iames the sixt, now Iames the first proclaymed,
 see how all hearts are heald, that earst were maymed.
The Peere is pleas'd, th'knight, the Clarcke, the Clowne,
 the Marke at which the malcontent *had* aymed,
Ys mist, Succession stablisht in the Crown./
 Ioy Protestant, Papist bee now reclaymed,
Leaue Puritan your supercillious frown.
 Ioyne voyce, hart, hand, all discord bee disclaymed,
Make all one flocke by one great Sheapheard guided,   [10]
 No forrayn wolfe can force a fold so fenced,
God for his house this Steward hath provided,
Right to dispose what earst was wronge dispensed,
but in my loyall loue and long prepensed,
 With all, yet more then all reioyce do I
 to conster **Iam=es primus et non vj.**/

An Elegie written at the same time for
the welcome of Queene Ann into
England./

Great Queene belou'd, and blest in heav'n and earth,
 by humaine favour and by grace devyne,
 like peacefull oliue, and like fruitfull vyne
You banishe dreadfull warr and barren dearth,
To beare kings borne, and borne of princely birth,
 Whose lynage *moch*, whose yssew more shall shyne,
Restoring Englands now long faynting *myrth*
 and raysing vp their hopes that did declyne;
Let England be your sea of blissful pleasure,
 Where you like ship full fraught with balme and wine, [10]
With sweetly swelling sayles may swim at leasure,
 and stem all tydes that at your course repyne./
 Chast vessell whose deere fraught we pryse and measure,
 more then ten Carricks lade with Indyes treasure./

258

The Authors farewell to his Muse written
at Eaton the 14. of Aprill. 1603.

Musa iocosa, meos solari assueta dolores
    Et medijs mecum ludere docta malis.
Quæ peregrinantem comitata et castra sequentem
    Ausa mihi in tumidis et comes ire fretis,
Quæ me ruricolam, tractantem et aratra sequuta es,
    Nec poteras thalamis abstinuisse meis,
Te nunc Ætonæ, namque hinc es nata relinquo.
    Filius hic hæres te colet vsque meus,
Nunc iuvat oblitis meditari seria ludis,
    Hos annos, animum hunc vita severa decet   [10]
Iam pro fictitijs mihi gaudia vera relucent,   266.
    Cum Regem, dominum cum resaluto meum
Iam dabitur veras audire ac reddere voces
    Nostra sat est pietas dissimulata diu./
Quod superest ævi, patriæ patriæque parenti
    Dedico, nec levibus iam vacat hora iocis./
Huic mea mens soli, mea mens huic semper adhæret,
    Hunc solum, hunc semper promeruisse paro./
Seu libet Hispano bellum indixisse potenti,
    Iusta sub invicto principe bella sequar./   [20]
Seu pacem mavult, antiquaque fœdera iungi,
    Quam cupidus pacis nuncius ire velim?
Siue satis domitis, Leges perscribere Hibernis,
    In me consilium sentiet esse pium./
Digna vel Augusto struxisse palacia Rege,
    Ah nimis his operis ingeniosus eram./
Seu velit infames patriæ punire tyrannos,
    Tela tyrannorum tendet ad ora manus./
Sive suæ interdum sacræ dare tempora Musæ,
    Lector et auditor non malus esse queam./   [30]
Quid velit incertum est, sed quod velit impiger illud
    Exsequar hoc certum est, Musa iocosa. Vale.

Finis.

Critical Apparatus

Conventions

Italics: Harington autograph

[ ]: editorial intervention and comment

[margn.]: marginal gloss

H: Sir John Harington

S: Scribe

[Preliminaries]

A Letter	[Copied, in later hand] [om.] *BL*
Dedication	To . . . Prince Henry] [om.] *BL*
Dedication.2	[margn. in later hand] Eliz: Hoyle
Dedication.6	(Candidi et Cordati Lectores,)] Candidi et Cordati Lectores, *BL*
Dedication.18	younge yeares, and the barbatula, or] *young* years *and the barbatula or* ~~and the~~ *BL*
Dedication.	[picture, now missing, probably that in *Orlando Furioso*]
Dedication.date	*19 Iune. 1605.*] [om.] *BL*
To Iames.title	*1602.*] [om.] *BL*
To Iames.1	O Ioy to present] ~~O~~ °Ioy to ~~the~~ present *BL*
To Iames.8	I] ~~I~~ *we BL*
To Iames.9	my] ~~my~~ *owr BL*
To Iames.13	We do] we, ~~do~~ *wee BL* vices] ~~vices~~ *errors BL*
To Iames.14	'Tis you great Prince, that one day] Tis you *tis you* great prince, that ~~one day~~ *BL*

The first booke

1.title	how] ~~that~~ *how BL*
1.8	Raysons] Reasons *BL*
1.13	*the* Readers ~~with~~] reeders with *BL*
1.15	~~leeve you did sitt still~~ *rather you sate still*] *BL*; leeue you did still *F*
2.2	How Momus found] *how* Momus ~~had~~ found *BL*
2.3	~~abuse~~ *abews*] abu*ew*se *BL*
3.title	Table frends] table ~~talk~~ friends *BL*
3.1	Thinke you] *Yow* Think ~~you~~ *BL*
4.1	Of wryters all, Sextus a known dispyser] ~~Of writers all, Sextus a known despiser~~ *Old Sextus of al vers a known dispyser}* *BL*

4.2   sayth that vpon] *doth* sai~~th~~ that ~~uppon~~ *BL*
4.5   sir)] *BL*; sir [closing lunula omitted] *F*
5.3   for ^*his*^] for his *BL*
6.1   heard] *BL*; hard *F*
6.2   thin*ey* lord an *A*sse] thy ~~lord an~~ *husband* ass *BL*
8.2   self] ~~life~~ *selfe C*
8.3   Ioynt] Ioynte~~s~~ *BL*; Ioynts *C*
8.5   but] though *C*
8.10   foyle] foyle *BL*; foyl *C* ['f' in all three mss; error for 'soyle'?]
8.14   loves like force] Loues-like-force *C*
12.1   consider*e*d] considered *BL*
12.2   on] one *BL*
13.2   sho*ou*te] sho*ou*te *BL*
13.5   them of the meaner] ~~those of~~ the ~~meaner~~ ^*modest playner*^ *BL*
13.6   credit doth so] credit ^*them*^ doth ~~so~~ *BL*
14.5   roomes] Roomes *C*
14.10   roome] Rome *C*
19.10   ~~in buying of thy lyving~~ *to buy thy sonne a lyving*] in buying of thy lyving *BL*
19.12   when they nothing giue, vse] ^*giving*^ ~~when they~~ nothing ~~give~~ vse ^*their*^ *BL*
20.title *1592.*] [om.] *BL*
20.2   gratious] sovraign *BL*
20.14   docillity] *BL*; docillty *F*
21.5   But] *and* ~~but~~ *BL*
21.7   by] ~~by~~ ^*in*^ *BL*
21.8   shall] ~~shall~~ ^*may*^ *BL*
22.8   ~~he~~ ^*who*^ swears] who sweares *BL*
23.4   purge] ~~powre~~ ^*purge*^ *BL*
23.9-28.8 And then . . . all disturbe./] [om.: one fol. missing] *BL*
26.9   *w*brought] [om. fol.] *BL*
27.title of Cannington . . . mother] [om. fol.] *BL*; [om.] *C*
28.4   c*a*ought] [om. fol.] *BL*
29.3   fourth] foorth *BL*
29.8   And ~~after~~ let him warde, and after] and let him ward and after *BL*
29.9   ble*i*ss] bliss *BL*
29.17-24 A flattring slut . . . at Ancor] [8 lines with 3 vertical deletion marks] *BL*
31.2   and whispers] ~~and whispers~~ ^*still wispring*^ *BL*
31.3   soft~~ly~~ ^*doth*^] softly wrings *BL*
31.4   his ^*her*^ ring . . . his ^*her*^ finger [superscript revisions in lead, without
         deletion] *F*; ~~his~~ her ring . . . ~~her~~ his finger *BL*
32.8   that] th*y*at *BL*
36.4   deale] ~~write~~ ^*deale*^ *BL*
37.4   and askt] ~~and~~ ^*I*^ askt *BL*   why] why? *BL*
37.7   there] the*n*ere *BL*; then *C*
37.11   before] afore *C*
38.4   brybed by one side] ~~brybd~~ by *t*one side ^*bribde*^ *BL*
38.9   First I could] I fyrst ~~I~~ would *BL*

38.10   next I] I next ~~I~~ *BL*

41.1   Proud Paulus] *Proud* Paulus ~~of~~ *BL*

41.5   Fer~~d~~inandos] Fernandos *BL*

41.10   mai~~e~~y] may *BL*

41.12   my Lord ^{keepers}] my Lord (.) ^{good} *BL*

42.7   finishe] ~~fynish~~ *fade BL*

42.8   Nor doth her Ware ought lessen or diminishe] ~~nor doth her ware ought lessen or dyminish~~ $^{\text{whose ware growes greater by hir gentle Trade}}$ *BL*

43.5   hospitally*ty*] hospytallity *BL*

43.7   see~~a~~is] see~~a~~ys *BL*

43.14 ^{not} no*r*] not ^{nor} *BL*

45.8   so] ~~so~~ that *BL* ^{soche} ~~good~~] good *BL*

47.3   sweare'st] swear*e*st *BL*

47.4   thy lookes, thy lips] thy lips, thy lookes *C*

47.8   thy fayr smooth *b'*haunches] thy fayr smooth hawnches *BL*; *thy fayr smooth* (   ) [H draws sinuous lunulae] *C*

50.3   chaunge his life] ~~chawng~~ ^{mend} his life *BL*

50.6   and but perhap] (and but perhapp) *BL*

51.5   Aggat] aggat*ts BL*

51.8   of] ~~off~~ *of BL*

52.5   whish] *F, C*; ~~whi~~*u*sh *BL*

52.7   our] my *C*

54.4   bare] bare*s BL*

55.11   Yet seldom shewes any his own Endytings] yet selld*om* $^{\text{shewes any}}$ ~~any~~ *of* his ~~own~~ enditings *BL*

55.12   'his] his *BL*

55.14   of] ~~of~~ ^{in} *BL*

59.4   tyrye] tyr*e*ye *BL*

59.15   skant ore] $^{\text{skant ore}}$ ~~overe~~ *BL*

60.9   wicked ^{acts}] wickednes *BL*

61.4   no man] *for* no*ne* ~~man~~ *BL*

64.6   nor hardly] ^{nor} hardly ~~worth~~ *BL*

[65].title *of* Carnaruan] of Carnaruan *BL*

[65].3 ^{Dayly}] Dayly *BL*

65.6   sam*ence*] same *BL*

67.9   ase] ases *BL*

67.13   ~~his game~~ will ^{rather} venter] ~~will fyrst~~ $^{\text{his game will}}$ adventure *BL*

68.1   Once by mishap] ~~Once by mishapp~~ $^{\text{of late by hap)}}$ *BL*

68.7   sugar may please] ^{that} sugar ~~may please~~ ^{lykes} *BL*

68.8   my verse] ~~my~~ ^{a} verse *BL*

69.title Of Southsaying to the Queens Ma$^{\text{tie.}}$] Of Soothsaying to the Queen^{s} ~~of England~~ *Ma*^{tie} *BL*; Another to the Queene Of So~~u~~othsaying. *C*

71.1   ~~some~~ ^{young}] good *BL*

71.5   Prouerbe$_{s}$ [H corrects in lead and ink] *F*; prouerb *BL*

72.23   the warme . . . the warme] ~~the~~ warm$^{\text{th of}}$ . . . ~~the~~ warm$^{\text{th of}}$ *BL*

72.28   said ^{Sir}] said: Sir *BL*

74.1   Your servant] ~~Good Madam in this vearse~~ [rubbed start] Your servant *C*
74.6   plea] pl*ᵉ*a~~y~~ *C*
74.9   councell] cowncell~~s~~ *BL*
75.5   how his] how ~~my how~~ his *BL*
75.16   [From here till 84.8, pp. 45–8, minimal punctuation and revision by H] *F*
78.title *from Bathe./*] [om.] *BL* ; *from Bathe.* *C*
80.6   frend Misacmos] ~~friend Misacmos~~ *ᵍʰᵒˢᵗˡʸ ᶠᵃᵗʰᵉʳ* *BL*
80.7   that till] vntil ~~that till~~ *BL*
82.1   Henceforth for Pencions Poets] ~~Poets~~ hencefoorth for pensions *ᵖᵒᵉᵗˢ* *BL*
82. 3   For vearses grow] for verses ~~are~~ grow~~n~~ *BL*
83.1   first] furst [margn.] 20. A papist dwelling to a:/ *24 lynes bisyde tytle BL*
86-87   To the . . . Cooke./ [light vertical deletion, pp. 36–7] *BL*; [om.] *F*
89.1   Leeke*s* you leeke] Leeks you like *C*
89.6   *Tobacco.*] ~~(goe looke)~~ *tabacco. BL*; (*Tobacco./*) *C*
90.10   Deu'll he sayd] de*v*ill he sayd *BL*
93   Of Cloacina . . . Aiax./ [light vertical deletion, p. 39] *BL*; [om.] *F*
94   94] *BL*; 93 *F*
95   95] *BL*; 94 *F*
96   96] *BL*; 95 *F*
97   97] *BL*; 96 *F*
97.12   that] till *C*
98   98] *BL*; 97 *F*
98.4   *ʷw*that [H overwrites and superscribes] *F*; what *BL*
98.20   person face and manners] parson ~~manners &~~ *ᶠᵃᶜᵉ ᵃⁿᵈ ᵐᵃⁿⁿᵉʳˢ* *BL*
99   99] *BL*; 98 *F*
99.3   the' horned Ram doth rule in head] th horned Ramm *ᵈᵒᵗʰ* rewle~~s~~ in ~~my~~
          head *BL*; the'horned Ram rules in my head *C*
99.7   backe and hart] Hart and back *C*
99.15   each part is possest] is each part possest *C*
100   100] *BL*; [om. number] *F*

The second booke
1.1   Old Haywood wrytes] *ᴼˡᵈ* Haywood *ʷʳʸᵗᵉˢ* ~~affermes~~ *BL*
2.title   rent.] Rent. To my Lady Rogers *C*
2.14   in the'tennants] in the tennants *BL*; in ~~the~~ Tennants *C*
2.28   the Quittance] the quittance *BL*; the'Acquittance *C*
3.14   to leaue prayre a while, and] ~~to~~ leaue*ⁱⁿᵍ* prayre a while &*ᵗᵒ* *BL*
[4]   [number om.] *F, BL*
5.1   You Ladies] yow Ladies ~~yow~~ *BL*
6.1   Whether] ~~Whether~~ *ʸᶠ ˢᵒ* *BL*
6.6   many with paynes purge here] ~~many~~ *ᵐᵉⁿ ᵉᵛᵉʳ* with paynes *ᵈᵒ* purge ~~heer~~ *BL*
6.7   Frying and freezing are the paynes there told] *to* ~~ffrying~~ and freez~~ing~~ are
          ~~the~~ paynes thear ~~told~~ *cheefly told BL*
6.8   heer the chief payn] ~~heer~~ the cheefe payn *ʰᵉᵉʳ* *BL*
6.9   cryes, vapor, and smoake] cryes *ʷⁱᵗʰ* vapor & smoak *BL*
6.15   ~~some~~ *seure*] sewr *BL*

7.8   came] com *BL*

8.title   Of playn dealling] To a great Lady. *C*

9.8   the man ~~should~~ in Statute ^{should}] the man ~~should~~ in statute ^{should} *BL*

10.7   thereby thy remembrannce to] therb~~y~~^{withall} thy ~~remembrance to~~ ^{memory} *BL*

10.16   tis] ~~this~~ ^{tis} *BL*

10.26   table] Table *C*

10.32   much affinity] great affinity *C*

10.36   his] her *BL*; her~~is~~ *C*

11.1   doth to me] to me doth *BL*

12.1   malconten~~d~~ted] *BL*; malconted *F*

12.4   o~~r~~*ft*] or *BL*

15.2   gentlema~~e~~n] gentlemen *BL*

15.16-18   ryott./] ryet [autograph margn.] *this ep. may begin heer. thus Two sqwyres of wales arryved at a towne./* *BL*

17.title   ~~Purgatory~~*aradice*] ~~purgatory~~ paradice *BL*

19.4   number] *BL*; cumber [eyeskip repetition] *F*

23.2   what means] *BL*; what mean? *F* [S misreads 's' as interrogation mark?]

24.5   my] me *BL*

25.3   doubt*es*] doubtes *BL*

25.4   to any] ~~to~~ ^{or} any *BL*

25.6   appeach Leda for a Recusant] appeach ^{thee} Leda for ~~a~~ Recusant *BL*

26.title   To my Ladie Rogers the Authors wiues mother] To the Lady Rogers *C*

26.2   in sport] in ~~pleasing~~ sport *C*

26.4   forth] ~~forth~~ ^{out} *BL*

26.5   no word] no~~t~~ ~~a~~ word *C*

31.2   sayes*t*] says *BL*

32.9   my] ~~my~~ ^{me} *BL*

33.3   stand] *BL*; stands *F*

34.3   my misconceaued] ~~my~~ ^{our} ^{mis}conceaved *BL*

40.6   this ^{ys}] this ys *BL*

40.7   we ^{do}] we do *BL*

46.2   encurre'd] encurrd *BL*; incur'd *C*

46.10   dafter] *F*, *BL*; Daughter *C*

47.title   Poppeas] Poppea *C*

47.7   Poppea~~s~~] Poppeaes *BL*; Popeas *C*

50.2   doth not beleeue the] ~~doth not~~ beleeues the $^{no\ wit\ the}$ *BL*

50.5   things are fables all] ~~thinges~~ ^{stories} a~~r~~ fables all ^{are} *BL*

50.7   I haue (saith he) traveld] I ^{traveld} have ~~traveld~~ (sayth he) *BL*

50.12   in $^{all\ or}$ part ~~or all~~] in all or part *BL*

50.13   sea, land, hell] ~~by sea~~ land, ^{seas} hell *BL*

52.19   th'~~a~~opposites] *BL*; th'apposites *F*

54.2   poore soule] ~~poor sowle~~ $^{blind\ foole}$ *BL*

59.1   a gallant] A ^{gallant} great lord [ink and lead correction & underlining] *BL*

59.6   I hope Sir gallant you haue learnd to swim] Your Lordship hath I hope learned to swim./ [margn.] *I hope S galant you have learnt to swim BL*

61.10   ~~witt~~ *quick*] ~~witt~~ *quick* [H corrects in lead] *BL*

63.title Paraclesian] [sic] *F, BL*
63.16   loue spirit] love ^*the* sperit *BL*
65.title A Groome ... time] *Another to the Queen. C*
66.3   *the^m*] the^m *BL* [H in *F*, S in *BL* add 't', insert tilde]; them *C*
66.10   the hemp, the woll, the flax] the woll, the hemp, the flax *C*
66.15   ~~clothes~~ ^*looks*, good ~~lookes~~ ^*cloaths*] ~~clothes~~ ^looks good ~~lookes~~ ^cloaths *BL*; lookes, good cloths *C*
66.22   Heroy~~r~~ns] Heroy~~oi~~ns *BL*; Heroyns *C*
66.24   Anomelo~~u~~ns] Anomele~~o~~ns *BL*; Anomelons *C*
66.27   Curr~~oe~~ntos] C~~au~~rr~~oe~~ntos *BL*; Correntos *C*
66.35   kn~~oe~~w] kn~~oe~~w *BL*; kn~~ee~~w *C*
66.36   But ~~yet~~ in] But in *BL, C*   he~~oo~~eroycall] hooreoy^c all *BL*; Heoaroycall *C*
68.title An] A *BL*
68.4   to rule./] to rule./ *probatum est* [margn. autograph postscript] *BL*
69   69] *BL*; [om. number] *F*
69.21   ~~Marcus~~ ^*Paulus*] ~~Marcus~~ ^*Paulus* *BL*
70.4   extoll~~ing~~*ed*] extolled *BL*
73   73] 74 *BL* [after deleted 73 'To Webb':see Appendix]
74   74] 75 *BL*
75   75] 76 *BL*
75.4   government] *BL*; goverment *F*
76   76] 77 *BL*
76.2   merrit] ~~merrit~~ ^*deserve* *BL*
76.3   he~~r~~*is*] he~~r~~*is* *BL*
77   77] 78 *BL*
78   78] 79 *BL*
80   ~~79~~*80*] 80 *BL*
80*bis*   80*bis*] 81 *BL*
81   81] 82 *BL*
81.1   He that] ~~hee that~~ ^*who so* *BL*
82   82] 83 *BL*
83   83] 8~~3~~4 *BL*
83.4   one] *BL*; on *F*
83.6   ^*thou* ~~And~~] ~~and~~ ^*thou* *BL*
83.8   gr~~oe~~wst] gr~~oe~~wst *BL*
84   84] 8~~4~~5 *BL*
84.1   Madam with speeches kynde] Madam with ^*speeches* kind ~~speeches~~ *BL*; Good Madam with kynd speach *C*
84.9   no] ~~a~~ ^*no* *BL*
85   85] 8~~5~~6 *BL*
85.3   pantaffles] pantoffles *BL*
86   86] 8~~6~~7 *BL*
86.8   picture] ~~picture~~ ^*statue* *BL*
86.12   the Cart] ~~the~~ ^*his* carte *BL*
87   87] 8~~7~~8 *BL*
88   88] 8~~8~~9 *BL*

88   Of a fayr Shrow./] Of a fair Shrew. To his wife.*C*
88.1   ~~fortunate~~ young] ~~fortunate~~ ^{young} *BL*; young *C*   thy] her *C*
89   89] 89*bis BL*
91.4   ~~ye that are~~ $^{least\ for\ your}$] ~~ye that are~~ $^{least\ for\ your}$ *BL*
92.5   neuer] ~~never~~ $^{n'ere}$ *BL*
93.3   greatest] greatst *BL*
95.3   deceaud] ~~deceavd~~ ^{beguyld} *BL*
95.10   oft in courts, knaues goe] ~~oft~~ ^{knaves} in courts ~~knaves goe~~ $^{are\ oft}$ *BL*
96.5   I did] *BL*; I ~~sadid~~ [S overwrote 'a' as 'd' but failed to delete 's'] *F*
97.title *A distick of frends*] *C*; [om. title] *F, BL*
98.5   married] married $^{did\ take}$ *BL*
100.13 Forsake, wife] forsake ^{thou} wife *BL*
100.14 quickly, and] ~~quickly &~~ $^{strait\ and}$ *BL*
        The end of the second booke./] [Followed by] *Certayn epigrams that will not speak englysh. BL* [see Appendix]

The third booke

1.2   thi~~s~~y] thy *BL*
1.5   the~~y~~] the *BL*
1.12 ^{they}] they
1.20   en~~dyt~~^{ten}dement] endytment *BL*
2.title   Of an vnkynde *kynde*] Of a kind vnkind *BL*
2.2   goodly] *BL*; goody *F*
2.10   me] ~~her~~ me *BL*
7.2   prompt of his] *and* prompt of ~~his~~ *BL*
7.4   one that] *full* ^{well} ~~one that~~ *BL*
7.6   hapned] ^{did} hap~~n~~ed *BL*
7.9   He told the tale to me and other] ~~he told the tale to me & other~~ $^{And\ I\ that}$ $^{wedlock\ prayse\ to\ all\ my}$ *BL*
7.10   and straight I learn'd yt at my fingers ends/] ~~and streyght I learnd it~~ ^{had} $^{quickly\ got\ his\ speeche}$ at ~~my~~ fingers ends *BL*
7.11   which ioyes] $^{Thease\ the}$ ~~which~~ ioyes *BL*
7.12   one on each] ~~one~~ on ~~each~~ ^{evry} *BL*
7.13-36   [Marginal watercolours of hands; see Plate 6] *F*; [ink-drawn hands under pastels tipped in] *BL*
7.17   Then for her frends, what ioyes] ~~then~~ $^{and\ next}$ for ~~her~~ friends what Ioy *BL*
7.18   dwell they] ^{that} dwell ~~they~~ *BL*
7.20   of strife, frawd or] of ^{sutes} strife, frawd ~~or~~ *BL*
7.21   fouthly] fowrthly *BL*
7.25   Marke then] ~~mark~~ then ^{marke} *BL*
7.26   Which of theis Ioyes] which ^{Ioys} of these ~~Ioyes~~ *BL*
7.27   First for the wife, sure] ^{and} ffyrst ~~for~~ the wife, sewr *BL*
7.28   that for most part] ^{but} ~~that~~ for most parte *BL*
7.36   onely theise twayn] ~~only~~ ^{behold} these twayn *BL*
8.1   You sent to me Marcus] You ^{Marcus} sent to me ~~Marcus~~ *BL*
8.4   tell ^{me}] tell me *BL*

9.15   ~~and~~ *in*] midst *BL*
10.2   ~~you~~ that single you] that single yow *BL*
11.1   now haue I] I now haue *C*
11.4   to ~~bee~~ *too*] to to *BL*; to *to* ~~be~~ *C*
11.17   keepe] kept *C*
11.21   travayle] travell *BL*; travail *C*
11.22   still] yet *C*   in] at *C*
13.14   or Statute, ~~or~~] statute or *BL*
14.10   seemd now] ~~now~~ seem^e d now *BL*
17   17] ~~17~~16*bis BL*
17.3   ~~witts~~ *strength*] witts *BL*
18   18] 17 *BL*
19   19] 18 *BL*
20*bis*   20*bis*] 19 *BL*
20   ~~21~~20] 20 *BL*
20.1   ~~it~~ *that*] ~~it~~ *that BL*
20.8   much, and] much & *more BL*
22   22] 21 *BL*
23   23] 22 *BL*
23.4   ~~martiall~~ *valient*] martiall *BL*
24   24] 23 *BL*
25   25] 24 *BL*
26   26] 25 *BL*
26.7   runns mine estate] *doth* runn~~s~~ myne estate *BL*
26.12   straight to those eyes my soule is in subiection] ~~straight to~~ those eyes *to take* my soule ~~ys~~ in *theyr* subiection *BL*
26.30   C~~au~~rr~~oe~~ntoes] Caora^e ntoes *BL*
26.32   ~~giha~~ue] ~~geve~~ *take BL*
26.34   the*y* f*ill* a braue roome in the bed] they fill a ~~braue~~ *goodly* roome in ~~the~~ bedd *BL*
26.35   comlier] ~~comlier~~ *nimbler BL*
26.38   Were she attyrd?] ~~wear she~~ *In ritch* attirde: *BL*
26.47   contry] cuntrey *BL*
27   27] 26 *BL*
27.1   Queene] *C* ; Queen *BL*; queem *F*
27.7   *being*] being *C*; beeing *BL*
28   28] 27 *BL*
28.7   mourn^e d] mourn^e d *BL*
28.10   and yet sweet foole, I loue thee, thou beleeuest] and yet (Sweet foole) I loue thee thou beleeuest [H inserts lunulae] *C*
29*bis*   29*bis*] 28 *BL*
29*bis*.4   pardon is] *is* pardon ys *BL*
29*bis*.5   ys restority] *ys* restority *BL*
29*bis*.8   Lynus would *quickly* proue] *thou* Lynus *then* wouldst ~~quickly~~ proove *BL*
29   ~~30~~29] 29 *BL*
30   ~~31~~30] 30 *BL*

32	32] 31 *BL*
33	33] 32 *BL*
33.7	obtayned~~st~~ from] obtainedst of f'om *BL*; obtayned from *C*
33.22	consumedst] consum^e dst *C*
33.30	breake them] breake ^them *C*
34	34] 33 *BL*
34.8	from shame] ^for ~~from~~ shame *BL*
35	35] 34 *BL*
35.4	^and cryde] & cride *BL*
36	36] 35 *BL*
36.8	indiscreetly] undiscreetly *BL*
36.13	bee ^you] be yow *BL*
37	37] 36 *BL*
37.2	writes] ~~sayth~~ ^writes *BL*
37.7	~~n~~venerable] venerable *BL*
38	38] 37 *BL*
38.21	erre] err *BL*; arre *C*;
39bis	39*bis*] 38 *BL*
39	~~40~~39] 39 *BL*
40	~~41~~40] 40 *BL*
40.title	To King David] ~~To~~ Of king David written to the queene./ *C*
40.1	To] ~~To~~ ^Thou *BL*
40.3	the] they *BL*
40.5	dreadfull beare, and Lion] Beare and dreadfull Lyon *C*
40.12	taught'st, not ^once ~~not~~] taughtst ~~no~~ not ^once *BL*; taught'st not ~~not~~ ^once *C*
40.14	~~l~~hookes] hookes *BL, C*
40.15	lapt in the] *F, C*; lapt ^close in the *BL*
40.16	faultles] *F, C*; fauor ^mer ~~ltless~~ *BL*
40.23	godly] *BL, C;* gody *F*
42	42] 41 *BL*
42.8	wealth] ~~hell~~ ^wealth *BL*
42.13	that] ^what ~~that~~ *BL* sitts] sittseth *BL*
43	43] 42 *BL*
44	44] 43 *BL*
44.8	noblenes] nobles *C*
45	45] 44 *BL*
45.12	wh~~at~~ich] what *BL*
46	46] 45 *BL*
46.6	sto~~e~~ar'd] stooed *BL*
46.17	the~~is~~] the *BL*
47	47] 46 *BL*
48.title	in his wryting] in wryting *C*
48	48] 47 *BL*
48.2	the~~y~~] th~~y~~at *BL*; thy *C*
48.8	*So* learn'd to set] learned to set *BL, C*
48.12	walke] ~~hang~~ ^walke *BL*; walk *C*

49   49] 48 *BL*
49.5   'tis not the] ~~tis not the~~ ^{yt ys not} *BL*
49.6   hell de~~v~~nou~~r~~n^cing] hell=de~~v~~now~~r~~n^cing *BL*; hell=de~~v~~nou~~r~~ncing *C*
50*bis*   50*bis*] 49 *BL*
50*bis*.4 o're all the Byble to th'Apocalips./] ~~o're all the Bible to th'Apocalips.~~
         from thence to Iob and thence t'Apocalips./ BL
50   50 [Marked with large cross in Table of Contents] *BL*; 51 *F*
50.8   how them] how they *BL, C*
50.9   But by] *BL, C*; By by *F*
52   52] 51 *BL*
52.11   *which made my muse so wood she sayd in rage*] At which I waxt so wood
         I said in rage *BL*
52.12   *that thirst of gold makes this an Iron age.* [H adds last two lines] *F* ; that
         thirst of gold makes this an Iron age *BL*
53   53] 52 *BL*
53.3   thinkst] thinks *BL*
53.10   pull] *BL*; pall *F*
54   54] 53 *BL*
54.30   (thriue vnthrifty)] *BL*; (thrive (vnthrifty) *F*
54.35   ~~s~~pooyle] spoyle *BL*
54.38   ~~and~~ shift] and shift *BL*
55   55] 54 *BL*
56   56] 55 *BL*
56   *A wary aunswer*] [om. title] *BL*
56.6   to~~'~~envre] to ~~envre~~ ^{put} *BL*
56.12   a frend answer] a friend*s* ~~answer~~ ^{defence} *BL*
57   57] 56 *BL*
57.7   he, ev'n] he ^{ev'n} *BL*
58   58] 57 *BL*
59   59] 58 *BL*
60*bis*   60*bis*] 59 *BL*
60   ~~6160~~] 60 *BL*
62title Of Galla to his wife.] Of Galla: to his wife./ *BL*
62   62] 61 *BL*
62.1   a loftie] a ~~sumptuous~~ ^{lofty} *BL*
62.10   the latter./] *BL*; the latter, *F*
63   63] 62 *BL*
64   64] 63 *BL*
65   65] 64 *BL*
66   66] 65 *BL*
66.6   ~~trade~~ *frawd* [H corrects proleptic eyeskip] *BL*; trade *F*
66.7   theis lewd trades and sinister] ~~lewd~~ ^{stet} trades ^{most} & sinister *BL*
67   67] 66 *BL*
67.3   friendly] *BL*; frendy *F*
68   68] 67 *BL*
68.6   move him to some] ~~use~~ ^{move} him ~~to~~ ^{make} som *BL*

68.9   Foole (sayd he) thinke you I will] *thow* ffoole (said he) think*st* thow
        I *⁷* ~~will~~ *BL*
69   69] 68 *BL*
69.13   ^kinde^ Almes] *BL*; ^ Almes *F* [*F* has caret, but no insertion]
70*bis* 70*bis*] 69 *BL*
70*bis*.2 wanting] lacking *C*
70   70] *BL*; 71 *F*
70.11   dur'd] ~~dewrd~~ *^brookt^ BL*
72   72] 71 *BL*
73   73] 72 *BL*
74   74] 73 *BL*
75   75] 74 *BL*
75.2   Curtesies ^*and*^ Complements] curtesies complements *BL*
75.3   presses ^*mee*^] presses me *BL*
75.8   mee] ~~thee~~ ^mee^ *BL*
76   76] 75 *BL*
76.1   Mais~~ter~~ [mistaken deletion by S] *F*; Mʳ *BL*
76.6   yᵉt] yet *BL*
77   77] [om. number] *BL*
78   78] 77 *BL*
78.2   *Larks* [S leaves space, H makes linear addn.] *F*; ~~lo~~earks *BL*
78.3   ~~do~~ ^*not*^ weary] not werry *BL*
78.4   ^*weary*^ neuer ~~weary~~] never ~~v~~wery *BL*
79   79] 78 *BL*
80*bis* 80*bis*] 79 *BL*
80*bis*.16 too] ~~do~~ ^too^ *BL*
80   ~~81~~80] 80 *BL*
80.4   that] ~~that~~ ^*save*^ *BL*
80.7   lay] ^*lay*^ *BL*
82   8~~1~~2] 81 *BL*
83   83] 82 *BL*
83.2   learne'd] learn'd *BL*
84   84] 83 *BL*
84.1   a grace] ~~a~~ ^*some*^ grace *BL*
85   85] 84 *BL*
85.2   thinks their names are] *doth* thinks their names ~~are~~ *BL*
85.6   way] ~~way~~ ^*pryze*^ *BL*
85.7   Those that are] ~~those that ar~~ ^*Theyr prayse ys*^ *BL*
85.8   Do] ~~do~~ ^*that*^ *BL*
85.10   books are not] *no* books ar ~~not~~ *BL*
86   86] 85 *BL*
86.3   being thus] ^*thus*^ being ~~thus~~ *BL*
87   87] 89 [scribal error for 86] *BL*
88   88] 87 *BL*
89   89] 88 *BL*
89.1   that ^last^] that last *BL*

89.4   Yt] yet [scribal error] *BL*
91   9̶0̶*1*] 89 *BL*
91.1   layes yt] layes *yt* *C*
91.7   am] *goe* *C*
91.14 Nine] ~~Nine~~ *Seavn* [H marks loss of two children] *C*
90   9̶1̶0] 90 *BL*
90.5   the*is*] this *BL*
92   92] 91 *BL*
92.18   any man] *BL*; many men [scribal eyeskip] *F*
93   93] 92 *BL*
94   94] 93 *BL*
94.9   persons] parsons *BL*
95   95] 94 *BL*
96   96] 95 [poem, not title, deleted; inserted after IV.13] *BL*
97   97] [om. number] *BL*
97.1   Of*t*] Oft *BL*
97.7   After the conquests] & after ~~the~~ Conquests *BL*
98   98] 96 *BL*
98.4   tast] tak~~e~~*ste* *BL*
99   99] 97 *BL*
99.5   frendly] *BL*; frendy *F*
99bis   ~~100~~ *99bis*] 98 *BL*
99bis.14 one sells all] one *to* sells ~~all~~ *BL*
99ter   ~~101~~ [*99ter*] *F*; 99 *BL*
99ter.7 ~~wa~~*ra*yll] rayll *BL*
99ter.16 ~~and~~ *or*] & *BL*
100   10̶2̶0] 100 *BL* [with latin version *F, BL*]

The fourth booke

1.9   mend] *BL*; men *F*
5.7   Combe] combe *BL*
5.8   ~~blacke~~, *darke*]~~black~~ *dark* *BL*
7.6   thi*e*ᵃs] this *BL*; theis *C*
7.8   for yt, haue euer] for it ~~oft times~~ have ever *BL*
8.1   those] ~~those~~ *theis* *BL*
8.4   killing their frends and kin of their] *by* killing ~~their~~ friends & folk of ~~their~~ neer *BL*
8.5   By] w*ith* ~~by~~ *its* *BL*
8.11   ~~braue~~ *fayr*] ~~braue~~ *fayr* *BL*
8.12   Doth kiss her and] doth *kyndely* kiss ~~her and~~ *BL*
8.15   her husbands chiefest Iewell] *to wear* her ~~husbands~~ chiefest Iewell *BL*
8.17   Vowing] & Vow*ding* *BL*
8.19   Oh motion moving] Oh motion *moving* *BL*
8.20   either he dyes] ~~either~~ *Or* he *must* dye~~s~~ *BL*
8.21   subiects] subiects *BL*
8.23   Lo yet] ~~ah~~ yet *lo* *BL*

8.24 worthy a woman] *right* worthy a woman *BL*

8.25 more then her self] ~~more then her self~~ *beyond all show* *BL*

8.29 thou pollute her?] thow ~~pollute her~~ *her defyle* ?*BL*

8.30 She in thy filthy lap lyes vndefyled] ~~she in thy filthy lapp lies vndefiled~~ *her fayth with this thy filth* ys ~~un~~defiled *not* *BL*

8.31 Honour of matrons] ~~honor~~ of matrons *honor* *BL*

8.32 thy] thy*ne* *BL*

8.33 *or* If] or if *BL*

8.34 'Twas a most pretious] *y*twas a ~~most~~ precious *BL*

8.35 Yf ought I know by hearing, or by reeding] ~~yf ought I know by heering or by reeding~~ *Thy fame then Lucres bee resownded furder BL*

8.36 this act Lucretias deed is far exceeding] ~~this act Lucrecias deeds is far exceeding~~ *whose soule ys chast yet guilty was of murder. BL*

9.5 seave'n] vij *BL*; ~~seavn~~ *eight* *C*

9.8 thus that] thus *that* *C*

10.3 on] one *BL*

10.7 Both do] *for* both ~~do~~ *BL*

10.14 ~~dliue~~ in the new, *live* ~~dy~~ if you *list* ~~can~~ in th'old./] live in the new, dy yf yow can in th,olde./ *BL*

13.1 of high byrth, great] ~~of high birth~~ great *in birth and* *BL*

13.2 *all* clothe'd] *all* clothe'd *BL*

13.3 wearing a border of rich] & wearing ~~a~~ border*s* ~~of~~ ritch *of* *BL*

13.4 at] ~~at~~ *worth* *BL*

13.6 through a great press, vp a darke payr of Stayrs] ~~through a great press~~ *to shun the press* ~~upp~~ *by* a dark ~~pair of~~ *and privat* stayrs *BL*

13.8 ~~seing~~ *that saw*] ~~seeing~~ *that saw* *BL*

13.9 the Stayrs] the*is* stairs *BL*

13.13 Attempt] *thrust vpp* ~~attempt~~ *BL*

13.14 Rudely to thrust his hand vnder] ~~rudly to thrust~~ his hand*s* *most rudely,* vnder *neath* *BL*

13.17 vnpleasant] *vn* ~~displeasant~~ *BL*

13.21 Villayns] *out knaves* ~~Villains~~ *BL*

13.22 t'other] ~~tother~~ *rest* *BL*

13.26 theirs] ~~theis~~ *BL*

14 14] 15 *BL*

15 15] 16 *BL*

15.title my Lady *R*: and her musick.] my Lady and her musick./ *BL*

16 16] 17 *BL*

17 17] 18 *BL*

17.2 ~~in w*th*~~] in *BL*

18 18] 19 *BL*

20 20 ~~19~~] 20 *BL*

21 2~~0~~1] 21 *BL*

21.12 (for she . . . redoubled) [H adds lunulae] *F*; for she . . . redoubled *BL*

21*bis* 21*bis*] 22 *BL*

21*bis*.8 And*s* their's] and theirs *BL*

21*bis*.12 course] rule *BL*

22   22] 23 *BL*

23   23] 24 *BL*

23.6   defends] defend *BL*

24   24] 24*bis BL*

24.9   delicate] <u>delicat</u> ^{daintie} [underlined, not deleted] *BL*

26.7   ruft*l*y] rufty *BL*

27.2   me Ile repay't] ~~me~~ ^{him} I^{le have} repayt *BL*

27.4   three] ~~six~~ ³ *BL*

27.6   saue'd] sav'd *BL*

29.1   it] thee *C*

29.5   wantonise] wanton⁼ryse *BL*; wantonn*r*yse *C*

29.8   without mee] with^{out} ~~little~~ ^{mee} *BL*; without my *C*

30.8   onely God damn me, is] ~~only~~ God damn me ^{now} is ^{growne} *BL*

30.10   hauing lost] ~~having lost~~ ^{that loosing} *BL*

31.7   ^{content}] content *BL*

31.11   Y*e*t] yet *BL*

31.16   so ill fare] <u>so ill fare</u> ~~such march beere~~ *BL*

32   32] [om. number] *BL*

32.6   neither] nether *BL*

32.17   ~~nor~~ ^a] & a *BL*

34.10   brest salvagious] ~~brest salvagious~~ ^{haynous guilt} *BL*

35.7   ~~so~~ ^{both}] so *BL*

36.title   gaue me] gave this Author in latten verses./ *BL*

37.1   once] ~~once~~ ^{late} *BL*

37.4   Pallas, and] *dan* Pallas ~~and~~ *BL*

37.5   Pallas was foule and grim so] *but* Pallas ~~was~~ foule and grim ^{was} ~~so~~ *BL*

37.6   *as neither gods nor men in her had pleasure* [H transposes from l. 11] *F*

37.7   Iuno so curst and shrowd was of her tounge] *at* Iuno^s ~~so curst and shrowd was of her tongue~~ ^{shrowdnes all he most did wonder} *BL*

37.8   that all mislyked her both old and younge] ~~that all mislyked her both olde & young~~ ^{he feared her tongue above her husbonds thunder} *BL*

37.11   ~~That neither godds nor men in her tooke pleasure~~ [H deletes with ruler] *F*; that neither godds nor men in her tooke plesure *BL*

39.6   the ^a] the *BL*

40.9   bewar*e* [H clarifies scribal 'e', which looks like 'c'] *F*; beware *BL*

41.1   Late hauing] *C*; Late Hauing [margn.] *F* ; Late having *BL*   a] ^a *C*

42.9   well ^{well}] well well *BL*

42.10   care] ~~place~~ ^{care} *BL*

42.12   Nay nay] Nay ~~think~~ ^{nay} *BL*

43.title   to Sr. Iohn Ashley.] [om. from title; poem functions as envoi] *C*

43.4   inti*y*s't] entyst *BL*; intyst *C*

46.2   ~~Yet~~ ^{That}] yet *BL*

47.13   he^er] her *BL*

48.2   ~~her~~ *his*] his *BL*

49.title   ~~to~~ neuer ^{to}] to neuer *BL*

50.13-16 This side sayth . . . Dividatur] ~~this side sayth . . . dividatur~~ [two vertical
             deletion marks though these four lines] *BL*
50.15   commorse] ~~remorse~~ commorse *BL*
51.1   The great Assuerus] ~~The~~ great ~~Assuerus~~ *Artaxerxes BL*
51.9   portion] *dowry* ~~portion~~ *BL*
51.10   eminent] *e*~~imminent~~ *BL*
51.14   Councell] ~~councell~~ *sample BL*
52.8   place] place~~s~~ *BL*
53.4   this is your censure] *is* this ~~is~~ your censure? *BL*
53.5   thereto] hereto *C*
55.2   warn*e*d] warnd *BL*
page   ~~1~~*221* [S has slipped a hundred in numbering pp. 221 to 239; H corrects] *F*
57.3   leaned] *did leane* ~~leaned~~ *BL*
57.7   softly sayes] soft~~ly~~ *doth* sayes *BL*
57.8   kayes] kayes *BL*
58   58] *BL*; [om. number] *F*
61.6   name] ~~fame~~ Name *BL*
66.16   deadly] deady *C*
68.1   I late] *I* Late ~~I~~ *BL*
68.2   and hastend to] *and* hast~~ien~~gd ~~vnto~~ *BL*
72.16   (after long scilence)] (~~after~~ long silence) *BL*
73.4   Vn'wares] vnwares *BL*
73.9   requy*cy*tall [H corrects analeptic eyeskip] *BL*; requitall *F*
75.2   other] other~~s~~ *BL*
76.2   ~~gr~~neat [H corrects analeptic eyeskip] *F*; neat *BL*
78.1   On *lesbya* Lynus ~~Lesbia~~] *BL*; On Lynus Lesbia *F*
79.4   had bourded her] *hir* ~~had~~ bourded ~~her~~ *had BL*
80.2   that] ~~that~~ *once late BL*
80.3   late] ~~late~~ *graue BL*
80.7   beare] bare *BL*
85.17   inclyne] inclynd*e* *C*
85.19-20   *and that . . . thyne vndefiled bed*] and that . . . thy vndefiled bed *C*; [om.] *BL*
86.1-10   One that . . . haue yt] ~~One that~~ . . . have it *BL* [For heavily corrected
             version in *BL*, see Appendix]
87.title   *to wryte . . . the Queen* [H adds, with some duplication] *F*; om. *BL*
87.51   Rough*ffe*] roofe *BL*
88.6   *you reade*] yow reede *BL*
88.7   poore] ~~poore~~ *playn BL*
88.8   ~~but~~ *and*] but *BL*
89   89] [Deleted poem, ~~The Pater noster~~ playnly ~~translated~~: see Appendix] *BL*
89.7   Good Cozen said] *good* Cosen ~~replide~~ *sayd BL*
90.5   ~~into~~] to *BL*
90.16   and *all* our neighbor] and *all* our neighbour~~s~~ *BL*
92.6   sinns] ~~skinns~~ *synns BL*
94   94] *BL*; [om. number, throwing sequence from 94 to 99] *F*
94.1   One that was] One ~~that was~~ *lately BL*

94.2   and] & *that* *BL*
95   95] *BL*; 94 *F*
96   96] *BL*; 95 *F*
97   97] [and latin version] *BL*; 96 *F*
98   98] [and latin version; om. margn.] *BL*; 97 [autograph margn.] *F*
99   99] [om. margn.] *BL*; 98 [autograph margn.] *F*
100.4   doth] will *doth* *BL*
100.8   younge] whole *younge* *BL*
100.12 deare./] [followed by 'an addicion' and latin version: see Appendix] *BL*
101   101] 1 *BL*
102   102] 2 *BL*
103   103] 3 *BL*
104   104] [om. number, followed by deleted poem on Ely: see Appendix] *BL*
104.14 my booke] my book./ [add. line] Cassador./ *BL*
105   105] 5 *BL*
105.7   now] now *BL*
106   106 *The last Epigram*.] om. number and title *BL*
106.11 gotten] gott *BL*
Finis./ Finis./] finis. [Followed by letter, *To Mr Richard Langley*, and additional
        poems, pp. 195–205: for all these, see Appendix] *BL*
Painted lantern] *Mr Swizzer in Sho. Lane must grave in wood the lantern.*/ [Om.
        picture; blank page 206 with autograph instruction] *BL*
A Newyeares   A Newyeares guift sent to the kings Mat^ie· of Scotland. Anno.
        1602.] A new yeeres guifte sent by S^r· Iohn Haryngton of Bathe
        in the county of Somerset knight, to the kings Mat^ie: of Skotland.
        Anno 1602. and in the xliiij^or yeer of Queen Elisabeth. *BL*
Lant. El.   The Elegie . . . Englishe.] om. title *BL*
Lant. El.3   haollow] hollow *BL*
Lant. El.11   Pure silver i's] Silver is *BL*
Lant. El.29   th'emblen] th'Embleme *BL*
Lant. El.lat.1   *Brutus.*[margn.] *F*; om. *BL*
Lant. El.lat.27   scindiet] scindit *BL*
Lant. El.lat.28   feros] tuos *BL*
K. Iames El.5   malcontented *had*] mallcontent had *BL*
K. Iames El.12   God for his house this Steward hath provided] *This Stewart god
        hath for his hous provyded* God for his hous this Steward hath
        provyded [margn. autograph revision and underlining] *BL*
Q. Ann El.6   *moch*] much *BL*
Q. Ann El.7   breathe *myrth*] merth *BL*
Musa Vale.9   meditari] meditaris *BL*
Musa Vale.32   Musa iocosa. Vale.] *F, BL* [See Appendix for lost translation.]
Finis.]   Finis.] finis. [followed by untitled index to first lines and table of
        contents, pp. 219–250.] *BL*
[Terminal punctuation (./) added to I.21; II.34, 61; III.18, 39*bis*; IV.37, 75 and 84;
parentheses closed by final lunula at III.56.3 and IV.68.8.]

First-line Index and Table of Contents

In *BL*, an index of first lines and table of contents follows the poems. I have transcribed this, merely adapting numbers and spelling to correspond with *F*. In Harington's table of contents, every tenth poem, or theological decade, is marked in the left margin with a cross, and these appear to be autograph. Two, I.90 and I.100, have not been so marked. Other theological poems (not on the decade) have a smaller cross marked in a separate column, so I have represented these after the first line. There are Harington autograph indications of poems for which a Latin version exists. More enigmatically, Harington has marked some poems with an *H*. Autograph changes are represented by italics. I have not transcribed what looks like a later, and certainly muddled, attempt to number the Latin versions.

Italic: autograph addition or revision
†   Harington's cross (mostly larger) by every tenth 'decade'
†   Harington's cross (in separate column) by theological poems not on decade
Latin, lat or (rarely*) lat.*:   indicates one or more Latin versions available.

[First-line Index]

Madam with speeches kynde and promise fayr	II.84
Madame I read to you a little since	II.46
Mall in mine absence this is still your song	IV.18
Mall once I did but do not now envy	II.47
Many men mervails Lynus doe's not thriue	III.66
Marke heer my Mall how in a dozen lynes	I.99
Men say that England late is bank'rout grown	IV.1
Men talking as oft times it comes to pass	II.89
Might Queenes shunn future mischief by foretelling	I.69
Mine own when in your closet for deuotion	II.10
Misacmos hath long time a sutor beene	II.64
Momus that loues mens lynes and liues to skan	I.32
Most worthy Prophet that by inspiration	III.33
Musa iocosa, meos solari assueta dolores	Musa Vale
Muse you Misacmos failes in some endevor	II.39
My deare frend Davis some against vs partiall	IV.25
My frend you presse me very hard	I.63
My good frend Lynus still is vndermyning	II.29
My Lord thoughe I by you am often prest	IV.106
My louely Leda some at thee repyning	II.25
My Mall I marke that when you mean to proue me	I.47
My Mall if any fortune to accuse me	IV.67
My Mall in your short absence from this place	I.78
My Mall the former verses this may teach you	I.66
My Muse is like king Edwards Concubine	IV.43
My noble Lord, some men haue thought me proud	I.55
My soule one only Mary doth adore	IV.47
My wife at other times like other Shrowes	IV.84
My wrytings oft displease you, what's the matter	II.8
New frends are no frends how can that bee trew	II.97
No sooner Cinnas wife was dead and buryed	IV.79
Not any learning Lynus no god knowes	III.65
Not very long afore this latter Schisme	IV.72
Now Faustus sayth long Epigrams are dull	III.78
Now Sextus twise hath supt at Sarzens head	II.85
O Ioy to present hope of future ages	To Iames
Of all my vearses Faustus still complaynes	III.59
Of all this town old Codros giues most credit	II.54
Of late I wrate after my wanton fashion	II.20
Of late in pleasant company by chaunce	IV.85
Of wryters all, Sextus a known dispyser	I.4
Oft reading acts admir'd of Charles the fift	III.97
Old Cosmus hath of late got one lewd quallity	I.43
Old Cosmus to his frends this out doth giue	IV.58
Old Ellen had foure teeth since I remember	I.28
Old Haywood wrytes and proues in some degrees	II.1

[Table of Contents]

The first booke

The second booke

The third booke

The fourth booke

Lib. Quarti finis

[Lantern and Elegies]

A Newyeares guift sent to the kings Matie. of Scotland

When that wise Counterfect to Phœbus went
Cum Phœbum sapiens stulti simulator adiret

Prima salutatam monstrat pictura Mariam
The blessed virgins picture first hath place

Come triumphe enter, Church, Courte, citty, town

Great Queene belou'd, and blest in heav'n and earth

Musa iocosa, meos solari assueta dolores

Appendix

Additional material in BL Add. MS 12049

My Lady Rogers Epitaphe

Death to make vaunt of his prepostrows powre,
first tooke away one grandchild then his brothers
till wayting late for his long lingred howre
hee sent to them their mothers aged mother
And thus hee thinks to bee owr conqueror thought
that hath owr babes & parents thus exilde
But Death, hee liues that hath owr ransom wrought
and of this tryvmph thow art quyte beguild,
    their soules in hands of god from death are free
    their flesh must rise agayne to conquer thee.

Lynus when hee is fresh which is but seeld
fayns himself drunk & walks as yf hee reeld
laughs and talks lowd when better men speak soft
to th'end that being drunk, which happens oft
his frends may say to saue his reputacion
hee ys not drunk forsooth 'tis but his fashion
    oh wondrous witt; yet sure I rather had
    bee deemed somtymes drunk, then allways mad.

Sit simplex humilis confessio pura fidelis   b
Atque frequens

[. . .]

Si Reges et Reginæ sunt Roma tuorum   c
Tutores et Nutrices vt perfida iactas
Cur modo papa pius Quintus, sed non pius intus
Obstrinxit diro Reginam anathemate sacram?
Hoc non est animas hominum sed quærere numos
Innocuos homines diris violare profanis
Et solium Cathedræ Regum supponere vestræ
Rumpentes placidam pacem fera bella cientes
Sanguinori nostro satiantes corda cruore
Morsibus ambrosias fœdantes sanguine mammas
Discite lac mueum blandis deposcere votis
Ne Nutrix meritam reddat pro lacte securim./
                    Fra: Har:

Perfidious Rome if kings and Queens are your Tutors and
nurses, as thow dost bost, why did now holy Quintus
the Pope but not holy within, Cruelly Excomunicate
our sacred Queene, this is not to seeke mens sowles
but monyes, so to wronge Innocents, with profane
Curses, And to subiect kinges Thrones to your Chair
breaking quiet peace Stirring up Cruell warres
bloodsuckers that glut your harts with our blood
fowling with blood those heavenly breasts with your
bytings, learne to ask your snow white milke with
Gentle prayers, least your Nurse give you a de
served hatchet for (or in steade of) Milke./
                    Francis Harington

                                                       Aij

[. . .]

The second booke

~~To Webb, the buier of land~~   74

73   ~~Webb leave this buying humor or at last~~
     ~~you or your heires will sell agayn as fast~~
        ~~a high spring tyde hath still a swyfter ebb~~
        ~~leav then this buyeng humor gentle webb/~~

[. . .]

[After 'The end of the second booke' occur the following additional poems in autograph. In *F*, a page has been left blank at this point, possibly to allow these to be included:]

86

Certayn epigrams that will not speak englysh

To the Lady   {*Non male nostra socrus lectissima fœmina dicta es*
Rogers./   {   *In lecto recubans noctu dieque tuo*

[Not wrongly, mother-in-law, have you been called a most be[d]loved woman, on your bed day and night loving to lie.]

To the same for calling mee vnthrift.

Sperabam socrum præstas ingrata novercam
*   hic videor, volui qui gener esse ~~nurus~~. nepos*

[I was hoping for a mother-in-law; you unkindly show yourself stepmother; I wanted to be a son-in-law, but instead am seen as a prodigal.]

Vndique sacra legant homines cum scripta prophani
*   Non miror nostro tempore sacrilegos.*

[Since profane men recite holy scriptures everywhere
I do not wonder at the sacrileges of our time.]

Ad vxorem

Scripta quod ignota tibe mitto epigrammata lingua
*   id facio interpres natus vt esse queat*
Hoc quoque nunc absens notum tibi mitto monile
*   Tu mihi tu presens esse monile potes.*

The last in englysh.
Thease epigrams, when as your sonne hath skand them
Perhaps his help may make you understand them
Your pendaunt eake I send, by his attendawnt
and when I come your selfe ~~must~~ ˢʰᵃˡˡ ᵐᵃʸ bee my pendawnt./
    [Translation in autograph secretary hand]

[. . .]

The fourth booke

80[lat.]   The same in latten   175

> Quid narrare iuuat nec enim res digna relatu ~~est~~
>   Est tamen in nostris fabula ~~rara~~ *grata* iocis.
> Doctor erat teneræ correptus amore puellæ
>   postque aliquot coitus fœta puella manet
> Illa propinquantis cum sensit tempora partus
>   Numina, prægnanti si qua fauetis ait
> Vos rogo me quoniam compressit concionator
>   Hic quem parturio concionator eat.
> Vouerat hæc et iam mitis Lucina labori
>   Affuit ex partu est nata puella tamen.
> Illa cito grauium quamuis oblita laborum
>   Inque puerpaerij vix bene missa torum
> Dicite ait nobis? num mas an fæmina nata est?
>   Ridet et obstetrix talia verba refert
> Non erit hæc doctor redeat nisi papa Iohanna.
>   Non has doctores grammatica vlla feret
> Ista tamen teneris olim crescentibus annis
>   Concionatori pulpita forte geret.

> [...]

82[lat.]
                 The same in latten   176
> Parcus hero famulus turdos portabat olentes
>   Quos simul admouit naribus ille suis
> Qualia vah nobis obsonia furcifer inquit
>   Emisti? canibus vix perhibenda meis
> Non ita seruus ait sunt corpora dulcia verum
>   Forsitan ex caudis venit amarus odor
> Credo ego formosam dominam si olfeceris istic
>   Iurabis dominam non redolere tuam.

> [...]

86.   A certaine Publican as is their fashion
that fermd had a fatt impropriation
did make his neighbours oft an exhortation
to pay their tithes & other duties truly
for theis no taxes are invented newly)
but old as double right belonginge duly
to god and called god allmightys parte,
who first gaue all and then layd this apart
then neighbours pay vp said hee with all yowr hart
to thys made answere one among the rest
but one that crost him oft and never blest
When foxes preach the geese bee most distrest
gods parte quoth yow tis true whose goodnes gave it
but yet somtimes wee see the devill have it./
[Every line, but the last, has been corrected, but not in autograph]

[. . .]

89   ~~The Pater noster~~ playnly   181
            ~~translated~~

Our father that does dwell in starry sky
    among all nations hallowd be thy name
hasten thy kingdom that it may draw nye
    as heavn thy will lett earth obey the same
Give vnto us this day our dayly bread
    forgive vs lorde our sinns as we forgive
into temptations lett vs not be lead
but keepe vs safe from evill while we live
    ffor thine all kingdoms are all praise all powers
    & ay shall dure to everlasting howrs./
    [This poem has five vertical deletion marks]

[. . .]

97[lat.]   The like in latten./   185
Stirpis Haringtoniæ soboles pulcherrima Sara.
    Cuius adhuc faciem vellet habere Venus
Sara fidelis amansque viri dominumque salutans
    Et domino viuens obsequiosa suo
Sara viri stirilem quæ non sinit esse senectam
    Concipiens natam de seniore senex
Nescio an hæc facies et adhuc sub iudice lis est
    Digna tamen facies est tibi vt hæc facies./

[. . .]

98[lat.]   The same in latten   186
Fluctibus oppressus furijsque agitatus amoris
    Heu feror instabili perfreta sæua rati
Vnaque Nimpharum mox est mergenda duarum
    Aut mihi non requies non datur vlla salus
Quam cuperem seruare ambas nisi fata vetarent
    Vni charus ego ast altera chara mihi
Hic timor est vasto sorberi a gurgite at illic
    Illidat dubijs ne mea cumba vadis
Sic feror incertus ventis dubitantior ipsis
    Parcere an ingratæ gratus an esse velim./
Quid faciam? vtar ego te consultore Cupido?   }
    Has minuet flammas non aqua tota maris   }
Iam morietur amans vt viuere possit amatæ   }
    Heu quanta facio cum pietate scelus   }
Quare ago sic rogitas? respondet ad omnia quare?   }
    Nec properatus amor fert rationis opus.   }
Quid faciam? Vtar ego te consultore Cupido?   }
    Qui puer et cæcus qui ratione cares.   }
Non ita nam ingratum qui dixerit omnia dixit   }
    Ergo supersit amans viuere digna magis   }
Nimpha ingrata valeto, omnisque ingrata puella   }
    discat ab exemplo mitior esse tuo./   }
                         [. . .]

100[add.]   an addicion for the same Epigram   188
Peeter for Westminster & Pawle for London
waile and lament your churches will be vndon
yf Smithfield finde a fetch forth of a stable
Lawes to elude & Lords [&]~~of~~ councell table./
            The same in latten
Non populo infenso, non ~~fractis~~ legibus ^{obnoxius} vllis ^{vlle}   189
    Noster Lalus habet pingue sacerdotium
vnde sed hoc venit ~~si vis~~ tibi ^{venit} refferet eccho
    Eccho mihi sodes dicito an emit? emit:
Pernegat hoc Lalus. Divos testatur et omnes
    Pernegat a*h* tanto pe~~cc~~*i*erat ille magis
Illia ducentem fractumque senilibus annis
    Illi patronus vendit auarus equum,
Aurea pro vetulo dat bis centena caballo
    Cui nec turca pater nec patria Italia
Ergo sacerdocium regina pecunia donat
    Hoc Lalus gratis accipit emit equum,
Vile sacerdocium sed equus iam charior æquo
    Magno equitat precio prædicat exiguo./

The addicion

Iam vos templorum properam sperate ruinam
  Et tu Petre tui tuquoque Paule tui
Sordida fabrili si nata astutia campo
  Patribus et sanctis legibus imposuit./

[. . .]

192

~~The byshop of Ely present and that last~~
  ~~that was earstwhile schoolmaster of Eaton since~~
  ~~which that sea being long vacant gave occasi~~
4   ~~on to write this idle Epigram~~
~~Who tells tales out of school somtimes is beaten~~
~~such was the fashion of the schoole of Eaton~~
~~but vayn it is my wanton muse to threaten~~
~~ffor why: of Eaton somewhat she must say~~
~~since crowned birds flew thence to Ely sea~~
~~I hear some say that drained is that sea~~
  ~~Then sure my Muse is loath to vtter freely~~
  ~~And swear they now? Eaton hath eaten Eely./~~

[This heavily deleted, and subversive, poem can just be deciphered]

[. . .]

To Mr Richard Langley
Schoolmaster of Eaton.

194

Because my sonne should not loose all his tyme
beeing with mee heer at the court I have ym=
ployed him in exercyses to the queen and some of
my Lords, and yf they seeme a litle to rype for
a boy of the fift forme in Eaton yow must suppose
that a trewant once in the sixt forme theare hath
prompted him, and trewly since I came from
Cambridge (which ys now 20 yeares) I cannot
remember yf I haue written any latten verses
yet by this occasion of teaching my sonne *I see* I haue
not quite forgotten them: But for him
I fynd him apt enough to verses, and I desire not
hee should bee much addicted to them least yt hin=
der him (as yt hath done mee) of better studies:
So I bid yow farewell
    this 3 of december
        1602.
            Yo^r loving ffrend
            Io. Har./

[This letter, with autograph direction and subscription, follows *The last Epigram*]

Carmine prima mihi primo dicetur Eliza   195
    splendidius noster qua nihil orbis habet
Auspice, qua teneræ crescit fiducia musæ.
    sospite qua patriæ non dubitanda salus
Vosque canam magni proceres sanctique senatus
    Cura quibus legis debet et esse gregis
Te quoque maturo pollens facunde Cecili
    Consilio ~~patriæ~~ ^{dominæ} fida columna tuæ
Fas mihi sit sacros interpellando labores
    Hæc ex optatis promere vota meis
Reginæ exopto longeui Nestoris annos
    vobis heroes Nestoris ingenium./

Maxima cui magnum credit regina sigillum
    Tu quoque consilijs pectora nata geris
Delphica facunda promens oracula lingua.
    Qui sensum Legis Sinderisimque tenes
Ecce rudis pius at ludi Ætonensis alumnus
    Munera dat meritis inferiora tuis
Vivet Egertonus multos fœliciter annos
    Æger erit nunquam si mea vota valent./

Inclite quem comitem fœcunda Salopia nouit   196
    Diceris et <u>merito</u> ^{comes} de comitate ^{bonitate} comes ^{magis}
Non ego maiorum describam gesta tuorum
    Materia vires exsuperante meas
Gallia testis erat, populo tum infesta britanno
    Debellata ab auis a prauisque tuis,
Atque eadem meritis populo iam grata Britanno
    Vestræ virtutis Gallia testis erit
Nam te cuius auos acres persenserat hostes
    Gallia Legatum sensit amica pium
O quam magnificos fecisti prodige sumptus
    Nobilium atque equitum quam veneranda cohors
Quorum inter primos dominus congnomine Diues
    Diues agri diues sed pietate magis
Cuius ego natis nunc Ætonensibus opto
    gesta stilo scribant vberiora patris
Nec caruit merita tua magnificentia laude
    Reginæ et patriæ grataque parque tuæ
Ah quoties memini nostrum quod itineris huius
    Non fuerat socius pænituisse patrem
Nec tibi se iunxit Candish fortissime cuius
    gustavit lepidos gallica mense sales

Quo tu magne heros tanquam es comitatus Achate
    per mare per montes flumina perque vias
Auratoque equiti Portman qui multus in auro
    Aureus auratis moribus esse soles
Principibus quamvis gallis quandoque molestus
    Non gallo reddens gallica verba tono

                                                              197
Most noble and great peere her Eearle whome Shrewsbury   Calleth
    by cursye meriting the latten name of a Earl   Comes
I take not on me to describe the worth of your ellders
    a matter too farr placed above my power
That France shall witnes in those days enimy of England   Lord
    which your most noble Awncestors oft haried   Talbot
And now the same againe new growne so frendly to England
    of your great vertuw ffrance may be witnes ynough
ffor why that same ffrance that felt the force of yowr Ellders
    a peace most frendly by yow received it hath
Oh how magnificall was yours how prodigall expence?
    Of lords and great knyghts how brave a troupe of accounte
Of whome the cheife peere was he that hath such a rich name   My Lo:
    In tenements more rich honesty most rich of all   Rich
Whose sonns most towardly, my now schoole fellows of Eaton
    m[a]y write their fathers arts in a much higher stile
Nor did your bounties want that dew praise it deserved
    gratefull vnto the queen, fitt to the Queen and the realme
how oft tymes have I heard my father say he repented
    that he in that Iourney went not a frend with the rest
With Valarous Candish whose sharp witt company pleasant   Sr Charles
    made at the French tables sawce better taste then the meat Ca[ve]ndish
whome in your Iournies yow did vse as a faithfull Achates
    By seas by mountains by many brookes & high wayes
With guiltspur Portman that goes well garded of angels
    with good condicions more precious then his goulde.   Sir Hugh
Though som french nobles made a plesant quarrell against him   Portman
    for not pronouncing ffrench of the french fashion

    Nec tua præteream charissima pectora Cary   198
        qui non iuratus dicere vera soles
    Ausus es et pulchris caput obiectare periclis
        Si quando patriæ sit dubitanda salus
    Sed ne nulla graui turbentur gaudia luctu
        Stranguisius iuuenis peste peremptus obit
    Cuius adhuc fati nimium memor optima Coniux
        Nomine cum viduæ virginis ora geret

Tempore iam ex isto sanctissima fœdera seruat
  Firma manens nobis Gallia firma sibi
Hinc reducem proceres te complectuntur ouantes
  Oscula fert manibus cætera turba tuis
Publica sed lassus tua dicere munera cesso
  Annales potius quæ meruere suos
Nunc priuata cano, non te fælicior alter
  Cum datur in patria posse manere domo
Quam pia quam prudens quam formosissima coniux
  Est tibi quæ triplici prole beata, beat
Non Artemisia huic olim non Hectoris vxor
  Par erat aut forma vel pietate prior
Vidi ego (nuper erat) te fabricitante sedere
  Sollicitam et morbo condoluisse tuo
Quæ cum tu valeas tecum venatur et agros
  permeat et siluas insequituir canes
Audet et ipsa suis manibus tractare balistas
  Mittere in armatas tela cruenta feras
Atque ita par animis virtutisque æmula Phœbe
  Est inter nymphas vera Diana suas
Nec minus interea stat provuida cura suorum
  Cuncta tibi fuerint vt satis apta domi

	199
Nor may I forgett yow most worthily Cary beloved	Sir Henry
that never swearing truely doe say evermore	Cary
And with a stout corage dare atempt all daungerous exploits	
of countries peace when question is to be made	
But that all owr pleasures may bring some dolorous event	
That prety youth Strangwayes dide in the prime of his youth	Strang
whose kinde wife to too much of her husbands destiny mindfull	wayes
though callde a widdow lookes like a virgin agayne	died of the
Now France, hath ever since a peace most iustly preserved	plage
standing firme towards vs, firme doth abide in it selfe	my Lady
how did all our nobles, imbrace yow at the returning	Nortons
how came the rest with, Base lo mano to yow	daughter
But thease high matters my muse grows weary to talk of	
things far more fit for Chronicle than for a verse	of my Lo^s.
Now speake I but private, o my lorde how happily live yow	private
when free from busines yow may remain in your house	happines
How kinde your Lady how wise how bewtifull is she	my Lady the
blest with 3 daughters makes yow be blessed alike	young coun
Not Artemisia, nor wife of vallarous Hector	tesse./
past her in kindnes or had a bewtie like hers./	
I saw (twas tother day) your Lordshipp sick of an Agew	

how pensive sate she how busy went she aboute
who when yow are in health will cheerly go with yow on hunting   her
 ore feelds & pastures follow the cry of the hounds   sports
And with those fair hands boldly dare handle a Crossbow
 and shoote at harts & strike harts that she meant not to hurt./
And thus in Noblesse and vertews like a Diana
 Amids her fayr Nimphes like a Diana she goes   her care
yet not neglecting with this the care of a matron   of the house
 to your most noble minde that each thing may be fitt

 Seu vos mannerium Sheffield seu porticus vrsop   200
  Detinet opiparæ sunt in vtrisque dapes
 Ordine cuncta tamen sic dispensata decoro
  Vt tua credatur principis aula domus
 Hic tu quam largus quam sis iucundus amicis
  Audio multocies hoc referente patre
 Qui nisi quod nullos res tam testata requirat
  testes sat Locuples testis adesse potest
 Nec tua diuitibus patet omnis Ianua solis
  plurima pauperibus distribuenda dabis
 Qua tua forte tacet non ambitiosa voluntas
  Fama tamen didicit te renuente loqui
 Tu Gilberte tuos æquas pietate parentes
  Moribus ingenio consilioque preis
 Propterea et princeps et te res euocat istinc
  Publica priuatim nec sinit esse diu
 Sed secreta quibus committat et ardua regni
  Vnum ex iuratis patribus esse iubet
 Quid quod gemmatum gestas in crure ligamen
  Sisque ira Georgianis associatus eques
 Sic tibi crescit honor longum sic crescat in æuum
  Et tardo veniat sera senecta pede
 Quid precer vlterius quiddam tamen amplius opto
  Vt tibi cum magno crescat honore salus
 Febris, nodosa et procul hinc procul esto podagra
  Nec poteris dominis esse molesta meis
 Viuere posse nocet detur nisi posse valere
  Non est vita mihi vita salute carens
 At vos internam simul externamque salutem
  Denique et æternam posse tenere velim././
      finis./

          201
yf Sheffeild mannor best like, or gallery worsop Sheffield mannor
 in both is great cheer sutable & for an Earle   worsop

yet with a grave Steward so ruled & guided in order   with the
    your Lordships house seems a royall Courte of a prince   famous gallery.
Now to your friends how kinde yow remayn how bountifull allwayes
    of myne own father oft have I heard the reporte   bounty
And save a thing so knowne hath no greate neede of a wittnes
    himselfe might well be wittnes inough in the case
Nor only keepe yow your gates open, unto the best sorte   Almes./
    But yow pointe great Almes vnto the poore to be givn
And though yowr royall almes yow would not have to be talkt of
    yet maugre your mindes fame may reporte it aboute
Thus noble Gilbert to your parents equall in honour
    In witt in councell curtesie them yow do passe   employments
wherfore for this cause your prince calls yow from the cuntrey
    the realmes employments gives yow not leave to take ease   ease
To sit in councells to mannage afayres of the kingdome   sworn
    she chosen hath yow counsellor unto her selfe   of privy councell
Long since she calld yow to the noble crew of the garter   knight of
    made of St Georges excellent order a knighte   the garter
Thus honour increases thus long encrease may your honour
    and as for old age let it be long a coming
What should I now wish for yet one thing more will I wish for
    with honour sound health health to your honor I wish   the charme
ffar hence all Agews and as far hence may the gout be   against the
    nor Lord, nor Lady nere may they trouble againe   gout
To live is a pennance except we live with a sound health.
    Where health is wanting, thear life I count but a death
But health internall & health external I wish yow
    And last æternall so to remain in the heavens./
                  finis

              [Blank page]   202

    Tu qui regalis controrotulator es aulæ   203
        Tertius atque ab avo connumerare meo
    Carmine da veniam si te rudiore salutem
        Talia scripsisti carmina forte puer
    Namque videmus adhuc, nostris insculpta fenestris
        Nomina Knowlls nostri nec procul inde patris
    Te tamen a studiis dudum Mars vindicat istis
        Sic simul et Marti Mercurioque places
    Seu iuuat in Galea caput abscondisse decora
        Inque gyros cursum flectere fortis equi
    Sic puto quod Mauors tum cum Venus arsit in illo
        portabat galeam tergaque pressit equi

Siue placet sumptis arcus sinuare sagittis
    Stridula librata mittere tela manu
Sic Niobes quondam numerosam perdere prolem
    Cum voluit telis stabat Apollo suis
Seu querulas docto percurras pollice cordas
    De Phœbi merito pars eris vna choro
Siue togatus eas, æquus prudensque senator
    Assistes reliquis, consiliumque dabis
Hoc quoque quod geminos reddat tibi barba colores
    Indicium fœlix auguriumque fuit
Fortia membra tibi belloque sat apta gerendo
    Flauus et auratus denotat ille color
Sed color hic niveus, tibi candida pectora monstrat
    Consilijs sacris dedita plena fide./   finis./

Me caruit totis bis septem absente diebus   204
    Ætonæ celebris quæ schola nomen habet
Et verum vt fatear veniam des vera fatenti
    Hic septem plures velle manere dies
At pater indulgens alias hoc durus in vno.
    Abnegat vlterius sustinuisse moras
Te tamen haud dubito Sauel illustrissime nostrum
    Sic exorandum posse movere patrem
Tu generose Sauel noster præfectus et in me
    Audiat ipse licet plus patre iuris habes
Iam prope fit charam Reginæ aduentus in vrbem
    Hanc nunquam videor posse videre satis
Mox spectare licet simulantes bella triumphos
    Quos perhibet dominis Aulica turma suis
Quis nisi mentis inops spectacula talia vitet
    vnica tam Longus quæ semel annus habet
Hæc mihi quæ cupio per te si cernere detur
    Tu mihi tu merito vel patre maior eris./

Iosua deuictos cum iam prope senserat hostes
    Et metuens Lucis vix superesse satis
Mandauit soli sol ut mandata ferenti
    Parebat, properes sustinuisse gradus
Sic hostes patriæ debellaturus Iesus   205
    Angliginæ solem hanc occubuisse vetat
Sacra diu lux hæc nostro splendescat in orbe
    Anglica lux post hanc non habitura parem
Hoc campanarum sonitus clangorque tubarum
    Hoc tormentorum terrificus tonitrus

Hoc hominum mixtæ voces et vota loquuntur
　　Nulla fuit similis, nulla futura tibi./

I near desearvd that glorious name of Poet
　　no Maker I, nor doe I care who know it
Occasion oft my penn doth entertayn
　　with trew discourse, let others Muses fayn
Myne never sought to set to sale her wryting
　　In part her frendes, in all her selfe delighting
She cannot beg applause of vulger sort
　　ffree born and bred more free for noble sport
My Muse hath one still bids her in her ease
　　yf well disposed to write, yf not forbear.

[In marginal space at foot of p. 205, in autograph]
Sæpe meæ genius musæ sic suadet in aurem
　　Aut mihi musa place ~~aut~~ ᵛᵉˡ tibi Musa tace
　　Aut place musa mihi vel ~~p~~tace Musa tibi.

[. . .]

　　　　In Tabaco:　　　　　　　　　　　　　　　251
　　A: gwg, gyda mwg
　　A miin. gwyredig;
　　yn gwradwydd y werin;
　　O gna fo leas, y gnol flin,
　　Ny ddyly r iach, y ddilin:

Qua larva? quo rictu oris? quo denique fumo
　　Astantum tota est mox peritura cohors
Sit, licet, ægroto fumus Medicina cerebro
　　sano idem capiti nil nisi virus habet./

What visage? vizard like? what fuminge smoake?
　　The standers by with poysoned breath doth choake
Is't Phissicke? Nay, a fond fantasticke tricke
　　For I was well, but fye't hath made me sicke./

[On verso of p. 251, unnumbered and upside down, in a later hand]

　　qui mihi discipulus
　　Qui mihi discipulus puer es cupis atque doceri
　　　　Huc ades hæc animo concipe dicta tuo

[Transcript of translation of *Musa Vale*, p. 265 in *F*, from now lost original in Edinburgh University Library. Transcript by John Leyden in National Library of Scotland, Adv. MS 19.3.2: from *Nugæ Antiquæ*, I.333-4; copied by McClure, no. 427, pp. 321-2.]

> Sweet wanton Muse, that, in my greatest griefe,
>> Was wont to bring me solace and reliefe.
> Wonted by sea and land to make me sporte,
>> Whether to camp or court I did resorte:
> That at the plow hast been my wellcom guest,
>> Yea to my wedlock bed hast boldly prest;
> At Eton now (where first we met) I leave thee,
>> Heere shall my sonn and heire of me receave thee.
> Now to more serious thoughts my soule aspyers,
>> This age, this minde, A Muse awsteare requiers.
> Now for those fayned joyes true joyes do spring,
>> When I salute my sovraigne lord and king.
> Now we may tell playn truth to all that ask,
>> Our love may walke bare-faste without a mask.
> My future age to realme and king I vow,
>> I may no time for wanton toyes alow.
> Ever I wish, and only, him to serve,
>> Only his love ever I would deserve.
> If he be pleasd war to proclayme with Spaine,
>> With such a prince I'le follow wars agayne.
> If his great wisdome th'auncient peace renews,
>> How fayn of peace would I reporte the news.
> List he give lawes to th'Irish, now well tamed,
>> I could give sound advises, and unblamed.
> To build some statelie house is his intention,
>> Ah, in this kinde I had too much invention!
> Will he suppress those that the land oppress,
>> A foe to them myselfe I still profess.
> Liste he to write or study sacred writte;
>> To heere, reade, learn, my breeding made me fitt.
> What he commaunds, I'le act without excuse,
>> That's full resolvd: farewell, sweet wanton Muse!

Fountain of the Haringtons at Kelweston Court.

Plate 10: Fountain of the Haringtons at Kelweston Court: Collinson, 1791.

Tables

1. Concordance of numbered epigrams in manuscript and print

The primary aim of this table is to enable readers to identify the poems in this edition if they are using commentaries and catalogues based on earlier printed editions. The table is constructed so that McClure (1930), and the two printed texts on which he based his text, Budge's 1618 and 1615 editions, are on the left, while the two manuscripts, on which this edition is based, are on the right. For ease of reference, McClure is on the far left, this edition on the far right.

The more interesting consequence of being able to see the distribution of poems in the two early printed texts of 1615 and 1618, compared with the poems in the two manuscripts, is that the reader can see at a glance in what ways these early editions culled the manuscripts, changed the order and omitted poems.

In the presentation manuscript (*F*) Harington has gone to considerable lengths to ensure that the theological poems occur on the decade, sometimes changing the contiguous numbers, and sometimes not. I have aimed to allow readers to see this (retaining italics for autograph changes), but also to provide each poem with its own number by treating the superseded number as *bis*. At the end of Book III, Harington deleted two numbers, 101 and 102, so here I have used *ter*. For the last six poems of Book IV, and indeed for the final elegies, the scribe of *BL* has omitted the running heads with the book number.

The table makes clear that the 1615 text drew randomly on all four books (just over twenty from each of the first three books and over thirty from Book IV). Only twenty Book IV poems enter the 1618 edition directly, while thirty-three come through the much smaller collection of 1615.

Both the 1615 and 1618 editions divide and double-number poems. There are twelve poems included by Budge in 1618 that are not in any of the three authorial manuscripts. McClure thought there were five more, since I.24–8 were on a leaf missing from *BL*, the only complete manuscript available to him. To these McClure himself added a further poem (No. 428), neither in the printed texts nor in the manuscripts, but in Thomas Coryate's *Crudities* (1611).

McClure 1930	Budge 1618	Budge 1615	BL Add. MS 12049	Folger MS V.a.249	This edition 2009
1	[ ]		I.1	I.1	I.1
2	I.1		I.2	I.2	I.2
3	I.2		I.4	I.4	I.4
4	I.3		I.6	I.6	I.6
5	I.4		I.8	I.8	I.8
6	I.5		I.11	I.11	I.11
7	I.6		I.13	I.13	I.13
8	I.7		I.14	I.14	I.14
9	I.8		I.15	I.15	I.15
10	I.9		I.17	I.17	I.17
11	I.10		I.18	I.18	I.18
12	I.11		I.19	I.19	I.19
13	I.12		I.20	I.20	I.20
14	I.13		I.21	I.21	I.21
15	I.14		I.22	I.22	I.22
16	I.15		[om. fol.]	I.24	I.24
17	I.16		I.29	I.29	I.29
18	I.17		I.30	I.30	I.30
19	I.18		I.36	I.36	I.36
20	I.19		I.38	I.38	I.38
21	I.20		I.40	I.40	I.40
22	I.21		I.41	I.41	I.41
23	I.22		I.43	I.43	I.43
24	I.23		I.45	I.45	I.45
25	I.24		I.46	I.46	I.46
26	I.25		I.47	I.47	I.47
27	I.26		I.49	I.49	I.49
28	I.27		I.52	I.52	I.52
29	I.28	76	I.53	I.53	I.53
30	I.29		I.56	I.56	I.56
31	I.30		I.60	I.60	I.60
32	I.31		I.62	I.62	I.62
33	I.32		I.12	I.12	I.12
34	I.33		I.65	I.65	I.65
35	I.34		I.65	I.65	I.65
36	I.35		I.65	I.65	I.65
37	I.36		I.66	I.66	I.66
38	I.37		I.68	I.68	I.68
39	I.38		I.78	I.78	I.78
40	I.39		I.81	I.81	I.81
41	I.40		I.82	I.82	I.82
42	I.41		I.83	I.83	I.83
43	I.42		I.84	I.84	I.84
44	I.43		I.85	I.85	I.85

McClure 1930	Budge 1618	Budge 1615	BL Add. MS 12049	Folger MS V.a.249	This edition 2009
45	I.44		I.86 [del.]		I.86
46	I.45		I.87 [del.]		I.87
47	I.46		I.88	I.88	I.88
48	I.47		I.89	I.89	I.89
49	I.48		I.90	I.90	I.90
50	I.49		I.91	I.91	I.91
51	I.50		I.92	I.92	I.92
52	I.51		I.93 [del.]		I.93
53	I.52		I.94	I.93	I.94
54	I.53		I.95	I.94	I.95
55	I.54		I.96	I.95	I.96
56	I.55		I.98	I.97	I.98
57	I.56		II.5	II.5	II.5
58	I.57		II.6	II.6	II.6
59	I.58		II.7	II.7	II.7
60	I.59		II.8	II.8	II.8
61	I.60		II.12	II.12	II.12
62	I.61		II.14	II.14	II.14
63	I.62	107	II.15	II.15	II.15
64	I.63		II.17	II.17	II.17
65	I.64		II.18	II.18	II.18
66	I.65		I.5	I.5	I.5
67	I.66		I.10	I.10	I.10
68	I.67		I.16	I.16	I.16
69	I.68		I.23	I.23	I.23
70	I.69		I.32	I.32	I.32
71	I.70		I.35	I.35	I.35
72	I.71		I.37	I.37	I.37
73	I.72	62	I.42	I.42	I.42
74	I.73		I.48	I.48	I.48
75	I.74		I.50	I.50	I.50
76	I.75		I.51	I.51	I.51
77	I.76		I.55	I.55	I.55
78	I.77		I.58	I.58	I.58
79	I.78		I.59	I.59	I.59
80	I.79		I.67	I.67	I.67
81	I.80		I.69	I.69	I.69
82	I.81		I.71	I.71	I.71
83	I.82		I.72	I.72	I.72
84	I.83		I.73	I.73	I.73
85	I.84		I.74	I.74	I.74
86	I.84*bis*		I.75	I.75	I.75
87	I.85		I.76	I.76	I.76
88	I.86		I.77	I.77	I.77

McClure 1930	Budge 1618	Budge 1615	BL Add. MS 12049	Folger MS V.a.249	This edition 2009
89	I.87		I.79	I.79	I.79
90	I.88	93	I.80	I.80	I.80
91	I.89		I.97	I.96	I.97
92	I.90	38	I.100	I.[om. no.]	I.100
93	I.91		II.2	II.2	II.2
94	I.92		II.3	II.3	II.3
95	I.93		II.13	II.13	II.13
96	I.94		II.19	II.19	II.19
97	II.1		II.26	II.26	II.26
98	II.2		II.21	II.21	II.21
99	II.3		II.22	II.22	II.22
100	II.4		II.23	II.23	II.23
101	II.5		II.24	II.24	II.24
102	II.6		II.25	II.25	II.25
103	II.7		II.20	II.20	II.20
104	II.8		II.27	II.27	II.27
105	II.9		II.28	II.28	II.28
106	II.10		II.31	II.31	II.31
107	II.11		II.32	II.32	II.32
108	II.12		II.33	II.33	II.33
109	II.13		II.34	II.34	II.34
110	II.14		II.35	II.35	II.35
111	II.15		II.36	II.36	II.36
112	II.16		II.38	II.38	II.38
113	II.17		II.39	II.39	II.39
114	II.18		II.40	II.40	II.40
115	II.19		II.41	II.41	II.41
116	II.20		II.42	II.42	II.42
117	II.21		II.44	II.44	II.44
118	II.22		II.45	II.45	II.45
119	II.23		II.46	II.46	II.46
120	II.24		II.47	II.47	II.47
121	II.25		II.48	II.48	II.48
122	II.26		II.50	II.50	II.50
123	II.27		II.51	II.51	II.51
124	II.28		II.53	II.53	II.53
125	II.29	39	II.54	II.54	II.54
126	II.30		II.56	II.56	II.56

McClure 1930	Budge 1618	Budge 1615	BL Add. MS 12049	Folger MS V.a.249	This edition 2009
127	II.31		II.57	II.57	II.57
128	II.32		II.60	II.60	II.60
129	II.33		II.63	II.63	II.63
130	II.34		II.64	II.64	II.64
131	II.35		II.65	II.65	II.65
132	II.36		II.67	II.67	II.67
133	II.37		II.68	II.68	II.68
134	II.38		II.69	II.[om. no.]	II.69
135	II.39		II.70	II.70	II.70
136	II.40	45	II.72	II.72	II.72
137	II.41		II.75	II.74	II.74
138	II.42		II.76	II.75	II.75
139	II.43		II.77	II.76	II.76
140	II.44	36	II.78	II.77	II.77
141	II.45		II.79	II.78	II.78
142	II.46	10	II.80	II.*80*	II.*80*
143	II.47		II.81	II.80	II.80*bis*
144	II.48		II.82	II.81	II.81
145	II.49		II.83	II.82	II.82
146	II.50		II.84	II.83	II.83
147	II.51		II.85	II.84	II.84
148	II.52		II.86	II.85	II.85
149	II.53		II.87	II.86	II.86
150	II.54		II.88	II.87	II.87
151	II.55		II.89	II.89	II.89
152	II.56		II.90	II.90	II.90
153	II.57		II.91	II.91	II.91
154	II.58		II.92	II.92	II.92
155	II.59		II.93	II.93	II.93
156	II.60	109	II.95	II.95	II.95
157	II.61		II.96	II.96	II.96
158	II.62		II.99	II.99	II.99
159	II.63		II.100	II.100	II.100
160	II.64		III.1	III.1	III.1
161	II.65	114	III.2	III.2	III.2
162	II.66		III.3	III.3	III.3
163	II.67	106	III.4	III.4	III.4
164	II.68		III.5	III.5	III.5
165	II.69		III.6	III.6	III.6
166	II.70		III.7	III.7	III.7
167	II.71		III.8	III.8	III.8
168	II.72		III.11	III.11	III.11
169	II.73		III.12	III.12	III.12
170	II.74		III.13	III.13	III.13

McClure 1930	Budge 1618	Budge 1615	BL Add. MS 12049	Folger MS V.a.249	This edition 2009
171	II.75	112	III.14	III.14	III.14
172	II.76		III.15	III.15	III.15
173	II.77		III.16	III.16	III.16
174	II.78	89	III.16*bis*	III.17	III.17
175	II.79		III.17	III.18	III.18
176	II.80	70	III.18	III.19	III.19
177	II.81		III.19	III.20*bis*	III.20*bis*
178	II.82		III.21	III.22	III.22
179	II.83	54	III.22	III.23	III.23
180	II.84		III.24	III.25	III.25
181	II.85		III.25	III.26	III.26
182	II.86		III.26	III.27	III.27
183	II.87		III.27	III.28	III.28
184	II.88		III.28	III.29*bis*	III.29*bis*
185	II.89		III.29	III.*29*	III.*29*
186	II.90		III.30	III.*30*	III.*30*
187	II.91		III.31	III.32	III.32
188	II.92		III.40	III.*40*	III.*40*
189	II.93		III.41	III.42	III.42
190	II.94		III.45	III.46	III.46
191	II.95		III.46	III.47	III.47
192	II.96		III.47	III.48	III.48
193	II.97		III.51	III.52	III.52
194	II.98		III.52	III.53	III.53
195	II.99		III.53	III.54	III.54
196	II.100		III.54	III.55	III.55
197	II.101		III.55	III.56	III.56
198	II.102		III.56	III.57	III.57
199	III.1		III.59	III.60*bis*	III.60*bis*
200	III.2		III.73	III.74	III.74
201	III.3	19	III.83	III.84	III.84
202	III.4.	84	III.84	III.85	III.85
203	III.5		III.87	III.88	III.88
204	III.6		III.88	III.89	III.89
205	III.7		III.98	III.*99bis*	III.*99bis*
206	III.8		III.99	III.~~101~~	III.99*ter*
207	III.9		III.57	III.58	III.58
208	III.10		III.58	III.59	III.59
209	III.11		III.60	III.*60*	III.*60*
210	III.12		III.63	III.64	III.64
211	III.13		III.64	III.65	III.65
212	III.14		III.65	III.66	III.66
213	III.15		III.66	III.67	III.67
214	III.16		III.67	III.68	III.68

McClure 1930	Budge 1618	Budge 1615	BL Add. MS 12049	Folger MS V.a.249	This edition 2009
215	III.17		III.68	III.69	III.69
216	III.18	103	III.71	III.72	III.72
217	III.19	53	III.74	III.75	III.75
218	III.20		III.75	III.76	III.76
219	III.21		III.[om. no.]	III.77	III.77
220	III.22		III.77	III.78	III.78
221	III.23		III.78	III.79	III.79
222	III.24		III.79	III.80*bis*	III.80*bis*
223	III.25		III.80	III.*80*	III.*80*
224	III.26		III.81	III.*82*	III.*82*
225	III.27		III.82	III.83	III.83
226	III.28		III.85	III.86	III.86
227	III.29		III.89[6]	III.87	III.87
228	III.30		III.92	III.93	III.93
229	III.31		III.94	III.95	III.95
230	III.32	69	III.96	III.98	III.98
231	III.30*bis*		IV.3	IV.3	IV.3
232	III.31*bis*		IV.4	IV.4	IV.4
233	III.32*bis*		IV.5	IV.5	IV.5
234	III.33		IV.6	IV.6	IV.6
235	III.34		IV.7	IV.7	IV.7
236	III.35	55	IV.8	IV.8	IV.8
237	III.36		IV.13	IV.13	IV.13
238	III.37	88	IV.[om. no.]	IV.32	IV.32
239	III.38	41	IV.33	IV.33	IV.33
240	III.39		IV.39	IV.39	IV.39
241	III.40	32	IV.79	IV.79	IV.79
242	III.41		[om. bk no.] 2	IV.102	IV.102
243	III.42		IV.54	IV.54	IV.54
244	III.43		IV.16	IV.15	IV.15
245	III.44		IV.63	IV.63	IV.63
246	III.45		IV.75	IV.75	IV.75
247	III.46		IV.73	IV.73	IV.73
248	III.47		IV.74	IV.74	IV.74
249	III.48		IV.58	IV.[om. no.]	IV.58
250	III.49		IV.76	IV.76	IV.76
251	III.50		IV.77	IV.77	IV.77
252	III.51		IV.83	IV.83	IV.83
253	III.52		IV.78	IV.78	IV.78
254	III.53		IV.64	IV.64	IV.64
255	IV.1	1	II.43	II.43	II.43
256	IV.2	2	II.74	II.73	II.73
257	IV.3	3	I.3	I.3	I.3
258	IV.4	4	IV.9	IV.9	IV.9

McClure 1930	Budge 1618	Budge 1615	BL Add. MS 12049	Folger MS V.a.249	This edition 2009
259	IV.5	5	III.42	III.43	III.43
260	IV.6	6	III.37	III.38	III.38
261	IV.7	6bis	I.7	I.7	I.7
262	IV.8	7	I.99	I.98	I.99
263	IV.9	8	IV.30	IV.30	IV.30
264	IV.10	9	IV.59	IV.59	IV.59
265	IV.11	46	III.9	III.9	III.9
266	IV.12	11	IV.99	IV.98	IV.99
267	IV.13	12	IV.88	IV.88	IV.88
268	IV.14	13	III.39	III.39	III.39
269	IV.15	14	I.57	I.57	I.57
270	IV.16	15	IV.27	IV.27	IV.27
271	IV.17	16	I.70	I.70	I.70
272	IV.18	17	I.9	I.9	I.9
273	IV.19	18	II.49	II.49	II.49
274	IV.20	65	III.34	III.35	III.35
275	IV.21	21	I.44	I.44	I.44
276	IV.22	22	IV.82	IV.82	IV.82
277	IV.23	23	[om. bk no.] 5	IV.105	IV.105
278	IV.24	24	IV.81	IV.81	IV.81
279	IV.25	25			
280	IV.26	26	II.59	II.59	II.59
281	IV.27	27	II.71	II.71	II.71
282	IV.28	28	II.55	II.55	II.55
283	IV.29	29	I.34	I.34	I.34
284	IV.30	30			
285	IV.31	31	I.39	I.39	I.39
286	IV.32	113	IV.48	IV.48	IV.48
287	IV.33	33	I.61	I.61	I.61
288	IV.34	34	II.37	II.37	II.37
289	IV.35	35	[om. fol.]	I.27	I.27
290	IV.36	37	III.62	III.63	III.63
291	IV.37	40	II.89bis	II.88	II.88
292	IV.38	42	IV.86	IV.86	IV.86
293	IV.39	43	IV.100	IV.100	IV.100
294	IV.40	44	IV.100add.		Appendix
295	IV.41	100	III.49	III.50	III.50bis
296	IV.42	47	IV.35	IV.35	IV.35
297	IV.43	48	[om. bk no.] 1	IV.101	IV.101
298	IV.44	49	II.62	II.62	II.62
299	IV.45	50	IV.85	IV.85	IV.85
300	IV.46	51	IV.17	IV.16	IV.16
301	IV.47	52			
302	IV.48	91	I.69	I.69	I.69

McClure 1930	Budge 1618	Budge 1615	BL Add. MS 12049	Folger MS V.a.249	This edition 2009
303	IV.49	98	IV.95	IV.94	IV.95
304	IV.50	56	II.97	II.97	II.97
305	IV.51	57	I.54	I.54	I.54
306	IV.52	58	[om. fol.]	I.28	I.28
307	IV.53	59	IV.68	IV.68	IV.68
308	IV.54	60			
309	IV.55	61			
310	IV.56	63			
311	IV.57	64	III.97	III.99	III.99
312	IV.58	66			
313	IV.59	67	II.16	II.16	II.16
314	IV.60	68	II.58	II.58	II.58
315	IV.61	71			
316	IV.62	72	II.11	II.11	II.11
317	IV.63	73	III.48	III.49	III.49
318	IV.64	74	IV.46	IV.46	IV.46
319	IV.65	75	IV.89	IV.89	IV.89
320	IV.66	77	I.33	I.33	I.33
321	IV.67	78	[om. fol.]	I.26	I.26
322	IV.68	79			
323	IV.69	80	IV.41	IV.41	IV.41
324	IV.70	81	IV.56	IV.56	IV.56
325	IV.71	82	IV.2	IV.2	IV.2
326	IV.72	83	II.1	II.1	II.1
327	IV.73	115			
328	IV.74	85	I.63	I.63	I.63
329	IV.75	86	II.50	II.50	II.50
330	IV.76	87	IV.52	IV.52	IV.52
331	IV.77	95	IV.45	IV.45	IV.45
332	IV.78	90	III.69	III.70	III.70*bis*
333	IV.79	92	IV.37	IV.37	IV.37
334	IV.80	94	II.9	II.9	II.9
335	IV.81	96	I.31	I.31	I.31
336	IV.82	97	III.43	III.44	III.44
337	IV.83	99	III.50	III.51	III.50
338	IV.84	101	II.10	II.10	II.10
339	IV.85	102	IV.72	IV.72	IV.72
340	IV.86	104	IV.98	IV.97	IV.98
341	IV.87	105	IV.98	IV.97	IV.98
342	IV.88	108			
343	IV.89	110	[om. fol]	I.25	I.25
344	IV.90	111	III.35	III.36	III.36
345	IV.91	116	IV.87	IV.87	IV.87
346	IV.92				

McClure 1930	Budge 1618	Budge 1615	BL Add. MS 12049	Folger MS V.a.249	This edition 2009
347			To Iames	To Iames	To Iames
348			My Lady R.		Appendix
349			'Lynus when'		Appendix
350			I.64	I.64	I.64
351			II.29	II.29	II.29
352			II.30	II.30	II.30
353			II.52	II.52	II.52
354			II.61	II.61	II.61
355			II.66	II.66	II.66
356			II.94	II.94	II.94
357			II.98	II.98	II.98
358			III.10	III.10	III.10
359			III.20	III.*20*	III.*20*
360			III.23	III.24	III.24
361			III.32	III.33	III.33
362			III.33	III.34	III.34
363			III.36	III.37	III.37
364			III.38	III.39*bis*	III.39*bis*
365			III.44	III.45	III.45
366			III.61	III.62	III.62
367			III.70	III.71	III.70
368			III.72	III.73	III.73
369			III.89	III.*91*	III.*91*
370			III.90	III.*90*	III.*90*
371			III.91	III.92	III.92
372			III.93	III.94	III.94
373			III.[95]	III.97	III.97
374			III.100	III.*100*	III.*100*
375			IV.1	IV.1	IV.1
376			IV.10	IV.10	IV.10
377			IV.11	IV.11	IV.11
378			IV.12	IV.12	IV.12
379			IV.[14]	III.96	III.96
380			IV.15	IV.14	IV.14
381			IV.18	IV.17	IV.17
382			IV.19	IV.18	IV.18
383			IV.20	IV.*20*	IV.*20*
384			IV.21	IV.*21*	IV.*21*
385			IV.22	IV.21*bis*	IV.21*bis*
386			IV.23	IV.22	IV.22
387			IV.24	IV.23	IV.23
388			IV.25	IV.25	IV.25
389			IV.28	IV.28	IV.28
390			IV.29	IV.29	IV.29

McClure 1930	Budge 1618	Budge 1615	BL Add. MS 12049	Folger MS V.a.249	This edition 2009
391			IV.31	IV.31	IV.31
392			IV.34	IV.34	IV.34
393			IV.36	IV.36	IV.36
394			IV.40	IV.40	IV.40
395			IV.42	IV.42	IV.42
396			IV.43	IV.43	IV.43
397			IV.44	IV.44	IV.44
398			IV.47	IV.47	IV.47
399			IV.49	IV.49	IV.49
400			IV.50	IV.50	IV.50
401			IV.51	IV.51	IV.51
402			IV.53	IV.53	IV.53
403			IV.55	IV.55	IV.55
404			IV.57	IV.57	IV.57
405			IV.60	IV.60	IV.60
406			IV.61	IV.61	IV.61
407			IV.65	IV.65	IV.65
408			IV.66	IV.66	IV.66
409			IV.67	IV.67	IV.67
410			IV.69	IV.69	IV.69
411			IV.70	IV.70	IV.70
412			IV.71	IV.71	IV.71
413			IV.80	IV.80	IV.80
414			IV.84	IV.84	IV.84
415			IV.90	IV.90	IV.90
416			IV.91	IV.91	IV.91
417			IV.92	IV.92	IV.92
418			IV.93	IV.93	IV.93
419			IV.94	IV.[om. no.]	IV.94
420			IV.96	IV.95	IV.96
421			IV.97	IV.96	IV.97
422			[om. bk no.].3	IV.103	IV.103
423			[om. no.]	IV.106	IV.106
424			'I near'		Appendix
425			K. Iames El.	K. Iames El.	K.Iames El.
426			Q. Ann El.	Q. Ann El.	Q. Ann El.
427 [Engl.]			Musa Vale	Musa Vale	Musa Vale
428					
			II.4	II.4	II.4
			[om. no.]	IV.24	IV.24
			IV.26	IV.26	IV.26
			IV.38	IV.38	IV.38
			IV.62	IV.62	IV.62
			[om. no.]	IV.104	IV.104
			Lant. El.	Lant. El.	Lant. El.
			Rosary	Rosary	Rosary

2. Epigrams in Cambridge University Library Adv. b.8.1 (*C*)

These are given by title (with first lines from *C* in parenthesis where the title is generic) in the order in which they occur, so that changes of title can be seen, and with no added punctuation. The numbers in Tables 2–4 refer to the text in this edition. *Italic* is for autograph additions or emendations. Harington, as he makes clear in his letter of dedication (see Chapter 4), first instructed the scribe to copy forty-one familial poems (in the same order as in *BL* and *F*), and then added, at the end, eleven public poems, some with significant changes of title. The first four of these and II.8 are addressed to the Queen, which is not obvious in *F* or *BL*. The changes of title are particularly striking in the cases of II.65 and in II.8, where there is no hint in *F* that a 'Great Lady' is involved, since the title is 'Of playn dealing'. The poems are dated *1600*, in autograph, in the letter of dedication, and by the scribe at the end, a date confirmed by the emendation made to IV.9.5. Eleven of the poems come from III.27-50.

Book One

8	An Elegie of a poynted Diamond giuen by the Author to his wife at the birth of his eldest sonne
14	To my Lady Rogers the Authors wiues mother, how Doctor Sherwood commended her House in Bath.
27	To my Lady Rogers ('Frowr'd and yet fortunate, if fortune knew yt')
37	To his wife of stryking her Dogge.
47	The Author to his wife of a womans Eloquence.
52	To my Ladie Rogers of breaking her Bitches leg.
58	Of a speachles woman to his wife
74	To my Lady Rogers. of her Seruant Payne./
78	Of an accident of saying grace at the Lady Rogers who vsed to dyne exceeding late. written to his wife. *from Bathe.*
89	Of Garlick. To my Lady Rogers
97	To the Lady Rogers of her vnprofitable sparing
99	To his wife of the .12. signes how they rule.

Book Two

2	A Tale of a Baylie distrayning for Rent. To my Lady Rogers
10	To my dearest a rule for praying./
26	To the Lady Rogers ('Yf I but speake words of vnpleasing sound')
41	To his wife at the birth of his sixt child.
46	To pacifie his wiues mother when she was angrie
47	To his wife of Poppea Sabynas fayr hayr.
66	To his wife of weomens vertues
77	To his Wife. ('When I to thee my letters superscribe')
84	To my Lady Rogers ('Good Madam with kynd speach and promise fayr')
88	Of a fair Shrew. To his wife.

Book Three

Book Four

[Political poems]

Finis

1600

3. Epigrams in Inner Temple Petyt MS 538, vol. 43, fols 289v–290v:
presentation copy to Lucy, Countess of Bedford, dated 19 December 1600 (fol. 303v)

Titles and first lines in this selection

'Certaine Epigram's out of a Pamphlet called Misacmos: merriements, composed by Sir
Ihon Harryngton'.   fol. 289v.
III.*40*   Of King David. 'Prophet to Princes, and of Prophets king'.
I.70   Of an Elephant. 'The pleasant learn'd Italian Poete Dant'.
I.60   Of the cause of dearth. 'Hearing our Contrie-neighbors oft complaine'.
I.69   Of Soothsaying. 'Might man shunne future mischiefs by foretelling'.   fol. 290r.
III.50   Of reading Scripture. 'The Sacred Scripture, treasure greate afford's'.
I.10   Of an unlearned Minister. 'A Cobler with a Curate once disputed'.
I.80   Of a presumptuous Christian. 'Leda, now she is sure she is elected'.
IV.88   To hir Maiestie. 'Euer most deare, euer most dreadded Prince'.
II.10   To myne owne of the abuse of Images. 'My deare, when in your closet for deuotion'.
                                                                               fol. 290v.
II.50   Of Paulus, a Saduce. 'Paulus, seduc't by Saduce's infection'
                                                              [catchword] Of my readers

**4. Epigrams included in *Alcilia: Philoparthens louing Folly, Wherevnto Is Added
Pigmalions Image with The Loue of Amos and Laura And also Epigrammes by Sir I.H.
and others*, 2ⁿᵈ edn (London: Richard Hawkins, 1613), STC 4275, sigs M3r-M5v**

Titles and first lines in this selection

II.18   *Don Pedro's Debt. 'Don Pedro*'s out of debt, be bolde to say it'.
III.96   *Sextus Wit.* 'To haue good wit is *Sextus* thought by many'.
II.3   *Of Casting out Spirits by Prayer without Fasting.* 'A Vertuous Dame, who for
           her state and qualitie'.
IV.75   *Of wicked Prayers.* 'A Husband and a Wife oft disagreeing'.
I.56   *The Author, of his Fortune.* 'Take Fortune as it fals, so one aduiseth'.
1.65   *Of Misse-Pointing.* 'Dames are indu'd with vertues excellent'.
I.66   *To his Wife.* 'My *Mall*, the former Verses this doth teach you'.
I.40   *Of a Precise Taylor:* 'A Taylor thought a man of vpright dealing'.
I.5   *Of a Cittizen and his Sonne:* 'A Cittizen that dwelt neare Temple barre'.
IV.38   *Mistaking a word.* 'An English Lad long woed a lasse of Wales'.
II.8   *Of his Writings.* 'My Writings oft displease you. What's the matter?'
IV.57   *Of a Ladyes Cabinet.* 'A Vertuous Lady sitting in a muse'.
II.68   *Of Wiues ruling.* 'Concerning Wiues, hold this a certaine rule'.
III.3   *Of Gella's Periwig:* 'See you the goodlye hayre that *Gella* weares'.
II.81   *Of a Prater, out of Martiall.* 'Who so is hoarse, yet still to prate doth presse'.
I.77   *Of trusting to his Friend.* 'If you will shrowd your selfe from all mishaps'.
II.38   *Of Faustus, a stealer of Verses.* 'I Heare that Faustus oftentimes rehearses'.

All but three of these poems (III.96, IV.57 and IV.38) are also in the 1618 edition. *Alcilia*
also includes three other epigrams, not listed, that do not appear to be by Harington.

5. Chronology of editions of epigrams and emblems

1494   Greek Anthology, edited by Johannes Lascaris, published in Florence.

1503   Greek Anthology, edited from MS Marcianus 481, published by Aldus.

1515   Erasmus's revised and expanded *Adagia* published by Froben in Basel.

1516   Erasmus's *Institutio Principis Christiani* published by Froben.

1517   *Martialis Epigrammata* published by Aldus.

1518   Erasmus's revised *Enchiridion Militis Christiani* published by Froben.

1518   Sir Thomas More's *Epigrammata* and *Vtopia* published together by Froben.

1518   Erasmus's *Familiarium Colloquiorum Formulae* (*Colloquies*): first of many edns.

1529   Alciati contributed to *Selecta epigrammata Graeca Latine versa*, Basel.

1531   Alciati's *Emblematum Liber* printed in Augsburg.

1534   Alciati's second edition of 113 emblems published in Paris.

1539   Guillaume de la Perrière's *Le Théatre des Bons Engins* published in Paris.

1546   Alciati's *Emblematum Libellus* (incl. *Aduersus naturam peccantes*) publ. Aldus.

1549   First edition of John Heywood's epigrams on proverbs.

1550   Alciati's *Emblematum Liber* (211 emblems) published in Lyons.

1558   Martial in Jesuit expurgated edition published in Rome.

1562   John Heywood's *Workes*, first complete edition of six hundred 'Epigrammes'.

1566   Thomas Palmer's ms. translation of Alciati: *Two Hundred Poosees*.

1566   John Heywood's *Workes*, second complete edition of *Epigrammes*.

1568   Martial, unexpurgated, published by Plantin in Antwerp.

1576   John Heywoodes *Woorkes*, third complete edition of *Epigrammes*.

1585   Samuel Daniel's *The Worthy Tract of Paulus Iovius*, printed in London.

1586   Geffrey Whitney's *A Choice of Emblemes*, publ. by Plantin in Leiden.

1587   John Heywood's *Workes*, fourth complete edition of *Epigrammes*.

1591   John Harington's translation of *Orlando Furioso*, publ. by Richard Field.

1593   Thomas Combe's *The Theater of Fine Devices*, publ. by Richard Field.

1594/5 Sir John Davies, *Nosce Teipsum*, *Orchestra* and, probably, *Epigrammes* published.

1598   John Heywood's *Workes*, fifth complete edition of *Epigrammes*.

1599   John Weever, *Epigrammes in the Oldest Cut and Newest Fashion*.

1601   Charles Fitzjeffery, *Affaniae sive Epigrammatum Libri tres*.

1605   Sir John Harington presents 'All my ydle Epigrams' to Prince Henry.

1606/7 John Owen, *Epigrammatum Ioannis Owen . . . Libri Tres* (three edns).

1607   Sir John Stradling, *Epigrammatum Libri Quatuor*.

1610   John Davies of Hereford, *The Scourge of Folly* (292 epigrams).

1612   15 May, Stationers' register: 'A booke called Ben Ionson his Epigrams'.

1614   Thomas Combe, *The Theater of Fine Devices*, 2nd edn, Richard Field.

1615   Martial, *Epigrammata*, first Eng. edn, ed. Farnaby, one owned by Ben Jonson.

1615   116 of (mostly) Harington's epigrams published by John Budge.

1616   First Folio, *Workes of Beniamin Ionson* (including *Epigrammes*), publ. W. Stansby.

1617   Martial, *Epigrammatum Libri XV*, publ. C. Morell (Paris), owned by Ben Jonson.

1618   346 epigrams, mostly Harington's, published by John Budge.

1619   Martial, *nova editio* published in Lyons, and owned by Ben Jonson.

6. Chronology of the life of Sir John Harington

1560   4 August: christened, with Queen as godmother, Earl of Pembroke, godfather.
1569   Parents, John and Isabella (Markham) Harington move to Kelston, near Bath.
1567/8 John Harington (father) has Campion's poem transcribed in BL Add. MS 36529.
1570   'Scholler at Eton' with Thomas Arundell and Sir Edward Hoby: 'Musa . . . nata'.
1576   Matriculates at King's College, Cambridge.
1578   Graduates as Bachelor of Arts.
1581   Proceeds Master of Arts, and leaves Cambridge.
1581   27 November: admitted to Lincoln's Inn.
1581   1 December: execution of Edmund Campion at Tyburn.
1582   1 July, father dies; Walpole's poem on Edmund Campion 'the last . . . he redd'.
1582   Leaves Lincoln's Inn.
1583   26 June, comes into possession of inheritance; 6 September, marries Mary Rogers.
1583/4 Involved, with help of James Baker, in distributing Edmund Campion's books.
1584   Refuses to sign Bond of Association.
1589   In Bath, 'rubell from the Abbee to mende the waie by the burwales: 20s'.
1590   Sends some epigrams to Sir John Stradling.
1591   High Sheriff of Somerset.
1591   Richard Field publishes his translation of *Orlando Furioso*.
1592   Queen (supposedly) visited Kelston and 'dined right royally under the fountain'.
1593   9 May, registered, Thomas Combe, *The Theater of Fine Devices* (Field).
1595   Letter to Lord Burghley; describes progress of repairs to Bath Abbey.
1596   *A New Discourse* (Field): 'devise' in 'An Anatomie' by 'T.C. Traveller' (Thomas
        Combe): large-paper copies to Lord Lumley and, 3 August, to Thomas Markham.
1598   June, visits sick Lord Burghley at the Bathe; receives letter of Robert Markham.
1599   April: travels to Ireland with Earl of Essex.
1599   30 July: knighted by Earl of Essex in 'Irish action'.
1599   31 August: letter to Thomas Combe from Ireland, thanking for 'sundry letters'.
1599   18 October: reads 45th canto of *Orlando Furioso* to Earl of Tyrone and sons.
1599   November: returns to England with Essex; arrives Richmond Palace.
1600   19 December: 52 epigrams to Lady Rogers and Lady H. (*C*, Scribe A).
1600   19 December: gift copy to Lucy, Countess of Bedford (Petyt MS 538, vol. 43).
1601   25 February: Earl of Essex executed with Blunt and Sir Charles Danvers.
1601   September: at court; reads verse to Queen 'quite disfavourd, and unattird'.
1602   18 December: sends *A Tract on the Succession* to Tobie Matthew (Scribe A)
1603   6 January, '1602' [3]: 'A Newyeares guift to the kings Ma$^{tie.}$'.
1603   3 April: date of King's letter to Harington.
1603   Sir Griffin Markham, cousin, involved in Bye Plot; nearly executed.
1604   Translation of *Aeneid* VI presented to Prince Henry (Trumbull MS 23, Scribe A).
1605   19 June: 'All my ydle Epigrams' dedicated to Prince Henry (*F*, Scribe A).
1608   *A Supplie or Addicion* presented to Prince Henry (Royal MS 17.B.XXII, Scribe A).
1608   Restoration of Bath Abbey nearly complete; appeals to Thomas Sutton for money.
1612   6 November: Henry, Prince of Wales, dies.
1612   20 November: Sir John Harington dies.
1612   1 December: Sir John Harington buried at Kelston.

Bibliography

Early Modern Manuscripts

United Kingdom

Arundel Castle
    Arundel Harington MS (Collection includes: I.24, 65, 90; III.26, 30).

Bodleian Library
    MS Rawlinson D. 289 (Edmund Campion's *Sancta salutiferi*), Scribe A.

British Library
    Royal MS 17.B.XXII (Harington's 'Supplie or Addicion'), Scribe A.
    Add. MS 4379   (William Badger's Winchester College notebook).
    Add. MS 12047 (Harington transcription of Sidney translation of psalms).
    Add. MS 12049 (Harington transcription of *Epigrams*).
    Add. MS 61821 (Helmingham Hall copy of Sidney's *Arcadia*).
    Add. MS 27632 (Harington miscellany, list of plays, letter to Bishop Hall).
    Add. MS 36529 (Harington transcription of Campion's *Sancta salutiferi*).
    Add. MS 38892 (Harington transcription of Sidney's *Arcadia*).
    Add. MS 46368 (Printer's copy of *A New Discourse*).
    Add. MS 46372 (Harington transcription of Sidney translation of psalms).
    Add. MS 46381 (Dr Henry Harington's collection of family material).
    Cotton MS Titus D. IV (Sir Thomas More *Epigrammata*, presentation copy).
    Egerton MS 2711 (Harington collection of Wyatt poems, and psalms).
    Add. MSS 39828–38 (Tresham papers, including III.44, 70; IV.1) before 1605.
    Add. MS 10309 (II.94; III.44; IV.1, 30) coll. Margaret Bellasys, c. 1630.
    Add. MS 15227 (I.10, 30, 40; IV.30, 39, 57, 80, 88, 105) c. 1630.
    Add. MS 22118 (IV.57) c. 1630.
    Add. MS 22601 (III.44; IV.1) c. 1605.
    Add. MS 22603 (I.40, IV.30) c. 1650.
    Add. MS 24665 (III.84) c. 1618–25.
    Add. MS 29481 (III.84) c.1630.
    Add. MS 30982 (I.7; III.43, 84) c. 1631–33.
    Add. MS 38139 (II.94) c. 1618–25.
    Add. MS 44963 (IV.80) c. 1632–40.
    Egerton MS 923 (IV.57, 80) c. 1630.
    Egerton MS 2230 (IV.1).

Egerton MS 2421 (III.43; IV.30, 57) Francis Norreys & Henry Balle, c. 1650.
Harley MS 367   (III.10, 70).
Harley MS 1836 (I.7; IV.39).
Harley MS 4064 (I.40; IV.30, 88) c. 1620–33.
Harley MS 6193 (III.43) post 1650.
Harley MS 6913 (II.94).
Harley MS 7332 (IV.38, 57) c. 1625–50.
Lansdowne MS 740 (I.40; III.7) c. 1620.
Sloane MS 542   (IV.57) c. 1630.
Sloane MS 1446 (IV.30) Francis Baskerville, c. 1633.
Sloane MS 1489 (II.1; IV.30, 1615 edn: 63).

Cambridge University Library
Adv. b.8.1 (Gift for Lady Rogers and Lady Harington), Table 2, Scribe A.

Holkham Hall
Holkham MS 437 (Transcription of Campion's *Sancta salutiferi*), Scribe A.

Inner Temple Library
Petyt MS 538, vol. 43 (Gift for Lucy, Countess of Bedford), Table 3.

York Minster Library
York Minster Library MS XVI.L.6 (Treatise for Tobie Matthew, including: II.8; III.44; IV.1, 10, 90), Scribe A.

United States

Philadelphia: Rosenbach Library
Rosenbach MS 239/18 (IV.57, 80) c. 1660.
Rosenbach MS 239/22 (II.80; III.84; IV.80, 88) c. 1638–45.
Rosenbach MS 239/27 (I.7, 40; III.84; IV.32, 80, 84; 1615 edn:79) c. 1634.
Rosenbach MS 240/2 (IV.80).
Rosenbach MS 243/42 (IV.57, 80; 1618 edn: IV.92).
Rosenbach MS 1083/15 (I.65; II.94; III.3; IV.85) c. 1630.
Rosenbach MS 1083/16 (I.7, 40; II.2, 94; III.10, 84; IV.30, 35, 43, 57, 80, 82, 105 & reply; 1615 edn: 30,79) Robert Bishop, 1630.
Rosenbach MS 1083/17 (III.44).

Washington, DC: Folger Shakespeare Library
Folger MS V.a.249 (Copy of *Epigrams* for Prince Henry), Scribe A.
Folger MS V.a.97 (I.30) c. 1640.
Folger MS V.a.103 (III.44) c. 1630.
Folger MS V.a.124 (III.84; IV.57), Richard Archard, c. 1650–57.
Folger MS V.a.162 (I.7, 10, 30; II.1; III.43; IV.39) c. 1650.

Folger MS V.a.246 (IV.57) c. 1674–84.
Folger MS V.a.262 (I.7; III.84, IV.30, 57, 80, 82) c. 1650.
Folger MS V.a.276 (IV.57) William Jordan, c. 1674–84.
Folger MS V.a.319 (III.44; IV.39, 57) c. 1640.
Folger MS V.a.322 (III.44; IV.39) c. 1660.
Folger MS V.a.339 (I.89, IV.57) c. 1630–50.
Folger MS V.a.345 (I.65; II.94; III.44, 99*ter*; IV.57, 80, 82, 105 & reply)

Private Collection
Trumbull Add. MS 23 (Harington's translation of *Aeneid* VI), Scribe A.

Early Modern Printed Editions

Alciati, Andrea, *Emblematum Liber* (Augsburg: H. Steyner, 1531).
_____, *Emblematum Libellus, Nuper In Lucem Editus* (Venice: Aldus, 1546).
Aldus, Manutius, *Institutionum Grammaticarum Libri Quatuor, Addito in fine de octo partium orationis constructione libello. Erasmo Roterodamo auctore* (Florence: Philip Junta, 1519).
Aldus, (Filii), Ανθολογια διαφόρων Επιγραμματων . . . *Florilegium Diversorum Epigrammatum in septem libros distinctum, diligenti castigatione emendatum* (Venice: Aldi Filii, 1551).
Castiglione, Baldessar, *The Courtyer of Count Baldessar Castilio. diuided into foure bookes*, trans. Thomas Hoby (London: W. Seres, 1561), STC 4778.
_____, *The Courtier of Count Baldessar Castilio, deuided into foure bookes*, trans. Thomas Hoby (London: John Wolfe, 1588), STC 4781.
[Chalkhill, John?] I. C., *Alcilia. Philoparthens Louing Folly. Whereunto Is Added Pigmalions Image. With the Loue of Amos and Laura. And also Epigrammes by Sir I. H. And others. Never before imprinted* (London: Richard Hawkins, 1613), STC 4275.
Collinson, John, *The History and Antiquities of the County of Somerset*, 3 vols (Bath: R. Cruttwell, 1791).
Combe, Thomas, *The Theater of Fine Devices, containing an hundred morall Emblemes, First penned in French by Guillaume de la Perrière, and translated into English* (London, Richard Field, 1614), STC 15230.
Donne, John, *Paradoxes, Problems, Essayes, Characters Written by Dr Donne, Dean of Paul's, to which is added a Book of Epigrams: Written in Latin by the same Author, translated into English by J. Maine, D.D.* (London: Humphrey Moseley, 1652).
Erasmus, *De Octo Orationis Partium Constructione Libellus, tum elegans in primis, tum dilucida brevitate copiosissimus* (Strasbourg: Schurer, 1515).
_____, *De ratione studii, ac legendi, interpretandique auctores libellus aureus, Officium discipulorum ex Quintiliano. Qui primo legendi, ex eodem*, 2nd edn (Strasbourg: Schurer, 1513).

_____, μωρίας εγκώμιου, *id est Stultitiae laus, Libellus uere aureus nec minus eruditus, & salutaris, quam festiuus, nuper ex ipsius autoris archetypis diligentissime restitutus* (Strasbourg: Schurer, 1514 and 1515).

_____, *Familiarium Colloquiorum Formulae et Alia Quaedam* (Basel: Froben, 1518).

_____, *Pacis Querela, De regno administrando, Institutio principis Christiani, Panegyricus ad Philippum & carmen, Item Ex Plutarcho De discrimine adulatoris & amici. De utilitate capienda ex inimicis. De doctrina Principum, Principi cum philosopho semper esse disputandum. Item Declamatio super mortuo puero* (Venice: Aldus, 1518).

_____, *Enchiridion militis Christiani, saluberrimis praeceptis refertum, autore Des. Erasmo Roterodamo. Cuique accessit mireque utilis praefatio* (Basel: Froben, 1520).

_____, *Enchiridion Militis Christiani, saluberrimis praeceptis refertum, autore Des. Erasmo Roterodamo. Cuique accessit mireque utilis praefatio* (Mainz: Schoeffer, 1520).

_____, *Familiarium Colloquiorum D Erasmi Roterodami opus, ab autore postremum diligenter recognitum, emendatum & locupletatum, adiectis novis aliquot lectu dignis colloquiis cum indice Froben* (Basel: Froben, 1533).

_____, *Adagiorum Omnium Tam Graecorum quam Latinorum Aureum Flumen* (Cologne: John Prael,1533).

Estienne, Henri, *Ανθολογια διαφόρων Επιγραμμάτων . . . Florilegium diuersorum epigrammatum veterum, in septem libros diuisum* ([Geneva]: Huldrich Fuggerus, 1566).

Fitzjeffrey, Charles, *Caroli Fitzgeofridi Affaniae sive Epigrammatum Libri tres* (Oxford: Joseph Barnes, 1601), STC 10934.

Fuller, Thomas, *The History of the Worthies of England*, 2 vols (London: J.G.W.L. and W.G., 1662).

Harington, Sir John, *Orlando Furioso in English Heroical Verse by Iohn Harington Esquire* (London: Richard Field, 1591), STC 746.

_____, *A New Discourse of a Stale Subiect, Called The Metamorphosis of Aiax* (London: Richard Field, 1596), STC 12779. Large-paper copies: Lumley (Folger) and Markham (Princeton); parts bound by Nares (Folger) w. 12780.

_____, *The Englishmans Docter or The School of Salerne* (London: Helme and Busby, 1607), STC 21605.

_____, *Epigrams Both Pleasant And Serious, Written by that All-Worthy Knight Sir Iohn Harrington and neuer before Printed* (London: John Budge, 1615), STC 12775.

_____, *The Most Elegant and Witty Epigrams of Sir Iohn Harrington, Knight, Digested into Foure Bookes: Three whereof neuer before published* (London: John Budge, 1618), STC 12776.

_____, *The Most Elegant and Witty Epigrams of Sir Iohn Harrington, Knight. Digested into Foure Bookes.*(London: John Budge, 1625), STC 12777.

_____, *Orlando Furioso, In English Heroical Verse by Sr Iohn Harington of Bathe Knight Now thirdly revised and amended with the Addition of the Authors Epigrams* (London: George Miller, 1634), STC 748 (incl. 12778).

Heywood, John, *John Heywoodes Woorkes. A dialogue conteyning the number of the effectuall proverbes in the English tounge . . . With one hundred of Epigrammes: and three hundred of Epigrammes upon three hundred proverbes: and a fifth hundred of Epigrams. Whereunto are now newly added a syxt hundred of Epigrams by the sayde John Heywood* (London: Thomas Powell, 1562), STC 13285.

_____, *John Heywoodes Woorkes* (London: Henry Wykes, 1566), STC 13286.

_____, *John Heywoodes Woorkes* (London: Thomas Marsh, 1576), STC 13287.

_____, *The Workes of John Heywood* (London: Thomas Marsh, 1587), STC 13288.

_____, *The Workes of John Heiwood* (London: Felix Kingston, 1598), STC 13289.

Jonson, Ben, *The Workes of Beniamin Ionson* (London: Will Stansby, 1616), STC 14751.

Lily, William, *De octo orationis partium constructione libellus*, ed. Erasmus (Strasbourg: Matthew Schurer, 1515).

Martialis, M. Val, *Martialis cum duobus commentis* (Venice: B. de Zanis, 1493).

_____, *Martialis Epigrammata* (Venice: Aldus Manutius, 1517).

_____, *Epigrammata, Paucis admodum vel reiectis, vel immutatis nullo Latinitatis damno, ab omni rerum obscoenitate, verborumque turpitudine vindicata* (Rome: Soc. Iesu, 1558).

_____, *Epigrammaton Libri XII* (Antwerp: Christopher Plantin, 1568).

_____, *Epigrammaton Libri Animadversi, Emendati*, ed. T. Farnaby (London: William Welby, 1615), STC 17492, Ben Jonson's copy in Folger.

_____, *Epigrammatum Libri XV. Cum Variorum Doctorum Virorum Commentariis, Notis, Observationibus, Emendationibus & Paraphrasibus, unum in corpus magno studio coniectis. Cum Indice Omnium Verborum* (Paris: Claude Morell, 1517), Ben Jonson's copy in Folger.

_____, *Nova Editio Ex Museo Petri Scriverii* (Lyons: John Maire, 1619), Ben Jonson's annotated copy in Folger.

Meres, Francis, *Palladis Tamia. Wits Treasury: Being the Second part of Wits Commonwealth* (London: Cuthbert Burbie, 1598).

More, Sir Thomas, *De Optimo Reip. Statv, Deque noua insula Vtopia, libellus uere aureus, nec minus salutaris quam festiuus . . . Epigrammata clarissimi disertissimique uiri Thomae Mori, pleraque è Graecis uersa; Epigrammata Des. Erasmi Roterodami* (Basel: Froben, 1518).

_____, *Epigrammata Clarissimi Disertissimique uiri Thomas Mori Britanni ad emendatum exemplar ipsius autoris excusa* (Basel: Froben, 1520).

Nowell, Alexander and William Day, *A true report of the Disputation or rather private Conference had in the Tower of London, with Ed. Campion Iesuite, the last of August. 1581* (London: Barker, 1583), STC 18744.

Owen, John, *Epigrammatum Libri Tres: Secunda Editio* (London: John Windet, 1606), STC 18984.8; *Epigrammatum Ioannis Owen Cambro-Britanni Libri Tres: Editio Tertia* (London: Humfrey Lownes, 1607), STC 18986.
Stockwood, John, *Progumnasma Scholasticum. Hoc est Epigrammatum Graecorum, ex Anthologia selectorum ab He. Stephano duplicique eiusdem id interpretatione explicatorum* (London: Adam Islip, 1597).
Stradling, Sir John, *Epigrammatum Libri Quatuor* (London: George Bishop and John Norton, 1607), STC 23354.

Modern Editions and Secondary Sources

Alciati, Andrea, *Emblemata*, Lyons, 1550, trans. Betty I. Knott (Aldershot: Scolar Press, 1996).
Augustine of Hippo, *City of God*, trans. William M. Green, 2 vols (London/Cambridge MA: Harvard University Press, 1963).
Baldwin, T. W., *William Shakspere's Small Latine and Less Greeke*, 2 vols (Urbana: University of Illinois Press, 1944).
Barker, Nicolas and David Quentin, *The Library of Thomas Tresham and Thomas Brudenell* (London: Roxburghe Club, 2006).
Bath, Michael, "'Dirtie Devises": Thomas Combe and the *Metamorphosis of Ajax'*, in *Emblematic Perceptions: Essays in Honor of William S. Heckscher*, eds Peter M. Daly and Daniel S. Russell (*Saecula Spiritualia* 36, Verlag Valentin Koerner), 9–23.
Beal, Peter, *Index of English Literary Manuscripts*, vol. 1, *1450–1625* (London: Mansell, 1980).
————, *A Dictionary of English Manuscript Terminology 1450–2000* (Oxford: University Press, 2008).
Bennett, H. S., *English Books & Readers: 1475 to 1557* (Cambridge: University Press, 1952).
————, *English Books & Readers: 1558 to 1603* (Cambridge: University Press, 1965).
Binns, J. W., *Intellectual Culture in Elizabethan and Jacobean England: The Latin Writings of the Age* (Leeds: Francis Cairns, 1990).
Bolwell, Robert W., *The Life and Works of John Heywood* (New York: Columbia University Press, 1921).
Bowers, Rick, 'Sir John Harington and the Earl of Essex: The Joker as Spy', *Cahiers Élizabéthains*, 69 (Spring, 2006), 13–20.
Boyle, Marjorie O'Rourke, *Petrarch's Genius: Pentimento and Prophecy* (Berkeley and Oxford: University of California Press, 1991).
Carroll, Clare, *Circe's Cup: Cultural Transformations in Early Modern Ireland* (Notre Dame IN: University of Notre Dame Press, 2001).

Cloud, Random [Randall McLeod], 'from *Tranceformations in the Text of "Orlando Furioso"'*, *Library Chronicle of the University of Texas at Austin*, 20 (1990), 60–85 (p. 72 and p. 76).

Corbett, Margery, and Ronald Lightbown, *The Comely Frontispiece: The Emblematic Title-Page in England 1550–1660* (London: Routledge & Kegan Paul, 1979).

Collinson, John, *The History and Antiquities of the County of Somerset*, 3 vols (Bath: R. Cruttwell, 1791).

Combe, Thomas, *Theater of Fine Devices*, introd. Mary V. Silcox (Aldershot: Scolar Press, 1990).

Corbett, Margery and Ronald Lightbown, *The Comely Frontispiece: The Emblematic Title-Page in England, 1550–1660* (London: Routledge & Kegan Paul, 1979).

Craig, D. H., *Sir John Harington* (Boston MA: Twayne, 1985).

Crick, Julia and Alexandra Walsham, *The Uses of Script and Print 1300–1700* (Cambridge: University Press, 2004).

Croft, P. J., 'Sir John Harington's Manuscript of Sir Philip Sidney's Arcadia', in Stephen Parks and Croft, *Literary Autographs* (Los Angeles: University of California, 1983), pp. 39–75.

Daly, Peter M., *Literature in the Light of the Emblem: Structural Parallels between the Emblem and Literature in the Sixteenth and Seventeenth Centuries*, 2nd edn (Toronto: University of Toronto Press, 1979).

Davies, Sir John, *The Poems*, ed. Robert Krueger (Oxford: Clarendon Press, 1975).

Davies of Hereford, John, *Complete Works*, 2 vols, ed. Alexander B. Grosart (Edinburgh: University Press, 1878).

Donaldson, Ian, 'Jonson's poetry', in *Cambridge Companion to Ben Jonson*, eds Richard Harp and Stanley Steward (Cambridge: University Press, 2000), pp. 119–39.

Eliot, T. S., 'Epigrams of an Elizabethan Courtier', *TLS*, 17 February 1927, p. 104.

Erasmus, *Collected Works of Erasmus*, 23, *Literary and Educational Writings*, ed. Craig R. Thompson (Toronto: University of Toronto Press, 1978).

_____, *Collected Works of Erasmus*, 24, *Copia*, trans. Betty I. Knott (Toronto: University of Toronto Press, 1978).

_____, *Collected Works of Erasmus*, 27, *Moria, Institutio Principis Christiani, Querela Pacis*, trans. Betty Radice, Neil M. Cheshire and Michael J. Heath (Toronto: University of Toronto Press, 1986).

_____, *Collected Works of Erasmus*, 31, *Adages*, I.i.1 to I.v.100, trans. M. Mann Phillips, annot. R. A. B. Mynors (Toronto: University of Toronto Press, 1982).

_____, *Collected Works of Erasmus*, 32, *Adages*, I.vi.1 to I.x.100, trans. and annot. R. A. B. Mynors (Toronto: University of Toronto Press, 1989).

_____, *Collected Works of Erasmus*, 33, *Adages*, II.i.1 to II.vi.100, trans. and annot. R. A. B. Mynors (Toronto: University of Toronto Press, 1991).

_____, *Collected Works of Erasmus*, 34, *Adages*, II.vi.1 to III.iii.100, trans. and annot. R. A. B. Mynors (Toronto: University of Toronto Press, 1992).

_____, *Collected Works of Erasmus*, 35, *Adages*, III.iv.1 to IV.ii.100, trans. and annot. Denis L. Drysdall (Toronto: University of Toronto Press, 2005).

_____, *Collected Works of Erasmus*, 39, *Colloquies*, trans. and annot. Craig R. Thompson (Toronto: University of Toronto Press, 1997).

_____, *Collected Works of Erasmus*, 40, *Colloquies*, trans. and annot. Craig. R. Thompson (Toronto: University of Toronto Press, 1997).

_____, *Collected Works of Erasmus*, 66, *Spiritualia: Enchiridion, De Contemptu Mundi, De Vidua Christiana*, ed. John W. O'Malley. *Enchiridion* trans. and annot. Charles Fantazzi (Toronto: University of Toronto Press, 1997).

_____, *The Adages of Erasmus*, sel. William Barker (Toronto: University of Toronto Press, 2001).

Flynn, Dennis, *John Donne and the Ancient Catholic Nobility* (Bloomington: Indiana University Press, 1995).

Foot, Mirjam M. and Howard M. Nixon, *The History of Decorated Bookbinding in England* (Oxford: Clarendon Press, 1992).

Foot, Mirjam M., *The Henry Davis Gift: A Collection of Bookbindings*, 2 vols (London: The British Library, 1978).

Furnivall, F. J., 'Sir John Harington's Shakespeare Quartos', *Notes and Queries*, 7th series, 9 (1890), 382–3.

Graves, T. S., 'The Heywood Circle and the Reformation', *Modern Philology*, 10/4 (1913), 553–72.

Greg, W. W., *Collected Papers*, ed. J. C. Maxwell (Oxford: Clarendon Press, 1966).

Harington, Sir John, *Nugae Antiquae: Being a Miscellaneous Collection of Original Papers in Prose and Verse*, ed. Thomas Park, 2 vols (London: Vernon and Hood, 1804).

_____, *A Tract on the Succession to the Crown (A.D. 1602)*, ed. Clements R. Markham (London: for Roxburghe Club, J. B. Nichols, 1880).

_____, *The Letters and Epigrams of Sir John Harington, Together with The Praise of Private Life*, ed. Norman Egbert McClure (Philadelphia: University of Pennsylvania Press, 1930).

_____, *A New Discourse of a Stale Subject, Called the Metamorphosis of Ajax*, ed. Elizabeth Story Donno (London: Routledge & Kegan Paul, 1962).

_____, *Ludovico Ariosto's Orlando Furioso Translated into English Heroical Verse* by Sir John Harington (1591), ed. Robert McNulty (Oxford: Clarendon Press, 1972).

_____, *A Supplie or Addicion to the Catalogue of Bishops to the Yeare 1608*, ed. R. H. Miller (Potomac MA: Turanzas, 1979).

_____, *The Sixth Book of Virgil's Aeneid: Translated and Commented on by Sir John Harington (1604)*, ed. Simon Cauchi (Oxford: Clarendon Press, 1991).

Harp, Richard and Stanley Stewart, *The Cambridge Companion to Ben Jonson* (Cambridge: University Press, 2000).

Hecksher, William S., 'Pearls from a Dung-Heap: Andrea Alciati's "Offensive" Emblem: "Adversus Naturam Peccantes"', in *Art the Ape of Nature: Studies in*

Honor of H. W. Janson, ed. Moshe Barasch and Lucy Freeman Sadler (New York: Abrams, 1981), pp. 291–311.

Heywood, John, *The Proverbs and Epigrams*, repr. of Spenser Society publ. 1867 (New York: Franklin, 1967).

Heywood, John, *A Dialogue of Proverbs*, ed. Rudolph E. Habenicht (Berkeley: University of California Press, 1963).

Heywood, John, *Works and Miscellaneous Short Poems*, ed. Burton A. Milligan (Urbana: University of Illinois Press, 1956).

Hudson, Hoyt Hopewell, *The Epigram in the English Renaissance* (Princeton NJ: Princeton University Press, 1947).

Hughey, Ruth, *John Harington of Stepney: Tudor Gentleman* (Columbus: Ohio State University Press, 1971).

_____, *The Arundel Harington Manuscript of Tudor Poetry*, 2 vols (Columbus: Ohio State University Press, 1960).

Humez, Jean McMahon, 'The Manners of Epigram: A Study of the Epigram Volumes of Martial, Harington and Jonson', PhD dissertation (Yale University, New Haven, 1971).

Hutton, James, *The Greek Anthology in Italy to the Year 1800* (Ithaca NY: Cornell University Press, 1935).

Kay, W. David, *Ben Jonson: A Literary Life* (New York: St Martin's Press, 1995)

Kilroy, Gerard, *Edmund Campion: Memory and Transcription* (Burlington VT and Aldershot: Ashgate, 2005).

_____, 'Scribal Coincidences: Campion, Byrd, Harington and the Sidney Circle', *Sidney Journal*, 22 (Spring, 2004), 73–89.

Laurens, Pierre, *L'Abeille dans l'Ambre: Célébration de l'épigramme de l'époque alexandrine à la fin de la Renaissance* (Paris: Les Belles Lettres, 1989).

Lawrence, Jason, *'Who the devil taught thee so much Italian?': Italian Language Learning and Literary Imitation in Early Modern England* (Manchester: University Press, 2005).

Marks, P. J. M., *The British Library Guide to Bookbinding: History and Techniques* (London: British Library, 1998).

Martial, *Epigrams*, ed. and trans. D. R. Shackleton Bailey, 3 vols (London and Cambridge MA: Harvard University Press, 1993).

May, Steven W., *The Elizabethan Courtier Poets: The Poems and Their Contexts* (Columbia and London: University of Missouri Press, 1991).

_____, and William A. Ringler, Jr., *Elizabethan Poetry: A Bibliography and First-line Index of English Verse, 1559–1603*, 3 vols (London and New York: Thoemmes Continuum, 2004).

McKerrow, Ronald B., *An Introduction to Bibliography for Literary Students* (Oxford: Clarendon Press, 1927).

Milligan, Burton, *John Heywood's Works and Miscellaneous Short Poems* (Urbana: University of Illinois, 1956).

Miller, R. H., 'Sir John Harington's Manuscripts in Italic', *Studies in Bibliography*, 40 (1987), 101–6.

_____, 'Unpublished Poems by Sir John Harington', *ELR*, 84 (1984), 148–58.

More, Thomas, *The Latin Epigrams of Thomas More*, ed. and trans. Leicester Bradner and C. Arthur Lynch (Chicago: University of Chicago Press, 1935).

_____, *The Complete Works of St. Thomas More*, vol. 4, *Utopia*, eds Edward Surtz, S. J., and J. H. Hexter (New Haven: Yale University Press, 1965).

_____, *The Complete Works of St. Thomas More*, vol. 3, Part II, *Latin Poems*, eds Clarence H. Miller, Leicester Bradner, Charles A. Lynch and Revilo P. Oliver (New Haven: Yale University Press, 1984).

Mulryan, John, 'Erasmus and War: The *Adages* and Beyond', *Moreana*, XXIII, 89 (Feb. 1986), 15–28.

_____, 'Jonson's Epigrams and the Adages of Erasmus: A Holistic Analysis', *Ben Jonson Journal*, XII (2005), 73–92.

Nichols, John. *The Progresses and Public Processions of Queen Elizabeth*, 3 vols (London: 1788–1807; repr. J. Nichols and Son, 1823), vol. 3, pp. 250–51

Orgel, Stephen, 'Marginal Jonson', in *The Politics of the Stuart Court Masque*, eds David Bevington and Peter Holbrook (Cambridge: University Press, 1998), pp. 144–75.

Petrarch, Francis, *Petrarch's Lyric Poems: The Rime sparse and Other Lyrics*, trans. Robert M. Durling (Cambridge MA and London: Harvard University Press, 1976).

Pollard, Alfred W., *Early Illustrated Books: a history of the decoration and illustration of books in the 15th and 16th centuries,* 2nd edn (London: K. Paul Trench, 1893).

Praz, Mario, *Studies in Seventeenth-Century Imagery*, 2nd edn (Rome: Edizioni Di Storia e Letteratura, 1964).

Scott-Warren, Jason, *Sir John Harington and the Book as Gift* (Oxford: University Press, 2001).

Shell, Alison, *Catholicism, Controversy and the English Literary Imagination, 1558–1660* (Cambridge: University Press, 1999).

Strong, Roy, *The English Icon: Elizabethan and Jacobean Portraiture* (London, Routledge, 1969).

Tilley, Morris Palmer, *A Dictionary of The Proverbs in England in the Sixteenth and Seventeenth Century* (Ann Arbor: University of Michigan Press, 1950).

Trapp, J. B., *Studies of Petrarch and His Influence* (London: Pindar Press, 2003).

Weever, John, *Epigrammes in the Oldest Cut and Newest Fashion* (1599), ed. R. B. McKerrow (London: Sidgwick and Jackson, 1911).

Weston, William, *The Autobiography of an Elizabethan*, trans. Philip Caraman (London: Longmans, Green, 1955), pp. 10–11.

Whitney, Geoffrey, *A Choice of Emblemes 1586*, English Emblem Books No 3, ed. John Horden (Aldershot: Scolar Press, 1969).

Woodhouse, J. R., *Baldesar Castiglione: A Reassessment of The Courtier* (Edinburgh: University Press, 1978).

Woudhuysen, H. R., *Sir Philip Sidney and the Circulation of Manuscripts 1558–1640* (Oxford: Clarendon Press, 1996).

Index